1 MONTH OF
FREE
READING

at

www.ForgottenBooks.com

By purchasing this book you are eligible for one month membership to ForgottenBooks.com, giving you unlimited access to our entire collection of over 1,000,000 titles via our web site and mobile apps.

To claim your free month visit:

www.forgottenbooks.com/free848307

ISBN 978-0-364-72491-0
PIBN 10848307

THE FRASER RIVER

THE SEARCH FOR THE WESTERN SEA

THE STORY OF THE EXPLORATION OF NORTH-WESTERN AMERICA

LAWRENCE J. BURPEE

TORONTO
THE MUSSON BOOK COMPANY
LIMITED

THE FRASER RIVER

THE SEARCH FOR THE WESTERN SEA

THE STORY OF THE EXPLORATION
OF NORTH-WESTERN AMERICA

BY

LAWRENCE J. BURPEE

TORONTO
THE MUSSON BOOK COMPANY
LIMITED

PRINTED BY W. BRENDON AND SON, LTD., PLYMOUTH, ENGLAND

TO MY WIFE

PREFACE

BECAUSE the story of the exploration of North-Western America had never been told, and because it seemed so well worth the telling, this book has been written. If it falls short of the expectations of those who may read it, the fault lies with the writer, not with his subject. No man could ask for a theme of richer possibilities. The field is that marvellous land of prairie and woodland, lake, river, and mountain; that land of magnificent distances laid out by Nature in her most opulent mood; that land of incalculable resources, upon which the destiny not merely of a colony, but of an empire, may depend. This is the stage; and the men who move over it are men of equally heroic build, strong, fearless, clear-eyed, endowed with masculine faults and masculine virtues, dominated by the spirit of adventure of two great races, fit men to break a path through a continental wilderness. These men gave to England and to the world a heritage the value of which is only beginning to be understood.

The material from which the story of their lives and achievements had to be reconstructed was sometimes ample, sometimes extremely meagre. In a few cases their own narratives were available in print; in others the original manuscript journals could be consulted; while occasionally the story had to be pieced together from the fragmentary evidence of their contemporaries. In every case the original documents, in whatever form they might be, have been made the basis of the story, secondary authorities being used only to supplement the material obtained from the original documents. Most of the manuscript material was found in the Canadian Archives at Ottawa; and full advantage has been taken of the valuable collections of maps in the archives, as well as in the office of the Geographer of the Department of the Interior.

The author is indebted to Mr. D. B. Dowling and Mr. Owen O'Sullivan, of the Canadian Geological Survey, Mr. R. H. Hunter, of the Canadian Topographical Surveys, Mr. J. B. Tyrrell, F.G.S., Dr. A. G. Doughty, C.M.G., Dominion Archivist, Mr. Benjamin Sulte, the historian of French Canada, Miss Agnes Laut, and Mr. T. G. Marquis for information and advice in the preparation of this book, but above all to Mr. James White, F.R.G.S., Geographer of the Department of the Interior at Ottawa, without whose generous assistance and kindly criticism the book would never have been written. The author is also glad to avail himself of this opportunity of acknowledging the loan of an important manuscript by Mr. Philèas Gagnon, of Quebec; and of photographs for illustrations by Dr. A. P. Low, Director of the Geological Survey, Mr. E. B. Bates, of Ottawa, and Dr. Robert Bell, of the Geological Survey.

OTTAWA, *January 12th*, 1908.

CONTENTS

PART III

THE ROAD TO THE SEA

ILLUSTRATIONS AND MAPS

INTRODUCTION

A THOUSAND years ago the Northmen, responding to that mysterious attraction which has exercised such a compelling power over men of Aryan blood, pushed their way across the Atlantic to Iceland, from Iceland to Greenland, and from Greenland to America, where they stood first of white men on the shores of a new world. That they were quite unconscious of the magnitude of their discovery does not detract from its interest. The world's greatest discoveries have generally been made unwittingly.

The Call of the West, though the phrase may seem a somewhat fanciful one, has been from the beginning a vital factor in the exploration of America. It may perhaps be defined as the spirit of adventure of a vigorous people acting upon a deep-rooted racial tendency to follow the path of the sun. In any case it acted like a magnet to the nations of Western Europe. As it drew the Northmen across the Atlantic a thousand years ago, so it undoubtedly animated the Spanish and Portuguese and British and French adventurers who some centuries later reached, more or less independently, and more or less unconsciously, the same great goal. In their case, however, the Call of the West was combined with other and more tangible influences. Columbus, the Cabots, Verrazano, Jacques Cartier, and the rest of that wonderful group of transatlantic voyagers sought primarily a short western route to China and the Indies. Behind it all was the lure of the setting sun and the adventurous spirit of their race, but on the surface at least was the eminently practical incentive of reaching golden Cathay.

The growing power of the Turk, who guarded the gates through which flowed the trade of the Orient, made it imperative upon the nations of Western Europe to find other and independent routes to the Far East. Portuguese navigators turned to the south, and eventually discovered a road, though a very long and difficult one, around the coasts of Africa. This, however, gave no satisfactory solution of the problem. A short, direct route was wanted, and gradually, almost imperceptibly, the belief grew that such a route might be found by following the sun. No barrier presented itself to the eyes of those who looked out from the shores of Europe over the western sea. According to the very imperfect geographical ideas of those days, the coasts of Asia lay not more than a thousand leagues to the westward. The knowledge of a great continental barrier, or indeed of any intervening barrier, was not to come for many a long year.

Before the close of the fifteenth century much had already been accomplished. Columbus had performed his memorable voyages, discovering what he quite naturally supposed to be Cipango or the Spicy Isles, and seeking diligently but ineffectually for the Strait of

Malacca in the Caribbean Sea ; and the Cabots had not only reached the mainland of America, but had explored almost the entire coast-line from Labrador to Virginia.

Before the close of the century, too, the truth was already beginning to dawn upon men's minds that the newly discovered lands were neither Cipango nor Cathay —a momentous and far-reaching conclusion. Columbus and the Cabots, not to mention Leif Ericson, who was actuated by quite different ambitions, sought Cathay and found America — sought the treasures of the Orient and found something of infinitely greater moment.

Perhaps in these latter days, in the arrogance of modern achievement, we are prone to forget the full significance of these exploits and the character of the men who performed them. If Columbus and his fellows did indeed build better than they knew, they were men of heroic stature, types of an adventurous age, dowered with masculine virtues, strong, fearless, enterprising, and imbued with the divine gift of imagination. Dreamers they were, sailing out into the west in quest of they knew not what—puppets in the game of destiny. What splendid courage it must have needed to sail in their little cockle-shells of vessels over that untravelled sea, with its dangers all the more terrifying because unknown ; its reputed monsters of every hideous shape ; the absolute uncertainty as to where fate might lead them ; even the fearful possibility of sailing over the edge of the world !

These men had discovered a new world, a mighty continent, full of incalculable possibilities, but even when the fact that it was a new world began to take tangible shape, its importance was clouded by the additional fact that the original object of maritime ambition was still uppermost. The idea that the eastern shores of Asia were washed by the Atlantic had also taken too deep root to be lightly abandoned. The newly discovered lands were conceived for a time to be a fringe of islands upon the outermost coasts of Asia. Gradually, as exploration proceeded, this theory was found to be insufficient; the small islands coalesced theoretically into larger ones, and receded from the coasts of Asia. Finally the original idea had to be abandoned altogether, giving place to the assured belief that a vast continent was added to the known world.

But this was not what had been looked for; this was not Cathay. It was a barrier, and a very inconvenient barrier, upon the high road to Asia. How break through it? Men scoured the coasts of America from Florida to Labrador, exhausting one promising clue after another, exploring every bay and inlet that seemed to offer a passage, always hoping to win a way through the continent to that Western Sea that did in truth wash the shores of far Cathay.

As the voyages of Columbus and the Cabots marked the fifteenth century as one of high maritime emprise, so the only slightly less momentous voyages of Verrazano and Jacques Cartier added lustre to the next century. The expeditions of Verrazano and Jacques Cartier each marked the beginning of a new epoch in the history of the New World. The former, unless we admit the doubtful contention that one of the objects of the Cabot voyage of 1498 was the discovery of a passage through the continental barrier toward the north-west, was the first distinct effort in the long search for the North-West Passage. The latter marked the inception of an even more vital and far-reaching project—the search for the Western Sea and the consequent opening up of the vast interior of the continent by way of the St. Lawrence and its connecting waterways.

In Verrazano's quest of a passage he carefully examined the Atlantic coast from the Carolinas to Maine, adding materially to the knowledge of those shores. He did not find the passage, but, in the words of John Fiske, " he did discover in this connection one of the most extraordinary mare's nests on record." On two of the maps published shortly after his return to Europe North America is shown as a double continent, joined by a narrow isthmus along the Virginia coast, the entire central portion of what is now the United States being represented as an arm of the Pacific Ocean. This curious misconception seems to have arisen in an even more curious way. Verrazano, landing upon the Accomac Peninsula, crossed it to the opposite shore, and mistook Chesapeake Bay for the Pacific! For a hundred years this imaginary Sea of Verrazano served to confuse the minds of European explorers and map-makers, and its presence upon contemporary maps serves to explain the otherwise puzzling persistency with which every bay and river, however insignificant, was examined as a possible channel into this elusive sea. Later we shall find the Western Sea masquerading for a time as another Sea of Verrazano, but by this time the proportions of the continent were more fully realized, and the imaginary sea appears on the maps well over toward the Pacific, with a couple of thousand miles of dry land between it and the Atlantic.

With Jacques Cartier began the history of Canada, and began also the most determined and long-continued effort to discover a route to the Pacific. The circumstances of the project were largely determined by geographical conditions. The route by which it was followed —the St. Lawrence and the Great Lakes—affords the only great waterway into the heart of the continent between Labrador and Florida. Here if anywhere there was a chance of piercing the continent. To follow these waterways until they should lead to the *Mer de l'Ouest* was the guiding motive of all the explorers of New France, from Cartier to La Vérendrye. At first the sea was supposed to lie somewhere above Montreal. As the St. Lawrence and its tributary the Ottawa were ascended to the Great Lakes, the sea receded like a will-o'-the-wisp. Finally, when Lake Superior had been explored, it became apparent that the Western Sea must be looked for still farther afield, somewhere far out toward the setting sun.

Up to this point the search had been along broad,

almost sea-like waterways, but these were now at an end, and the explorers stood upon the threshold of a great plain—an ocean of waving grass. Here began one phase of the long-continued series of explorations which form the subject-matter of the following pages. But this route by the St. Lawrence and the Great Lakes was not the only one that led up to the overland expeditions. If it may be described as the southern gateway to the interior of the continent, there was also a northern gateway—through Hudson Strait and Hudson Bay. As the exploration of the southern entrance belonged to France and her sons, so the exploration of this northern entrance must be credited as indisputably to the sons of England. Without the fearless enterprise of such Englishmen as Hudson, Button, and Foxe, much of this story of western exploration must have remained unwritten.

The discovery of the vast inland sea that bears Hudson's name, as of the great lakes that lie to the south of it, was merely incidental to the search for a navigable waterway through the continent. In both cases the search for a passage proved fruitless. The Strait of Anian was as mythical as the Sea of Verrazano. The hopes held out by the two great entrances were delusive. Many a long league must yet be travelled before the explorer could hope to look upon the waters of the Pacific, and when, after three centuries of effort, the search for the Western Sea was at last crowned with success, it was by an undreamed-of route, so long and tortuous, and beset by such manifold difficulties, that even the strong hearts of the men who had explored its earlier stages might have been daunted could they have looked behind the veil and realized the extent of the task they had undertaken.

The title adopted for this book has been chosen because it is believed to express the key-note of exploration in North-Western America. While the efforts of that notable group of British and French explorers whose story is told in the pages that follow resulted in unfolding the whole interior of North-Western America, the object of their search was primarily the discovery of a feasible highway to the Pacific. This object possessed the imagination of the men of both nations; the love of adventure was in their blood, and they became not only rivals in trade, rivals in land-hunger, but rivals also in the nobler purpose of adding to the sum of geographical knowledge. Entering the unknown wilderness of the west through widely separated doors, and following for a time distinct routes, they came together in the end, for the expedition that first succeeded in reaching the shores of the Pacific overland consisted of a party of French-Canadian *voyageurs* under the leadership of a Scottish-Canadian. It may not be without significance that from beginning to end, from Hudson and Cartier to Mackenzie and Fraser, the men who were engaged in this long search for the Western Sea were for the most part men of Brittany and Normandy, of Scotland and the coast towns of England, legitimate descendants of those hardy Vikings who first of white men set foot on American soil.

It will be convenient to describe briefly in this introductory chapter the field covered in the following
pages, chronological as well as geographical. As the
title implies, the book is not designed to cover the
complete story of the exploration of North-Western
America, which would indeed bring it down to the
present day, but only that portion of it which closed
with Mackenzie's overland expedition to the Pacific,
Fraser's descent of the Fraser, and Thompson's exploration of the Columbia. Geographically, the field is fairly
well defined. Cut off Alaska and, broadly speaking,
North-Western America is a gigantic parallelogram,
bounded on the east by Hudson Bay and Lake Superior,
on the west by the Pacific, on the south by the present
International Boundary, and on the north by the Arctic
Sea. It is entirely confined within the boundaries of
what is now the Dominion of Canada, and embraces an
area of something like two and a quarter million square
miles. In following the lines of exploration it will rarely
be necessary to go outside these limits.

Professor Russell, in his *Rivers of North America*,
divides the continent into nine drainage slopes: the
Arctic, Pacific, Hudson Bay, St. Lawrence, Atlantic,
Gulf of Mexico, Bering Sea, Great Basin, and Caribbean
Sea. Of these the first six may be regarded as of
primary importance. The particular field now under
consideration is confined for the most part to the Hudson
Bay, Arctic, and Pacific drainage slopes.

That portion of the Hudson Bay slope which lies
within this field consists of a triangular or wedge-shaped

region, whose base rests on the south-western shores of Hudson Bay, and whose apex reaches the Rocky Mountains at the point where the International Boundary intersects them. It includes two great valleys: the valley of the Saskatchewan and the valley of the Red River, the river systems of both these valleys, as well as the Winnipeg and English rivers, draining into one common reservoir, Lake Winnipeg, and emptying thence through the mighty Nelson into Hudson Bay. The slope drops gradually from an elevation of four thousand feet in the foothills of the Rocky Mountains to less than a thousand feet on the eastern side of Lake Winnipeg, where it reaches the foot of the Laurentian highlands. Thus far the slope has been from west to east. From Lake Winnipeg it drops to Hudson Bay in a north-easterly direction. At the same time it may be noted that the whole continent slopes to the north.

This wedge-shaped slope divides itself into four fairly well-defined areas. The lowest of these lies between Lake Winnipeg and Hudson Bay. The other three consist of a remarkable series of plateaus or steppes separated by two distinct escarpments running parallel in a north-west and south-east direction.

The lowest of the three steppes embraces the valley of the Red River, with Lakes Winnipeg, Winnipegosis, and Manitoba. This plateau itself slopes from south to north, though not uniformly. The general elevation of the plateau is from 1000 to 1500 feet, but at the source of the Red River it is only 980 feet. From these elevations it descends to 710 feet at Lake Winnipeg. This lowest plateau covers what was once an immense glacial lake, to which Mr. Warren Upham has given the name of Lake Agassiz. Lake Agassiz is supposed to have extended north and south from about Sipiwesk Lake to Lake Traverse. Though the bed of this prehistoric lake slopes, as we have seen, from south to north, the lake drained to the south, the northern end being shut in by the edge of the great ice-sheet. To the eastward Lake Agassiz must have reached as far as Rainy Lake, and on the western side it was bounded by the series of hills now forming the escarpment of the lowest steppe, and known as Pembina, Riding, Duck, Porcupine, and Pasquia mountains, going from south to north. The area of Lake Agassiz was equal to the combined areas of the five Great Lakes. Its bed, floored with rich alluvial silt, constitutes to-day one of the most fertile areas in the world—the famous wheat-fields of Manitoba.

The second or middle steppe, which reaches an average altitude of about 1600 feet, is bounded on the west by the tableland known as the Missouri Coteau, and by a line of low hills which extend north-west from the Coteau. It occupies most of the southern portion of the Province of Saskatchewan, an immense fertile plain.

The upper steppe is the widest of the three, extending from the Missouri Coteau to the foot of the Rocky Mountains. Ascending from the second steppe, the true prairie is left behind, and in its place one finds one's self in a park country, partly open, partly covered with smaller timber, sometimes fertile, sometimes semi-arid. The greater portion of the upper and middle steppes is drained by the Saskatchewan with its many tributaries, while the lower steppe is drained by the Red River and its affluent the Assiniboine. The importance of these rivers, and especially of the far-reaching system of the Saskatchewan, in facilitating the exploration of North-Western America will be dwelt upon later.

Let us turn now to the Arctic drainage slope. This, like the western section of the Hudson Bay slope, is roughly wedge-shaped, its base resting on the Arctic coast, and its apex touching the Rocky Mountains at Athabaska Pass. To the eastward the Arctic slope is bounded by the Hudson Bay slope, while on the west it follows the eastern side of the Rocky Mountains northward and north-westward to lat. 54° 10'. From this point to the Arctic the watershed is to the westward of the Rockies, the western tributaries of the Mackenzie interlocking with tributaries of the Yukon. The chief rivers of this slope are the Mackenzie with its affluents or continuations, the Liard, Slave, Peace, and Athabaska rivers, the Coppermine, and Backs or Great Fish River.

The Pacific slope consists of a long and comparatively narrow belt lying for the most part between the Rocky Mountains and the sea, and extending north and south from Alaska to Panama. That portion which comes within the limits of our field runs from the southern boundary of the Yukon Territory to the mouth of the Columbia. Its chief rivers within these limits are the Columbia and Kootenay, the Fraser with its several branches, the Skeena, and the Stikine.

The rivers and lakes of North-Western America were essentially the highways of explorers as well as of fur-traders throughout the entire period of early western history. It is desirable, therefore, to describe these pioneer lines of communication with sufficient care to enable the reader to follow intelligently the movements of the different explorers whose labours added this immense region to the known world. It has already been pointed out that Hudson Bay and the St. Lawrence Valley constitute the two great entrances to this region from the east. It will be convenient, therefore, to make these our starting-points for a rapid survey of the water routes leading north to the Arctic and west to the Pacific.

Lake Winnipeg may be regarded as the pivotal point in the exploration of the North-West. As exploration proceeded beyond it, other points of vantage clouded to some extent the importance of Lake Winnipeg, but it was the first great objective of explorers approaching from the eastward. Magnified by Indian tradition, it was at one time thought to be an arm of the Western Sea. Those who penetrated to its shores discovered it to be, not indeed the sea, but a vital link in the chain of watercourses leading eventually to the sea. From Lake Winnipeg branched out several tentative overland expe-ditions to the south-west, which foreshadowed the Missouri route of Lewis and Clark, and from Lake

Winnipeg also proceeded those explorations toward the north-west which finally culminated in the first overland journey to the shores of the Pacific.

Lake Winnipeg, with Lake Manitoba, Lake Winnipegosis, and the other smaller bodies of water that occupy the same basin, represent all that is left of the once gigantic Lake Agassiz. Winnipeg, though small in comparison with its prehistoric parent, is nevertheless worthy to rank among the greatest of inland waters. It is two hundred and sixty miles long and sixty-five miles across at its widest point. It runs approximately north and south, and is divided at the narrows into two unequal parts, the northern of which is much the larger. Through its numerous feeders it drains an immense territory. At its north-west corner it receives the waters of the Saskatchewan. The Red River enters from the south and the Winnipeg from the east. From the continental divide of the Rockies, from the height of land near Lake Superior, and from the water parting that divides the waters of the Mississippi from those that flow into Hudson Bay, these water roads all lead to Winnipeg Lake.

From Hudson Bay and James Bay five distinct boat or canoe routes lead to Lake Winnipeg. Taking them from the north down, these routes follow the Churchill River, the Nelson, the Hayes, Severn, and Albany. As routes to Lake Winnipeg they are not all of equal importance, though all have been used at times for that purpose. The chief route from Hudson Bay to the lake was by

way of the Hayes River.   The Nelson, while furnishing
a direct route, was never popular, because of the difficulties of its navigation.   The heavier boats of the
Hudson's Bay Company's brigades could make shift to
navigate its turbulent waters, but it was not safe for
light canoes, and was seldom used.   The Churchill
offered a roundabout road to the lake, by way of Frog
Portage and Sturgeon-Weir River, with an alternative
by way of Grassberry River.   The Sturgeon Weir
River was the recognized route between the Saskatchewan and the Churchill, Grassberry River being
seldom if ever used.   Another route, for small canoes,
followed the Little Churchill to Split Lake on the
Nelson.   On the map the Churchill would seem to be
the natural route from the Bay to the Athabaska, Peace,
and Mackenzie districts, but as a matter of fact it was
never so used.   Hayes River and its connecting waterways, first utilized to reach Lake Winnipeg and the
Saskatchewan, continued to be used as the road to the
interior after the region to the far north-west had been
discovered and opened up to trade.   The traders naturally preferred to follow the roundabout route with which
they were familiar, and on which they had gradually
built a chain of posts, than to test the problematical
advantages of the more northerly route.   This explains
the otherwise puzzling fact that long after the upper
waters of the Churchill had become one of the main
thoroughfares of the western fur-trade, the lower part of
the river, from Frog Portage to Fort Churchill, was practically unknown.

South again of Hayes River, the Severn, with a series of small lakes and rivers that connect with it, lead also to Lake Winnipeg, but this route is so tortuous, shallow, and broken by rapids that it has seldom been used except for local purposes. The Albany, emptying into James Bay, offered another road, by a portage to English River, thence by way of Winnipeg River to the lake. The Albany, however, is primarily a route between James Bay and Lake Superior; it connects north and south rather than east and west, though its course is in the latter direction.

The Churchill rises in La Loche Lake, or to be strictly accurate, at the head of a small creek flowing into the northern end of La Loche Lake. From thence to where it empties into Hudson Bay the distance is almost exactly a thousand miles, so that the Churchill is no inconsiderable stream. From La Loche Lake, Methye Portage, famous in the annals of western exploration and the fur-trade, and of which more will be heard hereafter, leads over the height of land to waters flowing to the westward. One can imagine the interest with which the first discoverers must have noted the course of these waters, for from the very beginnings of inland exploration in the great north-west men had been seeking a westward-flowing river. They had, indeed, found such a river in the Winnipeg, but such hopes as were pinned to this stream were very quickly dissipated. The earliest French explorers confidently expected that the Winnipeg would take them directly to the Western Sea. By the time their British successors reached Methye Portage a clearer impression had been gained of the breadth of the continent; yet it is probable enough that the man who first crossed that portage and stood upon the banks of the Clearwater, felt that the solution of the great problem of an inland route to the Pacific was at last within his grasp.

Descending the Churchill from La Loche Lake, a short river bearing the same name leads to Buffalo Lake; thence a narrow strait opens into Clear Lake and from the southernmost corner of Clear Lake a river leads to Ile à la Crosse Lake, another notable spot in western exploration, taking its name from the Indian game of lacrosse which has since become so popular in Canada. Here the largest tributary of the Churchill, the Beaver River, joins it after a course of three hundred and five miles from its source far off to the westward in Long Lake. The striking tendency of the great river systems of North-Western America to approach each other at certain points, though widely separated in their main courses, is illustrated in the case of the Beaver. Its source is within a very few miles of the head-waters of White Earth River, a remote tributary of the Saskatchewan. The same close connections are found everywhere throughout the north-west, and their significance will be readily appreciated. They afforded explorers and fur-traders navigable routes from any point in the west to practically any other point. Descending the Beaver, another illustration lies close at hand. A small branch leads north to the height of land, where an easy portage brings the traveller to Lac La Biche, connecting by La Biche River with the Athabaska. Here canoe routes extend from the waters of the Churchill to the Saskatchewan on the one hand, and to the Athabaska and the immense water system of the far north-west on the other.

From Ile à la Crosse Lake continuing down the Churchill through a network of small lakes to Island Lake, Frog Portage is reached, first known as Portage de Traitte, where the two waterways already mentioned lead south to the Saskatchewan. A few miles farther down the Churchill, Reindeer River flows in from the north, bringing the waters of Reindeer Lake. Still farther down the Churchill another portage leads to Burntwood Lake, through which water routes conduct both to the Saskatchewan and the Nelson. Finally, after flowing through Granville, South Indian and North Indian Lakes, the Churchill empties into Hudson Bay. The mouth of the Churchill will be found figuring prominently in the exploration of Hudson Bay, and on its shores may still be seen the ruins of Fort Prince of Wales, around which cling many of the most romantic incidents of the fur-trade. The original fort was built in 1688, rebuilt in 1721, captured and destroyed by Admiral La Perouse in 1782. The story of its capture will be told later on. Both time and money had been spent lavishly upon its massive walls. Why the Hudson's Bay Company took it into its head to build such a fortress on the remote shores of Hudson Bay, with nothing to guard but a gateway in the wilderness, has always remained a mystery ; and why, having built the fort, they left it in the charge of the merest apology for a garrison is, if anything, a still greater mystery. Possibly realizing the folly of building the fort, they made up their minds not to throw good money after bad. However that may be, the fort was there when the gallant La Perouse appeared upon the scene, and he captured it under circumstances that lie midway between melodrama and farce.

It is uncertain when the mouth of the Churchill was first discovered. Sir Thomas Button passed it in 1612 in his stout ship the *Resolution*, but so far as is known he neither landed at the mouth of the river nor even came close enough inshore to sight it. Munk, a Danish navigator, who sailed into Hudson Bay seven years after Button, seems to have been the first to discover the mouth of the Churchill. Danish River is one of the many names the river has borne. It was known to the Indians as the Missinipi. Although the Hudson's Bay Company had a trading establishment at its mouth at a very early date, there is no evidence that they attempted to explore the river until many years after; not, in fact, until traders from Canada had penetrated to the upper waters of the river and threatened to cut off the trade to the bay.

Despite its famous fortress, Port Churchill did not remain for any length of time, if it ever was, the headquarters of the Hudson's Bay Company on the bay. That distinction belonged to York Factory, some distance down the coast. Nevertheless Port Churchill may awake some day to find itself a centre of trade infinitely beyond anything that York Factory could boast of in its palmiest days. Port Churchill happens to possess the only good harbour on the bay, and before many years have gone by it may become the ocean terminus of a railway from Winnipeg, and the shipping port for Canadian wheat exported to Europe. This, however, is getting away from the period of exploration.

Coming down the coast, the next river is the Nelson. This, though popularly credited with not much more than a third the length of the Churchill, is a much more important stream. It is, in fact, the largest and most important of all the rivers emptying into Hudson Bay. Nominally it rises in Lake Winnipeg, and from there to the bay is three hundred and ninety miles, but if traced to its ultimate source in the Rocky Mountains, its total course is sixteen hundred and sixty miles. The Nelson is thus the fourth river of Canada, the Mackenzie ranking first, the St. Lawrence second, and the Yukon third; while in its vital relation to the drainage systems of the interior the Nelson probably ranks second only to the St. Lawrence. It has already been seen that the main stream of the Nelson carries to the sea the waters of the Saskatchewan, Red, and Winnipeg rivers, with all their tributaries, as well as many smaller lakes and streams that drain into lakes Winnipeg, Manitoba, and Winnipegosis, and the direct tributaries of the Nelson proper.

Compared with the Churchill, the Nelson is not a clear stream; that is to say, the lower portion of it. It does not indeed bring down any appreciable quantity of sediment from Lake Winnipeg, for Lake Winnipeg is notably free from sediment in its northern end, the immense quantities brought down by the Red River being deposited at the bottom of the southern end of the lake, while the burden of the Saskatchewan gets no farther than Cedar Lake. A certain amount of earthy matter is, however, contributed to the Nelson by its own banks, though not to anything like the same extent as in the rivers of the plains. It has been argued that the delta at the mouth of the Nelson is formed of alluvium carried down by the river for centuries past, but it is improbable that this could have been more than a very minor factor in the formation of these shoals. Whatever the source of these shoals, they are a very serious impediment to navigation. Where the river enters the bay the channel is so shallow that only vessels of light draught can enter. The Nelson is about three miles wide at its mouth, and flows there between clay banks one hundred feet high, which appear inconsiderable by reason of the width of the stream. For some distance up the river the width varies from a mile to a mile and a half. This portion is navigable for light-draught vessels, but from the Lower Limestone Rapids up to Split Lake it is one long series of rapids, with but comparatively short stretches of navigable water. The worst of these are the Gull Rapids, at the entrance to Gull Lake, where there is a descent of fifty feet in less than half a mile. From Split Lake to Sipiwesk Lake the course of the river is comparatively clear. Dr. Robert Bell in his exploration of the Nelson found that this portion occupies a channel scooped out during the glacial period along the course of a great dyke and afterward filled with pebbly clay. From Split Lake canoe routes lead north by the Little Churchill to the Churchill, east to Fox River, a tributary of the Hayes, west by Burntwood River to the Churchill, and southwest by Grass River to the Saskatchewan.

The Hayes River, a much smaller stream than either the Nelson or the Churchill, is important as the main route of explorers and fur-traders to the interior. It enters the bay a short distance south of the Nelson, the mouths of the two rivers being separated by Beacon Point. The canoe route runs from York Factory, on the north bank a few miles above the mouth of the river, up the Hayes to Knee Lake, thence to Oxford Lake, on which Oxford House of the Hudson's Bay Company stands, and thence by Echimamish River and the East River to Norway House on Little Playgreen Lake. From there to Playgreen Lake and Lake Winnipeg the course is clear.

The next river to the southward is the Severn, a shallow stream flowing through a well-wooded country for some four hundred and twenty miles. Fort Severn of the Hudson's Bay Company is situated opposite the head of Partridge Island, which divides the river at its mouth. About forty miles upstream the river is broken by White Seal Falls, and a long succession of rapids follow. The canoe route leaves the main stream at the mouth of the Fawn River, and follows that branch to Trout Lake, from which a portage brings the traveller back to the Severn at Severn Lake, thus avoiding the difficult navigation of the river below Severn Lake. From thence it follows the north branch of the Severn, through Sandy Lake, to its head-quarters, where a portage leads to the head-waters of the Poplar, thence to Berens River, which is followed down to Lake Winnipeg. The mouth of the Severn was first discovered by Captain Thomas James in 1631, and it was evidently named by him, as it appears as "New Severne" on his map. Although the route above described was traversed by Hudson's Bay men at a comparatively early date, and the course of the river has been carefully explored from its mouth to Severn Lake, comparatively little is known to-day of the south branch above Severn Lake.

The Albany River is readily traced on any modern map of Canada, as it forms the northern boundary of the province of Ontario. It ranks among the large rivers of Canada, being six hundred and ten miles from source to mouth. Ten miles below the forks, where the Kenogami flows in, stood the first inland post of the Hudson's Bay Company, built in 1741. It was called Henley House, and was established to meet the competition of the French traders from Canada, who were boldly encroaching on what the Hudson's Bay Company considered their own peculiar territory. At the mouth of the river, as at the mouth of all important rivers flowing into Hudson or James bays, the Hudson's Bay Company maintains a trading establishment. Albany Fort, or its predecessor, dates back to the latter

half of the seventeenth century. Captain George Barlow
was governor of the post in 1704, when the French
attacked it, and changed the name for a time to Ste.
Anne's. Martin Falls, where the Company have a small
post, is the first considerable break in the navigation of
the river. Between Martin Falls and Lake St. Joseph
the river is broken by several rapids. The source of the
Albany is in Cat or Catfish Lake, about one hundred
miles north of Lake St. Joseph, close to the head-waters
of the English River. From the western end of Lake
St. Joseph a portage leads to Root River flowing into
Lac Seul; thence the route for boats and canoes follows
the English River and the Winnipeg to the lake.

So much for the routes from Hudson Bay to Lake
Winnipeg. Now as to the route or routes leading from
Lake Superior to Lake Winnipeg. Broadly speaking,
this is one route; that is to say, it has always been
followed in the same general direction, along the same
broad line, from Lake Superior to the foot of Lake
Winnipeg. There have, however, been variants in the
details of the route. Up to the close of the French
regime the route led sometimes up the Kaministikwia
by many portages to Dog Lake, then up Dog River
to the height of land, where a portage brought the
voyageur to Savanne River, and so to Lac des Mille
Lacs, from whence he threaded his way through
numerous small lakes and streams to Lac la Croix;
and sometimes over the Grand Portage to Pigeon
River, and thence along what is now the international
boundary between the United States and Canada to

Lac la Croix. From Lac la Croix the route was practically always the same, still following the international boundary to Rainy Lake, and by Rainy River to Lake of the Woods. From Lake of the Woods it descended Winnipeg River to the lake. At one time, as will be seen later, the North West Company attempted to open another route from Lake Superior to Lake Winnipeg, by way of Lake Nipigon, Sturgeon Lake, and the English River; but it proved impracticable, and the Canadian traders after the conquest, as before, followed the two routes above mentioned, first by way of Grand Portage and afterwards by the Kaministikwia.

Having now reached Lake Winnipeg, from Hudson Bay and from Lake Superior, the next stage leads to two great rivers, two great avenues seemingly designed by nature to point the way to the Western Sea. As the lines of exploration drew to a common centre at Lake Winnipeg, so they are found diverging again, on one side south-west to the Missouri, and on the other north-west to the Saskatchewan. In sketching this geographical sequence, however, the chronological order of events must be more or less disregarded. As a matter of fact, the forking of the lines of exploration in point of time antedated the converging of the lines upon Lake Winnipeg, for the early French explorers were already feeling their way from Winnipeg out into that vast prairie sea of the west, while the English, after their splendid period of activity in exploring Hudson Bay, were taking a long rest upon its shores before pushing inland. However, in this broad survey of the field it is

permissible and even necessary to disregard the chronological order of events, the better to grasp the significance of the whole movement.

Returning to the Missouri and the Saskatchewan.
Over the former it is not necessary to linger. Although
its possibilities as a route across the continent were
foreseen by several far-sighted French explorers, it was
abandoned at an early date in favour of the Saskatchewan route. After the cession of Canada to England,
an occasional half-hearted attempt was made, or
planned, to test the Missouri route, but nothing of
much moment was added to the geographical knowledge acquired by the latter in this direction until
1805–6, when Lewis and Clark made their successful
journey overland to the mouth of the Columbia. Lewis
and Clark approached the upper waters of the Missouri
from the south-east, not from the north-west. Their
expedition was independent of the movement traced in
the following pages, and more properly forms a part of
the history of the Trans-Mississippi exploration.

The course followed by French and English explorers
from Lake Winnipeg to the Missouri was by way of
the Red River, the Assiniboine, and the Souris, thence
over the height of land to the Missouri. This was
approximately the route, whether the expedition went
by land or water. As a matter of fact, most of the
journeys undertaken to the Missouri were overland
from the Assiniboine, past Turtle Mountain, a famous
landmark lying across the international boundary. Of
the rivers mentioned, the Assiniboine is an affluent of

the Red, and the Souris of the Assiniboine, so that these three streams furnished a continuous waterway from Lake Winnipeg to the upper waters of the Souris, well over toward the Missouri. This can hardly be said to have been much more than a theoretical waterway, however, as the Souris was frequently too shallow, especially in its upper reaches, to float even a light canoe. The Souris is nevertheless quite a long stream; exactly the same length, in fact, as its elder brother, the Assiniboine, four hundred and fifty miles. It rises north of the international boundary, almost due south of the town of Regina, and about half-way between there and the boundary. From its source it runs generally south-east, crosses the boundary, and swings well down towards the Missouri before turning north again into Canadian territory, where it joins the Assiniboine. The Assiniboine itself rises to the westward of Lake Winnipegosis, and sweeps half-way around that lake and Lake Manitoba on its way to join the Red River. The Assiniboine was known to the early Canadian traders as the Stone Indian River, and it is so marked on David Thompson's map, of which more hereafter. The name Assiniboine is said to mean "River of the Stony Sioux." Another tributary of the Assiniboine, the Qu'Appelle or Calling River, rises two hundred and seventy miles from its junction with the Assiniboine, close to the head-waters of a little creek that empties into the South Saskatchewan. A short portage connects the two waterways. The Qu'Appelle got its name in a rather picturesque way. "In olden times," says Masson, "the shores of this river were haunted by a spirit, whose voice, resembling that of a human being, was often heard wailing during the night. So said the natives, and the *Voyageurs* called it *Rivière qui Appelle*." Harmon gives a similar account of the origin of the name.

The Red River, or the Red River of the North, as it was formerly called to distinguish it from several other rivers of the same name, is some three hundred and fifty-five miles long from the head of Lake Traverse, and five hundred and forty-five from the head of the Sheyenne. This is the Rivière Rouge of the early French explorers, who built rude forts upon its banks, as well as upon the banks of the Assiniboine, and used these as starting-points for further explorations west and south.

Turning now to the Saskatchewan, which is entered at the north-western corner of Lake Winnipeg, this river drains the Rocky Mountains through four degrees of latitude, interlocking with Athabaskan waters in the far north, and with Mississippian waters below the international boundary. North and south it approaches affluents of the mighty Columbia. At one point or another, east or west, north or south, it affords a communication, direct or by comparatively short portages, to every quarter of the continent. Its own waters reach Hudson Bay; by way of Lake Winnipeg and the Rainy River routes it reaches portages to Pigeon River and the Kaministikwia, thence by the St. Lawrence waterways to the Gulf of St. Lawrence; through Red

River and Lake Traverse a short portage leads to the Minnesota and the Mississippi; practically every pass through the Rockies from Howse to the South Kootenay affords a communication with Columbian waters and the Pacific; while half a dozen portages lead from the Saskatchewan to the Churchill and Athabaska, thence to the Mackenzie and the Arctic Ocean.

Extensive as is the area of the Rocky Mountains drained by the Saskatchewan, it is inconsiderable when compared with the length of that waterway, and remarkably so if only the two main branches are considered. The North Saskatchewan, recognized as the main stream, although actually shorter than the south branch, is eleven hundred miles long from its source in Wilcox Pass, opposite the head-waters of the Sun Wapta branch of the Athabaska, to where it empties into Lake Winnipeg. The South Saskatchewan flows for twelve hundred and five miles from the head-waters of Bow River to Lake Winnipeg. It is only about forty-five miles as the crow flies from the head-waters of one branch to the head-waters of the other; and the source of Little Fork or the south branch of the North Saskatchewan lies within one mile of the source of the Bow. From where they rise, so close together, the north and south branches rapidly diverge until some three hundred miles apart; a direct line from the confluence of the Bow and Belly rivers on the south branch, to the mouth of White Earth River on the north branch, is a little over two hundred and eighty miles. From the point of widest separation they

gradually approach again, until at last they come to-
gether at the Grand Forks, a little west of long. 105°.
On their course to this point, the North Saskatchewan
receives a number of tributaries, of which Battle and
Brazeau rivers are the most important; while the South
Saskatchewan brings down the waters of the Bow,
Belly, and Red Deer rivers. From the Grand Forks
the two branches flow together in one mighty stream to
Cedar Lake and Lake Winnipeg.

The river system which finally debouches into
Mackenzie Bay, north of the Arctic Circle, is one of the
most remarkable on this continent of great river
systems. It has as tributaries rivers which themselves
rank among the largest of North America, and drains
three great lakes as well as many smaller ones. The
main stream extends from the Arctic to Great Slave
Lake; from Great Slave Lake to Lake Athabaska it
assumes the name of Slave River; a little north of Lake
Athabaska, one of its great tributaries, the Peace River,
joins Slave River; and south of Lake Athabaska it
receives the southernmost of its affluents, the Athabaska.
North of Great Slave Lake the Mackenzie receives the
Liard, Peel, and Arctic Red rivers. These three come
in from the west; to the eastward the short Bear River
brings down the waters of Great Bear Lake. The Peace
River itself has several important tributaries, the largest
of which is the Finlay. The Finlay rises in Thutage
Lake, a small body of water in Northern British
Columbia, just south of the 57th degree of north
latitude. Thutage Lake is regarded as the ultimate

source of the Mackenzie, and from there to its mouth is a distance of two thousand five hundred and twenty-five miles, making the Mackenzie the longest river in North America after the Mississippi and Missouri.

Although the Liard joins the Mackenzie opposite Fort Simpson, only a little south of lat. 62° N., and the Peace empties not only three degrees farther south, but over ten degrees farther east, a branch of the Finlay rises in Sifton Pass, lat. 58° N., long. 126° 20′, within a few miles of the Kachika branch of the Liard. Similarly, east of the mountains, affluents of the Liard and Peace, as well as of the Peace and Athabaska, approach or interlock with one another. West of the mountains again the Finlay and Parsnip branches of Peace River join to form the main stream, reaching the same point from diametrically opposite directions. The Parsnip will be met with again in connection with Alexander Mackenzie's epoch-marking journey to the Pacific.

Two other important rivers of the Arctic slope remain to be considered, the Coppermine and Backs River. The Coppermine will always be associated with the name of Samuel Hearne, who penetrated to its mouth, from Prince of Wales Fort, in 1771. In the next century it was visited by Franklin, Richardson, Dease, Simpson, and Rae. It rises in a small lake south of Hood River, and after flowing south and west through Lac au Gras, turns north-west through a number of small lakes, and finally north, emptying into the south-west corner of Coronation Gulf, after a course of five hundred and twenty-five miles. It is broken by many rapids and, a few miles from its mouth, by Bloody Fall, made famous by a tragic incident in Hearne's narrative.

Backs River, discovered and traversed by Captain Back in 1834, rises in Sussex Lake, a little north of Aylmer Lake, and flows approximately north-east, six hundred and five miles, to its mouth at the foot of the deep inlet east of Adelaide Peninsula.

Before leaving the Arctic slope it may be noted that Great Bear Lake, though so much more inaccessible than Great Slave Lake, and discovered many years later, has been more carefully and thoroughly explored. With the exception of the west end of Smith Bay, the shore-line of the lake may now be said to be fairly well known, while much of the shore-line of Great Slave Lake is still purely conjectural.

Turning now to the Pacific slope. To reach any of the rivers that drain that slope it is necessary to cross one or other of the Rocky Mountain passes. Here the rivers of the plains were still the friends of explorers, as they had been in the easy access they afforded from one to another. Their guiding fingers pointed the way, and their waters offered a certain, if not always easy, pathway to the eastern entrance of every pass through the mountains. The Peace River leads not only up to, but through the Peace River Pass; Pine River, a branch of the Peace, offers a passage-way through the pass of the same name, and connects with the Missinchinka, a small tributary of the Parsnip; the Miette, a mountain affluent of the Athabaska, rises near the summit of

Yellowhead Pass, close to the head-waters of a branch of the Fraser; Whirlpool River, another branch of the Athabaska, similarly rises in the Athabaska Pass, and down the western slope a small stream leads to the Columbia; a tributary of the North Saskatchewan rises in Howse Pass, almost within a stone's-throw of the source of the Blaeberry branch of the Columbia; similarly the Kicking Horse Pass, Simpson Pass, White Mans Pass, Kananaskis Pass, North Fork, the Crows Nest, and the North and South Kootenay Passes, are all approached by one of the numerous tributaries of the South Saskatchewan; and in every case on the other side of the summit a branch of either the Columbia or the Kootenay is ready to convey the traveller, or at least to lead him, to the main streams in the valleys below.

British Columbian rivers differ materially from those of the plains, and the explorer who travelled across the mountains from one to the other had to prepare himself for very dissimilar conditions; they are essentially mountain streams, rapid, turbulent, treacherous; but in one particular, at least, they resemble the rivers east of the mountains, and that is in the facilities they afford for getting from one to the other. It has already been noted how closely the Liard approaches the Finlay. Coming south, the same conditions are everywhere observable. From one of the sources of the Parsnip in Summit Lake, Giscome Portage brings the traveller to the main waters of the Fraser. Ascending the Fraser to its upper waters, he may portage over to Canoe

River, a branch of the Columbia; and a short distance down Canoe River another portage brings him to the North Thompson, which conducts him back again to the Fraser, far down toward its mouth. Descending Canoe River to the Columbia, and paddling up the Columbia to its source in the Upper Columbia Lake, he may by a short portage reach the upper waters of the Kootenay.[1] Similarly, in the north, the Skeena connects through Babine Lake with the waters of the Fraser; and a branch of the Stikine approaches Dease Lake, the source of Dease River, a tributary of the Liard.

Another peculiarity of British Columbian rivers is their tendency to return upon themselves. The Columbia, for instance, flows north-west as far as the mouth of Canoe River, then turns and runs parallel with its upper waters to the Upper and Lower Arrow lakes. From thence, crossing the International Boundary, it sweeps down in a series of giant bends to its mouth. The Kootenay, on the other hand, runs south

---

[1] At one point less than a mile separates the two rivers, and as the Kootenay is a little higher than the Columbia, an enterprising Englishman, Mr. W. A. Baillie-Grohman, conceived the idea of turning the waters of the Kootenay into the Columbia, to overcome the enormous freshets that every summer flood the lower Kootenay valley, where he had secured from the British Columbia Government a concession of forty-eight thousand acres. The Dominion Government forbade the open channel Baillie-Grohman proposed to dig, but permitted him to cut a canal with a lock to overcome the difference in level. The canal was built, but apprehensions being felt that it might, during exceptionally high water, break through the gates and flood the valley of the Columbia, the Provincial Government ordered it to be closed up. Otherwise the modern traveller might cross from the source of the Columbia to the upper waters of the Kootenay without leaving his canoe.

from its source for some distance parallel with the upper waters of the Columbia, and after crossing the boundary turns north to Kootenay Lake, and finally joins the Columbia. The Fraser flows north-west from its source, like the Columbia, and from the great bend runs almost due south to its mouth. This characteristic of British Columbian rivers is the result of the peculiar formation of the Pacific slope. The country consists of gigantic parallel ridges running approximately north and south, separated by long, narrow valleys, through which run the rivers of the coast, down one great valley, then back down the next, until finally they break away from the mountains and reach the sea.

Of these rivers of the Pacific slope the Columbia is by all odds the greatest. It bears the same relation to the Pacific coast as the St. Lawrence does to the Atlantic, the Mackenzie to the Arctic, and the Mississippi to the Gulf. Its discovery was one of the most notable achievements in the exploration of the north-west coast. Long before its actual discovery the maps of North America showed a great river emptying into the Pacific about the latitude of the Columbia. This supposed river was known as the River of the West, and was renamed the Oregon by Jonathan Carver. On August 15th, 1775, Bruno Heceta discovered the mouth of the Columbia, without, however, recognizing its character. John Meares passed the entrance in 1789, and named it Deception Bay. In May, 1792, Robert Gray, of Boston, crossed the dangerous bar that guards the entrance to the estuary, which he explored, and named the river the Columbia, after his own vessel. Gray is properly regarded as the true discoverer of the river, as he first recognized its character, and was first to enter its mouth. Lieutenant Broughton, of the Vancouver Expedition, entered the Columbia five months after Gray, and ascended the river in boats for about one hundred miles, taking possession of the country for the King of England. The Columbia was first reached overland by the Lewis and Clark Expedition in 1805, and first explored throughout its entire length of eleven hundred and fifty miles by David Thompson, of the North West Company, in 1807–11. The Kootenay is the main tributary of the Columbia, but in its long course to the sea the latter receives many other affluents, chief of which are the Okanagan, rising not far from the South Thompson, in Southern British Columbia ; the Pend d'Oreille, or Clarks Fork,[1] whose ultimate source is near Butte, Montana, and one of whose branches rises north of the International Boundary, between the Crows Nest Pass and North Kootenay Pass ; and the Snake River, by which Lewis and Clark finally reached the Columbia.

The Fraser ranks next in importance to the Columbia, and in its course to the sea of six hundred and ninety-five miles receives a number of tributaries, of which the Thompson, with its two branches, is the largest. The

[1] This river appears on Canadian maps as the Pend d'Oreille, and on United States maps as Clarks Fork. Like the Columbia and Kootenay, it traverses both American and Canadian territory.

Fraser was discovered at its mouth by Galiano in 1792; it was discovered and traversed in its upper courses by Alexander Mackenzie in 1793, who mistook it for the Columbia; and in 1808 Simon Fraser explored the river down to its mouth, one of the most notable exploits in the history of North American discovery.

Coming back then to the starting-points on Lake Superior and Hudson Bay for a rapid survey of the course of exploration westward to the Pacific and northward to the Arctic, it will be seen that the tide of discovery followed, inevitably, the waterways that cover North-Western America with such a remarkable network. From Lake Superior the course of exploration lay up the Kaministikwia on the one hand, and over Grand Portage on the other, to Rainy Lake, where the first of a long series of trading posts in the interior was built, trading posts which played an essential part in the discovery of the west. Descending Rainy River, the early explorers reached Lake of the Woods, where another trading post was established. From thence the next step brought them to Lake Winnipeg, by way of Winnipeg River, at the mouth of which a third fort was built. From Lake Winnipeg the course of western discovery forked, first up Red River and the Assiniboine and overland to the Missouri and beyond; later, northwest to the Saskatchewan. To the Saskatchewan and Lake Winnipeg came the explorers from Hudson Bay, overlapping the earlier discoveries. Exploration then moved up the Saskatchewan and for some distance up its two great branches. From Cumberland Lake it turned north to the Churchill by way of Frog Portage, west to the Athabaska by way of Methye Portage, and north to Lake Athabaska. From Lake Athabaska it was a comparatively easy step to Great Slave Lake and the Peace River. The explorers now commanded the approaches to the mountains, and the country west of the mountains, by three several routes; they invaded the Pacific Slope, first by way óf Peace River, then by way of the Saskatchewan, and later by way of the Athabaska, and all three routes finally brought them to the shores of the Pacific. Before all this was accomplished, however, they had boldly attacked the far north, reaching the mouth of the Coppermine by a long overland expedition from Hudson Bay, and the mouth of the Mackenzie from Athabaska and Great Slave Lake.

A word or two here as to the origin and significance of place-names that will come up in the following narrative will not be inappropriate. Place-names in Western Canada may be divided, broadly speaking, into two classes: those which bear Indian names or translations of Indian names, and those which have been called after explorers. To the former class belong such names as Winnipeg, Manitoba, Saskatchewan, Assiniboine, Athabaska, Kootenay, and Okanagan ; and to the latter such as Mackenzie, Fraser, Thompson, Backs, and Stuart. There are of course exceptions, but it will be found that the majority of the place-names of the west fall into one or other of these two categories, and in these may be included the names of lakes, rivers, mountains, mountain passes, portages, and trading posts. The same rule applies to the names of provinces, towns, and other political divisions, but these do not enter into the present narrative.

Taking the lakes, it will be seen that most fall into the first class—Winnipeg, Winnipegosis, Manitoba, Athabaska, Shuswap; while some, like Great Slave, Reindeer, and Great Bear, are translations of Indian names. Of the first three, Sir W. F. Butler says that Winnipeg means the Great Sea; Winnipegosis, the Little Sea; and Manitoba, the Strait of the Gods; but, like a good many of Butler's statements, this translation is fanciful and inaccurate. Dr. Elliott Coues properly translates Winnipeg, which is derived from the Cree word Wi-nipi or Win-nepe, turbid water. Mr. C. N. Bell has compiled the following list, showing the gradual evolution of the name: Ouinipigon, first used by the French-Canadian explorer Pierre Gaultier de Varennes, Sieur de La Vérendrye, in 1734; Ouinipique, by Arthur Dobbs, in 1742; Vnipignon, by Gallissonière, in 1750; Ouinipeg, by Bougainville, 1757; Ouinipique, on a French map of 1776; Winnipeck, Carver, 1768; Winipegon, Alexander Henry, 1775; Winipic, Sir Alexander Mackenzie, 1789; Winipick, Harmon, 1800; Winepic, Ross Cox, 1817; Winnipic, Schoolcraft, 1820; Winnepeck, Keating, 1823; Winipeg, Beltrami, 1823; Winnipeg, Back, 1833.

If, as is apparently the case, Mr. Bell means that the existing form was first used in connection with Back's Arctic Land Expedition of 1833–5, he is in error;

the form Winnipeg will be found on Franklin's map, 1818–23. It may be noted also that the form Vnipignon credited to Gallissonière (Galissonière) should be to La Vérendrye. It appears on La Vérendrye's map of 1750, which was merely transmitted to France by Gallissonière, then Governor of Canada. Another form that might be added to the list is Winnipeggon-e-sepe, Coats's *Geography of Hudson Báy*, 1727–51. Dr. Coues says that the lake first appeared on Franquelin's map of 1688. It is open to question whether the lake shown on Franquelin's map was not rather the Lake of the Woods, though no doubt Indian reports of Lake Winnipeg may have reached the French as early as 1688. In any event, there is no satisfactory proof of any white man, French or English, reaching the shores of Lake Winnipeg before La Vérendrye. An interesting account of the four distinct names applied to Lake Winnipeg at different periods, with their unnumbered variants, will be found on pp. 37–8 of the Henry-Thompson Journals (Coues).

The name Athabaska is applied to a lake, a river, a mountain pass, a tribe of Indians,[1] and was formerly given to the territory now merged in the two provinces of Alberta and Saskatchewan. Like all the Indian place-names in the west, it has been spelled in many different ways—Athapuscow, Athapuskow, Athapupuscow, Athapupuskow, Athapescow, Athapishow, Arabascow, Araubaska, Ayabaska, Athapapuskow, Athabasca, Athabaska. The latter is the form approved by the

[1] The spelling of the tribal name is "Athapascau."

Geographical Board of Canada, whose decisions are followed uniformly in this book, so far as Canadian place-names are concerned. The meaning of the Indian name is given as the Meeting-place of Many Waters. The singular appropriateness of Indian place-names must have struck any one who has looked into the subject. It is regrettable that more of these names have not been retained.

A good deal of confusion has arisen owing to the fact that Hearne on his way back from the mouth of the Coppermine crossed a great lake which he named Athapuscow. For some reason which is not altogether clear at this time, it was assumed by many that Hearne's Athapuscow was the lake now known as Athabaska, though it would seem to be plain to any one with a map of the North-West before him that the lake reached by Hearne on his journey south from the Coppermine must have been the Great Slave Lake. Nevertheless, the error had taken such deep root that even now one finds it repeated by otherwise accurate writers. Athabaska is found as Lake of the Hills on Mackenzie's and several other early maps, and the Athabaska River was at one time known as the Elk. Dr. George M. Dawson says in one of his survey reports that Lake Athabaska is called A-pē-pas-kow by the Crees; and that the upper part of the river is known as Mus-ta-hi-sī-pī, or Great River.

Sir Alexander Mackenzie gives this interesting account of the origin of the Indian names for the Peace and Slave Rivers: It appears that the river derived its

name from a place on its banks known as Peace Point.
This was " the point where the Knisteneaux [Crees] and
Beaver Indians settled their disputes, the real name of
the river and point being that of the land which was the
object of their contention. When this country was
formerly invaded by the Knisteneaux they found the
Beaver Indians inhabiting the land about Portage la
Loche [Methye Portage], and the adjoining tribes were
those whom they called Slaves. They drove both these
tribes before them; when the latter proceeded down
the river from the Lake of the Hills [Athabaska],
in consequence of which that part of it obtained
the name of the Slave River. The former proceeded
up the river; and when the Knisteneaux made peace
with them, this place was settled to be the boundary."
On Mackenzie's map the Peace is marked as the
Unjigah; another form of the same Indian name being
Unshagah.

Dr. Coues gives Lac des Bois (or de Bois or du Bois),
Lac des Sioux, Lac des Isles, as names current during
the French period for what is now known as the Lake
of the Woods. Keating says the Indian name was
Sakahigan Pekwaonga, and translates it Lake of the
Island of Sand Mounds. Lake of the Sand Hills is
said to be still in use, and the name is supposed to have
been derived from the sand-bars and sandy reaches
marking the south-eastern shores of the lake. The explanation of this confusing medley of names is simply
this, that the whole body of water now called Lake of
the Woods, broken up as it is by many large and small

islands, was treated by the Indians as several more or less distinct lakes, each of which bore a distinct name descriptive of its character. Mr. Andrew C. Lawson makes the matter perfectly clear. Quoting from a paper by J. J. Bigsby in the *Quarterly Journal of the Geological Society*, 1852, he says: "In this paper Dr. Bigsby mentions the various names applied at the time of his visit to different parts of the lake, as follows: 'Lake of the Woods or Kamnitic Sakahagan; Clearwater Lake; Lake of the Sand Hills or Pekwaonga Sakahagan; Whitefish Lake or Whitefish Bay.' The first of these names," says Mr. Lawson, "is more probably the Indian equivalent of 'Island Lake,' which was perhaps with more likelihood than 'Lake of the Woods' the original Indian name, the present name having arisen by mistranslation." Clearwater Lake Mr. Lawson considers "probably a confusion with the north-west part of the lake known as Clearwater Bay, or with the present Whitefish Bay, which is still called by the Indians Clearwater." The third name was derived, as already suggested, from the sand-dunes near the mouth of Rainy River. The fourth name is "only now applied by the Indians to the sheet of water east of the Sioux Narrows." It has also been suggested that the old French name, Lac du Bois (so spelled on La Vérendrye's 1750 map, though generally Lac des Bois in his narratives), was named by La Vérendrye after the Abbé (afterwards Cardinal) Du Bois, the King's minister, favourite, and confidant, and for a time practically the ruler of France; and it is pointed out in support o this theory that La Vérendrye was in the habit of thus honouring his patrons and other influential personages of the hour. Unfortunately, however, for the theory, it will be seen by a reference to any of La Vérendrye's maps that it was only in the case of forts or trading posts that he followed this practice, as witness Fort St. Pierre, Fort St. Charles, Fort Maurepas, Fort La Reine, Fort Dauphin, Fort Bourbon. When he was naming lakes or rivers, he either translated the Indian name, or called them after some natural characteristic, as, for instance, Lac de la Pluie, Lacs Vnipignon, Rivière Poskaïao, Rivière aux Biches.

The little river which has borne such an important part in the history of exploration in North-Western America, the Kaministikwia, carries to-day the same name which it went by when French explorers first penetrated to the western end of Lake Superior, early in the second half of the seventeenth century. Pierre Esprit Radisson and his brother-in-law Medard Chouart seem to have been the first to reach the neighbourhood of the Kaministikwia, but there is no record of their having actually discovered the river. Daniel Greysolon Dulhut built, or is supposed to have built, the first trading post at the mouth of the river about 1678, and ten years later De Noyon is said to have ascended the Kaministikwia to Rainy Lake and Lake of the Woods. In 1717 Zacharie Robutel de La Noüe built a post at the mouth of the Kaministikwia, and another on Rainy Lake, the native name of this lake in La Noüe's day being Tékamamiouen.

The earliest French explorers who reached the Saskatchewan found the river under an Indian name variously spelled Poskaïao, Poskoiac, Pasquayah, Pasquia, Basquia, etc. The name still remains, but is now applied to a tributary of the Saskatchewan that comes in from the south, about long. 101° 15′. One of La Vérendrye's posts, Fort Poskoyac, stood here for some time after 1755, and twenty years later there was an Indian village about the same spot, under a robber-baron of a chief named Chatique, who robbed Alexander Henry and some of the other traders in a delightfully original fashion. The existing name of the great river is also of native origin, and is said by Dr. Coues to mean "swift flowing."[1] The name has had very many variants, sometimes beginning with S, sometimes with K, such as Kisiskatchewan. One of the oddest of its numerous forms is Kejeechewon.

The Red River was known as Rivière Rouge during the period of French exploration, and both names are a translation of the original Indian name, Miscousipi. The Assiniboine has changed its name almost more than any other western river. It was first called Rivière St. Charles by La Vérendrye in 1738, but on his 1740 and 1750 maps it appears as Rivière des Assiliboille, or Rivière des Assiniboilles. Among the early English traders it was considered an essential part of the Red River, and often got the same name. It was also called the Stone Indian River. Finally it reverted to the Indian name, and after wavering in the midst of a

[1] Literally, swift current.

perfect maze of variants finally settled into its present form, Assiniboine.

Of the rivers and lake west of the Rocky Mountains, the Columbia, as has already been mentioned, was named after Robert Gray's ship. It probably had an Indian name, but that is not now extant. By stretching a point the Columbia may perhaps be identified with the more or less conjectural River of the West that figured so prominently on nearly all the early maps, even as late as Carver; though it is a question whether such slight foundation as the River of the West was built upon had its origin in the accounts of voyagers who had sailed up the north-west coast, or in the reports of Indians carried from tribe to tribe across the continent, and, of course, gaining nothing in accuracy or definiteness on the way.

The Kootenay, first discovered by David Thompson in 1808, was named by him McGillivray's River, after his friend Duncan McGillivray. It is also sometimes called the Flat Bow River in Thompson's journals. The names on Thompson's maps and in his journals, applied to rivers, lakes, and trading posts west of the Rocky Mountains, are, in fact, almost uniformly different from those now in use, so much so that it is very difficult to follow Thompson's course to the sea without a key to his place-names. As Dr. Coues has compiled a list of the more important of these names, with their modern equivalents, it will be convenient to copy it here, as a means of helping the reader to trace Thompson through the topographical labyrinth of Southern

British Columbia and the country south of the international boundary.

Thompson's *Kootanae* River is the Columbia above Canoe River.

His *Kootanae* lakes are the Upper and Lower Columbia lakes (the lower one also now called Windermere Lake).

His *Kootanae House* was on the Columbia just below Lower Columbia Lake, where he wintered 1807–8, and again 1808–9.

His *McGillivray's* or *Flat Bow* River is Kootenay River.

His *Kootenae* or *Flat Bow* Lake is Kootenay Lake.

His *Saleesh* or *Flat Head* River is Clark's Fork of the Columbia.

[This is now known in Canada as the Pend d'Oreille, and that name will be adopted in following Thompson's course.]

His *Saleesh* or *Flat Head* Lake is Pend d'Oreille Lake, Idaho.

His *Kullyspell* Lake is also Pend d'Oreille Lake.

His *Kullyspell House* was built on Pend d'Oreille Lake.

His *Saleesh House* was built on Clark's Fork [Pend d'Oreille River], in Montana, where he wintered 1809–10.

His *Skeetshoo* River is Spokane River, which flows through Cœur d'Alène Lake, Idaho.

The Fraser River was named after Simon Fraser, who explored it to its mouth in 1808, as already mentioned.

Fraser Lake and Fort Fraser, in Northern British Columbia, or New Caledonia, as it was called in the days of the fur-trade, were also named after Simon Fraser. Stuart River and Lake were named after John Stuart, who accompanied Fraser in 1808. The names of Mackenzie, McKay, Fraser, and Stuart, splendid types of Scottish pluck and endurance, are indissolubly linked with the exploration of what is now the province of British Columbia. One Indian place-name which enjoyed a brilliant though temporary fame was that of the great River Tacouche Tesse or Tacoutche Tesse. Known for some time by Indian report, Mackenzie at last discovered it and traced it south for some distance, under the firm conviction that it was the long-sought Columbia. Fifteen years later Simon Fraser proved that the Tacouche Tesse was not the Columbia, but another river of almost equal importance, the Fraser.

PART I

THE NORTHERN GATEWAY

B

THE SEARCH FOR THE WESTERN SEA

CHAPTER I

THE DISCOVERY OF HUDSON BAY

THAT portion of the search for the Western Sea which proceeded through the gateway of Hudson Strait and Hudson Bay may be said to have had its birth in Amsterdam, in the year 1609. In that year, and in that town, famous even then as the home of maritime enterprise, two men might have been found poring over certain log-books. The two men were Peter Plancius, one of the ablest geographers of his day, and Henry Hudson, destined to earn an imperishable name in the annals of North American discovery. The log-books were those of George Weymouth, who, seven years before, had sailed a hundred leagues up the strait that afterward bore Hudson's name. But before attempting to describe the momentous results of this meeting, it will be well to glance back for a moment to still earlier times.

The story of the discovery of Hudson Strait is itself full of interest, human as well as geographical, but it must be passed over very briefly here. The question of who first discovered this remarkable entrance to an even more remarkable sea has been for many years, and probably always will be, a moot point among geographers. It is not unreasonable to suppose that the Scandinavian voyagers of the tenth century may have passed close enough to the strait to have seen it, or may even have entered it, when they sailed over to the western main in their wonderfully seaworthy little vessels. One can only say that they may have done so, for it is all pure conjecture. No proof is available one way or the other, documentary or cartographical.

The strait appears to be indicated on the Cabot planisphere of 1544, and contemporary as well as later evidence points to the probability that the entrance to the strait was reached in the Cabot voyage of 1498. Portuguese navigators have also been given credit for not only discovering the eastern entrance to the strait, but sailing up it, and even into the bay, somewhere between the years 1558 and 1567. Dr. G. M. Asher, who made a study of the Portuguese voyages in connection with his *Henry Hudson the Navigator*, satisfied himself that they had actually entered the bay. "They seem," he says, "to have advanced slowly, step by step, first along the shores of Newfoundland, then up to the mouth of Hudson's Strait, then through that strait, and at last into Hudson's Bay." With the aid of maps ranging from 1529 to 1570, Dr. Asher traces their

progress from point to point.   In 1544 he finds that the Portuguese had seemingly not yet reached the mouth of the strait; in 1558 their geographical knowledge extended beyond its mouth; in 1570 they had apparently reached the bay.   The "ancient geographical delineations" upon which Dr. Asher bases his belief are not perhaps quite so conclusive as he would have us believe. Nevertheless, it seems reasonably certain that the existence of the strait, if not of the bay, had been ascertained, as Dr. Asher says, before the publication of Ortelius's Atlas of 1570, and perhaps even earlier, for Ruysch's map in Ptolemy's Geography of 1508 contains a legend which could hardly refer to anything but the mouth of Hudson Strait.

Both Frobisher and Davis have been credited with the discovery of the strait, the former in 1578, and the latter in 1587, on his third voyage to the north-west. A careful reading of the narrative of Frobisher's voyages, as given in Hakluyt, in connection with contemporary and modern charts, leads, however, to the conclusion that the "strait" up which he sailed "for sixty leagues" was not Hudson Strait, but rather Frobisher Bay.   On the other hand, Davis's description of the "inlet or gulfe" passed over in August, 1587, where, to his great astonishment, he "saw the sea falling down into the gulfe with a mighty overfall and roaring, and with divers circular motions like whirlpools," seems clearly to apply to the eastern entrance of Hudson Strait, where these characteristic features have been time and again noted by later navigators.   It is equally certain that Weymouth, in 1602, sailed up the strait for about one hundred leagues, his farthest point west, or rather north-west, being probably somewhere in the neighbourhood of Charles Island, on the south side of the strait.

Hessel Gerritz, in his *Detectio Freti*, says that Hudson in the 1609 voyage, which preceded the one about to be described, sailed to the westward " to attempt again the way searched out by Captain Winwood [Weymouth]; which way, after passing for about a hundred leagues through a narrow channel, leads out into a wide sea. Hudson hoped to find a way through this sea [to the western or southern ocean], though Plancius had proved to him the impossibility of success, from the accounts of a man who had reached the western shore of that sea." Despite the evidence of this problematical voyager, Henry Hudson, after his return from the 1609 voyage, on which he discovered not Hudson Strait, but Hudson River, far to the south, determined to search again for a passage through the continent. This was the situation when he set forth on his memorable fourth and last voyage in the well-named *Discovery*.

Though published nearly half a century ago, Dr. Asher's *Henry Hudson the Navigator* still remains by all odds the best account of this " worthy irrecoverable discoverer," as Purchas calls him. Dr. Asher brought together for the first time, with infinite patience, the scattered fragments of evidence bearing on the life and explorations of Hudson. With the exception of certain depositions of the survivors of the fourth voyage, found by Miller Christy at Trinity House, and published as Appendix A to his *Voyages of Captain Luke Foxe and Captain Thomas James*, very little, if anything, has been added to that which we owe to the industry and enthusiasm of Asher. His work may be safely accepted as a guide to the four voyages, and particularly to the last, the only one with which we are here concerned.

The materials bearing on the voyage of 1610 consist of an abstract from Hudson's own journal, which breaks off abruptly as the ship is entering Hudson Bay from the strait; the narrative of Abacuk Prickett, which covers the entire voyage both outward and home; a note found in the desk of one Thomas Wydowse, or Woodhouse, who accompanied Hudson on the voyage, and, as will be seen, was afterward turned adrift with him in the bay by the mutinous crew; and Hudson's chart, or rather Hessel Gerritz's copy of Hudson's chart. As we probably owe the loss of all but a fragment of Hudson's journal of the voyage to the fear of his guilty crew of the exposure that it would afford, so we also doubtless owe the preservation of the chart to the inability of the crew to navigate the *Discovery* without it. These documents, with some stray notes by Purchas, Gerritz, and Foxe, make the sum of the material on the fourth voyage.

Hudson left the Thames on April the 17th, 1610, stopped at Iceland, where he spent Whit-Sunday and enjoyed an afternoon's shooting, his bag embracing partridge, curlew, plover, mallard, teal and goose, " so much fowle as feasted all our company being three and

twentie persons," and with a fair wind sailed out into the
west. On the fifteenth of June he was off the southern
coast of Greenland, and a few days later sighted Resolution Island, "that iland which Master Davis setteth
downe in his chart." "Our master," says Prickett, "would
have gone to the north of it, but the wind would not suffer
him ; so we fell to the south of it, into a great rippling
or overfall of current, the which setteth to the west."

Hudson's course through the strait is not easily traced
with any degree of certainty. Dr. Asher, Miller
Christy, and others have attempted to do so, but at least
some of their conclusions are impaired by the fact that
the Admiralty charts upon which they relied are far
from accurate. We have now available comparatively
recent maps of the Geological Survey of Canada, embodying the astronomically checked surveys of Dr.
Robert Bell and Dr. A. P. Low, which, though they do
not cover by any means the entire coast-line of the
strait, at least enable one to correct certain misconceptions arising from the older Admiralty charts. They
enable us, for instance, to correct the size, direction, and
latitude of Akpatok Island, in Ungava Bay, which had
been very inaccurately charted hitherto ; the shore-line
of Ungava Bay ; and the shore-line of portions of the
strait. With these recent maps before us, and Hessel
Gerritz's chart showing the strait as Hudson conceived
it to be, as well as the original narratives of Hudson and
Prickett, it may be possible to throw a little additional
light upon the course of the *Discovery* from Resolution
Island to Cape Wolstenholme.

Leaving Resolution Island, Hudson steered to the north-west, aided by the current, and was presently struggling in a veritable sea of broken ice. By constantly changing his course and taking advantage of lanes and channels that offered a temporary passage, he was able to make some progress west and north-west, and finally sighted the north shore, somewhere in the neighbourhood of East Bluff. Fighting his way along the north shore in comparatively open water, a storm sprang up from the west, and the wind brought the heavy ice so fast upon him that he was for a time in serious danger. Only one thing was to be done. He forced the *Discovery* into the midst of the loose ice, where she was at least comparatively safe from the sledge-hammer blows of the larger cakes. "Some of our men this day fell sicke," Prickett dryly remarks; "I will not say it was for feare, although I saw small signe of other griefe." Hudson freed his vessel when the wind moderated, and tried to force a way through the broken ice, but fell back baffled at every turn, until at last a way opened out to the south. Crossing the strait, he entered what is now Ungava Bay, where the ice once more closed in upon him.

It was now the fifth of July; he had been struggling about the eastern end of the strait for the better part of a fortnight, and his men were on the point of mutiny. The ship was in a desperate situation. Many years afterward, on almost the same day of the year, Captain Coats had his ship crushed to kindling wood in the ice, at the entrance to the strait; and on another occasion he six times tried to enter the strait, between the first of July and the twelfth, but was finally compelled to abandon the attempt and stand out into the open sea. Henry Hudson, however, was not a man to be turned from his purpose either by shouldering ice or a mutinous crew. Calling his men together, he spread Weymouth's chart before them, and showed them that Weymouth had sailed a hundred leagues up this strait, in the very same ship. What Weymouth had done could be done again. A few still grumbled, but Hudson's enthusiasm was infectious. The ship was now fast in the ice, and the crew set to work with a will to free her. A channel was cut for her to the open water, and at last she was free.

On this fifth day of July Hudson sighted the east shore of Ungava Bay, and made his position to be 59° 16′ N. On the strength of this observation both Dr. Asher and Mr. Christy place the landfall at or near Ittimenaktok Island, but this deduction is open to question. Hudson's latitude, wherever it can be checked with any degree of certainty, is found to be anywhere from a few minutes to a degree and a half astray, and forms, therefore, a rather insecure foundation on which to build any very positive conclusions. A careful reading of his journal, in connection with the Gerritz chart, and a comparison of his supposed positions while in Ungava Bay with the evidence furnished by the best modern charts, rather leads one to think that the point which Hudson reached upon the eastern shore of Ungava Bay was probably half a degree farther north, at or about Uivaksoak.

From this point, or rather from the spot where the *Discovery* was "embayed" in the ice, Hudson steered north-west, and on the eighth was, as he supposed, in 60° north latitude, where he discovered land lying N.W. by W. ½ N., high land covered with snow, a "champaigne" land, which he called Desire Provoketh. This was obviously Akpatok Island, but Hudson was astray in placing it in 60° N., and Dr. Asher did not mend matters by making it 59° 15′ N. As a matter of fact, the extreme southerly point of Akpatok is about 60° 10′ N., and the northern end of the island, in all probability the spot to which Hudson more particularly attached the name of Desire Provoketh, is about 60° 40′ N. A century and a quarter later Coats named this island Amocomanko, or perhaps it would be more correct to say applied to it the native name then current. He describes it as "a large, bold island on the south side, about twenty leagues to westward of Button's Iles"—the small group south of Resolution.

From Akpatok Hudson "plyed up to the westward, as the land and ice would suffer," and on the 11th July anchored by three rocky islands, which he named the Isles of God's Mercies. The latitude of these islands he found to be 62° 09′. Prickett gives the course from Akpatok, or Desire Provoketh, to the Isles of God's Mercies as north-west, but adds that they raised the land to the north of their course. There is some uncertainty as to the identity of these small islands. Dr. Asher supposes them to be Saddle Back and the surrounding islands to the south of Jackman Sound.

This hardly fits in with Hudson's course, which would lead rather to the Upper Savage group, near Big Island, of which Captain Coats, in his *Geography of Hudson Bay*, says, " Some call it God's Mercys." [1] At the same time, when Hudson left the Isles of God's Mercies his course was south-west, and he continued down on that course to 58° 50', which could only be at or near the foot of Ungava Bay. Obviously he could not sail on any such course from the Upper Savage to the foot of Ungava Bay, and the probabilities point to Saddle Back and the Middle Savage group.

Without doubt Abacuk Prickett was a clever scoundrel. One turns with more than a small measure of relief from Hudson's dry recital of dates, distances, and directions to Prickett's narrative. Hudson's journal is a lifeless official statement; Prickett's a human document. The former is, of course, invaluable in the evidence it affords as to the course of the *Discovery* through the strait. Without it we would be hopelessly at sea, for here Prickett's narrative is comparatively useless. He was not only no sailor, but there is reason to suppose that his narrative was written entirely after his return to England. Its inaccuracy and hopeless confusion from a geographical point of view is as striking as its dramatic interest. Prickett was a born story-teller. Wherever he went his eyes were wide open, and what he saw was not forgotten. This was a new world he was sailing through—a very different world from any he had been

---

[1] Dobbs, on the other hand, applies the name to the easternmost group.

accustomed to as the servant of Sir Dudley Digges. Everything was fresh; everything interesting. Trivial incidents that Hudson would have scorned to put on record Prickett describes with graphic simplicity and effectiveness. "We raised land to the north," he says, "and comming nigh it, there hung on the easternmost point many ilands of floting ice, and a beare on one of them, which from one to another came towards us, till she was readie to come aboord. But when she saw us looke at her, she cast her head betweene her hinde legges, and then dived under the ice, and so from one piece to another, till she was out of our reach."

It was the 16th July when Hudson found himself "imbayed with land" in lat. 58° 50', as he made it, probably at the foot of Hope's Advance Bay, on the south-western side of Ungava Bay. He was driven thus far south in his efforts to get around the ice that beset him on every side. After an unsuccessful attempt to land on this southern coast, he stood to the north again, and on the nineteenth, having sailed between Akpatok and the mainland, sighted the north-western extremity of Ungava Bay, which he named Hold with Hope—now Cape Hope's Advance.

The Gerritz chart revealed a curious misconception, on Hudson's part, as to the coast-line of Ungava Bay; a misconception which he seems afterward to have fallen into even more deeply in charting James Bay. A glance at the chart will show two bays taking the place of Ungava Bay, the easternmost shallow, the western-most quite deep. It is clear that, having sailed a short way down the eastern coast of Ungava Bay, thence west or north-west to Akpatok, he mistook that large island for a cape on the southern coast of the strait. Returning again from the northern shore of the strait, he passed down the western side of Akpatok, still mistaking it for the mainland, to the foot of Hope's Advance Bay. Ungava Bay thus appears as two on the Gerritz chart, and so remained for some years, none of the explorers who immediately followed Hudson making any attempt to examine the eastern side of the bay.

Having come up out of Ungava Bay and the encumbering ice, the long-suffering *Discovery* was no sooner in open water than she was once more besieged. "We were enclosed with land and ice, for wee had land from the south to the northwest on one side, and from the east to the west on the other, but the land that was to the north of us and lay by east and west was but an iland." This situation would fit any one of half a dozen places on the south shore west of Cape Hope's Advance, but it is most strikingly applicable to Diana Bay. "On we went till we could goe no further for ice, so we made our ship fast to the ice which the tyde brought upon us, but when the ebbe came the ice did open and made away, so as in seven or eight honres we were cleere."

Hudson now stood along the southern coast to the westward and north-westward, naming a prominent cape Prince Henry's Foreland. He does not mention this cape in his journal, but it is so named both in Prickett's narrative and on the chart. In both cases it is clearly on the southern shore of the strait, but for some unexplained reason Dr. Asher identifies it as North Bluff, Big Island, off the northern shore.

Still following the southern shore, a portion of which he called Magna Britannia, Hudson reached, about the end of July, what Prickett describes as "the extreme point of land looking towards the north," evidently Cape Weggs, or as Hudson named it, King James his Cape.

"The first of August," says Hudson, "we had sight of the northerne shoare, from the north by east to the west by south off us." Here again he seems to have repeated the Ungava error. Sailing west from Cape Weggs, he caught sight of the southern shore of Charles Island, mistook it for the northern coast of the strait, and named it Queene Annes Foreland, or as Gerritz turns it into Dutch on his chart, Quine Annes Forlandt. Here we find a curious statement in Prickett's narrative. The chart follows Hudson's journal in applying the name to a cape on the north shore of the strait. Prickett, however, says: "To the north of this [King James his Cape] lie certaine ilands, which our master named Queene Annes Cape or Fore-land." Did Prickett discover, on the homeward voyage, that Queen Annes Foreland was on an island, not on the northern main?

"Beyond the Kings Cape there is a sound or bay— Deception Bay—that hath some ilands in it. . . . Beyond this lyeth some broken land, close to the mayne, but what it is I know not, because we passed by it in the night." From Charles Island to Cape

Wolstenholme, at the western end of the strait, the southern shore is a little better known to-day than it was in Hudson's day.

Some distance to the westward of the Kings Fore-land, or King James Cape, there is marked on the chart, though not mentioned in Hudson's narrative, a great cape running far to the north, and named Cape Charles. Prickett says that the name was applied to a high hill on the mainland, which was called Mount Charles. Dr. Asher takes it to be Charles Island, and supposes that Hudson mistook it for part of the main-land.

On the second of August Hudson had sight of "a faire headland on the norther shoare, six leagues off, which I called Salisburies Fore-land." Prickett applies the name to a headland on an island to the north of and beyond Mount Charles. The chart places "Salis-bery's Ilandt" almost due west of Cape Charles. Here is variety enough. However, what was seen was evi-dently the large island still bearing the same name.

Leaving Salisbury Island to the north-east, Hudson sailed south through "a great and whurling sea" and reached the western extremity of the strait at Cape Wolstenholme, so named after Sir John Wolstenholme, one of the "adventurers" who had equipped the ex-pedition. Here, as elsewhere, every variety of spelling is encountered. Hudson spells the name "Worsen-holme"; Prickett, "Worsenhams"; and the Gerritz chart, "Worsnam." A cape on one of the small islands that lie to the north-westward of Cape Wolstenholme

HONIATHICO RIVER

Face p. 16

was called Cape Digges, after Sir Dudley Digges, another of the "adventurers." Hudson supposed Cape Digges to be on the northern shore of the strait, as is borne out by Prickett's explicit statement, "wur master took this to bee a part of the mayne of the north land, but it is an iland, the north side stretching out to the west more then the south."

Traversing the narrow passage between Digges Island and Cape Wolstenholme, Hudson "sailed with an easterly winde, west and by south ten leagues, the land fell away to the southward, and the other iles, and land left us to the westward. Then I observed and found the ship at noone in 61 degrees, 20 minutes, and a sea to the westward." Here Hudson's journal abruptly breaks off, and for the remainder of the voyage we must fall back on Prickett's narrative and the chart. Up to this point Prickett's narrative has been reasonably clear and accurate, and has on more than one occasion corrected the evident misconceptions of his master; but for the voyage down the eastern coast of Hudson Bay, and among the islands and shoals of James Bay, it is next to useless. Prickett was a landsman, and the seemingly aimless wanderings of the *Discovery* around James Bay might have taxed the powers even of an expert seaman to describe with satisfactory clearness.

Sailing down the Eastmain coast, a word or two here and there in Prickett's narrative helps out the evidence of the chart, as where he refers to land bearing to the eastward as "the same mayne land that wee had all this while followed." The chart shows to the westward of Digges Island a large unnamed island, evidently intended for Mansfield. Foxe says that Hudson named Nottingham Island after Lord Charles Howard, Earl of Nottingham, then Lord High Admiral of England, and one of the supporters of his voyage. We have nothing but Foxe's word for this. So far as the journals and the chart go, and their evidence should be conclusive, Hudson never saw Nottingham Island, or if he did, supposed it to be part of Salisbury. The outer line of islands which follows the Eastmain coast through four degrees of latitude, from 60° down to 56°, is roughly represented on the chart by four small islands, lying approximately north and south. Below these again is shown an island almost as large as Mansfield. This may have been intended for Akimiski, or it may even represent that portion of Ungava lying between the mouths of the Great Whale and Big rivers which forms, at Cape Jones, the north-eastern point of James Bay. Hudson, touching this coast at intervals, and noting its formidable sweep to the westward, might easily have mistaken it for a great island lying off the eastern mainland.

But when we get down into James Bay we are confronted with a still more singular puzzle. The Gerritz chart shows James Bay divided into two by a great peninsula extending from the foot of the bay almost to its head. What gave rise to this imaginary peninsula can only be conjectured. It may be that it represents the string of islands down the middle of the bay, from Bear Island in the north to Charlton in the south. Presuming that Hudson, in his zigzag course down the bay, touched at some of the larger islands, or saw them from a distance, they might have given the impression of a continuous coast-line. It has been suggested that Akimiski Island represents all that is tangible of the famous peninsula, but this explanation is harder to accept than the first. How could any navigator in his senses mistake an island lying so close to the western shore that at one point only about ten miles of water separate them for a peninsula bisecting a great bay one hundred and fifty miles across?

There is another possible explanation of this cartographical problem, but it is one that must be advanced with a good deal of hesitation, for it involves a claim on Hudson's behalf to the discovery of a large part of the western coast of Hudson Bay, a claim which has never seriously been advanced since the publication of Hessel Gerritz's *Descriptio ac delineatio Geographica Detectionis Freti*, and which rests upon statements made in the Dutch as well as the Latin editions; upon the chart prepared by Gerritz, based upon Hudson's own chart; and upon Gerritz's printed summary on the back of his chart. That chart puts the north-western extremity of the easternmost bay, named on the chart " The bay of Goods merces," a little north of the 53rd parallel. Cape Henrietta Maria lies on the 55th. But as the foot of James Bay, on the Gerritz chart, is more than a degree too far south, the distance from the foot of the Bay of Gods Mercies to its north-western extremity corresponds pretty closely with the distance from the foot of James Bay to Cape Henrietta Maria.

Assuming, then, that the Bay of Gods Mercies really represents James Bay, and not merely a portion of that bay, what becomes of the deep bay lying to the westward, unnamed? The only answer seems to be that Hudson rounded Cape Henrietta Maria, sailed across the shallow bay lying west of it, came within sight of the mainland again somewhere west of the mouth of the Severn River, and assumed that the intervening bay was as deep as the Bay of Gods Mercies. After Hudson's experience with Ungava Bay, such a theory is possible, though, it may as well be admitted, not altogether probable.

The chart carries the western coast of the bay up to 60°. Gerritz's summary, printed in Dutch on the back of the chart, says : " Having thus left the latitude of 52°, where they had wintered, and having sailed up to 60° along the western shore of their bay, they fell in with a wide sea and with a great flood from the north-west." Dr. Asher takes this as fairly conclusive evidence that the point thus reached must have been Cape Henrietta Maria, where they would have encountered a "wide sea" and a "great flood from the north-west." Cape Henrietta Maria is several degrees lower than 60°, but that does not necessarily invalidate Dr. Asher's theory, as nearly all the observations made by the early navigators and embodied in contemporary charts are one or more degrees astray. In the Latin edition of Gerritz's work (1612) he says that Hudson " sailed along the western shore of the bay till up to 62° or 63° north"; and in the Latin edition of 1613 it is said that he "ran along the western shore for forty leagues, and fell in, under 60°, with a wide sea," etc. Here we have a difference of three degrees in Gerritz's several accounts of this fourth voyage. The chart shows several large islands lying off the western coast of Hudson Bay between 56° and 60°. From Roe's Welcome in the far north to the foot of James Bay, only two large islands lie off the western coast, Marble Island and Akimiski. The former being out of the question, we are reduced to Akimiski. That convenient island seems to be a peg on which to hang every theory of the fourth voyage that defies other solution. In Gerritz's 1613 edition, Hudson's wintering-place is fixed in 54° instead of in 52°, as in the earlier editions. The spot where he is supposed to have wintered is somewhere about 51° 30'.

It may be noted here that Hudson's double bays were repeated, in almost identical form, on the charts of James and Foxe. In both cases it is probable that Hudson's chart, either in its original form or as published by Gerritz, was largely drawn upon both for the delineation of the east coast and of the shores of James Bay or Bays. Foxe had no means of checking Hudson's work, as he never went south of Henrietta Maria; and James explored only the western shores of the bay that bears his name, so that he could have no exact knowledge of what might lie to the westward of his course, and would naturally suppose himself to be in the westernmost of the two bays. Returning to the original problem, on the whole the more probable solution seems to be that the double bays were simply the result of confusion arising out of Hudson's rambling course in and around the inlets and islands of James Bay; and that his farthest point up to the west coast was Cape Henrietta Maria.

Three months had been spent in cruising about James Bay, "a labyrinth without end," as Prickett calls it. On Michaelmas Day they had gone down into a bay, which Hudson accordingly named Michaelmas Bay. There are many bays around the southern coast, and this one might have been almost any of them. The utter hopelessness of attempting to follow the course of the *Discovery* around James Bay may be illustrated by a single passage. They had come to the bottom of the bay, into six or seven fathoms of water. This tells us nothing. James Bay is shallow everywhere, with the exception of a channel somewhere about the position of Hudson's peninsula. In the lower part of the bay men have been out of sight of land, in water so shallow that bottom could be touched with an oar. However, from this problematical spot at the bottom of the bay they stood up to the north by the west shore till they came to an island in 53°. There is no means of knowing whether this was the west shore of the eastern bay or the west shore of the western bay. It might have been either, so far as the narrative goes. Lat. 53° cuts through the lower half of Akimiski Island. North Twin Island and South Twin Island are a little north of 53°, and Solomons Temples a little south. But, as

INDIAN BRIDGE OVER WATSONQUA RIVER

elsewhere suggested, it is not wise to hold Hudson, and if not Hudson, most decidedly not Prickett, too closely to his latitude. This island, where they landed to take water and ballast, may have been any one of a score of islands between 52° and 54°. Then when they took leave of this uncertain island, "up the north we stood," says Prickett, "till we raised land, then down to the south, and up to the north, then downe againe to the south, and on Michaelmasse Day came in and went out of certaine lands, which our master sets downe by the name of Michaelmasse Bay." Now can any one say where Michaelmasse Bay was? Dr. Asher suggests Hannah Bay. It is as likely to have been that as any other.

On the first of November, after further bewildering movements about the bay, the *Discovery* was brought aground for the winter in what has generally been supposed to be Rupert Bay, in the south-eastern corner of James Bay. Hudson's wintering-place is marked on the chart, but too vaguely to be of much service. Prickett's description of the locality is more definite than usual. "Wee stood up to the east and raysed three hills, lying north and south; we went to the furthermost, and left it to the north of us, and so into a bay, where we came to an anchor. Here our master sent out our boat, with myselfe and the carpenter to seeke a place to winter in; and it was time, for the nights were long and cold, and the earth covered with snow. . . . We went downe to the east, to the bottome of the bay, but returned without speeding of that we went for. The next day we went to the south and the south-west, and found a place, whereunto we brought our ship, and haled her aground." Sherrick Mountain, situated on a peninsula on the north side of the entrance to Rupert Bay, is described by Dr. A. P. Low as a very prominent landmark, rising as a granite hill about four hundred feet above the water. It is one of the very few hills on the southern coast of James Bay, which is generally low and flat, and may very well have been the hill or hills which the *Discovery* left to the north in entering the bay. The eastern side of Rupert Bay around the mouth of Rupert River is very shallow, while there is a comparatively deep channel leading down to the mouth of the Nottaway at the southern end of the bay. This agrees substantially with what Prickett has to say of their wintering-place, and but for a rather striking bit of evidence pointing to another spot, it might be reasonable to assume that Hudson wintered somewhere about the mouth of the Nottaway. The statement referred to is found in a memorial of the Hudson's Bay Company in 1699, in which it is said that Captain Gillam " built the said Fort Charles upon the ruins of a House which had been built there above 60 Yeares before by the English." The building of Fort Charles at the mouth of the Rupert, as will be seen in a later chapter, was in 1668, so that, if this statement is based on authentic knowledge, Hudson's winter quarters must have been at the mouth of the Rupert. The memorial should have said fifty-eight years instead of sixty.

By November 10th they were frozen in, and Hudson anxiously took stock of his provisions. The ship was victualled for six months, says Prickett. He must have meant six months from the time the ship was brought aground, as they had already been more than six months out of the Thames. Probably Hudson took a year's provisions with him when he set out on his voyage; but this was not enough, for they had still before them six long months before they could even begin the homeward voyage. To eke out the ship's stores Hudson offered a reward to every man that killed beast, fish, or fowl. For three months they had an ample supply of game. Of ptarmigan they killed about a hundred dozen, besides other birds. "All," says Prickett, "was fish that came to the net." With the approach of spring the ptarmigan left, and in their place came numbers of geese and duck, but to the bitter disappointment of Hudson and his men they flew on to their breeding-grounds in the remote north. The ship's stores were now almost exhausted. What little remained must be carefully husbanded for the voyage home. If they lasted until the ship reached Digges Island there was hope, as immense quantities of wild-fowl had been seen on Digges Island on the outward voyage. Meantime the land and the sea must feed them. "Then went wee into the woods, hilles and valleyes, for all things that had any show of substance in them, so vile soever; the mosse of the ground, then the which I take the powder of a post to bee much better, and the frogge (in his engendring time as loathsome as a toade) was not spared."

"Now out of season and time," writes Prickett, "the master calleth the carpenter to goe in hand with an house on shoare, which at the beginning our master would not heare, when it might have been done. The carpenter told him that the snow and frost were such as hee neither could nor would goe in hand with such worke. Which when our master heard hee ferreted him out of his cabbin to strike him, calling him by many foule names and threatening to hang him . . . the house was (after) made with much labour, but to no end." This is presumably the house referred to in the Hudson's Bay Company's memorial of 1699. It is an interesting point whether this same house might not also be the "old howse" of Radisson's narrative. Many curious possibilities suggest themselves in this connection, but the whole question is too intricate to attempt to unravel here. It must be left for a later chapter.

About the time when the ice began to break out of the bays there came a savage to the ship, the first that they had seen. Hudson "intreated him well and made much of him, promising unto himselfe great matters by his means." To conciliate the Indian he gave him a knife, looking-glass, and buttons. The next day the native returned, dragging a sled after him loaded with two deer-skins and two beaver-skins. "Hee had a scrip under his arme, out of which hee drew those things which the master had given him. Hee tooke the knife and laid it upon one of the beaver skinnes, and his glasses and buttons upon the other, and so gave them to the master, who received them ; and the savage tooke those things which the master had given him and put them up into his scrip againe. Then the master showed him an hatchet, for which hee would have given the master one of his deere skinnes, but our master would have them both, and so hee had, although not willingly. After many signes of people to the north and to the south, and that after so many sleepes he would come againe, he went his way, but never came more." So ended disastrously this earliest attempt at fur-trading on the shores of Hudson Bay. It was characteristic enough of the attitude of white men toward the natives that even on this first occasion, despite the honesty of the savage in bringing back a fair equivalent for the presents that had been given him, Hudson must squeeze two skins out of him as the price of one hatchet.

The bay being now clear of ice, Hudson had water, wood, and ballast taken on board, and sent some of the men fishing to supply immediate wants, while he himself set out toward the south in search of Indians, from whom he hoped to obtain a supply of meat. After some days he returned unsuccessful. There was nothing for it now but to make the best of their way to Digges Island, in the hope that there they might have better success. Before sailing Hudson called his men together and divided among them all the bread that remained, which came to a pound apiece. The men who had before been sent fishing had had some success, bringing in five hundred of fair size, and now as a last expedient they were once more sent out with the net. From Friday to Sunday noon they laboured, and brought in fourscore small fish, "a poore reliefe for so many hungry bellies."

Then at last Hudson weighed anchor and stood out of the bay. The bread was all gone. Five cheeses remained, and these too were divided equally. A further search brought to light thirty cakes of ship's biscuit in a bag. Plainly, on however small a ration. this would not carry them to Digges Island. Some of the crew were already ill, and the rest conspired to seize the remaining provisions and save themselves. Here is the story of what followed, as Prickett tells it. How much of it is truth and how much fiction will never be known, for Prickett alone told the tale.

"Being thus in the ice on Saturday, the one and twentieth of June, at night, Wilson the boatswayne, and Henry Greene, came to mee lying (in my cabbin) lame, and told mee that they and the rest of their associates would shift the company, and turne the master and all the sicke men into the shallop, and let them shift for themselves. For there was not fourteen daies victuall left for all the company, at that poore allowance they were at, and that there they lay, the master not caring to goe one way or other." According to his own account, which is not above suspicion, Prickett tried to dissuade them, but without avail. They would rather face the chance of hanging at home than the certainty of present starvation.

" It was not long ere it was day ; then came Bennet

for water for the kettle, hee [that is, John King, the carpenter] rose and went into the hold; when he was in they shut the hatch on him. . . . In the meantime Henrie Greene and another went to the carpenter and held him with a talke till the master came out of his cabbin; then came John Thomas and Bennet before him, while Wilson bound his armes behind him. He asked them what they meant. They told him he should know when he was in the shallop. Not Juet, while this was a doing, came to John King into the hold, who was provided for him, for he had got a sword of his own, and kept him at a bay, and might have killed him, but others came to help him, and so he came up to the master. The master called to the carpenter and told him that he was bound, but I heard no answere he made. . . . Then was the shallop haled up to the ship side, and the poore, sicke, and lame men were called upon to get them out of their cabbins into the shallop. The master called to me, who came out of my cabbin as well as I could to the hatch way to speake with him; where, on my knees I besought them, for the love of God, to remember themselves, and to doe as they would be done unto. They bade me keepe myselfe well, and get me into my cabbin. . . .

"Now was the carpenter at libertie, who asked them if they would bee hanged when they came home; and as for himselfe, hee said, hee would not stay in the ship unlesse they would force him; they bade him goe then, for they would not stay him. I will (said he) so I may have my cheste with mee, and all that is in it; they said he should, and presently they put it into the shallop. . . . Now were the sicke men driven out of their cabbins into the shallop. . . . They stood out of the ice, the shallop being fast to the sterne of the shippe, and so they cut her head fast from the sterne of our ship, then out with their top-sayles, and towards the east they stood in a cleere sea." Having turned Hudson adrift with eight others, one supposed to have been his son, the crew ransacked the ship, and found in the master's cabin two hundred biscuits, a peck of meal, and a butt of beer. This, however, it must be remembered, is Prickett's story, and Prickett held a brief for the guilty crew, who had spared his life that he might help them to escape the consequences of their deed when they returned home. While they were searching the cabin and the hold, it was said that the shallop was overtaking the ship. "They let fall the mainsayle, and out with their top-sayles, and fly as from an enemy."

From this time the shallop with Hudson and his eight doomed companions drops out of sight. What became of them will never be known. From a conversation that Prickett had with King, the carpenter, before he left the ship, there is reason to suppose that a wild attempt may have been made to sail the shallop up the eastern coast of the bay to Digges Island, in which case they probably struggled on for a few days until weakened by starvation, or perhaps a storm may have mercifully ended their sufferings. Another theory is that they made their way to one

CARIBOO BRIDGE, FRASER RIVER

Face p. 30

of the islands in James Bay and perished there. Twenty
years later Captain James found on Danby Island, on
the eastern side of Charlton Island, a number of stakes,
evidently cut with a hatchet, driven into the ground.
This little island may therefore have been the last
resting-place of Henry Hudson. "Of all the dark
mysteries of the merciless ocean," says Sir W. F.
Butler (of merciless men, might have been more appropriate in this case), "no mystery lies wrapt in deeper
shadow than that which hangs over the fate of Hudson."

It is, perhaps, hardly necessary to seek an explanation of the action of his crew in turning Hudson adrift.
The chief motive was obviously self-preservation. At
the same time there is evidence enough, even in
Prickett's biased statement, of the strained relations
that existed throughout the voyage between Hudson
and his crew. Hudson was a man of strong will and
strong passions. He was the leader of the expedition,
and would brook neither opposition nor even advice
from those under him. He ruled his crew with an iron
hand, and when at last their opportunity came they had
no mercy on him. The trying incidents of this first
winter spent by white men in Hudson Bay no doubt
added fuel to the resentment of the crew. The mutiny
that Hudson had crushed on the outward voyage was
still smouldering, waiting only the fanning of an evil
spirit to spring into fierce light again. This evil spirit,
if we may credit Prickett, was furnished by a vicious
young man named Henry Green, who is credited with
the engineering of the plot to drive Hudson out of

the ship. Green had been Hudson's own servant in England; Hudson had befriended him on the voyage; and now, after the manner of his kind, Green turned upon the hand that had fed him. It was a scoundrelly crew, and yet there were not wanting men of ability. One of the survivors was Robert Bylot, who returned to Hudson Bay in 1615 with Baffin, and made important discoveries in Fox Channel.

It has been suggested that one of the things that drove the crew to mutiny was Hudson's determination to make a final effort to discover a passage from the west side of Hudson Bay into the South Sea before returning home. There is nothing in Prickett's narrative to support such a contention, and however anxious Hudson may have been to attain this great object of his voyage, he would hardly have been guilty of the madness of a long and uncertain search with no provisions. In such a case, the mutiny would have been justified.

After Hudson had been turned adrift, the *Discovery* was sailed north to the strait, and, after many misadventures, finally reached Digges Island, where the crew were disappointed in their expectations of a supply of game. Henry Green and three others, discovering Eskimo on the shore, landed in hope of securing provisions, and were treacherously and most appropriately murdered. The rest continued their homeward voyage, under conditions so horrible that one is almost tempted to pity them. One died of starvation after they had cleared the strait. The others finally made the Irish coast, and secured food and a pilot to take them around to Plymouth. Why they were not all promptly hanged has always remained one of the mysteries of British justice. As to their master, whom they had so treacherously murdered, his name and fame will endure as long as the manly qualities of pluck, endurance, and steadfast purpose have any hold on human sympathy.

D

CHAPTER II

SEARCHING FOR THE NORTH-WEST PASSAGE

PRICKETT and his companions on the homeward voyage had managed to run the *Discovery* on a rock in the narrow channel between Digges Island and the mainland. "It was ebbe," says Prickett, "when they grounded, but the next flood floated them off againe." This incident, dismissed so lightly, was in reality one of those accidents out of which great movements are born, though not always great discoveries. In the present case men's minds had been prepared for the discovery of a passage through the new continent into the South Sea. When it became known that Hudson in his search for this channel had found a vast sea, which so far as he knew had no bounds towards the west; and when the survivors of the expedition brought back the significant news that, as Purchas puts it, "a great floud, which they by this accident tooke first notice of, came from the westward and set them flote"; there did not seem to be room for further doubt as to the existence of the passage. The great strait was there; all that remained was to sail through it into the South Sea. So fixed was this belief that nothing but the failure of many well-equipped expeditions served to wear it down. Even up to the middle of the eighteenth century enthusiasts like Arthur Dobbs were convinced that the passage must be looked for by way of Hudson Bay; as late as 1790 Alexander Dalrymple clung with characteristic obstinacy to the old theory; even a shrewd, practical seaman like Captain Coats, with a quarter of a century's experience in the bay, could argue for the probability of a passage. Captain Coats's expectations pointed to the wide opening in the western coast near Brooke Cobham, now Marble Island, and his hopes will not seem so absurd when it is remembered that this deep bay, Ranken Inlet, is even to-day practically unknown.   Dobbs's faith was pinned to the same inviting inlet, but not exclusively, for he had an alternative passage by way of Wager Inlet, or Wager Bay, as it is called on some of the latest maps.   After Dobbs the belief in a passage, by way of Hudson Bay, had few supporters, though for another quarter of a century it was still sought on the Pacific Coast of the continent, faith in the mythical Strait of Anian having taken even deeper root than the belief in a Hudson Bay passage.

But to get back to the early voyages to Hudson Bay. The mutineers had not returned to England much more than six months when a second expedition was sent forth, under command of Sir Thomas Button. Button's voyage was supported by a large and influential group of adventurers, one hundred and sixty in number according to Foxe. Three months after Button sailed, these one hundred and sixty adventurers, with one hundred and twenty-eight new members, were incorporated under

Royal Charter as The Company of the Merchants of London Discoverers of the North-West Passage. The patron of the expedition was Henry Prince of Wales, who gave Button a letter of instructions which throws an interesting light upon current opinion as to the prospects of the voyage. After certain directións as to the conduct of the expedition, the keeping of a journal, observations for the position of prominent points on the coasts, soundings, the height of the tide, etc., the Prince instructs Button to hasten to Digges Island, remembering that the way is already beaten thither. He will recognize the eastern entrance to Hudson Strait by the furious course of the sea and ice into it. He is advised to keep the northern side of the strait, as most free from ice, until past Cape Henry, and from thence to follow the ice between King James and Queen Annes forelands. Between Salisbury Island and the northern shore he is like to meet "a great and hollow billow from an opening and flowing sea from thence." Standing over to the opposite main, in about latitude 58°, he is to ride at some headland and observe well the flood; if it come in south-west, then he may be sure the passage is that way; but if from the north or north-west, his course must be to stand up into it, being careful not to waste time in exploring bays, inlets, or sounds that do not lead to the great passage. If his ships should become separated in traversing the strait, Digges Island is recommended as a suitable rendezvous; and if it should fall out that winter overtook him before he found the thoroughfare into the South Sea, his safest way would be to seek southward for some place to winter in; for, adds Prince Henry, "we assure our self by Gods grace you will not returne, without either the good newes of a passage, or sufficient assurance of an impossibility." He is to be careful to prevent all mutiny amongst his men, and to preserve them as much as possible from the "treacherie and villanie of the Saluages, and other Easterne people." Having found the strait, he is to explore it and look out for a good and strong port. If the strait does not afford one, he is to seek out some convenient place "on the back of America, or some island in the South Sea, for a haven or stacon for our Shippes and Marchaundizes." Finally he is urged to spend as little time as may be in this or any other search, saving of the passage, till he has dispatched the pinnace with news of his entrance into the South Sea, which must be done as soon as he shall be thereof assured. In the last edition of Hessel Gerritz's *Detectio Freti*, published before Button's return, the hope is expressed that he has passed through the strait, and that no news need be expected until he returns to England from India or China and Japan.

Button sailed from the Thames about the middle of April, 1612, with two ships, one the little *Discovery*, in which both Weymouth and Hudson had pursued their explorations towards the north-west, and which was still to carry two later expeditions before its course was run, and the other a larger vessel, the *Resolution*. Miller Christy notes the curious coincidence that the names of Captain Cook's two ships on his voyage in search of a north-eastern passage were also the *Discovery* and the *Resolution*. This expedition is notable in the number of men who took part in it whose names are otherwise connected with the exploration of Hudson Bay. Abacuk Prickett and Robert Bylot had already sailed to the bay with Hudson, and Hawkridge and Gibbons were each to command later expeditions, as was also Bylot. All these expeditions were to be equipped and sent forth by the same enterprising Company of the Merchants of London who were behind the present voyage, and the leading spirits in which had supported Hudson's expedition.

Button's journal was never published. For some reason that has never been very clearly ascertained, both Foxe and Purchas were refused the use of it, and the manuscript was subsequently lost. The available material consists merely of such fragmentary evidence as could be obtained from other contemporary sources. Purchas briefly notices the voyage. Foxe's material consists of a short narrative of the events of the voyage up to the time of wintering, obtained from Prickett; the report of Captain Hawkridge, who sailed as a volunteer on the expedition; and an abstract from Button's own journal, supplied to Foxe by Sir Thomas Roe. Hawkridge's account covers practically the same portion of the voyage as that of Prickett; the abstract from Button's journal embraces only part of the return voyage; the remainder of the voyage home is contained in another fragment written by Prickett. Purchas, in his *Pilgrimes*, refers to a chart of the voyage prepared

KANANASKIS FALLS, ROCKY MOUNTAINS

Face p. 38

by Josias Hubart, who accompanied Button, but this chart has disappeared.

So confident were those who had equipped Button that he would find the passage, and sail through it into the South Sea, that King James gave him this singular Letter of Credence, which he was to present to the Emperor of Japan, or any other eastern potentate with whom he might come in contact:—

"James, by the Grace of the Most High God, Creator and only Guider of the Universal World, King of Great Brittaine, France, and Ireland, Defender of the Faith, &c.

"Right high, Right Excellent, and Right mightie Prince, divers of our subjects, delighting in navigation and finding out of unknowne countries and peoples, having heard of the fame of you and of your people, have made a voyage thither of purpose to see your countries, and with your people to exercise exchange of Marchandize, bringing to you such things as our Realmes doe yield, and to receave from you such as y^{rs} affoord and may be of use for them, [it being] a matter agreeable to the nature of humane societye to have commerce and intercourse each with other. And, because, if they shalbe so happie as to arrive in yor Dominions, that you may understand that they are not persons of ill condition or disposition, but such as goe upon just and honest grounds of trade, Wee have thought good to recommende them and their Captain, Thomas Button, to your favo^r and protection, desiring you to graunt them, while they shalbe in yor country, not only favor and protection, but also such kindness and entertainment as may encourage them to continue their travailles and be the beginning of further amitie between you and us. And we shall be ready to requite it with the like goodwill towards any of y^rs that shall have cause or desire to visit our Countries."

Button entered Hudson Strait south of Resolution Island, which he so named, probably after his own vessel. Sailing a short distance up the northern shore, he crossed over to the south, which he reached at Cape Hopes Advance. This name, given apparently by Button to the same cape which Hudson had called Hold with Hope, still remains. From here his course was to the Savage Islands, which are named for the first time, and where Hawkridge says he tried the tide and found it to flow three fathoms. There is reason to suppose that the group so named was the Upper Savage. Leaving here, he sailed up the strait to the neighbourhood of Salisbury Island, then down between Digges and Cape Wolstenholme, where he found good anchorage in thirteen fathoms. Here the same fate overtook some of his men that had been meted out to Green and his companions the previous year. Attempting to go ashore to shoot guillemots, which were seen in immense numbers on Digges Island, they were attacked by Eskimo to the number of seventy or eighty. The Eskimo were fired on—one killed and others wounded; the remainder fled back to the shore in dismay, frightened by the noise and execution of this novel weapon. Yet they had their revenge. Before sailing Button sent the pinnace ashore for fresh water, when the natives, lying in ambush, succeeded in killing five of his men. One only escaped by swimming out to the ship. Hawkridge says that Button had already antagonized the Eskimo by seizing two of their "great canoes," otherwise kyacks.

From Digges Island his course was due west, around the northern end of Mansfield Island, to Coats Island, giving to a cape at the southern end of the latter island the singular name of Cary's Swans Nest. From here, still sailing west, he encountered shifting winds and shoal water, and finally, we may well believe to his infinite disappointment and disgust, struck the western coast of Hudson Bay, somewhere between Cape Eskimo and Driftwood Point. This unwelcome landfall he named "Hopes Checkt." He had confidently expected to sail on without impediment into the South Sea, never imagining that he would be checked by an impenetrable wall of barren, uninviting coast. North and south as far as he could see the same shore-line extended, without a break of any kind. There was nothing for it but to follow the coast until it should turn, as it inevitably must, into the great channel.

One hundred and twenty-five miles or so south of Button's landfall the great River Churchill flows into the bay, and just here is one of the most puzzling points in Button's voyage. Port Churchill, or the neighbouring bay now called Button Bay, was known in Foxe's day and earlier as Hubbart's Hope, and it clearly appears from both Foxe's and James's narratives that there was a strong expectation of finding here the long-sought passage. The narratives bearing on Button's voyage throw no light on this curious misconception, but Purchas says that when Button arrived in 60° he found "a strong race of a tyde running sometimes Eastwarde, sometymes Westwarde, whereupon Josias Hubbarde, in his platt, called yt place Hubbart's Hope." Under the circumstances one would naturally suppose that Button must have thoroughly explored such a promising opening; yet the evidence all points the other way. Had he explored the mouth of the Churchill, he would immediately have discovered that this was no strait or channel, but a large river, and we should have heard nothing more of Hubbart's Hope. On the contrary, nineteen years after Button's voyage Luke Foxe confidently looked for the passage in this very place, and was much disgusted to find it an illusion. One can only surmise that Button sailed around the bay without discovering the narrow entrance to Churchill Harbour, and departed leaving Hubbart's Hope an unsolved problem.

In any event, Button sailed down the coast from Hopes Checked to Hubbart's Hope, and from Hubbart's Hope down to a bay which he named Port Nelson, after his sailing-master, or it may have been the river itself which he so named. It was now late autumn, and as he could hope to do nothing more toward the search for a passage this year, he determined to make Port Nelson his winter quarters, and set out as soon as the ice broke up in the spring to continue his explorations. The exact spot where Button wintered has been matter of speculation, but the point is settled by John Thornton's chart of Hudson's Bay and Strait, 1685, discovered by Mr. Christy in the British Museum. On this chart Button's winter quarters are marked on a small creek on the northern side of the estuary of the Nelson, marked on the Admiralty chart as Root Creek.

He wintered in his ship, says Foxe, and kept three fires going all the time. Presumably he means the *Resolution;* but if Purchas is to be believed, the *Resolution* had to be abandoned, though he does not say when. Possibly she was crushed in the ice in the spring. In any event, Button and his men seem to have passed a wretched winter. In spite of the abundance of game, there was much sickness among the crew, several dying before spring. To relieve the tedium of inactivity, Button devised a series of questions to which his officers and men were invited to provide answers. One of the questions given to Josias Hubbart was as to the advisability of exploring the Nelson River, to which Hubbart replied: "I think it not amisse to search this River, if God give strength to our Men, before our departure from it, to have the knowledge how farre it doth extend; and that we may meet with some Inhabitants, which may further our expectations, but I cannot thinke of any profit to be made by it." To a further question as to the best course to pursue in the spring, Hubbart replied: "My answer to the 2 Demaund is to search to the Northward about this Westerne land, untill, if it be possible, that we may find the Flood comming from the Westward, and to bend our courses against that flood, following the ebbe, searching that way for the passage." Foxe was so delighted with this answer of Hubbart's that he added this characteristic foot-note, " Well guest Hubart ! "

Finally the long winter drew to a close, and with the spring the ice broke out of the bay. As soon as navigation was open, Button and the survivors sailed north again in the little *Discovery* to Hopes Checked. From here he explored the coast up to Cape Eskimo, sailed on past Ranken Inlet and Chesterfield Inlet, neither of which seems to have suggested the possibility of a passage, and up Roe's Welcome almost to the entrance to Wager Bay. He then turned south, apparently satisfied that no passage was to be found in this part of the bay ; sailed around the southern end of Resolution Island, passed Cary's Swans Nest, traversed the strait, and so home again.

The net result of Button's voyage, from a geographical point of view, was to add the entire western coast of Hudson Bay, from Port Nelson up to Roe's Welcome, as well as Southampton and Coats islands, to the known world. As has been seen in the preceding chapter, the eastern coast of the bay from Cape Wolstenholme to the foot of James Bay, and the west coast up to Cape Henrietta Maria, had already been explored by Hudson. Consequently all that remained now to be done to complete the general exploration of the bay was to examine the comparatively short bit of coast from Port Nelson to Henrietta Maria.

The disappointing results of Button's voyage, so far
as the passage was concerned, did not serve to dampen
the spirits of its promoters.   For the next decade
hardly a year went by without an expedition setting
forth from England to search for a passage by way
of Hudson Bay.   It will not be necessary, however, to
spend any time over these.   Gibbons in 1614, and
Hawkridge in 1617, did not succeed in adding anything
to what was already known of the great bay.   Gibbons
never even entered the strait.   Driven by contrary
winds and ice down the Labrador coast, he took refuge
in a bay, probably Saglek Bay, which his contemporaries
derisively called Gibbons' Hole.   Here he remained
ten weeks, and when finally he escaped, the season was
lost, and nothing remained but to turn ignominiously
homeward.   All this despite the fact that his vessel was
the "good and luckie ship *Discovery*."   Never had the
Discovery been engaged on such an unlucky voyage.
The voyage of Captain Hawkridge is clouded in
mystery.   If he sailed at all, it must apparently have
been in 1617.   Foxe's account of the voyage is very
confused, but as far as one can gather, Hawkridge sailed
through Hudson Strait and cruised about its western end
in an aimless fashion, up Fox Channel to about 65°, and
down the eastern coast of the bay to perhaps the Ottawa
Islands.   The geographical results of the voyage were
so slight that it was not worth while considering the
proofs for and against its authenticity.

Gibbons had been sent out by the Company of Merchants as a result of their settled policy to sift to the

bottom the question of a passage from Hudson Bay through to the South Sea. Button's voyage, in spite of its disappointing results so far as the main object was concerned, had by no means settled the question in the negative. Purchas records the fact that while at Digges Island Button had "found the comming in of the great and strong tide from the north-west, which feedes both those huge bayes, and leaves great assurance of nothing now left but a little sayling to the north-west for the finding of that Passage; or reason to looke no further for it." Consequently, when Gibbons returned with his story of abject failure, the matter stood where Button had left it. The adventurers, with commendable courage, immediately equipped another expedition, under Robert Bylot, who had taken part in three former voyages, and William Baffin, a "a navigator of exceptional ability and character." Bylot and Baffin sailed in March, 1615, in the same little *Discovery* that had carried so many adventurous hearts into Hudson Bay. They carefully investigated the source of Button's tide, and Baffin made the positive announcement, as the result of their discoveries, that no passage was to be found by way of Hudson Bay; that if the passage existed at all, it must be sought through Davis Strait. In the course of this voyage the western side of Fox Channel was explored for the first time, as far as Frozen Strait, and much additional information was added to the charts.

Jens Munk, a Danish navigator, sailed to the bay in 1619. He was sent out by Christian **IV**, with two

TRACKING ON ATHABASKA RIVER

Face p. 46

ships.   After experiencing great trouble with ice in the strait, he reached Digges Island, on the 20th August, and sailed across the bay to Port Churchill, where he wintered.   In the absence of any satisfactory proof that Button did so, Munk may be considered the discoverer of the mouth of the Churchill.   Otherwise he added nothing whatever to geographical knowledge of the bay. The story of his wintering is one of fearful mortality. Of the combined crews of sixty-four persons, Munk and two others alone remained the following spring. The survivors with much difficulty managed to navigate the smaller ship, and eventually reached the coast of Norway in September, 1620.

Up to the year 1631 the exploration of the western coast-line of Hudson Bay remained as Button had left it eighteen years before.   Of the several expeditions that had entered the bay in the interval, only one crossed to the western side, and that one had not, so far as is known, gone north or south of Port Churchill.   In 1631, however, two expeditions went forth from England, the results of which were to fill in the gap in the western coast between Port Nelson and Cape Henrietta Maria. These expeditions were commanded respectively by Captain Luke Foxe, of Hull, and Captain Thomas James, of Bristol.

Foxe was an enthusiastic explorer.   He had long harboured the ambition to become the discoverer of the North-West Passage.   In his own characteristic fashion he says that he " had beene itching after it ever since 1606."   His ambition did not need to be fired by the

example of Hudson, Button, and Bylot, but no doubt
the personal contact which he is known to have had
with several of the early voyagers added fuel to the
flame. He had already had many years' practical experience in seamanship, and joined to it a careful study
of the scientific side of navigation. The Company of
Merchants had dropped out of sight by this time, but
there were not wanting men of public spirit and enterprise to support Foxe's ambition. In 1629, or 1630,
Foxe, Henry Briggs, a well-known mathematician, and
Sir John Brooke, afterward Baron Cobham, petitioned
the King for the loan of one of His Majesty's ships to
go in search of the passage. After a long delay, official
red tape being then much what it is to-day, the prayer
of the petition was granted, and Foxe was given the
Charles, a 150-ton[1] pinnace, for the voyage. The delay, however, had made it impossible to sail in 1630,
and Foxe had to possess his soul in patience until the
following spring. In the meantime he had enlisted the
interest of a number of liberal-minded gentlemen,
among whom were Sir Thomas Roe and that old
friend of western exploration, Sir John Wolstenholme.
Finally, all preparations having been made, and the
ship victualled for eighteen months, Foxe was sum-
moned to His Majesty, and received a letter of instructions, with a map embodying the results of previous
explorations. He was also given a letter to the
Emperor of Japan, no doubt in the hope that he might
have better success than Button in delivering it.

[1] Seventy or eighty tons, by some accounts.

DANIEL WILLIAMS HARMON, ESQ.

Face p. 48

Before Foxe sails, it will be well to notice the some-what peculiar relations that subsisted between his own voyage and that of Captain James. Whether James got the idea of searching for a passage from Foxe, or planned it independently, is not certain. At any rate, James had wrought his fellow-citizens of Bristol to such a pitch of enthusiasm that they subscribed a sufficient sum of money to secure and equip a vessel of seventy tons, the *Henrietta Maria.* Not content with this very practical success, James wished to secure for himself the honours of discovery, whether he succeeded or not. He appealed to Henry Briggs, Foxe's friend and patron, and it was agreed that Foxe and he should have equal credit, no matter which might find the passage. Not content with this rather extraordinary arrangement, James posted off to Oxford and demanded, though on what grounds it would be hard to imagine, that his ship should have the precedence in any event. This amazing proposition was of course refused. As a matter of fact, if there was to be any precedence other than that which depended upon the achievements of the two men, it belonged to Foxe, whose expedition was at least semi-official, Foxe sailing "under the imme-diate patronage of the King," while James's voyage was a local venture of the Bristol merchants. The whole in-cident is rather trivial, but is interesting as bringing into striking contrast the characters of the two ex-plorers. Foxe was first and always a man of action; with him the accomplishment of his object would be of first importance ; any honour that might flow therefrom

E

of only secondary moment. James was differently constituted; he hungered for the applause of men before he had achieved anything.

Foxe and James sailed from England within two days of each other, the former from Deptford, the latter from Bristol. Curiously enough, they never met until nearly four months later, though from England to the western end of Hudson Strait, and later from Port Churchill to Cape Wolstenholme, both sailed over practically the same waters. Foxe's course, after reaching the western end of the strait, was between Mansfield and Coats islands, thence south of Southampton Island, and up the channel separating Southampton from the mainland. He made the western coast some distance north of Cape Fullerton, and landed on a small island lying off the coast, which he made to be in 64° 10'. This would be somewhere about Whale Point, the first prominent cape north of Cape Fullerton. He found upon the island certain " poles erected, and buildings of stone, and other hillocks like haycocks "; no doubt Eskimo huts with their treasured piles of driftwood. Foxe gives an interesting account of Eskimo graves found on this island, which may be regarded as the earliest contribution to the ethnology of Hudson Bay. This island he named Sir Thomas Roe's Welcome, after the eminent diplomatist who was one of the promoters of his voyage. The name was applied later to the strait in which this island lies.

From Sir Thomas Roe's Welcome Foxe sailed down the western coast to Marble Island, which he named

Brooke Cobham, after Sir John Brooke, another of his patrons. He was much impressed with the appearance of this island. "It is all of a white marble," he says in one place, and elsewhere describes it as "like Alabaster, but I take it to be such as they pave their houses with in Holland—they say brought out of the Mediterranean." Marble Island is constantly referred to in the journals of later expeditions to the bay, and has been for a number of years the head-quarters of New England whalers. It was the scene of one of the most tragic incidents in the exploration of Hudson Bay, the story of which will be told in another chapter. Before leaving Brooke Cobham, the master's mate urged Foxe to take the vessel into a convenient harbour, because there was a bolt in the stem that was exposed, and which he thought might cut the cable. Foxe would have none of it. The time was too far spent to neglect the opportunity of discovery by putting into harbour for such a trifle. "So long as I am sailing I bless God and care not," concludes this bluff navigator.

Leaving Brooke Cobham, he stood down the coast, trying to keep always within sight of the mainland, so that the entrance to the channel might not escape him, but sailing very warily, for these were dangerous waters, even in the clearest weather, thickly studded with reefs, ledges, and shallow ground. Sailing through what is now known as Mistake Bay, Foxe gave to a group of small islands the quaint name of Briggs his Mathematickes, in honour, or rather in memory, of his friend Henry Briggs, for Briggs had died before the expedition set forth. Passing Cape Eskimo and Button's Hopes Checked, Foxe reached Port Churchill, or Hubbart's Hope, on the 2nd August. He anchored that night two or three leagues from shore, in twenty fathoms, and in the morning stood into the bay. The land was low, and reminded him of the coasts of Holland and Flanders. Both Foxe and James looked confidently for a passage at Churchill. James says in his narrative, "We entered that inlet which heretofore was called Hubbart's Hope; which was the very place where the Passage should be, as it was thought by the understandingest and learnedest intelligencer of this Business in England." Foxe, as he approaches Churchill, says, "I hoped now for a sight of *Hubbert's comfortable Hope*"; and as he sails into the bay, "Hubbert makes me hope"; but having reached the foot, he exclaims disgustedly, "I could see the bottome of *Vainely Hoapt Hubbert*, for so I call it." Foxe throws light upon the origin of this singular idea that the entrance to the passage was at Port Churchill, when he says, "The Tyde came N.W., and this is that supposed Tyde that set E. and W., which was no more but the same Tyde I brought along with mee from *Sir Th. Roe's Welcome*, coming all along the coast S.W. by S., and falling into this Vaine *Hope* is enforced to alter his course by opposition of the S. side of this large Bay, and there to set E. and W."

From Churchill Foxe sailed down the coast to Port Nelson, where it will be remembered Button had wintered in 1612-13. Foxe was in doubt whether he had better go on, or run into Port Nelson for a few days. He decided in favour of the latter, and gives his reasons. He had on board a small pinnace, which had not yet been put together for lack of opportunity, and it was important that this should be done without further delay, as the safety of the crew might depend upon it in case the ship should be wrecked. He also hoped to get in touch with the savages to further his design; it was possible they might be able to impart some definite information as to the whereabouts of the passage. He thought it well to examine the Nelson River, which had not been done by Button. Possibly, if a suitable harbour could be found, and he was compelled to winter in the bay, this might be a good place to return to; but it is learned from his manuscript journal that Foxe had already made up his mind to return if at all possible before winter set in. It was therefore all the more necessary that the pinnace should be set up, as much could be done with her in shoal waters, where it would not be safe to take the ship, and there was no time to be lost, the days were already lengthening.

With much difficulty he crept up the dangerous channel, taking advantage of the flood tide, and, after grounding once or twice, managed to get into a creek on the north side, which offered a convenient place to put the pinnace together. This creek proved to be Button's wintering-place, for Foxe found on shore a quantity of hogsheads and barrel-staves, a maintop-mast, a topgallantmast, blocks, the remains of chests, and other relics. Searching along the shore for a tree suitable for a mainyard, he discovered other relics— broken anchors, bits of cable, a broken gun, lead and iron shot, a grapnel, an old tent, and a cross which had been set up, but was since fallen down. Foxe raised the cross, and nailed the following inscription, in lead, to it :—

"I suppose this Cross was first erected by Sir Thomas Button, 1613. It was againe raised by Luke Foxe, Capt. of the Charles, in the right and possession of my dread Soveraigne Charles the first, King of Great Brittaine, France and Ireland, Defender of the Faith, the 15 of August, 1631.

"This land is called New Wales." [1]

Further search brought to light a board broken in two, on which Button had placed an inscription. Only one half of the board could be found, but that Foxe brought home with him, and a copy of the inscription is given in his manuscript journal. This fragment Mr. Christy has very cleverly restored, and in all probability his version is substantially correct. It is given below, the words in brackets being supplied by Mr. Christy :—

"In . the . right . and . to [the honour of God]
and . our . dread . souera[igne, by the grace of]
God . King . of . Great . Bre[tagne, France, and Ireland,]
defender . of . the . tru[e faith of Christ,]

---

[1] On Foxe's map the west coast is called New Yorkshire. Button had first named it New Wales, and James afterward subdivided the coast into New North Wales and New South Wales. Munk called it New Denmark. None of these names had any particular vogue.

WADDINGTON'S BRIDGE.

this . coast . of . New . W[ales was discovered and

possession]

thereof . taken . and . i[t was so named by Thomas]

Button . Gentleman . of [Cardiff, when sailing to]

the . northwest . under . I [. . . . . . raised]

this . memoriall . with . h[. . . . . .]

Britainis . to . gether . with [. . . . . .]

and . our . most . hopefull [Prince Henry of]

Wales . heir . aparent . to [the Throne of]

Brittaine . the . Great . and [at the expense of the]

honorable . companie . incor[porated for discovering a

north]

west . passage . and . mygrations . a [. . . . . .]

I . thus . erected . on . the . S[eventh (?) day]

of . July . and . in . the . year [of our Lord]

1613."

On the other side of the board was the following
inscription :—

"[To this P]orte, I came the 27th of August, 1612,
[by foul] weather, where I wintered the
[before] written time, and then by reason o[f]
[wants] and sickness amongst my Company, [I]
[was] forst to leave my owen Ship, [and with the]
[Pinnas to] prosecute my discovery [for the North]
[West] the day and yeare afores[aid.]

"*Per me* Thomas Button,

"Gentleman."

After eleven days spent at Port Nelson, Foxe got the
Charles safely out of this apology for a harbour and

continued his voyage. "Now betweene Port Nelson and Hudson's W. Bay (all yet for a great distance not looked upon by any Christian), wee were to discover," he says. Foxe had already examined the western coast from Roe's Welcome to Port Nelson, and satisfied himself that no passage existed anywhere along that shore. He was reasonably certain that it need not be looked for farther south, but his instructions required him to complete the exploration of the coast, and he felt bound to do so. From Button's farthest at Port Nelson, Foxe was now sailing along the almost straight bit of coast that ends abruptly at Cape Henrietta Maria. Up to then this part of the bay had been represented by a gap on the charts.

While Foxe had been doing all this, Captain James had sailed across the bay from the western end of Hudson Strait to Port Churchill, which he reached on the 11th August, some time after Foxe had gone south. Foxe, in fact, although he had sailed north to Roe's Welcome and examined the coast carefully to the southward, had actually reached Port Nelson several days before James arrived at Churchill. Leaving Churchill, James followed Foxe down the coast, but did not land at Port Nelson. He passed outside the harbour while Foxe was putting his pinnace together in the creek, and, therefore, was first to explore the unknown coast beyond, or rather a portion of it, for Foxe overhauled him on the 29th August, somewhere near the mouth of the Winisk River.

Captain James invited Foxe to dine with him on

board the *Henrietta Maria*, but the meeting does not seem to have been a very pleasant one; in fact Foxe was at no pains to conceal his contempt for one whom he describes as "no Seaman." The politeness was all on James's side. Foxe laughed at him for flying his flag in such waters. James replied that he was on his way to the Emperor of Japan with letters from His Majesty, and that if it were a ship of forty pieces of ordnance, he could not strike his flag. "Keepe it up, then," quoth Foxe, "but you are out of the way to Japon, for this is not it." James urged him to winter in the bay, and pointed out that it was high time they sought a harbour. Sir Thomas Button had gone into winter quarters the fourteenth of this very month. (The 27th August, according to Button's inscription.) "Hee is no precedent for me," replied Foxe. "I must paralell my pouerty with poore Hudson's, who tooke no harbour before the first of Nouember." In spite of Foxe's unpleasant tongue, the two captains seem to have made a night of it, for, says Foxe, "wee parted not vntill the next morning's dawning." Foxe sailed away, and did not meet James again during the rest of the voyage. He continued his careful examination of the coast, sailing as close inshore as he dared, and on the 2nd September reached the south-easternmost point of Hudson Bay proper, which he named Wolstenholmes Ultimum Vale. "For," said he, "I do beleeve Sir John Wolstenholme will not lay out any more monies in search of this Bay." Foxe was now convinced that, so far as Hudson Bay was concerned, the passage had no existence. The only point that remains a little puzzling is how, examining the coast as carefully as he did, he could have escaped the wide entrances to Chesterfield and Ranken inlets, so suggestive of a possible passage.

James reached Foxe's Ultimum Vale the following day, September 3rd, without knowing that Foxe had already been there. He named the point Cape Henrietta Maria, after his own ship. Foxe's grotesque name is long since forgotten, but the cape still bears the name bestowed on it by James.

From here Foxe turned north, satisfied of the futility of any further search for a passage to the south-west. He sailed up the east coast of the bay, outside the islands, passed between Mansfield and Coats, thence over to the north shore of Hudson Strait, the western extremity of which he named King Charles Cape. He then explored the unknown western coast of Fox Land, and towards the end of September reached a point in about 66° 47′ north, which he named "Foxe his farthest." Curiously enough Foxe is still our only authority for this coast, which from his northern point around to Fury and Hecla Strait has never yet been explored. Foxe returned to the strait, sailed along the north shore to Resolution Island, and so home.

Captain James meanwhile had rounded Cape Henrietta Maria,[1] and sailed down the practically unexplored western shore of Hudson's West Bay, in future to be

---

[1] Mr. D. B. Dowling, in his *Exploration of Ekwan River* (Geol. Survey, 1901, F. 12), praises the accuracy of James's description of the coast from Port Nelson to Cape Henrietta Maria.

known as James Bay.   His course was so erratic that it is difficult to follow him, and it can hardly be said that he added materially to the existing vague knowledge of the bay.   Furthermore, as already mentioned, he quite failed to correct Hudson's curious double bays.   All that we can gather from James's narrative and chart is that he passed between Akimiski Island and the mainland, and then sailed south-east to Charlton Island, where he wintered.

From the end of November, 1631, to the beginning of July, 1632, James and his men lived on Charlton, if it can be called living.   The narrative of their experiences is one of the dreariest and most painful in the annals of northern discovery.   They seem to have had ample provisions, but suffered intensely from cold.   They were never free from sickness, several members of the crew dying during the winter.   Even the approach of summer, that brief, fierce summer of the north, brought only a variety of suffering, for James complains bitterly of " such an infinit abundance of bloud-thirsty Muskitoes, that we were more tormented with them than euer we were with the cold weather."   Mr. Christy comments on this, " James must surely have been exaggerating"; which only goes to show that Mr. Christy had never encountered the fierce and irrepressible mosquito of the far north.

James's tale of woe becomes very wearisome.   His perpetual complaints are by no means confined to his wintering on Charlton Island, where there was fair justification, but punctuate the entire narrative.   Remembering that they were in the bay at the same time, one is struck with the marked contrast between the lugubrious tone of James's narrative and the manly way in which Foxe made the best of his circumstances. Contrast with James's doleful story such a passage as this from Foxe: "I hope faire weather to come, yet have wee had such as I pray our neighbours in England have no worse, and then they cannot have better harvest weather to have in their crop; and, though this may be thought nothing pertinent to the history of a Sea Journall, yet, having been disswaded from this voyage in respect of the ice, I may thus much write for the incouragement of others that may happen to navigate this way, God giving good successe to this enterprise, that a Sea voyage of discovery (to a place unknowne, and farre remote, and in the like clime) cannot be taken in hand with more health, ease, and pleasure. I am sure it hath beene warme ever since we came from the yce."

Up to the time of wintering it must be borne in mind that Foxe and James had been sailing over practically the same waters; they were about equally well equipped for their work; their vessels, the *Charles* and *Henrietta Maria*, were of about the same tonnage; the *Charles* was possibly the larger vessel, but on the other hand she was from all accounts anything but seaworthy. Yet Foxe, despite constant difficulties with the lazy and sulky master of his ship, managed to accomplish in one season more than James did in two, and returned to England with a record of but one slight mishap to his vessel, while the *Henrietta Maria* was in constant tribulation. Foxe was, in fact, essentially a man of deeds; a bluff, fearless, boastful, more or less uneducated sailor; a man of no refinement, but of tireless energy and resourcefulness. James, on the other hand, though in general education and technical knowledge Foxe's superior, lacked his practical seamanship; lacked also his power to command, and his capacity for meeting circumstances as they arose, and, instead of surrendering to them, turning them to his own advantage.

James left his winter quarters at Charlton Island on the 3rd July, 1632, and, apparently still pursued by his evil fate, made his way up the west coast to Cape Henrietta Maria, where he landed and erected a cross bearing the King's arms and those of the city of Bristol. Still retracing his course up the western coast of the bay proper, he reached Cape Eskimo on the 19th August. From there he sailed east to Coats Island, or Cary's Swans Nest, and two days later made the north-western point of Nottingham Island. Here he turned north-west up Fox Channel, to the eastward of and parallel with the course of Bylot and Baffin seventeen years before. On the 26th he had reached a point near Winter Island, off the south-eastern coast of Melville Peninsula, but was so thickly beset by ice that he called his officers together to ask their advice as to the wisdom of proceeding any farther. A formal opinion was forthwith drawn up, under six heads, the gist of which was that they should immediately turn the ship homeward. James confesses that the reasons were just, and that he was unable to oppose them with any promise of a passage to the westward; he was now outside the closed door of the Frozen Strait, and even had he been able to penetrate this icy barrier, would have been no nearer his object. Wherefore with a sorrowful heart he consented that the helm should be borne up and the course shaped for England. "Although wee have," he concludes, "not discovered populous kingdomes, and taken speciall notice of their Magnificence, power, and policies, brought samples home of their riches and commodities, pryed into the mysteries of their trades and traffique, nor made any great fights against the enemies of God and our Nation; yet I wish our willingnesse in these desart parts may be acceptable to our Readers." It is an interesting fact that this *Strange and Dangerous Voyage* of Captain James formed one of the main sources of Coleridge's *Ancient Mariner*. Indeed Mr. Ivor James, in his ingenious study *The Source of the Ancient Mariner*, argues that it was *the* source of the poem.

The return of Foxe, and then James, with no hope of a passage, proved bitterly disappointing to those who had counted on a successful issue to one or other of these voyages, and practically put an end to the search by way of Hudson Bay. For a quarter of a century the great bay was abandoned altogether, and when ships again ploughed its waters the search was for peltries rather than for a passage. Eventually, however, the old quest was renewed, but the waterways by which it was followed were not the broad sea channels of the problematical passage, but the narrow, broken waters of the rivers of the west.

INDIANS OF THE GREAT PLAINS

Face p. 62

Reviewing the geographical results of these several voyages into Hudson Bay, up to and including 1642, it is seen that Hudson discovered for the first time the general features of the strait, and the eastern coast of the bay down to its extreme foot.   Button made known the rough outlines of the west coast, from Wager Bay to Port Nelson.   Foxe and James both contributed to a more exact delineation of the coast covered by Button, and both almost simultaneously, though quite independently, explored the hitherto unknown coast from Port Nelson to Cape Henrietta Maria, while James alone explored the eastern shores of James Bay, without correcting Hudson's error in dividing it into two.   This odd mistake was not, in fact, rectified until many years later, when the explorations of the Hudson's Bay Company dispelled the illusion, and Cape Monmouth, with the long peninsula that lay behind it—on the maps—disappeared into thin air.   Although the primary object of all these voyages was not accomplished, they resulted in a very important piece of exploration, the charting of the entire coast-line of one of the largest and most remarkable of inland seas.

CHAPTER III

THE HUDSON'S BAY COMPANY AND ITS EXPLORATIONS

ON June 3rd, 1668, two vessels sailed out of the Thames, bound for Hudson Bay. One was the *Eagle*, Captain Stannard master; the other the *Nonsuch*, Captain Zachariah Gillam master. They had been fitted out by a group of English adventurers, at the head of whom was that versatile cousin of Charles II, Prince Rupert, to sail to Hudson Bay on a voyage of exploration and trade. The command of the expedition was entrusted to two Canadians, Medard Chouart, Sieur des Groseilliers, and Pierre Esprit Radisson. The early history of these soldiers of fortune has been the subject of warm controversy, and all because Radisson, with no thought of the trouble he was storing up for future historians, neglected to make it plain where he and his brother-in-law Chouart went, and how they got there. *Radisson's Voyages, 1652–84*, was published by the Prince Society of Boston in 1885. These narratives cover four journeys—the first and second to the Iroquois country, south of Lake Ontario; the third and fourth to the far west, and possibly the far north. The war of words has gathered around the latter two.

Radisson, a Frenchman with a very imperfect knowledge of English, wrote the accounts of his travels in
English—fearful and wonderful English.   One group of
historians insist that on his third journey he discovered
the upper waters of the Mississippi; the others are
equally positive that he did nothing of the kind. The
former interpret the narrative of his fourth voyage to
mean that he reached the waters of James Bay, and
that his was therefore the first overland expedition to
the bay; the latter are divided in their minds; they are
confident that Radisson never saw these northern
waters, but hesitate between two theories, one that
Radisson falsely claimed to have reached the bay, the
other that he made no such claim and that those who
suppose he did misinterpret his language.   However,
though the whole question of Radisson's inland voyages
is most interesting, it is impossible to consider it here.
The essential point to be noted is that, in the course of
his fourth "voyage," putting aside the probability or
otherwise of his actually having reached the shores of
James Bay, he undoubtedly obtained valuable information as to the geography of the regions about Hudson
Bay, and the inexhaustible harvest of furs that awaited
those enterprising enough to establish trading posts in
this northern country.   Armed with this information he
returned to Quebec and tried to enlist the interest and
support of the Government of New France.   Failing in
this, he tried New England, with indifferent success.
A small vessel was secured after many difficulties, in
which Radisson and Chouart sailed for the bay, but

were driven back by ice and stormy weather before they reached the strait. Finally Radisson crossed the Atlantic determined to place his knowledge and skill at the service of King Charles, or of any of King Charles's subjects who might have sufficient faith or enterprise to take hold of the project. Charles was interested in the graphic story that Radisson and Chouart had to tell, but neither the public nor the privy purse would at that time bear any further pressure. His cousin, however, took up the scheme with enthusiasm; succeeded in interesting some of his moneyed friends; and among them they scraped together enough to fit out two small vessels and equip them with a correspondingly small cargo of trading goods, odds and ends such as were thought suitable to the Indian trade.

Stormy weather buffeted the vessels at the outset, and the *Eagle*, after a brief struggle, was driven back into port, to the deep disgust of Radisson, who had sailed on her. The *Eagle* was so badly damaged that the voyage, so far as she was concerned, had to be abandoned for that year. The following year Radisson made another effort to reach the bay, sailing in the *Waveno*, with the same Captain Stannard, but again they were driven back. In an affidavit made before Sir Robert Jeffery the 23rd August, 1697, Radisson says that the *Eagle* and *Nonsuch* sailed in 1667, and the *Waveno* in 1668, and that in 1669 he sailed in the *Waveno*, with Captain Newland, and reached Port Nelson the same year. Oldmixon, quoting from an original draft of an answer of the Hudson's Bay Company to a French paper justifying the pretensions of France to Fort Bourbon, gives the dates for these three voyages as 1667, 1668, and 1669. On the other hand, Gillam's journal of the first voyage, quoted in Joseph Robson's *Account of Six Years' Residence in Hudson's Bay*, says that they sailed from Gravesend the 3rd of June, 1668. Of the three, the last is most credible. It is to be borne in mind that Radisson's affidavit was made nearly twenty years after the events he describes, and that he was then sixty-one years of age; his recollection of the dates of the several voyages might easily be at fault.[1] Oldmixon's statement traces back to this same affidavit of Radisson's, so that it lends no additional weight to the earlier dates. Gillam's journal was presumably written while the voyage was actually being made, and there is no reason for questioning his statement that the *Nonsuch* sailed in 1668, or for doubting that Radisson's second ineffective voyage, and his final successful voyage, were made in 1669 and 1670 respectively, rather than in 1668 and 1669, as stated in Radisson's affidavit.

But to return to Chouart. When Radisson was driven back in the *Eagle*, Chouart with Gillam in the *Nonsuch* managed to weather the storm and continued the voyage. On August 4th they were off Resolution, at the eastern entrance of the strait; by the 19th they

---

[1] This is borne out by the fact that in a petition dated in 1698 Radisson vaguely describes the voyage as having been made "about the year 1666."

had reached Digges Island, without any serious difficulty from ice ; on the 31st they anchored at an island
near the Eastmain coast in 57° 49′, possibly Cotter
Island ; on the 4th of September they again approached
the coast in 55° 30′ ; and on the 25th were in a
bay near 51° 20′—Rupert Bay. Four days later the
anchor was dropped off the mouth of a river which
they named Rupert River, after their princely patron.
The course down the east coast of the bay has been
followed with some minuteness, because as a matter of
fact this voyage of the *Nonsuch* was the first to follow
Hudson's track, and the *Nonsuch* was the first vessel to
reach this out-of-the-way corner of the great bay since
the memorable voyage of 1610–11.

Chouart, Gillam, and their men landed at the mouth
of the river, and under Chouart's expert direction a
stockaded log fort was soon built, such as he had been
familiar with in Canada. This they named Fort
Charles after the King. Stores and supplies were taken
ashore ; the ship made snug and safe ; and the party
settled down for the long northern winter. The natives,
who had stood strangely aloof from all the earlier expeditions to the bay, were induced to visit and trade at
the fort, chiefly, no doubt, through the influence of
Chouart, an old and experienced fur trader. These
Indians would be Crees, members of the same tribe
with which Chouart and Radisson had come into contact on the shores of Lake Superior. Before spring a
respectable cargo of furs was ready for shipment to
England. A curious sidelight is thrown on this expe-

dition by an entry in the Jesuit Relations for the years 1669–70. "I heard," says the writer of the Relations, "that there was in their [the Assiniboine] country a great river leading to the Western Sea; and a Savage told me that, being at its mouth, he had seen Frenchmen and four large canoes with sails." Making due allowances for an Indian account, interpreted with some freedom, this may very well have referred to the voyage of the *Nonsuch*.

Thus was established the first fur-trading post on Hudson Bay, or to be more exact, on James Bay, the nucleus of that great system that was afterward to spread its mighty arms far and wide over the northern half of the continent, and which, after the lapse of nearly two hundred and forty years, is still lusty and prosperous. Thus also were planted the seeds of that fierce rivalry between the British fur traders in the north and the French fur traders in the south, a rivalry which even survived the British conquest of Canada, for the antagonism of the French toward those whom they regarded as interlopers was taken over as a legacy by the Anglo-Canadian traders who succeeded them, and, characteristically enough, burned with a fiercer flame between British and British than between British and French.

Meanwhile, at Charles Fort, Chouart and Gillam were busily engaged in the profitable exchange of penny gewgaws for prime beaver skins, establishing an economical precedent to which those who followed them religiously adhered, at least until competition

among the traders themselves brought about a more
equitable exchange of commodities. The available
narratives throw very little light upon the events of
the winter. No doubt Chouart and Gillam spent the
time not altogether unpleasantly. The severity of
weather that had taxed the endurance of earlier
voyagers would not seriously inconvenience these
hardy and seasoned colonials. Gillam was a New
Englander; it was in fact in his own vessel that
Radisson and Chouart had made their first and unsuccessful voyage to the bay. He and Chouart were
therefore old acquaintances, and many a yarn of the
Atlantic coast or western camp-fire must have enlivened the long evenings in the little log fort on
Rupert River.

When the ice broke up in the spring of 1669, Gillam
and Chouart sailed for England in the *Nonsuch* with
the first cargo of furs. It has been stated that Chouart
remained behind in the bay to look after the fort, but
Radisson's affidavit shows conclusively that he returned
with Gillam in the *Nonsuch*. Upon Radisson's return
from his second unsuccessful voyage, that is the voyage
which he places in 1668, but which there is every
reason to believe was in 1669, he "found the said
Grosillier [Chouart] safely arrived with the said Gilham
in England." The cargo was not a large one, but it
more than met the expectations of those who had pro-
moted the venture; met them so fully that in 1670
the *Waveno* and the *Rupert* were sent out with a much
larger cargo, including, on the advice of Radisson, a

FUR TRADER COMING IN FROM THE FAR NORTH

Face p. 70

number of fowling-pieces, with a quantity of powder and shot, which would not only command fabulous prices in exchange for furs, but incidentally would increase the future harvest by placing a more efficient weapon in the hands of the hunters. King Charles was so well pleased with the results of the voyage that he gave Radisson and Chouart " a gold chain and medal as a mark of his royal favour, and recommended them to the Company of Adventurers of England trading into Hudson's Bay, to be well gratified and rewarded by them for their services aforesaid." So Radisson says in his petition of 1698, though so far as the first voyage was concerned the " services aforesaid " were performed by Chouart alone. Evidently the will was taken for the deed, and Radisson got credit for what he might have done, rather than what he actually had accomplished. In any event, his subsequent services entitled him to this signal mark of the King's favour.

As a result of this initial venture, Prince Rupert and his associates applied to King Charles for a monopoly of the fur trade of Hudson Bay, and on May 2nd, 1670, the King granted a charter incorporating them as The Governor and Company of Adventurers of England trading into Hudson's Bay. It is significant that one of the main grounds for granting the charter was stated to be because the adventurers had " at their own great cost and charges undertaken an expedition for Hudson's Bay, in the north-west parts of America, for a discovery of a new passage into the South Sea." Here the old project was cropping up once more. That the adventurers had seriously entertained any such object in their first voyage is open to grave question, but, at any rate, they were credited with it, and it is clear from the language of the charter, with its amazingly wide privileges, that they were expected to continue the search for a passage. How far they fulfilled this implied contract will be seen later. They themselves claimed in after years to have amply performed their part of the agreement, while their enemies charged that they had altogether neglected it. As in most other like controversies, the truth lies somewhere between. They did not entirely ignore their undertaking to explore the west and search for a passage, but their efforts in that direction were both spasmodic and half-hearted. The very real profits of the fur trade proved more alluring than the very problematical advantages of discovering a passage into the South Seas.

Radisson sailed in the *Waveno* direct to the mouth of the Nelson River. Chouart went with Gillam in the *Nelson*. It does not appear whether the two vessels left England together. All that Radisson says is that Chouart sailed that year to the bottom of the bay. Radisson and Captain Newland landed at Port Nelson, built some kind of a rough fort, left some of their men there with an assortment of trading goods, and then sailed down to James Bay, where the two ships wintered at Charles Fort. In the spring Chouart sailed over to Fort Nelson with a further supply of goods. The Hudson's Bay Company now had a good footing on the bay, a footing which they held, with various interruptions from the French, from that time forward.

Radisson and Chouart returned to England after the second voyage, and not being able to make satisfactory arrangements with the Hudson's Bay Company for future expeditions, crossed over to France in December, 1674. This is the date as given in Radisson's Relation, in the Hudson's Bay Company's archives.   In his affidavit of 1697 he says that he remained in England until the year 1673, the implication being that in that year he crossed over into France.   At any rate, Radisson and his brother-in-law offered their services to the French Government.   Colbert, Louis XIV's great minister, received the adventurers and advised them to return to Canada, where the Governor would, no doubt, gladly equip an expedition to Hudson Bay.   They sailed for Canada, but on their arrival at Quebec found the Governor, Frontenac, in no friendly mood.   The powerful interests of the Canadian fur trade had his ear, and he would do nothing for Radisson and Chouart.   Radisson accordingly returned to France, leaving Chouart and his family in Canada.

After serving for a time in the French navy, Radisson, to whom the wilderness had always greater charms than any of the pleasures of civilization, sailed once more for Canada.   La Chesnaye, an influential merchant of Quebec, had promised to equip a vessel for him. Caution had to be exercised, as the authorities were still hostile to Radisson and his projects.   He and Chouart, therefore, sailed around to Acadia and spent the winter there, the understanding being that La Chesnaye would have two ships ready in the spring. As soon, therefore, as navigation opened in the spring of 1683, Radisson and his brother-in-law repaired to the place agreed upon and found to their disappointment that the two stout vessels well fitted and stored with provisions, promised by La Chesnaye, had resolved themselves into a couple of leaky little craft, one fifty tons, the other even smaller, very poorly equipped for a long and difficult sea voyage.

Having determined to carry out the expedition, they would not turn back. The odds were that the ships would sink ere they reached the bay; nevertheless, they sailed on July 11th, got safely through the Strait of Belle Isle, and coasted up the Labrador. The nineteenth day out Chouart's men mutinied and refused to go any farther, fearing that the vessel would be caught in the ice, and that if they were not drowned they would in any event be reduced to starvation. Their fears were by no means groundless, but by threats and promises the leaders managed to pacify them.

A day or two later a hostile sail was sighted in lat. 57° 30', but by running close inshore where the larger vessel could not follow, they managed to escape. At Nachvak Bay, or Saglek—Gibbon's Hole—Eskimo came out to the ships in kyacks with "sea-wolf-skins" to trade. As they approached the strait the fears of the men again taxed Radisson's leadership, but once more he carried the day. They entered the strait with favourable winds, but harassed by a good deal of ice.

Keeping close to the north shore, they managed to get through without serious mishap, though once a gale struck them and drove them into the ice. "Wee had," says Radisson, "much adoe to recover out of the ice, and had like divers times to have perish'd, but God was pleas'd to preserve us." Chouart in the smaller ship fell behind, and Radisson reached the western side of the bay before him, on August 26th. September 2nd Chouart overtook him at the mouth of a river called by the Indians Ka-Kiwa-Kiouay; "Who goes, who comes," translates Radisson; probably a reference to the rise and fall of the tide. This was Hayes River, a few miles south of the Nelson. Both rivers had been visited on the second voyage from England, and Radisson was already familiar with Button's wintering-place.

Entering Hayes River, their first care was to find a convenient place to secure their vessels. This they found in a creek on the north shore, about fifteen miles upstream. Leaving Chouart to build a small fort, Radisson with Chouart's son, who had accompanied the expedition from Canada, ascended the river for forty or fifty miles, hoping to get in touch with the natives. On the eighth day, having taken shelter upon an island to rest, an Indian appeared on the opposite shore. He was following a deer, which had taken refuge on another island above them. Seeing Radisson's canoe on the beach, he supposed that a party of Indians was encamped on the island, and whistled to warn them of the deer. Radisson, more interested in the Indian than the deer, ran to the shore and called out to him. The

Indian stood for a moment in amazement, cried out in his own language that he did not understand him, and then made off into the woods.

The Frenchmen kept guard all night, and in the morning made a large fire on the shore to attract the attention of the Indians. Nine canoes were presently discovered coming toward the camp. When they got within speaking distance, Radisson asked them who they were. They replied in friendly terms. Radisson told them who he was, and explained the object of his visit. These were evidently Crees, a tribe whose hunting-grounds extended from Lake Superior to Hudson Bay. Some of them Radisson may have met on his fourth voyage. At any rate, he was familiar with their language, and they evidently knew who he was, and even seem to have expected him. An old chief, armed with a spear, club, and bow, rose in his canoe, drew an arrow from his quiver, pointed to the east and the west, the north and the south, then broke the arrow in two and threw it into the river. Addressing his companions he said, "Young men, you have no longer anything to fear. The sun is favourable unto us, for this is the man that we have wished for ever since the days of our fathers." So saying he sprang overboard, followed by the others, and they swam ashore. Radisson made them leave their weapons on the shore, and then invited them to the camp fire. Addressing the old man, he asked who was their chief. The chief bowed, and another answered, "You are speaking to him." Radisson made a speech; assured the Indians that their friends would be his friends; that he had brought them arms to destroy their enemies; food to keep them from starvation; raiment to clothe them. He invited them to visit the fort. In a long harangue the old chief thanked him, promising eternal friendship between his tribe and the French. Radisson gave presents to each; a musket, powder and shot for the chief; knives for the rest. Overwhelmed with gratitude, the Indians threw their robes at his feet, and brought presents of beaver-skins from their canoes. Promising to bring all their furs down to him at the fort, the Indians departed, and Radisson paddled down the river, delighted with the result of the expedition.

On the day of his arrival at the new fort he was alarmed by a cannon shot. Taking a canoe, he went down to the mouth of the river, but discovered nothing. Again the shot was heard, this time unmistakably from the north. Taking three men with him, Radisson crossed by a channel through the low, swampy lands between the two rivers, and found a ship anchored in the Nelson. This proved to be a New England trading ship, commanded by a son of Zachariah Gillam, whom Radisson had met in Boston. The rival traders professed to be delighted to meet again. Radisson went on board the ship, impressed Gillam with the fact that he was in command of a large expedition from Canada, that he was expecting another ship daily, and that he had secured the allegiance of all the Indians. Finally he magnanimously permitted Gillam to remain, and even to build a house, but it must not be fortified. Radisson would guarantee the New Englanders against insult from the Indians, over whom he had absolute power. "We parted after that," says Radisson, "well satisfied with each other, he fully convinced that I had the force of which I had boasted, and I resolved to keep him in this good opinion, having the design to oblige him to retire, or if he persisted in annoying me in my trade, to await a favourable opportunity to seize his ship, which was a good prize having neither a commission from France nor England for the trade, but I would not undertake it unseasonably for fear of failure."

Leaving young Gillam, the astute Frenchman paddled down the Nelson, but had scarcely made three leagues when he discovered another ship entering the river under sail. Hastily making for the south shore, he landed and raised a thick smoke to attract the attention of the newcomers. It was now toward dusk, and the vessel anchored opposite the place where Radisson was in hiding. He and his men watched all night to see what would happen. In the morning he saw a boat put off from the ship and come toward him. Posting his three men fifteen or twenty paces apart, at the edge of the wood, where they might do duty for a large party, he himself advanced alone to the water's edge. The ship proved to be a vessel of the Hudson's Bay Company, and in the boat that was now approaching was the new Governor, Bridgar, Radisson's old friend Captain Gillam, and six sailors. After some parleying Bridgar landed. Was not this, he asked, the River Kakiwakiouay? "No," replied Radisson, "that was farther to the south." The river on which they were was called by the Indians Kawirinagaw, or the wicked river. Bridgar asked if it was not here that Sir Thomas Button had wintered. " Yes," said Radisson, and showed him the place to the north. Bridgar invited him to go on board. Radisson's nephew tried to dissuade him; but though he and Gillam had fallen out in England, and he had reason to fear that if he went on board Gillam would arrest him, he nevertheless resolved to go. As a precaution, however, he insisted that two of Gillam's men should remain on shore as hostages. Then Radisson went out to the ship and dined with his British hosts, to whom he related the same fairy tale that had so impressed young Gillam. Bridgar was equally credulous, to Radisson's relief, "for," says he, "if he had taken the trouble which I had done to go forty leagues through the woods, to lie on the hard ground, in order to make discoveries, he would soon have noticed my weak points."

Radisson returned to Hayes River with his men, while Bridgar proceeded to build a fort on the Nelson. The situation was a peculiar one, and Radisson thought he saw a way to turn it to his own advantage. Bridgar had come to open an establishment on behalf of the Hudson's Bay Company. He considered Radisson an interloper, but believed him to be too strong to interfere with, for the present at any rate. So far he knew nothing of the New Englanders, but would certainly eject them if he did find them out. Here was Radisson's opportunity. Captain Gillam and his son were in collusion. The former was in the pay of the Hudson's

Bay Company, and at the same time had sent his son to poach on the Company's preserves. If the two British ships could be kept apart, he might deal with each at his leisure. The Gillams were only too anxious to keep the matter from the Governor, and Radisson so played on young Gillam's fears that he agreed, in case any of Bridgar's men should ascend the river, to pass his vessel off as a French ship.

All went smoothly for a time, until the Governor grew suspicious, and took steps to test the accuracy of Radisson's statements. He sent men out to ascertain the whereabouts and strength of the French forts and the number of their ships. Two of them discovered the New Englanders, and hastened back with the news that one of the French forts and one of their vessels were on the river above. Other of Bridgar's men were captured by Radisson in the bush, and taken to his own fort on Hayes River, where they were detained but treated civilly. They told Radisson that Bridgar's ship had been crushed in the ice, and that Captain Gillam with his lieutenant and four sailors were lost. About the same time letters were intercepted from young Gillam, from which it appeared that he too had become suspicious as to the strength of the French, and was making preparations to seize Radisson's fort. The latter promptly decided to anticipate him. He visited Gillam in his fort, and, knowing his anxiety to find out his strength, invited him to visit the French establishment. Gillam eagerly consented, taking several of his men with him. They remained for a month. Radisson says

CARRYING FURS OVERLAND FROM FORT SMITH

Face p. 80

that he treated Gillam well and with all sorts of civili-
ties, which he abused on several occasions. Gillam saw
the weakness of the French, and grew insolent. Finally
Radisson told him that he was about to take both his
fort and his ship. Gillam answered haughtily that even
if he had a hundred men he could not succeed. His
people would kill forty before they could reach the
palisades. Radisson, nettled at the taunt, asked him
how many men there were in the fort. " Nine," replied
Gillam. " Choose an equal number of my men, myself
included," cried Radisson, "and I promise to give a good
account of both your fort and your ship in two days."
Gillam picked out eight men, confident that he was
sending them to certain destruction.

Radisson and his men set out, taking one of Bridgar's
men as a witness. Arrived within half a league of the
fort, he left the Englishman with one of his own men,
commanding them not to leave until they had his
orders. He then sent two of his men to approach the
fort boldly, while he and the remaining five crept up
behind to watch the proceedings. The two were
stopped outside the gate by three of Gillam's men, who
asked if they had letters from their master. The French
replied, as Radisson had instructed, that Gillam was
following with him, and that they had been sent on
ahead for some brandy. They were told to go into the
fort, while one of the New Englanders started off with
the brandy to meet the main party.

This was just what Radisson had hoped for. One of
his men was already in the fort, left there a month

G

before as hostage for Gillam. The orders were that, at the right moment, he was to take possession of the door of the guardhouse, while the other two were to watch the door of the main house and keep the gate open. But as it turned out there was no need of even these precautions. Radisson and his men were inside the gates before those who should have guarded them were aware of their presence. The surprise was complete, and there was nothing for it but to surrender the fort. Radisson had won a bloodless victory. He ordered the lieutenant in charge to bring him the keys of the fort, with all the arms and ammunition. When this had been done he took possession of the fort in the name of the King of France. Forcing the lieutenant to accompany him to the ship, this was also seized with equal ease.

Meanwhile a young Scotchman had escaped to warn Bridgar of what had happened. His flight was not discovered for a time, and when at last men were sent in pursuit he had gained too great a start. Anticipating that Bridgar would probably attack him, Radisson sent to Chouart for reinforcements. During the night one of the dogs gave the alarm. Bridgar's men were about to storm the ship. Radisson with five of his men rushed out of the fort, and ordered the attacking party to lay down their arms, which, if he is to be believed, they ingloriously did. Of course, all this is Radisson's side of the story. Unfortunately there is no authentic account of the other side. Bridgar was not found among the prisoners, and it turned out that he had "remained half a league off to await the success of the enterprise," as Radisson contemptuously remarks. The remainder of the winter passed in diplomatic fencing between Radisson and Bridgar, but the former had now completely the upper hand. His troubles were not over though by any means. He had to guard both Gillam's and Bridgar's men; feed them from his own stores to a large extent; and to crown all, the Indians came down, and could with difficulty be made to understand that though the English were Radisson's enemies, he did not wish them destroyed.

As soon as navigation opened Radisson made preparations to depart. He had determined to send the English down to their posts at the bottom of the bay, and gave them one of his own small vessels for that purpose, while he sailed for Quebec in the New England ship, taking Bridgar and young Gillam with him. Chouart's son remained in command of the fort on Hayes River, and before Radisson left both the English establishments were burnt. Thus ended for a time the English fur trade at Port Nelson. The Hudson's Bay Company was never a very militant organization when it came to actual fighting. Time and again their forts were captured by French expeditions, generally without firing a shot. But they possessed wonderful pertinacity. As soon as the coast was clear, back they came to re-establish their interrupted trade with the Indians.

It is as explorers rather than as traders, however, that their history is now being examined. In its evidence before the Parliamentary Committee, in 1749, the Company submitted copies of instructions sent to its governors in the bay, urging them to explore both the coast and the interior. The first of these letters was addressed to Governor Bayly in 1676, who was directed to use his utmost diligence in making discoveries both of the coast and the country, of mines, and of all sorts of commodities which the country might produce. Bayly replied that he had already done so; that for six years past he had had three men engaged in a constant discovery of the regions about the bay; but though he enlarges upon the dangerous character of the work, and the extreme difficulty of inducing his men to undertake it, he omits to say what has actually been accomplished; he gives in fact no hint whatever as to where his men had gone or what they had discovered.   Instructions to later governors were to the same purport, and their replies are equally unenlightening.   Vague generalities fairly describes them.   It is sufficiently clear that about all the Company had in view in these proposed explorations was the furtherance of their own direct interests; their men were to spy out the land and ascertain its capabilities from a fur trader's point of view; make treaties with the Indians; and induce them, if possible, to bring their furs down to the forts on the bay.

There is nothing to show that exploratory parties were not sent out, but with one or two exceptions there is little or nothing to prove that they were. Of these exceptions the first in point of time relates to a journey made, it is alleged on behalf of the Company, by a young boy Henry Kellsey, whose journal has been preserved. This overland journey will be dealt with in the following chapter; for the present it may be convenient to consider briefly certain voyages along the north-western coast of Hudson Bay, undertaken under the directions of the Hudson's Bay Company for, among other reasons, the discovery of a passage to the Western Sea.

Among the papers presented to the Committee appointed to inquire into the affairs of the Hudson's Bay Company, in 1749, was a list of vessels fitted out by the Company for the purpose of discovering a North-West Passage. The list is worth reproducing as it stands, as furnishing a concise statement of this particular phase of the subject.

1719. *Albany*, frigate, Capt. George Berley,[1] sailed from England on or about 5th June. Never returned.

1719. *Discovery*, Capt. David Vaughan, sailed from England on or about 5th June. Never returned.

1719. *Prosperous*, Capt. Henry Kelsey, sailed from York Fort, June 19th. Returned 10th August following.

1719. *Success*, John Hancock master, sailed from Prince of Wales's Fort, July 2nd. Returned 10th August.

1721. *Prosperous*, Capt. Henry Kelsey, sailed from York Fort, June 26th. Returned 2nd September.

1721. *Success*, James Napper master, sailed from York Fort, June 26th. Lost 30th of the same month.

1721. *Whalebone*, John Scroggs master, sailed from

[1] Hearne spells the name *Barlow*.

Gravesend, 31st May; wintered at Prince of Wales's Fort. Sailed from thence 21st June, 1722. Returned July 25th following.

1737. *Churchill*, James Napper master, sailed from Prince of Wales's Fort, July 7th. Died 8th August; and the vessel returned the 18th.

1737. *Musquash*, Robert Crow master, sailed from Prince of Wales's Fort, July 7th. Returned 22nd August.

The two vessels first mentioned, the *Albany* and the *Discovery*, constituted the first expedition sent out by the Hudson's Bay Company for the discovery of a passage, or as they themselves put it, to "find out the Streight of Anian." This expedition was under the command of Captain James Knight. Hearne, in the introduction to his *Journey*, says that Captain Knight was a man of great experience in the Company's service, but adds that he had nothing but the imperfect accounts of the Indians to guide him in the exploration he was now about to undertake. Knight must have been a man of unconquerable energy, for he was nearly eighty years of age at the time he started out on this voyage of discovery. He had himself suggested the voyage to the Company, and was so confident that it would not only lead to the discovery of the elusive Strait of Anian, but, what seems to have been really uppermost in his mind, to the discovery of mines of fabulous richness, that he took with him on one of the vessels a number of large iron-bound chests, which were to be brought back loaded with treasure.

The intention was that the *Albany* and *Discovery*,

after discovering the strait, were to return, if possible, the same year to England.   They failed to turn up, but no particular anxiety was felt, as they had on board an ample stock of provisions, a house in frame, and other conveniences.   When, however, neither vessel appeared the following year, grave apprehensions were entertained as to the fate of the expedition, and the Company sent out Captain Scroggs, in the *Whalebone*, to search for the missing vessels.   The *Whalebone* had a difficult passage out, and did not reach Churchill until late in the autumn of 1721, too late to do anything that year.   In June following Scroggs set out for the north, and followed the coast as far as Whale Point, in Roe's Welcome, without, however, discovering any vestige of the missing ships or their crews.   He returned to Churchill on the 25th July.

Scroggs's failure to find the *Albany* and *Discovery* served to confirm the strong opinion which, as Hearne says, then prevailed in Europe respecting the probability of a North-West Passage by way of Hudson Bay, and it was believed in many quarters that Knight had found the passage, had taken his ships through, and would eventually turn up by way of Cape Horn.

It was not until the summer of 1767 that the fate of the expedition was discovered.   In that year one of the Company's vessels, engaged in the whale fishery, visited Marble Island, and happened upon a harbour toward the east end of the island, which had hitherto been overlooked.   Sailing into this harbour, they found relics on every side of the lost expedition.   The shores were strewn with guns, anchors, cables, bricks, a smith's anvil, and many other articles which the Eskimo had found too heavy to carry away. The remains of the house, as well as the hulls of the two vessels, were still to be seen, the latter lying sunk in about five fathoms water, toward the head of the harbour. The figure-head of the *Albany* was sent home to England, as evidence of the fate of the expedition.

Three years later a number of Eskimo were met with at Marble Island, among whom were several aged men. Through the medium of an interpreter the old men were questioned, in the hope that they might have some knowledge as to the disastrous history of the expedition; and from them was obtained the following circumstantial account:—

When the vessels arrived at Marble Island it was very late in the fall, and in getting them into the harbour the largest received much damage; but, on being fairly in, the English began to build the house, their number at that time seeming to be about fifty. As soon as the ice permitted, in the following summer (1720), the Eskimo paid them another visit, by which time the number of the English was greatly reduced, and those that were living seemed very unhealthy. According to the account given by the Eskimo, they were then very busily employed, but about what they could not easily describe, probably in lengthening the long-boat; for at a little distance from the house there was still to be seen a quantity of oak chips, which had been most assuredly made by carpenters.

ESKIMO AT FISHER BAY, HUDSON STRAIT

Face p. 83

Sickness and famine occasioned such havoc among the English, that by the setting in of the second winter their number was reduced to twenty. That winter (1720) some of the Eskimo took up their abode on the opposite side of the harbour to that on which the English had built their houses, and frequently supplied them with such provisions as they had, which chiefly consisted of whale's blubber and seal's flesh and train oil. When the spring advanced the Eskimo went to the mainland, and on their visiting Marble Island again, in the summer of 1721, they found only five of the English alive, and those were in such distress for provisions that they eagerly ate the seal's flesh and whale's blubber quite raw, as they purchased it from the natives. This disordered them so much that three of them died in a few days, and the other two, though very weak, made a shift to bury them. Those two survived many days after the rest, and frequently went to the top of an adjacent rock, and earnestly looked to the south and east, as if in expectation of some vessels coming to their relief. After continuing there a considerable time together, and nothing appearing in sight, they sat down close together and wept bitterly. At length one of the two died, and the other's strength was so far exhausted, that he fell down and died also, in attempting to dig a grave for his companion. Hearne, who gives the foregoing account as it was received from the Eskimo, adds that the skulls and other large bones of two of the men were still lying above-ground close to the house in 1769, which seemed to confirm the story told by the Eskimo.

It is singular enough that although the Company's vessels are said to have frequently passed Marble Island, and to have made use of one or other of its harbours, nearly half a century went by before any trace was found of the *Albany* and *Discovery*.

Of the two expeditions of the *Prosperous* and *Success*, in 1719 and 1721 respectively, nothing is known beyond their bare mention in the foregoing list. They are not found in the Orders given by the Hudson's Bay Company to sundry persons with regard to the discovery of a North-west Passage, copies of which form part of the Appendix to the Report of 1749. Probably the Henry Kelsey named as captain of the *Prosperous* was the same whose overland expedition has already been mentioned.

Of the expedition of the *Churchill* and *Musquash* in 1737 no details are extant except the instructions to their masters, James Napper and Robert Crow. These officers were ordered to sail close along the western shore, making discovery into Sir Thomas Roe's Welcome and elsewhere along the coast; to observe bearings and distances of each remarkable headland; to take soundings; watch and report upon the set of the tide; the rise and fall at ebb and high water, and the distance of the time of flood; to study the character of the coast, its soil, trees, and possible minerals. The instructions close with the pious prayer, "So God send the good Sloops a successful Discovery, and to return in Safety. Amen." Whether the good sloops accomplished all or any of the important objects of their voyage there is no means of knowing.

It will be seen that from a geographical point of view these several expeditions sent out by or on behalf of the Hudson's Bay Company for the discovery of the Strait of Anian, and other objects geographical, scientific, or commercial, added practically nothing to what was already known of the north-western coasts of the bay.

In 1741 an expedition was dispatched independently of the Company, and toward which it showed itself none too friendly. This expedition, commanded by Christopher Middleton with H.M.S. *Furnace* and *Discovery* (how often the latter name crops up in northern voyages!) was more successful. Material additions were made to the geography of the north-west coast of the bay, including Roe's Welcome, Wager Bay, Repulse Bay, and the Frozen Strait. Incidentally this voyage disposed of the vexed question as to whether or not there was a channel from Hudson Bay to the western ocean; though that fierce pamphleteer Arthur Dobbs and a few other enthusiastic advocates of the theory of a strait through the continent refused to be convinced.

Middleton sailed from England in the summer of 1741, and reached Port Churchill about the beginning of September. Here he wintered in Sloops Cove, intending to sail north with the breaking up of the ice in the spring.

" In the course of one of our outings," says Mr. J. W. Tyrrell,[1] " we reached a place called Sloops Cove, about half-way to Prince of Wales Fort, and there made some

---

[1] *Across the Sub-Arctics of Canada*, pp. 214-15.

interesting observations. This cove owes its name to the fact that in the year 1741 the two sloops, *Furnace* and *Discovery*, sent out from England in command of Captain Middleton to search for the long-looked-for North-West Passage, spent the winter there. How two vessels could have been forced into this cove is a question which has given rise to much speculation on the part of Canadian scientists, for the cove does not now contain more than sufficient depth of water, at high tide, to float a small boat, and it is doubtful if even such a boat could get in through the rocky entrance. The historical fact remains, however, that this cove was the winter quarters of these two sloops, and as proof of the fact a number of ring-bolts to which the vessels were secured may still be seen leaded into the smooth glaciated granite shores. Besides the ring-bolts, many interesting carvings are to be seen cut on the surface of the smooth rocks. Amongst them are the following: '*Furnace* and *Discovery* 1741,' 'J. Horner 1746,' 'J. Morley 1748,' 'James Walker May ye 25 1753,' 'Guillford Long May ye 27 1753,' 'J. Wood 1757,' 'Sl Hearne July ye 1 1767.' In addition to many other names are several picture carvings, and notably one of a man suspended from a gallows, over which is the inscription, 'John Kelley from the Isle of Wight.' According to local tradition, Mr. Kelley is said to have been hanged for the theft of a salt goose."

Leaving Churchill on July 1st, 1742, by the 12th Middleton was well into Roe's Welcome, off what he calls Whale Bone Point—Whale Point of the modern charts.   North of this point he passed another headland in 65° 10', which he named after his worthy but unbelieving friend Arthur Dobbs, and discovered an inlet opening to the north-west, into which he was glad to run his ships to escape the ice.   He named this inlet Wager River, in honour of Sir Charles Wager, then First Lord of the Admiralty.   In Wager River he was compelled to stay for three weeks, the Welcome being filled with ice.   Vexatious though the delay seemed to him, he managed to improve the time by making a fairly thorough examination of the inlet, or bay as it is more properly called, an examination which confirmed the conclusion he had already reached, because of the strong set of the tide into the bay, that here at least was no Strait of Anian.

On August 3rd, the mouth of the inlet being comparatively clear of ice, he sailed carefully out and pursued his voyage north up the Welcome.   At noon on the fifth he was in lat. 66° 14', off a headland which, as it seemed to mark the extreme northern limit of the coast, he called Cape Hope.   But this was another case of Hope Checked, for on rounding the cape and sailing a few leagues to the westward, Middleton found himself at the foot of a bay with the coast still blocking his passage to the westward.   This he appropriately named Repulse Bay.

He had now established beyond reasonable controversy, though not to the satisfaction of Arthur Dobbs and Alexander Dalrymple, that no passage existed anywhere on the western coast of Hudson Bay up to

66° 40′ N. Before entering Repulse Bay Middleton had observed a very strong tide coming into Roe's Welcome from the east by south. Crossing to the Southampton side of the strait to discover, if possible, the origin of this tide, he landed south of Cape Frigid, the extreme northern point of what was until recently supposed to be Southampton Island, but which Dr. A. P. Low has found to be another island, unnamed, to the north of Southampton. Travelling inland ten or twelve miles, he came to a high mountain, climbed to its summit, and had from there a splendid view of the ice-burdened waters of the Frozen Strait. He plainly saw that this was the strait through which the flood entered Roe's Welcome. From his high vantage point it was visible from end to end, dotted with many small islands, and packed with ice from shore to shore. The Frozen Strait he correctly supposed to run toward Fox Channel, and he had consequently connected his own explorations with those of Foxe, James, and Bylot on the eastern side of the strait. Plainly no passage for his ships was to be hoped for through Frozen Strait, and after consulting his officers Middleton turned south again down Roe's Welcome, and so home, to face the fiery denunciation of the disappointed Dobbs.

Only one other attempt was made in the eighteenth century to explore Hudson Bay. Captain Duncan sailed to the west coast in 1790, but accomplished nothing of any moment. Hearne lent a copy of a Chipewyan vocabulary which he had prepared to the Secretary of the Hudson's Bay Company, to make a copy for Captain Duncan, but the latter apparently made no use of it.

Of later explorations in and about the northern waters of Hudson Bay it will be sufficient to note that Parry in 1821–3, starting where Middleton left off in Repulse Bay, explored the entire eastern coast of Melville Peninsula, finally discovering, in Fury and Hecla Strait, the nearest approach to a North-West Passage by way of Hudson Bay.   Back, in 1836–7, explored the northern coast of Southampton Island ; and Rae, in 1846–7, followed Middleton's track to Repulse Bay on his way to the north.   In still more recent times Dr. Robert Bell and Dr. A. P. Low, of the Canadian Geological Survey, have added to and corrected the geography of the bay.   As recently as 1903–4 Dr. Low discovered that the so-called Bell Island was merely an extension of Southampton, the strait shown on the maps separating Bell from Southampton being purely imaginary.   He also found Tom Island, supposed to lie in 63° 15′ N. and 87° W., had no existence. Dr. Bell and Dr. Low have added materially to our knowledge of the coasts of Hudson Bay proper, as well as James Bay.   They have also done good work in Hudson Strait, or rather the eastern half of the strait, the western half being still very imperfectly known.

CHAPTER IV

THE HENRY KELLSEY PUZZLE

HENRY KELLSEY[1] is first heard of in the annals of the Hudson's Bay Company in 1688, in which year instructions were given Governor Geyer, at Port Nelson, to send "the boy, Henry Kelsey," to Churchill River, "because we are informed he is a very active lad, delighting much in Indians' company, being never better pleased than when he is travelling amongst them." Presumably Kellsey was to bring the northern Indians—probably Chipewyans—down to Port Nelson, as the Company had not yet any establishment at the mouth of the Churchill. There is nothing to show that the journey was ever made; but on September 8th, 1690, Geyer writes: "This summer I sent up Henry Kelsey (who chearfully undertook the journey) into the country of the *Assinæ Poets* [Assiniboines], with the Captain of that Nation, to call, encourage, and invite the remoter Indians to a trade with us." The following year Geyer writes that he has received a letter from Kellsey saying that the Indians are continually at war, but have promised to get what beaver they can, and to

---

[1] The name is generally spelt "Kelsey," but as the signature at the end of the narrative in the Hudson's Bay Report, 1749, is "Henry Kellsey," that spelling has been adopted.

ON THE FIRST PORTAGE, SLAVE RIVER

bring it down with them the following year. He adds
that he has ordered Kellsey to return to the fort in
1692, and bring the Indians with him, and in the meantime to "search diligently for mines, minerals, or drugs
of what kind soever, and to bring samples of them down
with him." In 1692 Geyer writes again: "Henry Kelsey
came down with a good fleet of Indians, and hath
travelled and endeavoured to keep the peace among
them, according to my orders."

From all this it would appear that Kellsey had been
sent inland by the Hudson's Bay Company for the
special object of making discoveries, and bringing the
western Indians down to trade at the bay; but Joseph
Robson, the English engineer who planned Fort Prince
of Wales, and who spent six years on the bay, takes
quite a different view. He was at some pains to
ascertain the true history of Henry Kellsey, and the
account he obtained from old employees of the Company was about as follows:—[1]

Henry Kellsey, a little boy, used to take great delight
in the company of the natives and in learning their
language, for which, and some unlucky tricks that boys
of spirit are always guilty of, the governor would often
correct him with great severity. It may be explained
that the Company, from some accounts at least, strongly
discouraged the learning of native languages, or any
intercourse with the natives except on the Company's
business. Kellsey resented the governor's severity, and

---

[1] *Account of Six Years' Residence in Hudson's Bay, 1733–36 and
1744–47* (London 1752), p. 72 *et seq.* and App.

H

when he was advanced a little in years and strength, took an opportunity of going off with some distant Indians, to whom he had endeared himself by a long acquaintance and many little offices of kindness. A year or two afterward the governor received by an Indian a letter written with charcoal on a piece of birch bark. This was from Kellsey, and was to ask the governor's pardon for running away and permission to return to the fort. The pardon being granted, Kellsey came down with a party of Indians, dressed after their manner, and attended by a native wife, who wanted to follow him into the factory. The governor opposed this, but upon Kellsey's telling him in English that he would not go in himself if his wife was not suffered to go in, the governor relented.

There seems to be some confusion as to the years covered by Kellsey's expedition. Geyer's correspondence leads one to suppose that Kellsey left Port Nelson for the interior during the summer of 1690, and returned the summer of 1692. Kellsey's own journal, however, which forms part of the Appendix to the Hudson's Bay Report, 1749, is dated 1691, while a duplicate of the journal, also included in the Appendix for some unexplained reason, is dated July 15th, 1692. From the wording of the first copy of the journal one gets the impression that Kellsey left on his journey in July, 1691, while according to the duplicate he left a year later. The two copies are otherwise identical, and leave no room for doubt that they refer to one and the same journey, though in neither case do the dates fit in

with Governor Geyer's account of the expedition.   The
only rational explanation seems to be that the substitu-
tion of the date July 15th, 1692, in the duplicate, for
July 5th, 1691, in the original, was due to a clerical
error.   Why the Company thought it worth while to
offer both in evidence remains a puzzle.   In fact, the confusion does not end even here.   Three titles are given
in the Appendix.   The first reads : " A Journal of
Henry Kelsey in the years 1691 and 1692, sent by the
Hudson's Bay Company to make discoveries, and increase their trade inland from the Bay."   No journal
follows this title.   The second reads : " A journal of a
voyage and journey undertaken by Henry Kelsey to
discover and endeavour to bring to a commerce the
Naywatamee-Poets, 1691"; and the third: " A journal
of a voyage and journey undertaken by Henry Kelsey,
through God's assistance, to discover and bring to a
commerce the Naywatamee-Poets.   Duplicate."   These
latter are the two already referred to.   It has been suggested that the Company wished to create the impression
that Kelsey had been sent on two distinct expeditions, the
first in 1691 and the second in 1692 ; but this is altogether
improbable.   No one who took the trouble to read the
two journals could for a moment be deceived, as the
duplicate follows the original almost word for word.
The true explanation is probably found in the concluding words of the two journals.   The first ends as
follows : " Sir, I remain your most obedient and faithful
servant"; and the second : " I rest, honourable masters,
your most obedient and faithful servant, at command."

As Robson suggests, the former was no doubt addressed to Governor Geyer; the latter to the Company. The Company having both copies, one received direct from Kellsey, the other through Geyer, submitted them to the Parliamentary Committee, and both consequently found their way into the 1749 Report. As to the reference, in the first title, to the years 1691 and 1692, the explanation of that may simply be that Kellsey went out in 1691 and returned in 1692.

Now as to the more vital question—in what direction, and how far, did Kellsey travel, if he went anywhere? The last proviso is necessary, for it has been maintained by competent writers that Kellsey's expedition was a pure myth invented by the Hudson's Bay Company to meet the attack of those who had charged it with bad faith in neglecting to explore the west. It is pointed out by those who believe the narrative to be a fabrication that the statements of Geyer are at variance with the narrative; that neither one nor the other fits in with the evidence obtained by Robson; that the narrative bears internal evidence of its spuriousness, as in the extraordinary vagueness of its topography; that although the Hudson's Bay Company had time and again been put on its defence to prove its title by occupation to the territory draining into Hudson Bay, it never once mentioned Kellsey's journal after the investigation of 1749, although if Kellsey's exploration were authentic it would have been evidence of the greatest importance on the Company's behalf. These are weighty arguments, and yet a careful study of

Kellsey's journal in the light of all the surrounding circumstances tends rather to confirm its authenticity. This does not necessarily imply, however, that the claim put forth on behalf of the Company that Kellsey had been sent forth by them on discoveries was true, but merely that Kellsey actually performed the journey described in his journal. As to this latter point, the evidence adduced by Robson, though he himself was not an unprejudiced witness, is almost overpoweringly against the Company's contention.

Assuming, then, that Kellsey performed the journey; that he had already been in the interior for some time before the authorities of the Hudson's Bay Company discovered that his presence there might be turned to their own advantage; that he penetrated farther to the westward either on his own account, or possibly at the instance of Governor Geyer. How far did he go; and what direction did he take? The popular theory among Canadian historians has been that his general course was south-west, from Port Nelson or some point up the river, and that he reached either Lake Winnipeg or the country north of the Saskatchewan. An instance is found here of the danger of relying on second-hand authorities when the original documents are available. The late Dr. Elliott Coues, one of the most industrious, painstaking, and accurate of historians, made it almost his invariable practice to dig back to the original documents. One of the very rare instances in which he departed from this practice occurs in his *New Light on the Early History of the Greater North-West.* In a foot-note (p. 38) he says: "I should not omit to note the journal of Henry Kellsey, of the H. B. Co., showing that he was on Lake Winnipeg in July and Aug., 1692: see Bell." Turning to Mr. Bell's paper,[1] to which Dr. Cones refers, this passage is found: "In 1749 the H. B. Co. produced before a committee of the British House of Commons the journal of an employee named Henry Kellsey, dated July and August, 1692, which seems to show clearly that he was at Lake Winnipeg on an exploring trip made in the interests of the H. B. Co., and with the object of inducing the Indians of the interior to take their furs down to the posts on Hudson's Bay. The journal is printed in detail in the above report, which I have in my possession." If Dr. Coues had gone direct to the journal in the 1749 Report, he would have found that there is not one word to indicate that Kellsey was on Lake Winnipeg in 1692 or any other year; that he ever saw Lake Winnipeg; or even heard of it through the Indians, which he must have done had he been anywhere in the neighbourhood.

The more general theory has been that Kellsey's journey took him to the open country north of the Saskatchewan, some investigators assuming that he reached almost to the foothills of the Rockies, others more conservative taking him only to the vicinity of the main Saskatchewan below the forks. The former supposition seems to have been based solely on Robson's

---

[1] "Some Historical Names and Places of the Canadian North-West," by Mr. Charles N. Bell, F.R.G.S. *Transactions of the Manitoba Historical and Scientific Society*, No. 17, 1885.

story that Kellsey had encountered grizzly bears. " He
and an Indian were one day surprised by two grizzled
bears, having but just time to take shelter, the Indian in
a tree and Kellsey among some high willows ; the bears
making directly to the tree, Kellsey fired and killed one
of them ; the other, observing from whence the fire
came, ran towards the place, but not finding his prey,
returned to the tree, which he had just reached when he
dropped by Kellsey's second fire.   This action obtained
him the name of Miss-top-ashish, or Little Giant."
Knowing the limited range and effectiveness of the old
muzzle-loading trading gun of the Hudson's Bay Company, and the immense strength and tenacity of life of
Ursus horribilis, this story is to say the least improbable; but even admitting its accuracy, there is no
necessity to carry Kellsey to the foothills of the Rocky
Mountains, or anywhere near the foothills, to bring him
into contact with grizzly bears.   The narratives of many
of the early fur traders show that grizzly bears were
met with all through the west.   Hearne speaks of them
east of the Coppermine, and Alexander Henry says
they were numerous in the Red River country.   Between these two extremes they might have been encountered almost anywhere west of Hudson Bay.   The
probabilities are that Kellsey's encounter was with some
less ferocious and powerful member of the bear family.

    There are strong grounds for the belief that Kellsey's
discoveries were neither in the vicinity of Lake Winnipeg nor of the Saskatchewan River, but farther north.
Mr. R. H. Hunter, of the Canadian Topographical

Surveys, who is familiar with the character of the country, says that, after a careful study of Kellsey's narrative, he is convinced that his course could not have been in the direction of Lake Winnipeg or the Saskatchewan. To have gone this way Kellsey would have had to travel through a country occupied by a network of lakes, rivers, morasses, and bogs, the intervening lands being covered with coniferous woods, interspersed with poplar, birch, and willow, obstructed everywhere with fallen timber, and thick and tangled underbrush. The difficulties of travelling by land through such a country would be almost insurmountable, and it is estimated that two or three miles a day in a given direction would be fast travelling. Kellsey's journal shows that he abandoned his canoes so as to travel faster, which would be utterly impossible through this part of the country. On the other hand, if it is assumed that his course was west, rather than south-west, the natural conditions meet those of his narrative much more exactly. This will be made clear in following the journal.

Kellsey took his departure from Deerings Point the 15th of July, 1691, having received his supplies from Governor Geyer on the 5th, and sent ahead to hunt a party of Assiniboines who were with him. There is no certain evidence as to the whereabouts of Deerings Point. The name, which has long since disappeared, was doubtless given in honour of Sir Edward Dering, who was Governor of the Hudson's Bay Company towards the close of the seventeenth century. From Geyer's

FORT GOOD HOPE, MACKENZIE RIVER

Face p. 104

correspondence this point was evidently somewhere on the Nelson, and Dr. A. P. Low identifies it with Split Lake, though he does not say on what authority. Kellsey toward the end of his journal refers to Deerings Point as the place of rendezvous of the Indians coming down to trade at Port Nelson, or York Factory, as it was afterward called. This would fit in with the theory that Deerings Point was on or about Split Lake. Split Lake is the meeting-place of many waters. It marks the junction of Burntwood and Grass rivers with the Nelson, and through a small tributary it connects with the Little Churchill, all furnishing important canoe routes from the hunting-grounds of the western and northern tribes to Port Nelson. Split Lake finds a prominent place on all the early maps ; in fact often out of all proportion to its geographical importance. It was for many years supposed to lie at the height of land, its waters draining north-west to Hudson Bay and south-east to Lake Winnipeg. This point will be referred to again. Split Lake was unquestionably well known to the Indians, a convenient rendezvous, or "Place of Resortation," as Kellsey calls it, for trading parties from the Churchill, the Saskatchewan, and Lake Winnipeg, coming down to Port Nelson.

Setting out, then, from Split Lake, Kellsey paddled until noon on July 18th, when finding his progress too slow, by reason of the strength of the current or the difficulties of navigation, and being entirely dependent for provisions on what he might kill by the way, he decided to cache his canoe with the heavier parts of his outfit, and push forward on foot, carrying on his back what was absolutely necessary. From Deerings Point to the place where he abandoned his canoe Kellsey gives the distance as seventy-one miles. One can only conjecture on which river he paddled these seventy-one miles, but the balance of probabilities points to the Burntwood. Throughout his narrative Kellsey gives not the slightest indication as to his courses. All that serve as a guide are certain meagre indications of the general character of the country he travelled through, the kinds of trees met with in the course of his march, and the game. For three hundred and sixteen miles he tramped through a wooded country, first covered with spruce and pine, and afterward, as he drew near the open country, with poplar and birch. The open plain that followed was traversed for forty-six miles, and this was succeeded by a park country, through which he journeyed for eighty-one miles, making his total distance from Deerings Point five hundred and fourteen miles. In all this distance he only mentions crossing one river, and that a small stream, shallow, and but a hundred yards from bank to bank. This fact alone has served to throw discredit on Kellsey's narrative, for it is impossible to travel five hundred miles from any point on the Nelson River, in any conceivable direction, without striking many rivers and lakes. It is true that from Split Lake west and north-west to the Churchill the maps show no rivers or lakes of any kind, but this absence of topographical features does not necessarily mean that no rivers or lakes exist. It simply means that this is one of a number of unexplored areas in the Canadian West, which will probably be found to contain as many rivers and lakes as the surrounding regions. Apart, however, from the probability that if Kellsey's course was west or north-west from Split Lake, he would still have had to cross not one, but several rivers, this country, so far as it is known at all, fits more nearly the descriptions given in the journal than do any of the more southerly regions.

Coming back to the narrative. After abandoning his canoe, **Kellsey** travelled on foot through the bush, as already mentioned. It was impossible to carry provisions of any kind. He must rely absolutely on what might be picked up by the way. For some days game was scarce ; exceedingly scarce ; barely sufficient to keep him alive. On the 24th July, however, he overtook a party of Indians who had killed a buck moose, part of which they gave to him. Eleven days later he overtook the party of Stone Indians, or Assiniboines, whom he had sent on ahead from Deerings Point. These are the same called Assinæ Poets by Governor Geyer. With them were a number of Nayhaythaways, or Crees.[1] The Stone Indians brought word that the Naywatamee Poets, whom Kellsey was seeking, had killed three Nayhaythaway squaws in the spring. This was bad news from every point of view. The Nayhaythaways would be on the war-path to avenge the death of their

---

[1] Umfreville, in his *Present State of Hudson Bay*, speaks of the Assinepoetuc, or Stone Indians, and the Nehethawa, or Kalisteno. Knisteneaux or Cristineaux, with innumerable variants, was the French name for the Crees.

squaws, and, what was much more serious, the shock to their own dignity. The Naywatamee Poets would be harder to get at than ever. From now on Kellsey had all he could do to restrain the enraged Crees. They were incapable of understanding why their tribal affairs must give place to the white man's commerce. The Indian had not yet learned his lesson, that neither he nor his affairs were of any importance as compared with the white man's greed for peltries.

August 6th they camped by the side of a small stream which the Crees called Wasskashwsebee. With the exception of Deerings Point this is the only place-name in Kellsey's journal, and it is even harder to identify than the former. Mr. Hunter suggests that Kellsey may have reached Reindeer River, though he would have had to cross the Churchill on his way, between Nelson and Granville lakes. He points out the significant fact that Reindeer River is about three hundred miles from Split Lake, which agrees with the distance from Deerings Point to the Wasskashwsebee; and the further fact that the native name of Reindeer River is Wahwasskais-seepee. Too much must not be built, however, on the similarity of these two names, for they, or their English equivalent Deer River, have been applied to innumerable rivers throughout North-Western America.

Wherever this particular Deer River was, it ran through a pretty fair country. Game was plentiful, and Kellsey and his Indian friends at last had enough to eat. Continuing the journey, on the sixth day after leaving the Wasskashwsebee the country began to grow heathy and barren.   They were not on the open plains, but in a park country, wooded land interspersed with open spaces.   Fir trees gave place to poplar and birch.   On August 15th one of the Indians took sick, and after lingering for a couple of days, died.   The following morning the body was " burnt in a fire, according to their way, they making a great feast for him that did it ; so after the flesh was burned, the bones were buried, with logs set up round it."   The companions of the Indian, by a characteristic course of native reasoning, blamed Kellsey for the man's death.   Kellsey had prevented them from avenging the murder of their squaws ; the Gods were angry ; hence this additional victim. Kellsey felt the need of placing the situation squarely before them.   He accordingly gave a " Feast of Tobacco," as he calls it ; otherwise smoked the ceremonial pipe ; told the Indians that they were not supplied with guns and ammunition by the Company to kill their enemies, and that if they went to war, in spite of his remonstrances, they need not go down to Port Nelson, for the governor would not look upon them with favour.

August 19th found Kellsey near the open country, and the following day he camped on the outermost edge of the woods, the plains stretching out before him as far as eye could see.   Buffalo had been seen the previous day, and were now found in abundance.   These were " not like those which are to the northward, their horns growing like an English ox, but black and short." Although the sentence is not very clear, it is evident that the description is meant to apply to the buffalo now met with, not to "those which are to the northward." The latter were probably not buffalo at all, but musk ox. The musk ox during the winter season migrate from the barren lands to the wooded districts farther south, for shelter and food. There is evidence of their having been found in the neighbourhood of Wollaston and Reindeer lakes. How far the buffalo ranged to the northward is not certain, but it will be seen in the next chapter that Samuel Hearne found them in immense herds immediately south of Great Slave Lake, and they probably roamed wherever there was open ground and grass to feed upon. The fact that Kellsey met with buffalo does not therefore throw much light upon his whereabouts. He might have seen them anywhere from Lake Winnipeg to Reindeer Lake.

"On the 22nd," says Kellsey, "we pitched into the barren ground. It is very dry ground and no water, nor could we see the woods on the other side." The ground was covered with "short, round, sticky grass." Over this wide plain he journeyed for seven days, a distance of forty-six miles, when he again reached wooded country, a high "champain" land, covered with poplar and birch, and everywhere an abundance of small ponds, and quantities of beaver. They camped for a day to hunt beaver. Kellsey's party had been joined by another band of Assiniboines, under a chief named Wassha.

September 2nd a large herd of buffalo were seen, and the entire party gave chase, with satisfactory results.

They were nearing the country of the Naywatamee Poets, and Kellsey sent several of his Indians ahead to look out for hunting parties. On the 7th they were again on the open plain, and the following day four of the Naywatamee Poets arrived in camp. Kellsey entertained them as well as his narrow means would permit, and sent them back with a message to their chief. The evening of the 11th he himself arrived at the camp of the Naywatamee Poets.

Kellsey pitched his tent, filled his pipe of ceremony, and sent for the chief of the Naywatamee Poets, to whom he presented, on behalf of the Hudson's Bay Company, a coat, cap, and sash, one of his own guns, with knives, awls, and tobacco, and a small quantity of powder and shot; with all of which one can readily believe the Naywatamee Poet was well pleased. The chief expressed his sorrow that he had nothing worthy to offer in exchange, but promised to meet Kellsey the following spring at Deerings Point and go down with him to Port Nelson. True to his promise, he did set out in the spring for Deerings Point with a quantity of beaver-skins, but being set upon by a band of Crees, who had a bone to pick with the Naywatamee Poets, he was forced to turn back to his own country. Who these Naywatamee Poets were, whose allegiance was so highly prized by Governor Geyer, there is no means of knowing. The name suggests that they might have been the Nodwayes or Sioux, but the home of the Sioux was too far south to have been reached by Kellsey with any degree of probability.

Kellsey's journal is certainly one of the most puzzling in the literature of American exploration. The closest study of his narrative leaves one in doubt as to how far he travelled and in what direction, and even his starting-point is by no means certain. There does not, however, appear to be any good reason for denying that the journey described in this narrative was actually made, and, without exaggerating its importance, there is no question but that from several points of view it was a notable achievement. It was the first serious attempt, indeed the first attempt of any kind, to explore the interior from Hudson Bay; it foreshadowed the awakening of the Hudson's Bay Company from its comfortable sleep by the shores of the bay, and the far sweep of its trading ventures throughout the length and breadth of the great west. Kellsey was the first white man, if we except the case of Radisson, to explore any portion of the north-west; he was first to visit one of the western tribes; he was first to see and hunt the buffalo. Unconscious though he and those that sent him were of any such object, his journey forms a link, and not an unimportant link, in the chain of exploration toward the Western Sea.

One or two random glimpses are had of Henry Kellsey's later history. Robson mentions that he was deputy governor of York Fort in 1697, when it was taken by the French under D'Iberville; and that he was afterward made governor of the same fort. This, no doubt, was in or after the year 1713, when by the Treaty of Utrecht the forts on Hudson Bay were restored to

THE SEARCH FOR THE WESTERN SEA

Kelsey's journal is certainly one of the most puzzling in the literature of American exploration. The closest study of his narrative leaves one in doubt as to how far he traveled and in what direction, and even his starting-point is by no means certain. There does not, however, appear to be any good reason for denying that the journey described in this narrative was actually made, or, without exaggerating its importance, there is no question but that from several points of view it was a notable achievement. It was the first serious attempt, indeed the first attempt of any kind, to explore the interior from Hudson Bay; it foreshadowed the awakening of the Hudson's Bay Company from its comfortable sloth by the shores of the bay, and the far sweep of its trading ventures throughout the length and breadth of the great west. Kelsey was the first white man, if we except the case of Radisson, to explore any portion of the north-west; he was first to visit one of the western tribes; he was first to see and hunt the buffalo. Unconscious though he and those that sent him were of such object, his journey forms a link, and not an unimportant link, in the chain of exploration toward the Western Sea.

One or two random glimpses are had of Henry Kelsey's later history. Robson mentions that he was deputy governor of York Fort in 1697, when it was taken by the French under D'Iberville; and that he was afterward made governor of the same fort. This, no doubt, was in or after the year 1713, when by the Treaty of Utrecht the forts on Hudson Bay were restored to

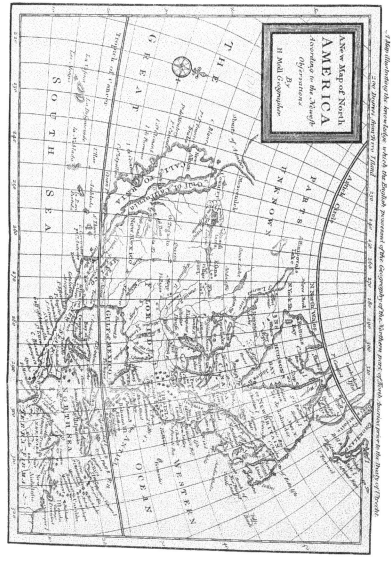

A New Map of North
AMERICA
According to the Newest
Observations
By
H. Moll Geographer

the Company.   Robson also mentions that while governor of York Factory Kellsey prepared a vocabulary of
the Indian language (presumably Cree), and that the
Company ordered it to be suppressed.   It has already
been seen that in 1719 a Captain Henry Kelsey sailed
from York Fort, in command of the *Prosperous*, on a
voyage of exploration up the west coast of the bay.
No doubt this was the same man.   It is unlikely that
two of the same name would have been in the Company's service on the bay at the same time.   There is
nothing in Kellsey's earlier history to show that he
knew anything about navigation or maritime affairs;
but there is nothing to show that he did not.   He may
have gone up in charge of the expedition, with a naval
man in command of the ship.   At all events, this is the
last that is heard of him, beyond the fact that he
returned from his voyage in September of the same
year, having accomplished nothing in the way of further
geographical discovery, so far as is known.

CHAPTER V

OVERLAND TO THE SASKATCHEWAN

AMONG the countless manuscript journals at Hudson Bay House is one that is of exceptional interest, for it represents the first authenticated journey from the shores of Hudson Bay to Lake Winnipeg, the Saskatchewan River, and the great plains of the far west. This journey was made in 1754–5 by a young officer of the Hudson's Bay Company named Anthony Hendry.[1] From marginal notes on the manuscript by Andrew Graham, who had been writer at York Fort at the time of Hendry's expedition, it appears that Hendry was born in the Isle of Wight. Having been outlawed in 1748 for smuggling, he two years later entered the service of the Hudson's Bay Company, the directors not knowing that he was under sentence of outlawry. Graham describes him as bold and enterprising, and adds that he voluntarily offered his services to go inland with the natives and explore the country. He was "the first person who ventured inland." Graham was either ignorant of Henry Kellsey's journey, or

---

[1] The name is spelt Hendey in a copy of the journal in the archives at Ottawa, but the writer learns from Miss Agnes Laut that in the minutes of the Hudson's Bay Company at Hudson Bay House, London, the name is invariably spelt Hendry. That form has consequently been adopted.

perhaps had reason to doubt its authenticity. He adds in another place: "Before this time none of the Servants at the Factories had ventured to winter with the Natives."

Hendry left York Factory with a company of Indians, probably Crees, on June 26th, 1754, and paddled up Hayes River to Amista-Asinee or Great Stone, twenty-four miles from the fort, where he camped for the night. This is present Stoney River, the Penny-cut-a-way of Lindsay Russell's 1882–3 map of the North-West Territories. Dr. Robert Bell calls it the Penneygutway on his 1878 map of Nelson River and the boat route between Lake Winnipeg and Hudson Bay. Continuing up Hayes River, the following morning, Hendry came to Steel River—Apet-Sepee or Fire-Steel River he calls it—which he ascended that day and the next, until he came to Pine Reach, sixty miles from York Factory. He paddled the following day twenty-five miles up Steel River, the banks high with tall woods. He passed what he calls four large falls, but which in reality were not very serious rapids. Sunday, the thirtieth, he made twenty-eight miles, passing seventeen places where the water was so shoal that portages became necessary. The next five days were spent in struggling upstream, the constant portages proving very fatiguing to Hendry's men. Provisions were scarce, and the Indians smoked constantly to allay their hunger. July 6th he reached Attick-Sagohan or Deer Lake. His courses and distances are not always to be relied on, but there can be no doubt that his Deer Lake is the present

Oxford Lake. Mathew Cocking, second factor at York Factory, fortunately paddled over the same route in 1772, and although most of his place-names differ from Hendry's, and neither agree with those found on old or modern maps of the region, he was in every way a more scientific traveller, and his journal affords valuable data with which to check Hendry's narrative.

Where Hendry went after leaving Oxford Lake is at first very puzzling. All the maps, old and new, show but one route to the westward from Oxford Lake, that is by way of the Echimamish, but neither his distances nor directions, nor even the character of the country through which he travelled, admit of such a solution of the difficulty. Fortunately the missing link is supplied by a member of the Canadian Geological Survey Staff, who travelled through this part of the country in 1906. While at Oxford House, on Oxford Lake, he met a Roman Catholic missionary who had come over from the Nelson by a route hitherto unknown, and of which no indication is given on the maps. This is undoubtedly the lost route of Anthony Hendry, followed also by Mathew Cocking eighteen years later. The fact that neither Hendry nor Cocking, so far as can be ascertained, prepared any sketches of the route he followed, may explain why this waterway from Oxford Lake to Cross Lake does not appear on any of Arrowsmith's maps.

Crossing Deer or Oxford Lake, Hendry came to a river. "The natives," he says, "are divided as to the name of the river; however, it cannot with propriety be called Apet-Sepee or Steel River"; meaning thereby, no doubt, that it could not be regarded as part of the same direct waterway in the sense that Steel River is now looked upon as forming part of Hayes River. He paddled twelve miles up this river, and the next day twenty-six miles, the direction west-north-west, islands and rocks all the way. The evening of the second day he came to a large lake which he calls Christianaux. It is fortunate that the Echimamish route has been eliminated, as otherwise one might be tempted to assume that Hendry had now reached Lake Winnipeg, which during the French period bore for a time the name of Christinaux.

Hendry camped on an island in "Christianaux" Lake, and the next day, July 9th, traversed the lake in a south-west and south-west-by-southerly direction, passing twenty-two woody islands, on one of which he stopped for the night. The following day he paddled twenty-five miles west-south-west and came to a river on the west side of the lake, where he put up for the night. All this agrees with the account of the Roman Catholic missionary.

July 11th Hendry turned up the river, meeting on the way twenty canoes of natives on their way to York Fort, by whom he sent a letter to the factor, James Isham. Continuing his course upstream for twenty-eight miles, he camped, and the next day made twenty-five miles, his course both days being south-west. Monday, July 15th, he paddled twenty-four miles south-west-by-south, and met four canoes of Indians under a leader named Monkonsko, who informed him that he was on the confines of the dry inland country called by the natives the Muscuty Tuskee, and that he would soon come to a French trading post. The following day he paddled twenty miles, in the same direction, and came to Othenume Lake.

It is evident that at some point on this part of his journey Hendry must have traversed Cross Lake; probably on the 13th, when he describes the river as "wide with small islands." The remainder of the journey was up Pine River, and his Othenume Lake was the present Moose Lake. Cocking, following Hendry over this portion of his route in 1772, calls Hendry's Christianaux Lake, Pimochickomow. He definitely names Pine River, which is of material assistance in tying Hendry down to that stream; and he has an entirely new name for Moose Lake — Oteatowan Sockoegan. This lake, says Hendry, is a good day's paddle either way, and the woods around it are tall and well-grown timber—all of which applies to Moose Lake. A half-breed named Joseph La France, whose journey from Sault Ste. Marie to York Factory by way of Lake Superior and Lake Winnipeg will be described in a later chapter, reached Moose Lake in March, 1742, and named it Lake Cariboux. Here is quite an interesting collection of names for the same lake.

Hendry paddled twenty miles across Moose Lake, in a south-west-by-south direction, and then came to a river, which he ascended for twenty-six miles. There was good water for the canoe, the river was wide, with

high banks, and no woods to be seen. The next day
he paddled another twenty-six miles. July 20th he
made six miles, when he left this river, and after
dragging his canoes three-quarters of a mile through a
swampy drain, intermixed with willows, came to Nelson
River. This is part of the waterway connecting Moose
Lake with the Saskatchewan. It is part of the
perversity of the man that, after puzzling one with
unknown names of important lakes and rivers, he
should now give this well-known name to an insignificant stream. However, the following day he had the
satisfaction of paddling out on to the broad waters of
the Saskatchewan—the first Englishman to see this
great river of the western plains. Twenty-two miles
upstream from the point where he entered the river he
came to a French fort, built, as will be seen in a later
chapter, by De La Corne the previous year. "On our
arrival," says Hendry, "two Frenchmen came to the
water-side and in a very genteel manner invited me
into their home, which I readily accepted. One of
them asked me if I had any letter from my master, and
where, on what design I was going inland. I answered
I had no letter, and that I was sent to view the country,
and intended to return in the spring. He told me the
Master [presumably De La Corne] and men were gone
down to Montreal with the furs, and that they must
detain me till their return. However, they were very
kind, and at night I went to my tent and told Attickasish or Little Deer, my leader that had the charge
of me [his Indian guide, in other words], who smiled

and said they dared not. I sent them two feet of tobacco, which was very acceptable to them."

This meeting of the young English explorer from Hudson Bay with French traders on the Saskatchewan is of somewhat exceptional interest. It is the only case, of which there is any record, direct or indirect, of French and English coming face to face west of the Great Lakes while the former were still in possession of Canada. They had met and fought, time and again, in the border country between New England and New France, and on the shores of Hudson Bay, but hitherto the French had remained in undisputed possession of the vast fur country of the north-west. It is easy to imagine, therefore, that despite all surface politeness Hendry was anything but welcome to the French traders on the Saskatchewan. Hendry reports the conversation, but leaves in doubt the curious point as to the language in which the conversation was carried on. It was probably in French. Under ordinary circumstances an English trader from Hudson Bay would be as little likely to understand French as a French trader from Canada would be to understand English, but in this particular case it will be remembered that Hendry had begun his adventurous career as a smuggler, and must have picked up at least a smattering of French in his dangerous calling.

The day after his arrival at the fort Hendry was invited to breakfast and dinner with the French traders. They thanked him for the tobacco, and returned the compliment with a gift of moose flesh. Nothing more

OLD BATTLEFORD, NORTH SASKATCHEWAN

[Face p. 120

was apparently said of the idle threat of detaining him at the fort until De La Corne's return from Montreal, for the following morning Hendry continued his journey up the Saskatchewan. It is interesting to note that when Cocking reached the same spot at the end of July, 1772, the French post was still standing, though doubtless in a ruinous condition. "This is a long frequented place," he says in his journal, "where the Canadians rendezvous and trade with the natives." Cocking made the distance from York Fort to Basquia, as he travelled it, four hundred and fifty miles. Hendry estimated it to be five hundred and twenty-eight miles. As they apparently followed substantially the same route, the discrepancy is singular. As a matter of fact, Hendry's distances are uniformly unreliable. Cocking's figures are much nearer the true distance.

Hendry paddled six miles up the Saskatchewan from the French fort. He then left the river and paddled sixteen miles across a lake on the south side, now known as Saskeram Lake. From here he crossed over to Carrot River, which he ascended for fifty-five miles. On July 27th he left the canoes and continued his journey by land, to the immense satisfaction of the Indians. The whole party had lived on fish for a month past, and were heartily tired of the monotonous diet. Now that they were travelling towards the open plains there was every prospect of securing buffalo or deer. Provisions being low, they had to travel rapidly, and for the first day or two the pace told on them, after their long period of water travel. It was not until the 30th that fortune favoured them. On that day the Indians brought two moose into camp. They were now well out on the plains; game was plentiful; and they could cut their day's march down to a more moderate figure.

July 31st Hendry met a small party of Asinepoet Indians or Assiniboines. He smoked with them and urged them to bring their furs down to York Factory the following summer, but they replied: "We are conveniently supplied from the Paqua-Mistagushewuck Whiskeheginish," that is, the Frenchmen's trading house. Everywhere Hendry got the same answer. The Indians were accustomed to the French; they got on admirably together; the French supplied them with all they needed; why, then, should they attempt the long and dangerous journey to Hudson Bay to secure what the French brought to their very doors? It took some little time to convince the officers of the Company that it was not sufficient to send their men inland to invite the natives down to the forts on the bay. They must bring their goods inland if they would secure the furs of the far west. From a trading point of view, therefore, Hendry's journey was not destined to be of much value, though from the standpoint of exploration it was a notable achievement. Hendry had already won for the Hudson's Bay Company the honour of reaching the Saskatchewan overland from Hudson Bay thirteen years before the arrival of the first English traders from Montreal. As he leaves the Saskatchewan he is about to explore a country never before traversed by white men. By the time he has completed his outward journey he will have won the distinction of exploring for the first time the broad country between the North and the South Saskatchewan, nearly as far west as long. 114°. Whether he is entitled to be called the discoverer of the South Saskatchewan is a debatable point. As will be seen in a later chapter, the French explorer De Niverville, or his men, ascended one of the branches of the Saskatchewan in 1751, three years before Hendry, and the evidence seems to point to the South Saskatchewan. It is, however, by no means certain that De Niverville got as far west as Hendry, and in any event Hendry's is the first circumstantial account of the South Saskatchewan and its tributary the Red Deer, as well as of the great plain enclosed by the two branches.

After leaving Carrot River Hendry's course was generally south-west, over the Pasquia Hills. Not far from the Carrot he found the families of his Indian guides in a starving condition. August 9th he passed two small salt lakes or ponds, lumps of salt lying everywhere around the edges of the water. A few days later he found himself in a network of similar saline ponds. "We are now," he says on the 13th, "entered the Muskuty plains, and shall soon see plenty of buffalo, and the Archithinue Indians hunting them on horseback." Up to this time nothing had been heard at Hudson Bay of these mounted huntsmen and warriors of the far western plains, and so incredulous were the officers of the Company that when Hendry, upon his return to York Factory, told them of his adventures among the Blackfeet, he was treated as a malignant type of Baron Munchausen. Hendry never speaks of these famous horsemen except as the Archithinue Indians, and there might be some doubt as to their identity but that Cocking supplies the missing link. Under date of December 1st, 1772, he says in his journal: "Our Archithinue friends came to us and pitched a small distance from us. . . . One of the leaders talks the Asinepoet language well, so that we shall understand each other, as my leader understands it also. This tribe is named Powes- tic-Athinuewuck [i.e.] Water-fall Indians. There are four tribes or nations more, which are all Equestrian Indians, viz: Mithco-Athinuwuck or Bloody Indians, Koskitow-Wathesitock or Blackfooted Indians, Pegonow or Muddy-water Indians, and Sassewuck or Woody Country Indians." The Archithinue were therefore members of the great Blackfoot Confederacy of the far west.

August 15th Hendry saw several herds of buffalo grazing on the plains, the first encountered on his journey. These, however, were but small, isolated bands, the main bodies having moved towards the North Saskatchewan. From signs that his guides had no difficulty in reading, it was evident that the Blackfeet whom he was seeking had followed the buffalo to the north-west, and Hendry promptly changed his course to the same direction. A month later he was in the midst of countless herds of buffalo; so numerous that, as he puts it, "we had to make them sheer out of our way."

August 20th he came to the banks of Wapesewcopet

River, a large stream with high banks covered with birch, poplar, elder, and fir. The Indians made temporary canoes of willows covered with moose-skins, and in these frail craft the entire party was safely ferried across to the other side. The Wapesew-copet was undoubtedly the South Saskatchewan, and from Hendry's distances and directions since leaving the lower waters of the Carrot, as well as in the light of his subsequent movements, it is tolerably clear that he crossed the South Saskatchewan somewhere about Clarke's Crossing, not far from the old telegraph line.

Three days after crossing the South Branch he sent his guide Attickasish with two other natives to look for the Blackfeet. The same evening he reached Seconby River, about two furlongs wide, full of sandy islands, the current rapid and flowing in an easterly direction, water deep, high banks clothed with birch and hazel. This was unquestionably the North Saskatchewan, which Hendry reached somewhere between the mouth of Eagle Hill Creek and the Elbow. The North Sas-katchewan at this place is exactly as Hendry describes it. Following the Indian trail, he travelled two miles up-stream in a westerly direction, then fourteen miles west-by-north, still on the trail ; saw a couple of buffalo feed-ing on the other side of the river, and met an aged man and a horse loaded with moose flesh, which he distributed among the party—whether voluntarily or not Hendry does not say. The next day he left the river and struck out to the westward. September 4th Attickasish re-joined the party with two of the long-sought Archithinue

Indians on horseback. The main body was still some distance off, following the buffalo. The next day Hendry came up with a small party of Mekesue or Eagle Indians, a branch of the Assiniboine tribe. They differed from other tribes of the plains in dispensing with clothing of every description. Their leader promised Hendry to collect furs and go down to York Fort with him in the spring, a promise which he faithfully kept. This was one of the few instances in which the explorer succeeded in inducing the western Indians to undertake the long journey to the bay.

On the 13th Hendry saw many herds of buffalo on the plains "grazing like English cattle." His Indians killed seven. The flesh was "sweet but coarse." For a man who had lived a month on fish, and had since been more than once next door to starvation, this was almost hypercritical. Hendry was being spoiled by a surfeit of good things, for this prairie country between the two branches was a huntsman's paradise, abounding in buffalo, moose, deer, hares, pheasants, geese, and several varieties of wild duck. "I went," says Hendry, "with the young men a buffalo hunting, all armed with bows and arrows; killed several; fine sport. We beat them about, lodging twenty arrows in one beast. So expert are the natives that they will take the arrows out of them when they are foaming and raging with pain, and tearing the ground up with their feet and horns until they fall down."

September 16th he came to a small river or creek which he calls Chacutenah. Buffalo were numerous.

The Indians killed a great many, taking only their tongues and some other choice pieces, leaving the remainder to the wolves. The next day two of the natives were horribly mangled by a grizzly bear. Hendry was still in what he calls the Muscuty plains. "I cannot describe," he exclaims, "the fineness of the weather, and the pleasant country I am now in." On the 1st of October a party of Blackfeet met him, all mounted on horseback, armed with bows and arrows, bone spears and darts. He made presents to the leader and smoked a ceremonial pipe. Through an interpreter he learned that the main body of the Blackfeet were still some distance away. The leader promised to inform the Great Chief of the coming of the white men, and so left them.

Since leaving the North Saskatchewan Hendry's course had been about south-west, and he had travelled, on October 11th, as he reckoned it, about two hundred and seventy miles. On that day he came to a river which he calls the Waskesew, which he crossed "on a fall about two feet high and much the same depth, and twenty poles wide." On both banks he found round stones of different sizes and of an iron colour, and a little distance from the river were veins of iron ore running along the surface of the ground. No woods were to be seen. In a foot-note, apparently added to the manuscript by Andrew Graham, it is said that "Keskatchew and Waskesew River is all one river, and is called by the French Christianaux River, from the Lake of that name." This identifies the Waskesew as the Saskat-

chewan, or one of its tributaries.   Upon the evidence of
Hendry's courses and distances, with his description
of the river and the surrounding country, it is reasonably safe to say that the river crossed on October 11th
was the Red Deer, and the point where he crossed
it was probably between the mouths of Knee Hills
Creek and Three Hills Creek, or a little north of
51° 30'. It may be noted in passing that Waskesew
was one of the Indian names for the red deer, though
this is of no practical service in identifying the particular stream, North-Western America abounding in
rivers and lakes bearing that familiar name in one or
other of its native forms.

Three days after crossing the river Hendry came up
with the Blackfeet.   Four men came out to meet him
on horseback.   They said they were sent out from the
main body to see whether they were friends or foes.
"We are friends," promptly replied Hendry.   Four
leading Indians of Hendry's party marched on in front,
and he with the remainder followed some distance behind.   So they came to the temporary village of the
Blackfeet.   Two hundred teepees were pitched in two
parallel rows.   Down the thoroughfare marched the
English explorer, watched from each tent door by
many curious eyes, looking for the first time upon a
white man.   He was conducted to the lodge of the
Great Chief at the farther end of the village.   It was large
enough to contain fifty persons.   The chief received
him seated on a sacred white buffalo skin, attended by
twenty elders.   He made signs for Hendry to sit down

on his right hand. The calumet was produced and passed around in ceremonial silence. Boiled buffalo was then brought to the guests in willow baskets. Through Attickasish, his interpreter, Hendry told the Great Chief of the Blackfeet that he had been sent to his country by the Great Leader of the white men, who lived by the side of the great eastern waters, to invite his young men down to see him and to bring with them beaver and wolf skins, for which they would get in return guns, powder and shot, cloth, beads, and other commodities. The Great Chief listened patiently, but made little answer. The white man's fort was far off, and his young men knew nothing of canoes. Then he diplomatically turned the conversation into other channels until it was time for his guests to depart.

The following day Hendry had another interview with the chief, urging the advantages of going down to the bay. "Let some of your young men come down to the fort with me," he said, "and I can promise that they will be received with every kindness. They will get guns and everything else they desire." The shrewd old warrior was not greatly impressed. It was far off, he repeated. His young men could not live without buffalo flesh. They were accustomed to travel on horseback, not in canoes. They knew not the use of a paddle, and could not live on fish. Why should they go, in any event? They never wanted food on these boundless plains. They followed the buffalo from place to place, taking what they needed from day to day. Their bows and arrows were all they required. He

K

had been told that those who frequented the settlements of the white men oftentimes starved on their journey. "Such remarks," Hendry candidly admits, "I thought exceeding true." After an exchange of gifts, the explorer left the lodge and took a view of the camp.

The horses of the Blackfeet were turned out to grass, tied by long thongs of buffalo hide to stakes driven into the ground. They had hair halters, buffalo-skin pads, and stirrups of the same material. They were fine tractable animals, about fourteen hands high, lively and clean made. The Blackfeet were then, as now, excellent horsemen and expert buffalo-hunters. Strict discipline was maintained in the camp. Parties of horsemen were sent out evening and morning to reconnoitre; and others were regularly detached to secure provisions for the camp. This Blackfoot camp was twenty-three miles south-west-by-west from where Hendry crossed the Red Deer. Having spent three days with the Blackfeet, he took his departure and pursued his journey toward the south-west. Sixty miles from where he had crossed the Red Deer he came to another stream, which he again calls the Waskesew. If his previous positions have been correctly interpreted, this was undoubtedly Knee Hills Creek.

After fording this stream Hendry kept to the same course for six miles, and then swung gradually around through west, west-by-north, and north-west, to due north. This brought him up almost parallel with the

Calgary and Edmonton trail. Three days after crossing Knee Hills Creek he left the Muscuty plains, through which he had travelled since August 13th, when it will be remembered he was south of Carrot River. He was now entering a comparatively wooded country watered by many small creeks, in which beaver were plentiful. November 1st marked the approach of cold weather, and by the middle of the month the squaws were busily engaged in dressing skins for winter clothing. Hendry was struck with the improvidence of the Indians. Their days were spent in dancing, conjuring, drumming, and feasting, although many of them had not yet half enough skins for clothing. "What surprises me most," he says, "they never go out of their tents but when they want provisions, altho' the beaver and otters are swarming about us in the creeks and swamps." November 21st Hendry reached his farthest point to the westward. According to a note by Andrew Graham, he was on this day in lat. 59°, eight hundred and ten miles from York Fort. Lat. 59° crosses Peace River and Lake Athabaska, and by no process of reasoning can it be supposed that Hendry got anything like as far north as this. Even though his courses were entirely wrong, his descriptions of the country through which he travelled make it impossible to suppose that he was at any time north of the North Saskatchewan. Graham's latitude is quite out of the question. His estimated distance from York Factory is almost equally unreliable. Checking Hendry's distances and directions with the safe test of the character of country through which he travelled, it is pretty safe to say that on November 21st he was in about lat. 51° 50', long. 113° 50'. Since leaving York Fort he had travelled, by his own reckoning, in the neighbourhood of twelve hundred and fifty miles, and if his position on November 21st was as above indicated, he would be at his turning-point nine hundred and forty-five miles from York as the crow flies.

Hendry had now gone as far as he intended to the westward, but still had five months to put in before it would be possible, or at any rate desirable, to turn his steps homeward. He wintered in the Blackfoot country west of Red Deer River, sometimes travelling short distances, oftener camping for days where game or beaver were plentiful. There was no monotony in this life. Every day brought something of interest, and there was not lacking the occasional touch of danger that lends spiciness to life in the wilderness. The weather was so mild that up to the 1st of December Hendry was still wearing his summer clothing. That day he notes in his journal, "No frost here more than in the middle of summer," but the very next day he had a different tale to tell. A strong gale with snow and sleet, followed by a heavy frost, made him glad to put on the winter rigging that the squaws had been preparing for him. The biting frost stirred the Indians out of their laziness, and they busily bestirred themselves to secure the skins necessary to complete their winter clothing. One man while hunting beaver wounded a grizzly bear. The animal turned on him ferociously, and he narrowly escaped by flinging his beaver coat

FALL ON SPRAY RIVER, WHITE MAN'S PASS

Face p. 132

from him, which the bear tore to pieces. This, says Hendry, the natives always do when forced to retreat. Herds of moose and red deer passed and repassed within two hundred yards of the tent, but the ammunition was getting low, and as long as they were in the beaver country, where the day's provisions could be trapped without difficulty, Hendry did not think it wise to waste precious powder and shot on larger game.

December 23rd he crossed "a branch of Waskesew river," otherwise Three Hills Creek. On a rising ground on the east side of the creek he "had an extensive view of the Muscuty country, which will be the last this trip inland." He was looking over the level plains lying between Three Hills Creek and Devils Pine Creek, before turning north-east into the wooded country. Hendry was now busily engaged trapping wolves, and reproached his Indians because they sat idly in their tents. "The Archithinue," they replied, "would kill us if we trapped in their country." "Where, then," asked Hendry, "will you get the skins to carry down in the spring?" They made no answer, but laughed among themselves at the unsophisticated white man. When Hendry pressed them, they told him impatiently that they could get more skins than they could carry from the Blackfeet in the spring. Why, then, should they labour when both prudence and common sense pointed to a better and easier way?

February 27th Hendry came to Archithinue Lake, about one mile broad and a good day's journey in length, with tall woods on both sides, mostly pines, the largest he had yet seen. Since crossing Three Hills Creek his course had been a zigzag one, first north-east to Devils Pine Creek, then back again to Three Hills Creek, thence to the north-west of that stream, and finally north-east to Archithinue Lake, which may be identified with reasonable certainty as present Devils Pine Lake, lat. 52° 5′, long. nearly 113° 30′. This was a pleasant and plentiful country. Buffalo, which had not been seen for some time past, were again abundant. A number of unknown Indians joined the party, bringing with them several women and children captured from the Blackfeet. They offered Hendry the embarrassing present of a boy and a girl, which he declined as modestly as he could.

March 3rd he came to another river, north-east of Archithinue Lake, evidently the Red Deer, to which he had now returned after a roundabout course to the west and north. He struck the river in about lat. 52° 15′, above Tail Creek, and travelled down with sleds on the ice for a few miles. The rest of the month was spent in hunting, and building canoes for the return journey. Game was plentiful, and that and the approach of spring put every one in good humour. April 12th a party of Assiniboines pitched their tents below Hendry's camp, and in the evening came over to smoke with him. They promised not to trade with the French at Pasquia, and to go down with him to York—much to his satisfaction.

April 23rd he displayed his flag in honour of St. George, and his Indians did the same after he had explained to them the significance of the ceremony. That evening the ice in the river broke up. The canoes were now ready for the long journey back to the bay, and on the 28th he embarked on the Red Deer and paddléd. rapidly down to the Saskatchewan. At this time of the year the river was deep and free, though Hendry was informed by the Indians that in summer it was almost dry and full of small rapids.

May 23rd he reached a French trading post in charge of six men. This was the fort built some years before a few miles below the Grand Forks of the Saskatchewan. Hendry was invited to supper by the officer in charge of the post, who told him that this establishment was subordinate to Basquea or Pasquia. " It is surprising," says Hendry, " to observe what an influence the French have over the natives. I am certain he hath got above 1000 of the richest skins." Six days later he reached the lower fort, which he had visited on his outward journey. De La Corne had returned in the interval, and received the English explorer in person. He invited him to sup with him, and was very kind. He was dressed " very genteel," no doubt in the uniform of a French officer of the period. De La Corne was captain in one of the colonial regiments. In contrast to the finery of their leader, the men wore " nothing but thin drawers and striped cotton shirts ruffled at the hands and breast," a rather inadequate costume at that time of the year. Hendry describes the fort as twenty-six feet long by twelve wide, and nine feet high to the ridge. It had a sloping roof, and the walls were built of logs, the top covered with birch bark fastened together with willow thongs. It was divided into three rooms: one for trading, one for furs, and the third the living-room.

The following morning De La Corne took Hendry into his storeroom and showed him his stock of furs—"A brave parcel of Cased Cats, Martens, and parchment Beaver." The birch-bark canoes of the French "will carry as much as an India Ships longboat, and draws little water; and so light that two men can carry one several miles with ease. They are made in the same form and slight materials as the small ones, only a thin board runs along their bottom; and they can sail them before the wind, but not else." "The French," he adds, "speak several [Indian] languages to perfection; they have the advantage of us in every shape; and if they had Brazile tobacco, which they have not, would entirely cut off our trade. They have white tobacco made up in Roles of 12 lb. wt. each. The Master desired me to bring or send him a piece of Brazile tobacco, and a quart or pint japanned drinking mug." De La Corne told Hendry that he would shortly set out with his furs for one of the chief settlements, as soon as he received the returns from the upper post, which would be in a few days.

June 3rd Hendry took leave of his kindly hosts and paddled down the Saskatchewan, followed the same route as on his outward journey to Moose Lake and Cross Lake, and reached York Fort on June 20th, 1755, after an absence of nearly twelve months.

CHAPTER VI

SAMUEL HEARNE DISCOVERS THE COPPERMINE

OF the early life of Samuel Hearne, as of the early life of so many of the world's great explorers, next to nothing is known. He himself tells us that, when he first entered the employment of the Hudson's Bay Company, it was as mate of one of their sloops employed in trading with the Eskimo. In this way he probably acquired much information that was afterwards turned to good account in his overland journey to the mouth of the Coppermine River. He was still a young man when he set forth on the expedition which was to make his name famous. One glimpse of his whereabouts at this time is afforded by the inscription found carved on the granite face of Sloop Cove, near Port Churchill—" Sl Hearne July ye 1, 1767."

The Northern or Athapascan Indians who visited Fort Prince of Wales, at the mouth of the Churchill, had from time to time brought reports of a great river that lay far to the north-west, near the south of which rich copper deposits were to be found. Moses Norton, the half-breed governor of the fort, represented to the Company the advantages that would follow the discovery of this river, and upon his representations the

Company decided to equip and send an expedition under the command of Samuel Hearne.

Evidence, though not of a convincing character, points to an earlier visit to the Coppermine than that about to be described; or perhaps it would be more exact to say, an attempt to reach the Coppermine. Joseph Robson quotes a letter from the Hudson's Bay Company to Richard Stanton, at Prince of Wales Fort, 4th of June, 1719. "You having one Richard Norton[1] our apprentice under your command, whom we are informed by Captain Knight has endured great hardship in travelling with the Indians, and has been very active and diligent in endeavouring to make peace among them, we being always desirous to encourage diligent and faithful servants, upon application of his mother in his behalf, have ordered him a gratuity of fifteen pounds."

Captain Caruthers, in his evidence before the Parliamentary Committee, testified that Knight, who was at the time governor of Nelson Factory, "was very inquisitive with them [the Indians] about a copper-mine north of Churchill. . . . That Knight was very earnest about this discovery, which was always his topic . . . and that he [Caruthers] carried Norton, who was afterwards governor, and two northern Indians to Churchill, where he put them in a canoe; and the purport of their voyage was to make discoveries, and encourage the Indians to come down to trade, and to bring copper-ore."

[1] The Richard Norton referred to is said to have been Moses Norton's father.

DOG TRAINS AT JASPER HOUSE

Face p. 138

Hearne was instructed to make his way overland to the mouth of the Coppermine River, or as it was called by the Indians, the Neetha-san-san-dazey—Far-Off-Metal River; to ascertain its course, and the latitude and longitude of its mouth; to examine the much-talked-of copper-mines; and to endeavour to discover, either by his own explorations or from Indian reports, whether a passage existed through the continent. " It will be very useful," adds Governor Norton, " to clear up this point, if possible, in order to prevent further doubts from arising hereafter respecting a passage out of Hudson's Bay into the Western Ocean, as hath lately been represented by the American Traveller." And as if all this were not enough, Hearne is instructed in the event of his failing to reach the Coppermine to return to the northern coast of the bay and endeavour to trace the course of Wager Strait to the westward ; and if no passage should be discovered here, to make a similar examination of Chesterfield Inlet; and in either case to report whether it would be advantageous for the Company to establish trading posts in these far northern latitudes. " There is," dryly remarks Hearne, "certainly no harm in making out all instructions in the fullest manner, yet it must be allowed that those two parts might have been omitted with great propriety."

Commenting after his journey upon his instructions to search for a passage, Hearne says : " The Continent of America is much wider than many people imagine, particularly Robson, who thought that the Pacific Ocean was but a few days' journey from the west coast of Hudson's Bay. This, however, is so far from being the case, that when I was at my greatest western distance, upward of five hundred miles from Prince of Wales Fort, the natives, my guides, well knew that many tribes of Indians lay to the west of us, and they knew no end to the land in that direction ;- nor have I met with any Indians, either Northern or Southern, that ever had seen the sea to the westward." Hearne mentions having met several Indians who had been so far west as to cross the top of the immense chain of mountains which runs from north to south of the continent, and he adds, " Beyond those mountains all rivers run to the westward." He shows, in fact, a much more exact knowledge of the breadth and character of the continent than was possessed by even the most eminent geographers of his day ; and ridicules the very possibility of a passage existing anywhere through the continent of North America.

The vagueness of geographical knowledge in Hearne's day, as regards North-Western America, is illustrated in the following extract from a memorial of the Hudson's Bay Company, describing the territory alleged to have been covered by their grant from the British Crown: " And towards the west all the land that lye on the west side or coast of the said Bay and extending from the Bay westward to the utmost limits of those lands, but where or how those lands terminate to the westward is unknown, though probably it will be found they terminate on the Great South Sea."

But to return to Hearne's journey, or rather journeys,

A SOUTH-WEST VIEW OF PRINCE OF WALES'S FORT, HUDSON'S BAY

Face p. 140

for three times he started out from Prince of Wales
Fort in search of the Coppermine. Nothing could have
been more inspiriting than the circumstances under
which he began his first expedition. He had under
his command what the governor, at least, conceived to
be an exceptionally efficient party, consisting of two
Englishmen, volunteers; two of the Home-guard
Southern Indians (Crees), in whom Norton had special
confidence, perhaps because they were of his own particular tribe; and a picked body of Northern Indians
(Chipewyans), under their leader Chawchinahaw; he had
been equipped with instruments, maps, and ammunition
and supplies sufficient for two years. As he marched
out of the gates of the fort on the 6th of November,
1769, under the salute of seven cannon, Hearne must
surely have felt confident of success. Yet within a
little more than a month he had the mortification to
find himself again within sight of the walls of Prince
of Wales Fort. He had hardly begun his journey
before the Indians, particularly Chawchinahaw, began
to give him trouble. Unfortunately Hearne, though
gifted with wonderful pluck and perseverance, lacked
that power of command so necessary in dealing with
Indians. Chawchinahaw, with the keen perception of
his race, was not long in discovering signs of weakness,
and set himself deliberately to thwart the expedition in
every possible way. Finding after a time that Hearne
was not to be turned from his purpose by petty annoy-
ances, he and his men coolly deserted and set off in
another direction, making the woods ring with their

derisive laughter. Hearne was left to find his way back to the fort, nearly two hundred miles, as best he could.

On the 23rd of February, 1770, Hearne started out again. This time he took with him a smaller party, three Northern Indians and two of the Home-guard—Indians settled around the fort. He left the two Englishmen behind, convinced that they were more of a hindrance than a help. The snow at this time was so deep on the top of the ramparts that few of the cannon were to be seen. A salute was consequently dispensed with, but the governor, officers, and people lined the walls and gave the plucky explorer three cheers as he started forth on his second attempt to discover the Coppermine.

His course was again to the westward, up Seal River to Lake Shee-than-nee or Sheth-nanei (the high hill), where he wintered. In the spring he turned north, by way of Lakes Nejanilini and Baralzone and the headwaters of the Tha-anne and Maguse rivers, and on June 30th reached the Kazan River at a place which he calls Cathawachaga, about a day's journey south of Yath-Kyed Lake. Here he says he made several observations for the latitude, and found it to be 63° 4' N. As the Kazan empties into Yath-Kyed Lake about lat. 62° 38', and the crossing-place which he calls Cathawachaga must have been a couple of minutes farther south, the mean of his observations was nearly half a degree too far north. In his third and final journey he was to make a much more serious error in fixing the position of the mouth of the Coppermine, but there he at least had the excuse of a cumbersome and unreliable quadrant, which was not the case at Cathawachaga. As a matter of fact, his astronomical observations throughout are so inaccurate that it is extremely difficult to trace his course either north or west with any degree of accuracy.

Again Hearne experienced the annoyance of being at the mercy of his Indian guides. The best part of the summer was wasted in wandering hither and thither in search of caribou and musk ox, working gradually to the north and west, until about the end of July they had reached the northern end of Dubawnt Lake. The Indians now said plainly that the year was too far advanced to admit of their reaching the Coppermine that summer, and advised Hearne to winter with them and push on to the Coppermine the following spring. As he had no choice, Hearne submitted to the inevitable as gracefully as he could.

On the 11th of August his cup of bitterness was filled by the breaking of his quadrant; left standing while he ate his dinner, and blown over by a sudden gust of wind. There was nothing for it now but to return once more to the fort. He travelled down the west side of Dubawnt Lake, crossed the Dubawnt River a few miles above where it flows into the lake, then crossed the Kazan somewhere above Lake Angukuni, and on November 25th was again at Fort Prince of Wales, after an absence of eight months and twenty-two days; "a fruitless or at least unsuccessful journey," as he bitterly remarks.

On the way down to the fort he was joined by a famous North Indian named Matonabbee, who treated him with extraordinary kindness, clothed and fed the half-frozen and more than half-starved explorer, and gave him much excellent advice out of his abundant experience as to how an expedition across the barren grounds must be conducted to be successful. He asked Hearne if he would make another attempt to reach the Coppermine, and upon Hearne's emphatic statement that he was determined to complete the discovery even at the risk of his life, Matonabbee volunteered to accompany him as guide, an offer which the explorer accepted with unfeigned delight.

On their way to the fort they matured their plans for the third expedition. Matonabbee thoroughly disapproved of Governor Morton's idea of sending out an exploring party without women. That, in his opinion, was the most fatal of errors. Women were indispensable. They were obviously made for labour; they could carry, or haul, as much as two men; they could pitch the tents; make and mend clothing; in fact, said he, there was no such thing as travelling any considerable distance or for any length of time in this country without their assistance. Moreover, he shrewdly added, "though they do everything, they are maintained at a trifling expense; for as they always stand cook, the very licking of their fingers in scarce times is sufficient for their subsistence." This last picture of native economy rather shocked Hearne, but he comforted his conscience with the thought that probably the women helped themselves

131

Face p. 144

INDIANS OF NORTHERN BRITISH COLUMBIA

when the men were not present. In any event, it was decided that when they set forth on the third attempt to reach the Coppermine the party should consist of Matonabbee with some of his immediate followers and their wives.

Armed with renewed instructions from the governor, Hearne once more left Fort Prince of Wales on the 7th of December, 1770. They travelled with dogs and sledges, and, on the advice of Matonabbee, the course was more to the south than on the previous expedition, so as to avoid the barren lands as much as possible. On the last day of the year they reached Island Lake (Nueltin Lake on the present maps), where the wives and families of some of the party had been awaiting their return from the fort. This lake was in fact a general tarrying-place for the families of the Northern Indians; bearing the same relation to Fort Prince of Wales as Split Lake did to York Factory. While the men went down to Prince of Wales Fort to trade their furs for powder and shot and gewgaws, the wives and children camped on the islands of Nueltin Lake, which was celebrated in Hearne's day for the abundance of fish that were to be caught in its waters.

The united party set forward with an ample supply of pemmican and other provisions. Their course was west-by-north, and on the 6th of February they crossed the main branch of Cathawhachaga River (now the Kazan), and after walking three miles came to the side of Crossed Whole or Partridge Lake (Kasba), which they crossed on the ice. Leaving Partridge Lake, the course was west-by-south. Deer was so plentiful that though they moved slowly, camping three, four, and five days at a place, they were unable to use more than a fraction of the spoils of their hunting. Their wastefulness worried Hearne, who could never get used to the improvidence of the Indians. With them life was always either a feast or a famine. They gave no thought to the morrow; but Hearne was compelled to admire the fortitude, even cheerfulness, with which they would bear actual starvation. On the 21st of February they crossed Snowbird Lake, and on the 2nd of March camped by the side of Wholdiah, or Wholdaia, Lake.

Matonabbee now explained fully his plan of campaign. He proposed that they should proceed leisurely to the westward, living upon the country as they went. It was useless to attempt to turn north yet, as at this season of the year they would all starve on the barren grounds. As the spring advanced, however, and the caribou returned to their summer haunts in the far north, the party could follow them and have the assurance of an ample supply of meat, or, at any rate, carry a sufficient stock of provisions to take them through. Their immediate destination was a small lake named Clowey, in the heart of a great unexplored district. Even to-day it is known only by Hearne's course through it.

They reached Clowey Lake in May, 1771, and were joined here by upwards of two hundred natives. Hearne was puzzled to account for this great addition to his party, but it gradually leaked out that these Indians (probably Chipewyans) proposed to join the expedition as a convenient way of reaching their hereditary enemies the Eskimo. Hearne made an attempt to turn them from their purpose, but finding that they simply interpreted his remonstrances as a sign of cowardice, he, perhaps rather weakly, yielded to the force of circumstances, hoping that something would turn up to prevent the intended massacre. It may be urged in Hearne's defence that his instructions from Governor Norton particularly enjoined him to do nothing to antagonize the Indians, one of the primary objects of his journey being to induce the tribes of the far north-west to come down with their furs to the bay.

The whole party rested at Clowey Lake for about a month, completing their preparations for the dash over the barren lands to the Coppermine. Leaving Clowey, their course was almost due north. On the 30th of May they reached Peshew Lake. Here most of the women were left behind to follow at a more leisurely pace, and await the return of the expedition from the Coppermine at a well-known rendezvous. With the women were left all the heavier parts of their equipment, and the men, accompanied only by a few of the younger and more energetic squaws, pushed forward with renewed energy. On their way north they passed Catt Lake (probably Artillery Lake, north-west of Great Slave Lake), and then Thoy-noy-kyed, which may perhaps be identified with Clinton-Colden. On the 20th June they reached Cogead Lake (Contwoyto, or Rum Lake of the present maps). Daylight was now continuous, which Hearne accepted as proof that they were now well within the Arctic circle.

The following day they reached a branch of the Conge-ca-tha-wha-chaga River (which still bears the same name abbreviated). A number of Copper Indians were hunting caribou on the opposite bank. Hearne had brought one or two small canoes to be used in ferrying the party over such lakes and rivers as might lie in their course; but as it would have been a long and tedious task to get their large party across the Conge-ca-tha-wha-chaga—there were still one hundred and fifty—they induced the Copper Indians to bring over a number of their own canoes to their assistance. Arrived on the other side, they were hospitably entertained by the Copper Indians, who took the keenest interest in Hearne—the first white man they ever had seen. Here the remainder of the women were left behind, and the men set out on the last stage of their journey to the Copper-mine, guided by some of the Copper Indians.

Their way lay for fourteen miles over a trail which crossed what the Indians called the Stoney Mountains. The trail was often so steep that they were compelled to crawl on hands and knees. This was one of the main Indian thoroughfares to the copper-mines, and the road had been so well travelled that, in Hearne's words, it was " as plain and well-beaten as any bye foot-path in England." By the side of the trail were several large flat stones covered with thousands of small pebbles, which the Copper Indians informed him had been deposited there, as a kind of tribute to the gods, by those who were travelling to and from the mines. Bowing to the force of custom, Hearne and his Chipewyans added each a pebble to the pile.

The weather now became very unpleasant, culminating on the 6th of July in a violent snowstorm. A number of the Indians turned back in disgust, and the rest had to seek such shelter as might be found in the crevices of the rocks. As soon as the storm had abated they pushed on once more. On the 8th they reached Grizzly Bear Hill, so named by the Copper Indians because of the numbers of grizzly bears that resorted thither. On the 12th they crossed a branch of the Coppermine, and the following day arrived at the main stream, about forty miles from its mouth.

The first sight of the Coppermine proved rather disappointing to Hearne. The Indians had represented it to be a mighty river, navigable for large vessels for many miles from the mouth. Instead, it was found to be at this point scarcely navigable for canoes, being no more than one hundred and eighty yards wide, everywhere full of shoals, and with no less than three rapids in sight.

Meanwhile the Chipewyans had sent spies down the river to look out for the Eskimo. These scouts presently returned, reporting an Eskimo encampment on the west side of the river, about twelve miles down. Preparations were immediately made for a surprise. The war party crossed the river, stripped, put on war paint, armed themselves with spears and shields—all this to fall upon a party of inoffensive Eskimo not half their own number. With characteristic Indian strategy it was decided to surprise the Eskimo in the early morning, before they had left their tents.

Everything favoured the Indians. They were in the midst of the encampment before the unhappy Eskimo were aware of it. Hearne graphically describes the scene that followed: "The poor unhappy victims were surprised in the midst of their sleep, and had neither time nor power to make any resistance; men, women, and children, in all upwards of twenty, ran out of their tents stark naked, and endeavoured to make their escape; but the Indians having possession of all the land side, to no place could they fly for shelter. One alternative only remained, that of jumping into the river; but, as none of them attempted it, they all fell a victim to Indian barbarity."

To his horror Hearne saw a young girl speared at his very feet, so close that when the first spear was thrust into her side she fell down, writhing round his legs. He pleaded for her life with the Indians, but as they transfixed her body to the ground with their spears, they asked him contemptuously if he wanted an Eskimo wife. Hearne could hardly restrain his tears at the horror of the scene and his own utter inability to prevent it.

One of the most pitiful incidents of the massacre was the finding of a poor old woman, blind and deaf, sitting placidly on the banks of the Coppermine fishing, while her friends and relatives were being butchered within a few yards of where she sat. The Indians fell upon her before she had any conception of who or what they were. In her case, at least, murder was perhaps the best thing that could have happened. A handful of Eskimo, who were fortunately on the opposite bank of the river at the time of massacre, escaped. This wanton massacre had such an effect upon the Eskimo that when David T. Hanbury visited the Coppermine in 1899 it was still talked of. Sir John Franklin visited the scene in 1821 and found ample corroborations of Hearne's story. Among other things he discovered a number of human skulls bearing marks of violence. While on Great Slave Lake he had met an old Indian who said that he had accompanied Hearne on his journey, though very young at the time, and still remembered many of the circumstances, particularly this massacre.

The site of the massacre has ever since been known as Bloody Fall. The fall was only about eight miles above the mouth of the river, and from the high ground where he stood Hearne could distinctly see the sea. He had already made a rough survey of the Coppermine from the point at which he reached it to Bloody Fall. He now continued it down to the mouth of the river, but, as the sequel shows, it must have been a very perfunctory piece of work. A thick fog prevented observations, but because, as he says, of the extraordinary care taken in observing the courses and distances from Conge-ca-tha-wha-chaga, where he had two good observations, he was satisfied that the latitude of the mouth of the river might be depended upon within twenty miles at the utmost. As a matter of fact it proved to be two hundred miles too far north. Hearne made the mouth of the river to be in lat. 71° 54′ N., and long. 120° 30′ W. Franklin found the true position to be 67° 47′ 50″ N., and 115°⁻36′ 49″ W. Hearne, by some extraordinary blunder, recorded a rise and fall of fourteen feet at the mouth of the river. Franklin found only four inches.

Hearne erected a mark and took formal possession of the country on behalf of the Hudson's Bay Company. He then returned up the river to examine the much-talked-of copper-mines. These he found as disappointing as the river itself. They were "nothing but a jumble of rocks and gravel." The Indians had represented the mines to be so rich and valuable that, if a factory were built at the mouth of the river, a ship might be ballasted with the ore instead of stone. By their accounts Hearne expected to find hills entirely composed of the metal, in handy lumps like a heap of pebbles. In reality, after searching with all his party among the rocks for nearly four hours, their united efforts were rewarded with one piece of ore, about four pounds in weight, which Hearne brought back with him to Prince of Wales Fort.

On his homeward course Hearne retraced his steps as far as Cogead Lake, and then turned south-by-west between the upper waters of the Coppermine and the Yellowknife River on one side, and Lac de Gras and Lake Mackay on the other, until he reached on the

24th of December the "north side of the great Athapuscow Lake." This has sometimes been taken to
mean that Hearne reached Lake Athabaska on the
24th of December, but there is no foundation for any
such assumption. His narrative and map show clearly
that the lake reached was Great Slave Lake, not Athabaska. The misunderstanding was doubtless due to the
similarity of the names Athapuscow and Athabaska,
but it is certain that the lake known to the Indians in
Hearne's day and later as Athapuscow was the Great
Slave Lake of the present time. One singular feature
of Hearne's journey to the Coppermine is that he
apparently got no hint from either the Chipewyans or
the Copper Indians of the presence, only a comparatively short distance west of the Coppermine, of that
immense inland sea Great Bear Lake.

Crossing Great Slave Lake, somewhere in the vicinity
of Reindeer Islands, Hearne reached the southern shore
about the mouth of Slave River, which, under the name
of Athapuscow River, is indicated on his own map.
The south shore of the lake he describes as "a fine
level country, in which there was not a hill to be seen,
or a stone to be found," in striking contrast to the
country north of the lake, which is "a jumble of rocks
and hills." His description of the Grand Athapuscow
River is so exact as to leave no doubt as to its identity
with present Slave River. He estimates the length of
Athapuscow Lake, from Indian reports, at one hundred
and twenty leagues, and its width at twenty leagues.
The actual length of Great Slave Lake is about three

hundred miles, and its greatest width fifty-five miles, so that Hearne was not far out in his estimate.

Following the course of the Athapuscow River for forty miles, he turned off to the eastward, on the final stage of his homeward journey, leaving the river "at that part where it begins to trend due south." About the end of February he came to a curious bit of wood-land standing isolated in the heart of the barren grounds—an oasis in the desert. For more than a generation one family or clan had made this their winter home. Hundreds of miles from the wooded country to the east and west, it was quite out of the regular track of the Indians, either on their hunting or trading expeditions, and the family who made it their home held undisputed possession. Through these small woods ran a considerable stream which, according to the Indians, communicated with several lakes. As the current set to the north-east Hearne conjectured that it emptied into Hudson Bay, probably by way of Baker Lake and Chesterfield Inlet. Possibly this may have been the Thelon River, in which case he would be quite right; but so far as one can follow his course from Slave River to the eastward he would seem to be at this time some considerable distance west of Thelon River, or rather of the supposed position of the upper waters of Thelon River, for as a matter of fact this part of the country has never been explored since Hearne crossed it in 1771, and the position of the upper waters of the Thelon as laid down on the maps is purely conjectural. On the whole it is

"THE LAST OF A NOBLE RACE." (In Banff National Park)

more probable that this was one of the rivers emptying into Great Slave Lake, possibly the Rivière du
Rocher.

It is interesting to note from the narrative that in
Hearne's day vast herds of buffalo ranged as far north
as the southern shore of Great Slave Lake. Travelling
east from Slave River, the buffalo were still numerous,
but were left behind about the end of February, as he
got out of the level plains and approached the comparatively hilly country toward the Dubawnt River.
When the camp could no longer be supplied with
buffalo, moose were fortunately encountered in sufficient
numbers to keep the party going.

Not the least interesting feature of Hearne's book is
the graphic pictures it affords of big-game hunting in
the far north in the eighteenth century. But for limita-
tions of space one would be tempted to quote his
admirable descriptions of moose hunts, caribou "parks,"
and the hunting of the musk ox. Hearne had no very
high opinion of the musk ox as an article of diet—
especially in the raw state. On one of his journeys,
fuel being unobtainable, he was compelled to eat his
musk - ox steaks raw. There is abundant evidence
throughout the narrative that Hearne was not squeamish,
but raw musk ox was too much even for his seasoned
stomach. He describes it as coarse, tough, and rank of
musk, worse than raw fish—which was saying a great
deal. Warburton Pike and other later travellers give a
somewhat less repulsive account of the meat; no doubt
Hearne's experience was with an old bull; but it is

improbable that the flesh of the musk ox will ever be considered as a delicacy.

The explorer seems to have been very unfortunate with his instruments. His second journey had to be abandoned because of the loss of the quadrant, and now on his third expedition the old Elton's quadrant, "which had been upwards of thirty years at the fort" —the only instrument he could obtain—followed the example of its predecessor. " I cannot," says Hearne, "sufficiently lament the loss of my quadrant, as the want of it must render the course of my journey from Point Lake very uncertain." He had lost it on the return journey from the Coppermine, before he reached Great Slave Lake. While there his watch stopped, which added greatly to his misfortune, as he was now deprived of every means of estimating distances with any degree of accuracy.

On March 19th he passed Wholdyeah-chuck'd Whoie, or Large Pike Lake, and soon after Bedodid and Hill Island lakes. The two latter find a place on the latest official Canadian maps, though their position is more or less guesswork. They form part of one of the great unexplored areas of the north-west. On April 7th they crossed the Thele-aza River; and on the 28th were once more at Thleweyaza Yeth, where the woodwork for their canoes had been prepared the previous spring. On the 11th of May they camped by the side of a river that was said by the Indians to empty into Dubawnt Lake. Here they threw away their snowshoes, as the ground was getting so bare of snow that they were no longer of any assistance. Wholdiah and Snow Bird lakes were crossed, and on the 30th May the party was again at the Cathawhachaga (Kazan) River, which must not be confused with the Conge-ca-tha-wha-chaga of the Coppermine country. On June 26th they reached Seal River, and the last of the month saw them back in Fort Prince of Wales—after an absence of eighteen months and twenty-three days, or two years, seven months, and twenty-four days since setting forth on the first expedition.

Hearne concludes his narrative with the statement that his journey had "put an end to all disputes concerning a North-West Passage through Hudson's Bay." If he had done nothing else, the achievement would have been notable enough, but this was but one of many results of his journey. Inaccurate· though his observations were, he added materially to the geography of the far north, and it is a fact that Hearne is still the authority, and the only authority, for the topography of much of this unexplored part of Canada. He preserved, too, many valuable data with regard to the northern tribes and the northern fauna at the period of his journey. And, perhaps most important of all from the point of view of this book, his expedition paved the way to further explorations toward the west and north, by showing that a man possessed of sufficient perseverance and endurance could safely penetrate every quarter of the unknown west.

Hearne's narrative had almost as remarkable a history as the man himself. It is said that the famous French

admiral, La Perouse, when he captured Prince of Wales
Fort in 1782, found among the papers a manuscript
account of Hearne's journey. La Perouse, himself no
mean traveller, saw the value of the narrative, and
would only agree to Hearne's urgent request that the
manuscript should be returned, upon the latter's promise that he would print and publish it immediately
on his arrival in England. It is further related that
La Perouse afterward complained of Hearne having
broken his promise, and expressed the hope that the
pledge might still be redeemed. In 1795 the fine quarto
edition of the *Journey from Prince of Wales's Fort, in
Hudson's Bay, to the Northern Ocean* appeared; but as
a matter of fact Hearne had already put the results of
his journey before the public in pamphlet form in 1773,
and again in 1778–80. These were, however, but very
modest forerunners of the ambitious work of 1795. If
one may judge from Hearne's preface to the latter, it
was designed more as a reply to the severe strictures
of that fierce critic Alexander Dalrymple, than as the
fulfilment of any promise made to La Perouse.

This Alexander Dalrymple,[1] whose vitriolic criticism
hurt Hearne so deeply, was the same that so violently
attacked Captain Cook, for no more sufficient reason
than that Cook had been preferred before Dalrymple in
the command of the expedition to the South Seas. In
Hearne's case, Dalrymple's criticism—of his latitude
of the mouth of the Coppermine—was certainly well

---

[1] For some years hydrographer to the East India Company, and afterward hydrographer to the Admiralty.

founded, and, though Hearne was not disposed to admit that he had made such a serious blunder, it was not the charge itself, but rather the venomous tone, that hurt.

The geographical results of Hearne's journeys are not easily defined in precise terms. That they were important, both intrinsically and in their influence upon future explorations, is beyond question ; but it is equally certain that a great deal of their effectiveness was lost through the inaccuracy of Hearne's observations, both for latitude and longitude, and the consequent uncertainty as to the identity of many of his lakes and rivers. This difficulty has been increased—though here at least the fault was not Hearne's—by the fact that a considerable portion of the ground he covered has never since been explored.

The first journey was, from a geographical point of view, of little or no importance, as Hearne did not get beyond what was already familiar ground. On the second expedition, though he failed to accomplish his main object, he discovered at least two important lakes—Dubawnt and Yath-Kyed, besides a number of smaller lakes, with their connecting waterways. How far north he got on this journey is not known. Certainly he was north of Dubawnt Lake, and possibly came within sight of Aberdeen Lake, but this is mere conjecture. Only one explorer has been over the same ground, or any portion of it, since Hearne's day. In 1893 Mr. J. B. Tyrrell, of the Canadian Geological Survey, explored the Dubawnt River down to Aberdeen Lake ; and the following year he explored the Kazan to a point about twenty miles below Yath-Kyed Lake, thence tracing a river, which he named the Ferguson, to its outlet into Hudson Bay.

Hearne's third journey was of course by all odds his greatest achievement. In it he accomplished his primary object—the discovery of the mouth of the Coppermine River. Despite all errors of latitude and longitude, no one since Sir John Richardson has seriously questioned Hearne's claim to this discovery. Sir John Franklin, visiting the river in 1821, clearly recognized both Bloody Fall and the mouth of the river, from Hearne's description. Hearne reached the Coppermine somewhere about the Sandstone, or perhaps the Musk Ox Rapids, and explored the river thence to its mouth. This was his most important discovery. By it he not only added an important river to the maps, but he performed at the same time the double service of proving the non-existence of a channel through the continent in any of the latitudes of Hudson Bay, and the existence of a salt sea to the north into which the Coppermine emptied its waters.

Hardly less important, from other points of view, was Hearne's discovery of Athapuscow or Great Slave Lake, and the Athapuscow or Slave River. There is no difficulty in identifying the Coppermine and Athapuscow, but beyond this all is more or less guesswork. On the outward journey he mentioned Catt Lake, which he crossed on his way north from Clowey. Catt Lake has been identified, with some show of probability, as Artillery Lake. Similarly his Thoy-noy-kyed Lake would seem to be either Aylmer or Clinton-Golden Lake, perhaps both. His Cogead Lake was probably the present Rum or Contwoyto. The Conge-ca-tha-wha-chaga River still appears on the maps under the same name or a slightly abbreviated version thereof, though there is no absolute certainty that the stream that now bears the name was the one discovered by Hearne. It may be assumed that Hearne crossed Lac du Sauvage and Lake Paul on his way to the north-west from Thoy-noy-kyed, but he does not appear to have seen Lake Mackay or Lac de Gras on either the outward or home-ward journey.

Hearne's discoveries to the northward of Great Slave Lake have been supplemented by a number of later explorations, notably those of Sir John Franklin (1820–1–2), Sir John Richardson (1826 and 1848), Sir George Back (1833), Dease and Simpson (1839), Dr. John Rae (1853–4). In 1889 Warburton Pike explored a portion of the Barren Grounds; J. B. Tyrrell and his brother J. W. Tyrrell covered substantially the same field in 1893; Caspar Whitney in 1895; and David T. Hanbury in 1899. J. W. Tyrrell surveyed the canoe route from Clinton-Golden Lake to Chesterfield Inlet in 1900. The extensive tract of country lying between Great Slave Lake on the west and the Dubawnt on the east, and between Lake Athabasca and the Thelon River, has never been explored since Hearne crossed it in 1771–2. Clowey, Bedodid, Hill Island, and the other lakes visited and named by Hearne appear on most modern maps, but their positions and proportions are

M

purely conjectural, and there is very little uniformity in either.

Two years after his return from the Coppermine, Hearne was sent inland again, but upon a quite different errand. The Canadian traders were pushing the old Company hard; they had reached the Churchill while Hearne was returning from his last expedition, and their work had already borne fruit in diminished receipts at the posts on the bay. This was too much for the Hudson's Bay Company—at last effectually awakened from its dream of a peaceful and benevolent monopoly. Unless it was to throw up the sponge, that must be done at once which should have been done long ago —trading posts must be established at all important points in the interior.

Hearne was accordingly proceeding to the Saskatchewan to build a post at some point on the river that would most effectually serve the double purpose of protecting the trade of the old Company and hampering that of the new. He found the very spot he was looking for on Cumberland or Pine Island Lake, on the Lower Saskatchewan. This was the key to the entire system of waterways: westward to the Rockies; north to Athabaska, the Peace River country, and the vast unknown beyond Great Slave Lake; east to the Churchill and the Nelson, on the one hand, and Lake Winnipeg and Red River—the citadel of the North West Company—on the other. Here Cumberland House was built, to become a thorn in the flesh to the Canadian traders, and the turning-point in the career of the

Mʀ. SAMUEL HEARNE,
late Cheif at Prince of Wales's Fort,
Hudson's Bay.

Published as the Act directs by J. Sewell, Cornhill, Augᵗ. 1ˢᵗ 1796

Hudson's Bay Company. Had they continued to re-main inactive on the shores of the bay, there is no doubt that the North West Company would before long have wrested from them the entire fur trade of the great west. The establishment of Cumberland House, and the consequent acceptance of the policy of interior trading posts, gave to the Hudson's Bay Company a new lease of life.[1]

In 1775 Hearne returned to the bay, having been appointed governor of Prince of Wales Fort. He was still in command of the fort in 1782 when La Perouse appeared in the harbour with his fleet, landed with his men, and demanded the surrender of the fort. Although the fort was probably at the time the strongest on the continent outside of Quebec, Hearne surrendered it without even a show of resistance. For this he has been severely censured by historians, though Umfreville, who was present at the time, states that the garrison of the fort was only thirty-nine men, but a fraction of the force needed to garrison it effectively.

A very interesting bit of evidence was secured by Dr. Robert Bell, of the Canadian Geological Survey, some years ago when at Fort Churchill. There lived at the fort an extremely ancient pensioner of the Company,

---

[1] While the building of Cumberland House is properly regarded as the first effective step taken by the Hudson's Bay Company in the develop-ment of trade in the interior, it may be noted that between 1740 and 1760 they had established three inland posts: Henley House, on the Albany River; Split Lake House, on the Nelson; and Fort Nelson, on Footprint River. These, however, were all within easy reach of the bay, and were only nominally inland posts.

a centenarian by his own account, and remarkably well preserved for his years. Getting into conversation with him one day, Dr. Bell asked him if he remembered hearing about the surrender of Prince of Wales Fort. The old fellow had not merely heard of it, but had himself been present. "When the French appeared outside the walls," said he, "there were not sufficient men inside to have manned one gun. The majority were all away in the marches, duck shooting." He described graphically how La Perouse appeared before the gate and demanded the surrender of the fort; how Hearne, hastily doffing the rough working clothes in which he had been doing work not consistent with his dignity as governor of the fort, and tumbling into his uniform, marched out through the gates, his sword drumming against the stones as he went, and presented the keys of the fort to La Perouse on a silver salver—doubtless to the latter's no small delight; and how La Perouse, having stripped the fort of everything of value, tried to pull down the walls, but as these had been built to resist all ordinary weapons, his men could make no impression. Finally, the admiral ordered them to mine the walls, which they did, firing the trains of gunpowder far out toward the beach, and then hastily entering their boats and pulling off to a safe distance. The work was so thoroughly done that Prince of Wales Fort thereupon became a thing of the past. The ruins, still visible, bear mute witness to the thoroughness alike of the British engineer who built the fort, and the French admiral who destroyed it.

Mr. J. W. Tyrrell, in the course of his journey across the Sub-Arctics of Canada in 1893, visited the ruins of Prince of Wales Fort. "As La Perouse left the Fort," says he, "so did we find it. For the most part the walls were still solid, though from between their great blocks of granite the mortar was crumbling. The guns, spiked and dismounted, were still to be seen lying about on the ramparts and among the fallen masonry. In the bastions, all of which were still standing, were to be seen the remains of walls and magazines, and in the centre of the Fort stood the walls of the old building in which Hearne and his men had lived. The charred ends of roof-beams were still attached to its walls, where, undecayed, they had rested for the past one hundred and eleven years."

CHAPTER VII

LAST PHASES OF INLAND EXPLORATION
FROM HUDSON BAY

THE Hudson's Bay Company was profoundly sceptical as to the material advantages to be derived from explorations of any kind, marine or inland. So far as the North-West Passage was concerned, the Company believed that if it were not the wildest kind of a myth, they at least had the best of reasons for discouraging a discovery which must inevitably destroy their monopoly. Periodically some enthusiast like Arthur Dobbs or Alexander Dalrymple[1] managed to strike so effectively the chord of British love of adventure that the Company was forced for a time to swim with the tide, and to sanction with the best grace they could muster an expedition which seemed to their practical minds hopelessly and perhaps dangerously quixotic. And how can we blame them? Whatever their charter might say, they had not built forts on the inhospitable shores of Hudson Bay to further the interests of science or the advancement of human knowledge. Dividends, not discoveries, was the prize they sought. All they asked was to be left alone, and it must have been peculiarly exasperating when some

---

[1] Reference may be made to Alexander Dalrymple's curious Memorandum on the Route for Discoveries, in the Appendix.

officious individual insisted on dragging the affairs of the bay into the light, and stirring the Government or the public to demand a *quid pro quo* in the way of geographical discoveries for the Company's extraordinary privileges. The Company's attitude toward interior exploration was equally consistent, but here, curiously enough, the pressure came not so much from the outside as from its own officers. Extensive discoveries were made, from time to time, on behalf of the Hudson's Bay Company, mainly because the enthusiasm of certain of its officers could not be restrained. Samuel Hearne's was a case in point. So also were those of Anthony Hendry, Peter Fidler, and David Thompson, and, to a less extent, Henry Kellsey. Philip Turner, on the other hand, was sent out at the instance of the Imperial Government. These men went inland, so far as the Company was concerned, primarily to drum up trade, and it was due almost entirely to their own initiative that they accomplished so much in the cause of exploration. And it was not, as already noted, until the energy and resourcefulness of the Montreal traders had thoroughly alarmed the Hudson's Bay Company that it awakened to the necessity of carrying its trade into the Indian country. Up to that time the Company had been content to bring the Indians down to the bay. The North West Company pursued a more enlightened policy in the matter of exploration. At the same time it must be said in all fairness that in its case also much of what was accomplished was due to the tireless enthusiasm of its men.

Among the Canadian traders who were stirring the old Company out of its comfortable dream of a perpetual monopoly was one Peter Pond, an extraordinary character, whose story will be told in a later chapter. It is sufficient to say here that he drew a series of remarkable maps of North-Western America, embodying his own discoveries with such additional information as he was able to procure from the Indians. He laid down the western coast of the continent with tolerable accuracy from Captain Cook's charts, but owing to his own lack of scientific knowledge and the reliance he placed upon the estimates of the *voyageurs* or canoemen, who, like all unprofessional travellers, were inclined to overestimate distances, Pond succeeded in bringing Lake Athabaska within a comparatively short distance of the Pacific coast. Charles Lindsey, in his *Investigation of the Unsettled Boundaries of Ontario*, says that Sir Hugh Dalrymple,[1] on comparing Pond's map with Cook's charts, found that the former brought the western end of Lake Athabaska within less than one hundred miles of the Pacific. This was perhaps something under the mark. None of Pond's maps now available bring the lake anything like so near the Pacific. However, one at least puts the western end of Athabaska three-quarters of the distance across the continent from Hudson Bay, whereas it should be less than half-way. The map in question was sent to the British Government in 1785, and attracted a great deal of attention at the time—though it was most unfortunately forgotten

[1] He probably meant Alexander Dalrymple.

some years later, when it would have been of important service to the nation, or at any rate to those who cared to preserve the territorial rights of British North America. However, in 1785, taking the longitude of Athabaska as approximately correct, every one was naturally struck with the apparent fact that exploration had already proceeded to within a short distance of the Pacific, and that little effort would be required to connect Pond's discoveries with Cook's.

So much having already been accomplished by or on behalf of the North West Company, the Government naturally turned to the Hudson's Bay Company to complete the gap, or at least ascertain beyond peradventure the true longitude of Lake Athabaska. The Company could not readily avoid the task, but altogether missing its importance, it was placed in the hands of a boy of fifteen, one George Charles. This boy is said to have spent one year at a mathematical school, where, armed with a quadrant, he thrice performed the feat of bringing down the sun to a chalk line on the wall, after which he was pronounced competent for a task demanding much more than average ability. Of course he achieved nothing, and it was not until five years later that, upon the urgent representation of the Colonial Office, the Company sent out a qualified surveyor, Philip Turner. A manuscript map inscribed "Chart of Lakes and Rivers in North America, by Philipp Turner," in the archives of the Hudson's Bay Company at London, embodies the results of his explorations between the years 1790 and 1792. A copy of this map was made by or for Dr. John G. Kohl, the eminent geographer, and forms part of the Kohl collection of maps relating to America, in the Library of Congress.

Turner is said to have entered the service of the Hudson's Bay Company about 1779. He is described by Kohl as "surveyor and astronomer of the Hudson's Bay Company." Materials for an account of his explorations are extremely meagre. Kohl says that Turner wrote a circumstantial report of his explorations in 1790–2, of which "the manuscript is preserved in the archives of the Hudson's Bay Company in London, and which has the title 'Journal of a Journey from Cumberland-house towards the Athapiscow Country and back to York Factory 1790–1792.'" The present map, he adds, was probably particularly made to illustrate this journal. Recent inquiries have failed to elicit any information as to this journal at Hudson's Bay House. Unless it should at some future time come to light, the reconstruction of Turner's work in the north-west must depend upon his map, with the assistance of Kohl's notes appended to the Library of Congress copy, and a few random references in the journals and letters of Turner's contemporaries in the west. Kohl may have had the opportunity of reading Turner's journal at Hudson's Bay House. If so, it is regrettable that he did not procure a copy with the map, or at least take such notes as might now be of service in tracing Turner's course.

Turner's map begins on the east at Cumberland House, and extends to Great Slave Lake. Its most *cr. 1790.*

Face p. 170

N SEA

eminent
ction of
gress.
of the
escribed
tudson's
of his
ys that
explora-
is pre-
company
tal of a
e. Atha-
1792."
ticularly
ies have
ournal at
ne future
er's work
with the
ibrary of
es in the
f reading
f so, it is
with the
ow be of
mberland
Its most

HUDSON'S-BAY-COUNTRY by Turner, 1790.

notable feature is the delineation of Lake Athabaska, which appears here for the first time in its correct form. Both the outline and position of Lake Athabaska are in fact remarkably accurate. The west end, which Peter Pond had placed as far west as 131°, on Turner's map corresponds almost exactly with the position on the latest official map of the country, while the east end of the lake was equally accurate. The difference of over twenty degrees in the longitude of the west end of Lake Athabaska threw out the calculations of those who had been, on the strength of Pond's map, figuring on an easy linking up of Cook's explorations with Pond's.

While the mapping of Lake Athabaska is the most striking feature of Turner's map, his survey of the canoe route from Cumberland House north-westward to Great Slave Lake is almost equally remarkable. A comparison of Turner's map with this portion of Pond's brings out the crudity and inaccuracy of the latter ; and yet previous to Turner's, Pond's map was far and away the most accurate delineation of north-western America ; in fact it was the only map that gave any even approximately accurate details of the country between Lake Winnipeg and the Rocky Mountains. Turner's map shows both Methye Portage, the famous carrying-place from the waters of the Churchill to those of the Athabaska, and also the water communication by way of Red Willow (now Pembina) River and Swan Lake.

That Turner was a careful and painstaking as well as a competent surveyor, his map bears ample witness. He clearly distinguishes the results of his own surveys from what was merely information gathered from the Indians. In this way it becomes possible to arrive at a tolerably close estimate of the extent of territory actually covered by Turner in the course of his explorations. He marks by two crosses the waterways which he knows only by Indian report. It appears, then, that he made a careful survey of th Saskatchewan up to the Forks, and a short distance up the north branch to Hudson's House;[1] also of Sturgeon-Weir River and its connecting waterways to Frog Portage; of the upper waters of the Churchill to Mithy or La Loche Lake; of the Clearwater River, and as much of the Athabaska as lies between the mouth of the Clearwater and Athabaska Lake; of Athabaska River, Slave River, and a small portion of the south shore of Great Slave Lake. From Indian report, he laid down the North Saskatchewan and indicated the South Saskatchewan; laid down Beaver River and the chain of lakes which empty into it from the westward (these latter even to-day are imperfectly known);[2] laid down the Peace River and indicated the upper waters of the Athabaska. The two branches of the Saskatchewan, the Athabaska and the Peace rivers, are all marked as taking their rise in the "Stony Mountain." Turner shows on his map the post built by Peter Pond on the lower waters of the Athabaska. He also shows establishments of the Canadian traders on the Saskatchewan, the Churchill, at Ile à la

David Thompson says that this establishment was built by Turner.
[1] The lakes as they appear on Canadian Government maps are taken Thompson's map, but are to be supplied in a year or two.

FORT McLEOD, McLEOD LAKE, B.C.

FON DU LAC, LAKE ATHABASKA

Face p. 172

from what was merely information gathered from the
Indians. In this way it becomes possible to arrive at a
tolerably close estimate of the extent of territory
actually covered by Turner in the course of his explorations. He marks by two crosses the waterways which
he knows only by Indian report. It appears, then, that
he made a careful survey of the Saskatchewan up to the
Forks, and ˌa short distance up the north branch to
Hudson's House;[1] also of Sturgeon-Weir River and its
connecting waterways to Frog Portage; of the upper
waters of the Churchill to Methye or La Loche Lake;
of the Clearwater River, and so much of the Athabaska
as lies between the mouth of the Clearwater and Athabaska Lake; of Athabaska Lake, Slave River, and a
small portion of the south shore of Great Slave Lake.
From Indian report, he laid down the North Saskatchewan and indicated the South Saskatchewan; laid
down Beaver River and the chain of lakes which empty
into it from the westward (the latter even to-day are
imperfectly known);[2] laid down the Peace River and
indicated the upper waters of the Athabaska. The two
branches of the Saskatchewan, the Athabaska and the
Peace rivers, are all marked as taking their rise in the
"Stony Mountain." Turner shows on his map the post
built by Peter Pond on the lower waters of the Athabaska. He also shows establishments of the Canadian
traders on the Saskatchewan, the Churchill, at Ile à la

---

[1] David Thompson says that this establishment was built by Turner.

[2] The lakes as they appear on Canadian Government maps are taken
from Thompson's map, but are to be surveyed in a year or two.

FORT McLEOD, McLEOD LAKE, B.C.

FON DU LAC, LAKE ATHABASKA

Face p. 172

Crosse, on the Beaver, on Athabaska Lake, on the Peace River, and on Great Slave Lake. Curiously enough, although he surveyed Lake Athabaska so carefully, he altogether omits from his map Lake Claire, lying immediately to the westward, and which is shown on Pond's map. How much work Turner accomplished in the west outside the limits of this map there is no present means of knowing. Dr. A. P. Low suggests that the surveys in the Severn River country laid down on Arrowsmith's map may have been Turner's work, and it is not at all unlikely that that industrious map-maker may have been indebted to Turner for many other additions to the geography of North-Western America.

Kohl says that Turner was accompanied in his explorations by Peter Fiedler or Fidler. This may very well have been the case, as Fidler entered the service of the Hudson's Bay Company about 1791. Alexander Mackenzie, in his letters to his cousin Roderick, refers several times to Turner and his work. In a letter dated at Opas (now The Pas), on the Lower Saskatchewan, June 24th, 1790, he writes: "We were at Cumberland House yesterday and learnt that Mr. Turner was sent out on discoveries. He is to winter at Athabasca next year." In another latter, dated at Lac des Bœufs (Buffalo Lake, below Lake La Loche), June 1st, 1792, he says: "I met ¹⁷⁹¹ Mr. Turner here this morning. I find the intention of the expedition is discoveries only. I also find the party ill-prepared for the undertaking. Mr. Ross [evidently another Hudson's Bay man assisting Turner] wishes to obtain storage from you for some baggage, should the expedition proceed further than your place, where, they say, they intend to pass the winter." Roderick McKenzie was at that time stationed at Fort Chipewyan, on the south shore of Lake Athabaska. Whatever might be the attitude of the rival companies in matters of trade, it is clear that hostility went no further, at least in the case of men like Mackenzie and Turner. Alexander Mackenzie had already written Roderick a fortnight earlier: "Endeavour to see the house put in proper order before the arrival of the English, who, if there is room, will lodge at the Fort"; and on August 10th following he writes again: "Give my compliments to Mr. Turner, the English astronomer, and tell him I am sorry I cannot have the pleasure of his company this winter." Turner seems to have returned to England in 1792, upon the completion of his surveys.

Peter Fidler, described as the successor of Turner in the office of surveyor and astronomer of the Hudson's Bay Company, was born on August 16th, 1769, and if his birthplace was not Bolsover, in the county of Derby, England, he at least spent his early years there. From the fact that he kept a diary of his service and explorations in the Indian country beginning in 1791, it is inferred that he entered the service of the Hudson's Bay Company in that year, in his twenty-second year. As already mentioned, he is said to have been associated with Philip Turner in his western surveys. His own explorations were extensive and important enough to stand alone. Unfortunately, although he left journals whose voluminousness were rivalled in the annals of

Canadian exploration and fur trading only by those of David Thompson, no trace can now be found of them. All the material extant, apart from the valuable manuscript map of the North-West, now in the office of the Geographer of the Department of the Interior at Ottawa, and the indirect evidence furnished by some of Arrowsmith's maps, is a copy of his will, in the possession of the Reverend George Bryce, of Winnipeg, and certain meagre references in contemporary journals.

It is of course well known that Arrowsmith obtained most of the data for the north-western portion of his maps of North America from the Hudson's Bay Company or its officers. In some cases he even indicated the routes of explorers whose discoveries were incorporated in his maps. Fortunately this was done in the case of one at least of Fidler's journeys. In Arrowsmith's 1802, as well as in the 1811 map, Fidler's route is laid down from old Fort George to the Little Bow River. Fidler left Fort George, on the North Saskatchewan, four and a half miles above the mouth of Moose Creek, in 1792, and travelling in a south-westerly direction, crossed the Battle, Red Deer, and Bow rivers, the first a tributary of the North Saskatchewan, the other two of the South Saskatchewan, and finally reached the Little Bow River somewhere about the foot of the mountains. He returned to Fort George in 1793 by a route somewhat to the eastward of that followed on the outward journey, crossing the Red Deer at the mouth of Rosebud Creek, which he calls " Edge Coal Creek," the origin of the name being explained by a note on the map: "Great quantity of coals in this creek." "With the exception of the coal seam mentioned by Sir Alex. Mackenzie," says Mr. J. B. Tyrrell, who first noted the above particulars of Fidler's journey, "as having been seen by him on Great Bear River in 1789, this is the first record of the discovery of coal in the Canadian North-West Territory." This is hardly accurate. Apart from the fact that Mackenzie's discovery of coal was on the Mackenzie River, not the Great Bear River, he is not entitled to the credit of original discovery, Edward Umfreville having been the first to record the presence of coal in the north-west.[1]

Arrowsmith's 1802 map gives the South Saskatchewan as unexplored from Chesterfield House, at the mouth of the Red Deer, down to South Branch House.[2] In his 1811 map the missing link is supplied. Evidently this portion of the river was explored in the interval, and as Arrowsmith's information came almost entirely from the Hudson's Bay Company, the probabilities point to its having been the work of Peter Fidler, a supposition confirmed by a reference to a manuscript map prepared by George Taylor from Fidler's surveys.

David Thompson met Fidler at Cumberland House on August 18th, 1798; and in his 1799 journal, under

[1] *Present State of Hudson's Bay*, p. 149.
[2] The original Chesterfield House was built in 1791. It was rebuilt by John McDonald, of Garth, in 1805. South Branch House was built some time before 1790. Harmon says it was about 120 miles above the Forks of the Saskatchewan, at a place where the two branches approach within fifteen miles of each other. There was another post six miles below. South Branch House was abandoned, and afterward rebuilt in 1805, when Harmon was there.

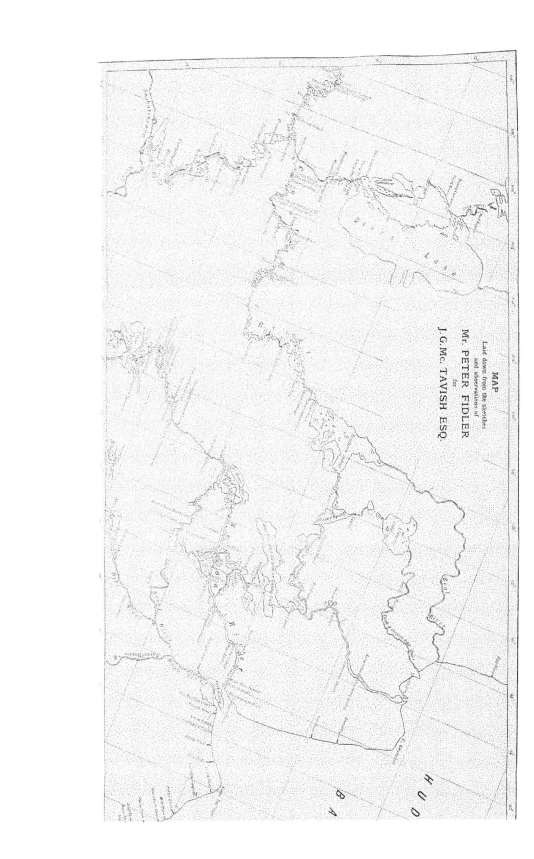

date of September 5th, he mentions Fidler at Green Lake, a long, narrow body of water lying a little east of long. 108°, at the northern end of which the Hudson's Bay Company and North West Company both built small posts. From Green Lake, Fidler evidently went to Ile à la Crosse, where Thompson gets word of him a week later.

In the journal of Archibald McDonald,[1] who accompanied Sir George Simpson to the Pacific in 1828, mention is made of a post built by Fidler on English Island, at the extreme western end of Lake Athabaska; Nottingham House, on Taylor's map. When the party passed English Island in that year, the chimneys of the old fort were still standing.

A curious bit of evidence is furnished by a map included in the Kohl collection at Washington. This map is described as a copy of a sketch of the Upper Missouri branches, made by an Indian, and preserved in the archives of the Hudson's Bay Company at London. Kohl says that the map was taken to Europe by Peter Fidler. As it is dated 1801, Fidler must have crossed the Atlantic early in the century. How long he remained in England there is no means of knowing, but, at any rate, he was back again in the west in 1806. The map, according to Kohl, bears the following inscription: "An Indian map of the different tribes that inhabit on the East and West side of the Rocky Mountains with all the rivers and other remarkable

---

[1] " Peace River. A Canoe Voyage from Hudson's Bay to Pacific, by the late Sir George Simpson, in 1828." *Journal of the late Chief Factor, Archibald McDonald.* Edited with notes by Malcolm McLeod. Ottawa. 1872.

places, also the number of tents. Drawn by 'The Feathers' or 'Ackomakki,' a Blackfoot chief, 7th Febr. 1801. Reduced from the original by Peter Fidler." The map is remarkable in that it names eleven peaks in the Rockies, between the head-waters of the South Saskatchewan and the head-waters of the Yellowstone. It shows and names Chesterfield House, on the South Saskatchewan. Two rivers are shown flowing westward from the Rocky Mountains and emptying into the Pacific Ocean, which may be intended to represent the Columbia and the Fraser, or perhaps the Columbia and its great tributary the Kootenay. This map is interesting as a probable source of some of the information on Arrowsmith's 1802 map. Apart from the fact that it brings out Fidler's presence in England in 1801 or thereabouts, it does not throw any particular light on his movements.

In 1806, when Daniel Williams Harmon was in charge of Cumberland House of the North West Company, Peter Fidler had control of the neighbouring Hudson's Bay Company's post of the same name. Though Harmon remained there for over eight months, he makes no further mention of his Hudson's Bay Company neighbour. It may be gathered, however, that their relations were not unfriendly, as Harmon notes in his journal during the winter : " The greater part of the North West and Hudson's Bay people live on amicable terms, and when one can with propriety render a service to the other, it is done with cheerfulness."

"From Churchill Factory in 1809," says Bancroft, " Peter Fidler went with eighteen men to establish a post at Ile à la Crosse, the Hudson's Bay Company having failed in previous similar attempts, being driven away by their rivals, who had secured the attachment of the natives of that locality. Mr. Fidler built his fort; but meanwhile the North West Company stationed a party of *battailleurs* or professional bullies in a watch-house built for that purpose, in order to overawe the natives and prevent them from trading at the Fidler fortress. Not liking his situation, Mr. Fidler retired, and his persecutors set fire to his fort."[1] The fierce rivalry between the two great fur companies, in which sometimes one, sometimes the other, got the upper hand, and which finally became so dangerous that union was resorted to as the only alternative to the extinction of one of the companies, constitutes perhaps the most dramatic chapter in the history of the fur trade. Unfortunately, as this is the story of western exploration rather than the story of the western fur trade, it must be left for another occasion. As Bancroft says, a complete history of this war between the rival companies would fill a volume, and a large volume at that.

These meagre details of Fidler's life have only an indirect bearing upon the history of western exploration. They serve, however, to throw a little light upon the character of one of the notable actors in this drama of western expansion, and furnish the atmosphere in which the story moves. Little as is now known of Fidler's early life in the fur country, his later years are shrouded in even deeper mystery. According to

[1] Bancroft's *History of the North-West Coast*, I, 570.

Dr. Bryce, he was entrusted with the conduct of one of the parties of settlers from Hudson Bay to the Selkirk Settlement. He is also said to have made the boundary survey of the district of Assiniboia, in the Red River Settlement, and to have prepared the plan of the settlement. He was placed in charge of the Red River department about this time, but on the arrival of Governor Semple was transferred to Brandon House, where his impulsive temper might expend itself harmlessly. He died in 1822 at old Norway House, at the southern end of Playgreen Lake, leaving an eccentric will, of which Dr. Bryce gives a synopsis.[1]

Under this will the residue of his property, after provision had been made for his children, was to be placed in the public funds and allowed to accumulate until August 16th, 1969, the two-hundredth anniversary of his birth, when the whole amount of principal and interest was to go to " the next male child heir in direct descent from my son Peter Fidler." He left a collection of five hundred books, besides printed maps, two sets of twelve-inch globes, a large achromatic telescope, a Wilson's microscope, and a brass sextant, a barometer, and all his thermometers, to the Selkirk Colony. It is said that the books were afterward absorbed into the Red River Library, and that volumes are still to be seen in Winnipeg.

But the most important provision of Fidler's will, from the point of view of this story, is the disposition he made of his own writings. His journals, covering

[1] *Remarkable History of the Hudson's Bay Company*, p. 284.

twenty-five or thirty years, also four or five vellum-bound books, being a fair copy of the narrative of his journeys, as well as astronomical and meteorological and thermometrical observations, also his manuscript maps, were to be given to the Committee of the Honourable Hudson's Bay Company. What became of these voluminous journals is at present a hopeless puzzle. Diligent search has failed to disclose them either at Hudson's Bay House, London, or at Norway House, where Fidler died. If they should turn up some day they may be expected to throw a valuable light upon the exploration of North-Western America between 1791 and 1822.

Meanwhile Taylor's map is invaluable in the evidence it affords as to the extent of Fidler's explorations. The map is entitled "A Map laid down from the Sketches and Observations of Mr. Peter Fidler, for J. G. McTavish Esquire, by G. Taylor, Junior." Unfortunately it is not dated. John George McTavish was a partner of the North West Company, and after the coalition of 1821 became Chief Factor in the Hudson's Bay Company. George Taylor was an officer of the Hudson's Bay Company. It is altogether probable, therefore, that his map was prepared subsequent to 1821, and probably after Fidler's death the following year. It is based, as the title indicates, on Fidler's sketches and observations, but also embodies a certain amount of additional information. Portions of the Winisk and Ekwan rivers, the former emptying into Hudson Bay, the latter into James Bay, are shown, with the connecting waterways,

from a survey made by Taylor himself in 1808. Taylor
spells the former Wenisk, and the latter Equan. Trout
River, with the Sutton Mill Lakes and Little Ekwan
River, are also shown, from Thomas Bunn's survey in
1803. Bunn, no doubt, like Taylor, was an employee of
the Hudson's Bay Company. The map also shows
waterways connecting Hayes River with the Severn.
The river is named Samattawah, and may have been
explored by Fidler. Falconer, of the Hudson's Bay
Company, however, had gone over this route some years
before, and as the results of his survey were incorporated in Arrowsmith's 1802 map, no doubt both
Fidler and Taylor were familiar with it. The river
appears on Arrowsmith's map as the Shemataway, with
the explanatory note, "Mr. Falconer with Indians in a
canoe in 1767."

A comparison of Taylor's map with the earlier manuscript maps of Peter Pond, Philip Turner, and David
Thompson, and the published maps of Arrowsmith,
reveals the extent and importance of Fidler's discoveries, though it does not settle the dates of his
several explorations, and leaves it an open question in
some cases whether Fidler or Thompson is entitled to
the honour of priority of discovery. A comparison of
the achievements of the two men is inevitable. Both
loom large in the story of Western American exploration. Many hitherto undiscovered sections of the
north-west were explored by both. Which was first in
each particular field will not be known until Fidler's
journals come to light, if that ever happens. One thing

from a survey   de by Taylor himself in 1808. Taylor spells the for   Wensik, and the latter Equan. Trout River, with t   Sutton Mill Lakes and Little Ekwan River, are al   hown, from Thomas Binn's survey in 1803. Binn,   doubt, like Taylor, was an employee of the Hudson'   ay Company. The map also shows waterways c   necting Hayes River with the Severn. The river is   amed Samattawah, and may have been explored b   idler. Falconer, of the Hudson's Bay Company, h   ver, had gone over this route some years before, and   the results of his survey were incorporated in   rowsmith's 1802 map, no doubt both Fidler and   aylor were familiar with it. The river appears on   rowsmith's map as the Shemataway, with the explana   y note, "Mr. Falconer with Indians in a canoe in 17   "

A compa   on of Taylor's map with the earlier manuscript map   f Peter Pond, Philip Turner, and David Thompson   nd the published maps of Arrowsmith, reveals th   extent and importance of Fidler's discoveries, t   gh it does not settle the dates of his several ex   rations, and leaves it an open question in some case   hether Fidler or Thompson is entitled to f priority of discovery. A comparison of ents of the two men is inevitable. Both t the story of Western American explora   tion. M   hitherto undiscovered sections of the north-we   ere explored by both. Which was first in each par   lar field will not be known until Fidler's journals   e to light, if that ever happens. One thing

SOUTH

MER DU NORD WEST

NEW MEXICO

HUDSON'S BAY'S COUNTRY

is practically certain: each operated independently of the other. For a number of years they were contemporaries in western exploration, but for the greater part of that period they represented rival interests; Fidler was a Hudson's Bay man, Thompson a Nor'-Wester. Thompson casually mentions Fidler on one or two occasions, as has already been shown, but says nothing whatever of his work as an explorer. What Thompson thought of Fidler, or Fidler of Thompson, we have no present means of knowing. In the extent of their respective discoveries, at least east of the Rocky Mountains, as well as in the courage, resourcefulness, and tireless energy that marked their characters, both are entitled to equal honour. No fair comparison can be made of the results of their labours as represented on their maps, Fidler's own maps not being available, but so far as Taylor's map correctly covers Fidler's work it is undoubtedly inferior to Thompson's in accuracy.

Taylor's map begins on the east with the west coast of Hudson and James bays, and extends west to the Rocky Mountains and north-west to the mouth of the Slave River. The international boundary marks its southern limits. Most of the rivers that find their outlet on the west coast of Hudson Bay are shown. Lakes Winnipeg and Winnipegosis—the latter named "Winipeg as sish"—are sketched in partially. The Red River is barely indicated, but the Assiniboine is carefully mapped. Characteristically enough, while this Hudson's Bay Company man shows in detail the waterways leading from the bay to Lake Winnipeg, he omits altogether the route from Lake Superior to Lake Winnipeg. The map is a blank east of Lake Winnipeg, with the exception of an isolated sketch of Lake Abitibi.

West of Lake Winnipeg, the Saskatchewan is shown with its two great branches, and many of their branches. A comparison of Taylor's map with that of Turner makes it clear that Fidler at one time or another explored both the North and South Saskatchewan from the forks to their sources in the mountains. From Cumberland House he went north by the Frog Portage route to the Churchill, thence west and north-west by way of Methye Portage to the Clearwater, Athabaska, and Lake Athabaska. This portion of the map is practically identical with Turner's. Turner had surveyed the route from Cumberland House to Great Slave Lake, and it is quite possible that Fidler accompanied him on that survey. Turner's map may have been drawn upon in the preparation of Taylor's. From Ile à la Crosse Lake, Fidler explored the Beaver River and crossed over the Athabaska to Lesser Slave Lake. He seems to have explored both the Athabaska and Peace rivers, although it is improbable that he could have gone up the Peace to the mountains before Alexander Mackenzie.

Fidler's most notable achievements in geographical discovery, however, lie in that vast and even to-day little-known territory between Lake Athabaska and Hudson Bay, and including the lower waters of the Churchill. There can be no reasonable doubt that Fidler was the first white man to explore the Churchill from Frog Portage to the bay. He is equally entitled to the credit of exploring Seal River from its mouth to the height of land leading to South Indian Lake on the Churchill, as well as Etawney Lake and the river which drains its waters into Hudson Bay ; though Hearne was on the Seal River in 1770, and, according to Arthur Dobbs, one Frost of the Hudson's Bay Company "travelled a considerable way in the country north-westward of the River of Seals" some time about 1730. Taylor's map also proves that Fidler explored the route by way of Reindeer Lake from the Churchill to Lake Athabaska. The map shows Deer River leading north into Deer Lake and Wollaston Lake, then Hatchet Lake, Porcupine River, Black Lake, and Stone River to Lake Athabasca or Athabaska. Here, as on the Saskatchewan and the Athabaska, Fidler and Thompson were independently working over the same field. Which first surveyed the Reindeer Lake route it is quite impossible at present to say.

On April 30th, 1770, there was born in the parish of St. John, Westminster, a man whose achievements in exploration were to be of even greater moment than those of Fidler or Turner. David Thompson is said to have been educated at the Blue Coat School. He entered the service of the Hudson's Bay Company in 1784, being sent as a clerk to Fort Churchill. There he began one of the most remarkable series of journals in the history of exploration. These journals, all in his own handwriting, and comprising over forty-five volumes of foolscap, averaging one hundred pages to a volume, are preserved in the vaults of the Surveys

Branch of the Crown Lands Department at Toronto. They cover the amazing period of sixty-six years, from 1784 to 1850.

The year after he landed at Fort Churchill, Thompson went overland to York Factory, where he remained until 1787. In that year he accompanied a trading expedition sent inland to the Saskatchewan, under the command of an officer of the Hudson's Bay Company named Tomison. Two new trading posts were established on the Saskatchewan above the forks. At the first, Manchester House, Thompson spent the winter of 1787–8, and the following winter at Hudson's House. In 1789 he returned down the river to Cumberland House, where he remained until May, 1791. At Cumberland House he had an opportunity of studying practical astronomy under Philip Turner, an opportunity of which he took full advantage, as his recorded observations amply show.

Even at this early age Thompson revealed the qualities of pluck and dogged perseverance which were afterward to carry him over obstacles that would have daunted any less unconquerable soul. Throughout his long career as an explorer there is but one recorded instance of his having set out to reach a definite point and turning back unsuccessful. Hunger nor thirst, disaster nor danger, threats of Indians nor mutiny of his men, had any power to turn him from his fixed purpose. In the single instance referred to he turned back, not because of any obstacle animate or inanimate, but simply because the guides whom he had relied

RUINS OF FORT PRINCE OF WALES, PORT CHURCHILL
By Courtesy of De Robert Bell, Ottawa

FORT SASKATCHEWAN

Face p. 186

upon, and who possessed the only available knowledge of the course to be followed, failed to put in an appearance.

While stationed at Cumberland House, Thompson took a series of astronomical observations to ascertain the true position of the fort, which he found to be in lat. 53° 56' 44", long. 102° 13'. It is a tribute to his accuracy and skill that the result of this first of his lifelong series of observations, taken when he was only twenty years of age, is almost identical with the position as laid down on the latest official maps of the Dominion Government.[1]

In June, 1791, he descended the Saskatchewan to Lake Winnipeg, and followed the Hayes River route to York Factory, where he wintered. September of the following year he ascended the Nelson to Seepaywisk House, where he remained until May 28th, 1793, when he travelled to Chatham House, on what is now known as Wintering Lake. He was back again at York Factory on July 21st.

September 1st he left for the Saskatchewan, reaching Cumberland House on the fifth of the following month. This, however, was not his objective. Ascending the river to the forks, he turned up the South Saskatchewan, reaching South Branch House on October 18th. Leaving here, Thompson travelled overland to Manchester House, on the North Saskatchewan, thence to Buckingham House. Mr. J. B. Tyrrell gives the position of the

[1] Malcolm McLeod, the editor of Archibald McDonald's journal, 1828, who knew Thompson intimately, pays a warm tribute to his conscientiousness, scrupulous accuracy, and devotion to what he conceived to be his duty.

former post as three and a half miles below the mouth of Horse Creek, and of the latter four miles above the mouth of Moose Creek. At Buckingham House Thompson remained until the spring of 1794, when he returned to York Factory, making as he went a survey of that portion of the Saskatchewan travelled over. At Cumberland House he left the Saskatchewan and surveyed a shorter route by way of Sturgeon-Weir and Goose rivers to Goose Lake and Athapupuskow Lake (the small lake of that name, not of course to be confused with Lake Athabaska). From Athapupuskow he portaged over into Cranberry Lake and followed the Elbow River to Ithenoostosequan (now Elbow) Lake, thence down Grassy River to Reed Lake; thence by way of Crooked and File rivers and Burntwood Lake and River, to Split Lake on the Nelson, and so to York Factory, which he reached on July 5th.

The two following years were spent in surveying routes through the intricate tangle of waterways lying between the Nelson and Churchill rivers, building trading posts at convenient points, trading with the Indians for his employers the Hudson's Bay Company, and filling in all his spare time with meteorological and astronomical observations. These latter tasks were indeed the really serious parts of his day's work. He was too conscientious a man to have neglected his commercial duties, but one can well believe that he made but an indifferent fur trader. He was first and always a man of science. He never missed an opportunity of surveying the routes he followed, fixing his

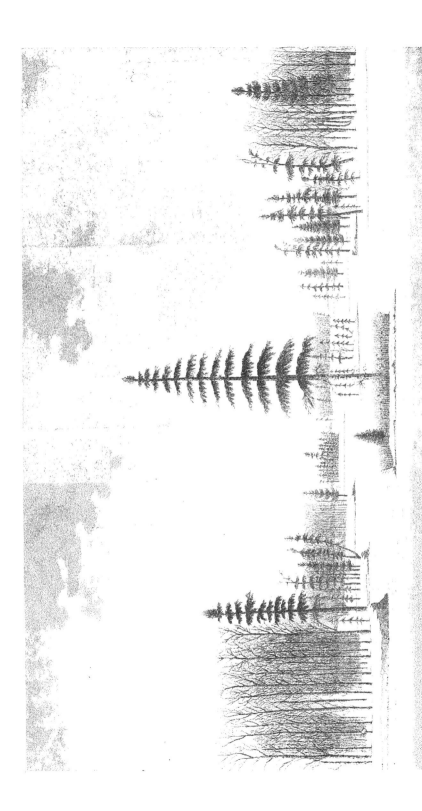

A WINTER VIEW IN THE ATHAPUSCOW LAKE, BY SAMUEL HEARNE, 1771

Face p. 188

positions by observations for latitude and longitude, and keeping a meteorological journal whenever the exigencies of trade compelled him to spend any considerable time at one post. His voluminous journals contain an enormous mass of astronomical calculations, traverse tables, meteorological and other scientific data, important enough in its way, though somewhat indigestible to any one attempting to tell the story of Thompson's life. In the present attempt free use has been made of the admirable paper of Mr. J. B. Tyrrell, already referred to, his statements having been checked by references to Thompson's map and Dr. Coues' elaborate notes.

In June, 1796, Thompson was at Fairford House, on the Churchill, one mile below the mouth of Deer River, in lat. 55° 33′ 28″. On June 10th he left Fairford House on an expedition to Lake Athabaska. He followed Deer River to the lake of the same name, thence into Hatchet Lake, and descended Black River to Athabaska Lake. On July 1st he camped at "Mr. Turner's lopt tree," thus connecting his survey with that of the English astronomer made a few years before. Returning to Deer Lake, he built Bedford House in lat. 57° 23′, long. 102° 58′ 35″, and wintered there, "keeping his customary meteorological journal, and taking a long series of observations for latitude and longitude." He was unfortunate enough to lose his notes in Black River, but saved a number of rough sketches, from which he worked out the route to Athabaska.

At Bedford House, on the 23rd of May, 1797,

Thompson left the service of the Hudson's Bay Company, having been notified that no further explorations could be sanctioned. He decided to try his luck with the North West Company, and left immediately for Cumberland House. Meeting three of the partners of the North West Company on the way, he talked the matter over with them, and received such encouragement that he determined to go down to the headquarters of the Company at Grand Portage, on Lake Superior. So closed David Thompson's career in the service of the Hudson's Bay Company. When we next meet him it will be under more favourable auspices, following his vocation with increased energy and a freer hand; unravelling the intricate skein of great river systems; opening new routes east and west, north and south; leading his men over the great continental barrier to that wonderland that lies beyond, that land of snow-capped mountains and deep valleys, of gigantic glaciers and turbulent rivers and forests of titanic trees, where nature seems to have compressed into a limited space the features of half a continent; always adding something to the sum of geographical knowledge, and always working with the same systematic and painstaking accuracy that has made all that he did of permanent value.

LAC SVPERIEVR ET AVTRES LIEVX OV SONT LES MISSIONS DES PERES DE LA COMPAGNIE DE IESVS COMPRISES SOVS LE NOM D'OVTAOVACS

MAP OF LAKE SUPERIOR, FROM THE "RELATION" OF 1670-71

Face p. 190

PART II

THE SOUTHERN GATEWAY

CHAPTER I

PLANS FOR WESTERN DISCOVERY

THE preceding chapters have been devoted to the story of British exploration in the north, first into and about Hudson Bay, then inland from the shores of the bay. The narrative covers a period of one hundred and sixty-five years, from the date of Henry Hudson's discovery of the great bay to the establishment of Cumberland House by Samuel Hearne.

The story now moves south to trace that other route by which the exploration of the west was accomplished. This southern or St. Lawrence route marks the line of French exploration as distinctly as the northern or Hudson Bay route marks the line of British exploration towards the west. For two hundred years the tide of exploration rolled westward up the great valley of the St. Lawrence, until it reached the head of the Great Lakes. Here for a time it paused, gathering strength, as it were, for the second stage of its progress across the continent.

During these two centuries much had been accomplished. Cartier explored the St. Lawrence from its mouth to the Lachine Rapids. Champlain paddled up the Ottawa, crossed over to Lake Nipissing, and then down the French River until he stood upon the shores

o 193

of Lake Huron, which Etienne Brulé, that intrepid pathfinder, had already discovered, by another route. Brulé also discovered Lake Ontario, and afterward Lake Superior. Champlain and Brulé between them explored a large part of what is now the province of Ontario. Jean Nicolet, under Champlain's inspiration, made an even more determined effort than any of his predecessors to reach the grand object of all western exploration in New France—the *Mer de l'Ouest*, and though he failed in this, he did succeed in discovering Lake Michigan and Green Bay, and tracing the Fox River to the height of land separating the St. Lawrence basin from the basin of the Mississippi, thus opening a direct route to the continental valley of the Mississippi. Radisson and Chouart followed Nicolet to the height of land by the Fox River, then crossed the portage to the Wisconsin, traced that river to its junction with the Mississippi, and perhaps went some distance west of the Mississippi. In a later voyage they explored the entire south shore of Lake Superior, and penetrated the land of the Sioux about Lac des Mille Lacs. What they accomplished beyond this, or may have accomplished, will be considered in the following chapter. Jolliet and Marquette explored the Mississippi down to the mouth of the Arkansas. La Salle, following in their track, traced the river to its mouth, and proved once for all that it flowed into the Gulf of Mexico—not into the Western Sea, as some had supposed. Father Louis Hennepin, despite his gigantic fabrications, really explored the Mississippi upstream from the mouth of the

Wisconsin to the Falls of St. Anthony. Finally, Dulhut ranged far and wide throughout the land that lies between Lake Superior and the head-waters of the Mississippi. These two hundred years of exploration had therefore, so far as the westward movement is concerned, opened up the entire valley of the St. Lawrence, from the Atlantic to the insignificant height of land that divides the waters flowing east to the Gulf of St. Lawrence from those that flow north to Hudson Bay and south to the Gulf of Mexico.

In the narratives of these early Canadian explorers one finds everywhere the same underlying motive—the strong desire to reach, to see, to stand upon the shores of the Western Sea. During the seventeenth and the early part of the eighteenth century a variety of projects were put on foot having the discovery of this sea for their definite object. Elaborate memoirs were drawn up for the French Government, of which two at least demand particular mention. These were prepared, the first by Father Bobé, one of the. Jesuit missionaries in New France, and the second by Father Charlevoix, the historian. The former is dated April, 1718, though the real date is 1720, and the latter is dated 1723.

Before taking up these memoirs, however, it may be well to glance back a few years and see what the state of geographical knowledge was, as regards the far west, in the last decade or two of the seventeenth century. In a petition, undated, but about the year 1685, Daniel Greyselon, Sieur Dulhut, says that in a voyage of three and a half years (1678–81), he discovered nations and lands hitherto unknown to the French or to any other European nation; and that being in the land of the Nadouesioux or Sioux, distant from Quebec as he computed more than seven hundred leagues, he learned from the Indians that not more than twenty days' journey from their villages, towards the west-north-west, there was a great lake or sea whose waters were not good to drink. The Indians even gave him salt which they said had been brought from this sea, which Dulhut believed to be the Mer Vermeille or Gulf of California. He asked permission from the French Government to establish a post in the Sioux country, to further his proposed discovery of the coasts of the Western Sea. While the great salt lake spoken of by the Indians had no existence where they described it to be, it is not necessary to assume that they were merely indulging in their popular pastime of hoaxing the credulous white man. All the early western explorers heard from the Indians of a great water to the west-ward, both the distance and direction of which varied. Sometimes it was only a few days' journey; at other times it was far towards the setting sun; and its position was placed anywhere from the south-west to the north-west. That the tribes of the interior knew, though not from personal knowledge, of a great sea whose waters were salt or bitter is perfectly credible. The more northerly tribes had knowledge of Hudson Bay, and those to the south of the Gulf of Mexico, and some account of the Pacific might have filtered from tribe to tribe across the continent until it reached those who lived about the upper waters of the Mississippi. It has even been suggested that some of these stories grew out of exaggerated accounts of Great Salt Lake, Utah. Naturally, Indian knowledge would be vague both as to distance and direction; and naturally also they would be inclined to meet more than half-way the eager questionings of explorers, predisposed to believe that the Western Sea could not be more than a few days' journey distant.

Six or seven years after Dulhut returned from his journey to the Sioux country, Jacques de Noyon,[1] a young *voyageur*, ascended the Kaministikwia River, which empties into Lake Superior where the town of Fort William now stands, and where Dulhut is said to have built the first trading post—the first of many at this historic spot. De Noyon got as far as Cristinaux Lake (Rainy Lake), and wintered at the mouth of Ouchichig River (Rainy River). Of De Noyon's route a detailed description is found in a memorandum of the Intendant Begon, dated 12th November, 1716. Leaving Lake Superior, he ascended the Kaministikwia for ten leagues to the first portage. Above this he encountered rapids for two leagues, then a short portage, when three leagues of paddling brought him to a long portage called the *Portage du Chien*, or Great Dog Portage. Passing through what is now known as Dog Lake, he entered Dog River. Following it for fifteen leagues, a

---

[1] Born at Three Rivers, 1668. He was baptized by François Dollier de Casson, February 12th, 1668. His father, Jean de Noyon, a locksmith, was born at Rouen in 1627, and settled in Three Rivers some time before 1659, marrying Marie Chauvin in 1665.

portage brought De Noyon into a small lake at the height of land, now called Height of Land Lake. At the end of this lake he portaged into a swamp; thence into a small stream, down which he paddled for ten leagues, and reached Canoe Lake (Lac des Mille Lacs). Six leagues brought him to a portage through a point of trembling poplars, to a small stream (Seine River) full of wild rice, or wild oats, as it was called. Down this stream he paddled for two days, making about ten leagues a day, to a waterfall (Sturgeon Fall), where a short portage brought him into a lake three leagues long, at whose western end there was a rocky strait opening into the lake of the Crists or Cristinaux (Rainy Lake), described as about eight leagues long. At the western end of this lake, or on the banks of the Taka-mimouez or Ouchichig River (Rainy River), he wintered, as already mentioned.

The Assiniboines offered to conduct De Noyon in the early spring to the Western Sea, where they were going on a war expedition to the number of one hundred, to fight a nation of dwarfs, whom they de-scribed as three and a half or four feet tall, and very stout. The Indians, never lacking in imagination, told De Noyon of fortified towns and villages where the men were white and bearded, and rode on horseback with the women behind. They spoke of having seen ships that fired great guns, of a city with walls of stone, and of other wonderful things. All this they told him, or De Noyon thought they told him, which perhaps is nearer the truth. The wish was perhaps father to the thought, and the imagination of the Indians may have been helped somewhat by his eager suggestions.

De Noyon did not accompany the Assiniboines to the Western Sea, but he does seem to have gone as far as Lac des Assiniboiles or Lake of the Woods. Of the route by way of Ouchichig River to Lac des Assiniboiles, Begon says: " About two leagues after entering the river there is a fall where a small portage is required, and there are also two other small falls where portages also require to be made, and then we come to Lac aux Iles, otherwise called Asiniboiles." The first fall mentioned is what is now known as Chaudière Fall; the two others are Manitou and Long Sault rapids.

" On entering this lake," continues Begon, " to the left the country is barren, and on the right-hand side it is provided with all sorts of trees and filled with numerous islands." At the end of the lake, according to Indian report, there was a river emptying into the Western Sea. The river could only be the Winnipeg River, and consequently the " Western Sea " as here mentioned was Lake Winnipeg. That the lake referred to by Begon as Lac des Assiniboiles was the Lake of the Woods seems clear from the description. At the same time, it may be said that Judge Prud'homme, of Winnipeg, in a paper read before the Royal Society of Canada in 1905, makes Lac des Cristinaux Lake of the Woods and Lac des Asiniboiles Lake Winnipeg. Undoubtedly the name Asiniboiles, or one of its countless variants, was afterward applied to Lake Winnipeg;

in fact, both the names of Asiniboiles and Cristinaux
were given to this lake, the former being applied particularly to the lower portion, south of the Narrows,
and the latter to the main upper portion; but there
is good reason to believe that the name Cristinaux was
first applied to Rainy Lake, and Asinipoiles to the
Lake of the Woods. In Franquelin's map of 1688—
apparently the very year of De Noyon's journey—both
" Lac des Assinibouels" and " Lac des Christinaux"
are shown. Franquelin also indicates the " Kamanisti-
gouian " River, but does not show its connection with
the upper lakes. The Mississippi is carried up to Lac
de Buade, in the country of the Sioux, north-west of
Lake Superior. From the northern end of Lac de
Buade a river runs to Lac des Assinibouels, and
another river connects this lake with Lac des Christinaux.
Lac des Christinaux lies east of Lac des Assinibouels,
and north of Lac Alepimigon or Nipigon, with which
it is also connected by a river studded with islands.
Another river, the Rivière des Bourbons, carries the
waters of Lac des Christinaux into Hudson Bay. In
Delisle's map of 1703 Lac des Assenipoels and Lac des
Christinaux are shown in the same relative position, but
Rivière de Bourbon flows out of Lac des Assenipoels to
Hudson Bay instead of out of Lac des Christinaux.

In a report made by De Vaudreuil, then Governor of
New France, and Intendant Begon, of the same date as
Begon's memorandum already mentioned, it is said that
the Indians had brought down from Lac des Asinipoiles
some pieces of silver money which appeared to bear

Chinese characters, stating that they had received these coins from a ship with which they traded on the sea-coast. They also said that they had axes which were round and not of the same metal as those of the French, Probably another case of the wish being father to the thought. Similarly, Hessel Gerritz, in speaking of Hudson's fourth voyage, says that Hudson met an Indian armed with a Mexican or Japanese poniard—"wherefrom it appears that the people of that country have some communication with those along the Pacific Ocean."

De Vaudreuil and Begon recommended to the King that as a preliminary step in the search for the Western Sea, three posts should be established in the upper country: one at Kamanistigoya, the second at Lac des Cristinaux, and the third on Lac des Asini-poiles. The project was of so great importance that they had already sent an officer with seven or eight canoes to erect the first post at Kamanistigoya, and if possible the second also. After the three posts had been built, and a line of communication established, the Asinipoiles post would become the base for a determined effort to reach the Western Sea. The plan was to collect there a party of fifty Canadians under a capable leader, and secure as guides some of the Indians who were supposed to have personal knowledge of the Western Sea. Two years would be required for the discovery, and the King was asked for a grant of fifty thousand livres to cover the expense. His Majesty approved the establishment of the three posts, which were to cost him nothing, but must have in minutest detail the expenses of the larger project before that could be approved.

Lieutenant Zacharie Robutel de La Noüe, the officer sent to establish the Kamanistigoya post, was a native of Montreal, and had already seen service with De Troyes in his expedition to James Bay in 1686. He reached Kaministikwia in the autumn of 1717, and before winter he and his men were safely sheltered in a small stockaded fort. The same year he is said to have built a post on Tékamamiouen (Rainy) Lake. Beyond this he does not seem to have gone. He wrote De Vaudreuil in 1718 that the Indians were well satisfied with the post and had promised to bring there all those who had been accustomed to trade with the English at Hudson Bay. But of the Cristinaux and Asinipoiles posts nothing further is heard at this time, nor of the great project of discovering the Western Sea. An officer named Pachot, writing in 1722, says that the road which was then thought the most favourable for penetrating the west was by way of a small river named Nantokoua-gane, said to be "about seven lieues from Kaministigoya." This was evidently Pigeon River, though the actual distance is more than seven French leagues (the "lieue" was about 2½ English miles). It is notable as the first mention of the long famous Grand Portage route.

About this time Father Bobé prepared and presented to the governor for transmission to the King his elaborate memoir on the means and routes to be adopted for a successful expedition toward the Western Sea.

The manuscript is entitled " Memoir for the Discovery of the Western Sea, prepared and presented in April, 1718, by Bobé, priest of the congregation of the Mission," but the document itself bears evidence of a later date, for he says, toward the end of his memoir, "This year, 1720, the King has given orders to make the discovery of the Western Sea through Canada."

"The Spanish, the French, the English, and the Indians," says Bobé, "have known for many years of a sea to the west of America, and separating that land from China and Japan. The French on account of their geographical position in New France, are more deeply interested.in the discovery of this sea than the Spanish or the English, and also have better facilities for discovering it."

Bobé's memorandum is a curious mixture of sense and nonsense ; of shrewd and penetrating criticism of some of the geographical theories of his day touching Western America ; and of unquestioning acceptance of others equally fantastic. For instance, he says of the marvellous city of Quivira, which found a place on many of the maps of his day, that it has no more foundation than Parma Lake, the city of Manoa, Eldorado, or the kingdom of King Doré. In the very next paragraph, however, he swallows Lahontan's elaborate hoax *La Rivière Longue*, though he seems to have found it just a trifle indigestible. Bobé was an omnivorous reader ; he was also familiar with all the maps then available ; and not content with the printed narratives of contemporary and earlier western explorers, obtained many unpublished memoirs, and supplemented the information contained in these by closely questioning every man he could find that had any direct or indirect knowledge of the west. In this way he possessed himself of all that was then known, or conjectured, of the western plains and the sea that lay somewhere beyond.

On these data Bobé built up an ingenious theory which, like all his conclusions, was partly right and partly very wrong. He believed that the Western Sea was not more than two hundred leagues distant from the source of the Missouri—which was not at all a bad guess; but he spoilt it by estimating the same distance from the source of the Mississippi to the Western Sea— a very wild guess indeed. The western coast he carried up as far as Cape Blanc, which he puts at 43° N. Above Cape Blanc, as he thought, the coast turned abruptly to the west or north-west, and so continued until it encountered D'Uriez Strait, the Strait of Anian, on the other side of which was the coast of Northern Japan. D'Uriez Strait led into a great sea called the Gulf of Amour. This immense tract of imaginary country between Cape Blanc and D'Uriez Strait Bobé speaks of as Bourbonnie.

"Bourbonnie according to some," says Bobé, "is separated from New France by a strait extending from Ne Ultra (the extreme north-western angle of Hudson Bay) to Cape Blanc. But," he adds, "they are wrong. There is truly a strait running inland from Ne Ultra, but instead of going to the south-west, it runs north-west to the glacial sea above Bourbonnie." He made this statement on the authority of Jérémie, who spent twenty years in Hudson Bay, 1694–1714, and for six years was in command of the French post, Fort Bourbon. Jérémie knew just about as much of the matter as Bobé.

Bobé was an enthusiastic advocate of the theory that America had been peopled by the Jews, or rather by Jews and Tartars. The Tartars, he says, were the first colonists, crossing from Asia to America by way of Bourbonnie. Later some of the Hebrews, who had settled in China after their dispersion by Salmanasar, followed the Tartars into America, and the two races became amalgamated in the new land. This Tartarized-Hebrew stock produced the North American Indian. To prove his theory Bobé presents a bewildering array of parallels between the religious and social customs of the Indians and those of the Hebrews. The problem as to how and when America was first peopled has puzzled many later scholars, and Bobé's ingenious theory has had more than one eminent supporter.

Finally, Bobé urged upon his Government the importance of at once sending an expedition overland to the Western Sea, and to the western extremity of Bourbonnie, so as to forestall the Spaniards in the one case and the Russians in the other. The discovery of the Western Sea, he said, was quite an easy matter, as the sea was really not far distant from the western boundaries of New France, and could be readily reached by way of several river systems. He suggested six feasible routes. The first by way of the upper waters of the

Mississippi. The Mississippi to be ascended to its source, which, it must be remembered, was thought in Bobé's day to be much farther to the westward than is actually the case. From the head-waters of the Mississippi a portage would take the explorer to the head-waters of another river coursing to the west, and which was believed to fall into the sea about Cape Blanc. " At Cape Blanc," says Bobé, " there is a great gulf into which the currents are very violent, a sign that several large rivers meet there."

The second route, recommended as easier and more agreeable than the first, was by the Missouri, or the Manigoua (Lahontan's *Rivière Longue*), or the St. Pierre. Ascending any of these rivers to their source, rivers would be found flowing westward, and which inevitably must fall into the Western Sea. All these west-flowing streams apparently emptied their waters into the sea at Cape Blanc. The third route was for the benefit of explorers setting out from Louisiana. Between New Mexico and the Missouri, rivers would be found flowing toward the west and into the sea of Western Louisiana. The fourth route was also south of the Missouri. From that river a tributary stream connected by a portage with the Colorado, which emptied into the Gulf of California. The fifth route, and the sixth, are of particular interest because they had to do with what is now Western Canada, and foreshadowed, if somewhat vaguely, the route that eventually carried the first successful expedition overland to the Pacific.

The fifth route Bobé thought would be found in some respects the surest and most convenient, and perhaps the shortest. A fort must be built on the northern shore of Lake Superior. From thence a party should be sent to discover Lake Des Chiens (Dog Lake), which, according to Jérémie, was not far from Lake Superior. From Lake Des Chiens, Lake Takamamiouen (Rainy Lake) could be reached by a connecting river. The country between Lake Superior and Lake Des Chiens was to be examined to discover if any river led from one to the other which could be used as part of the route. From what he had read, and from charts he had seen, Bobé believed such a river would be found at "Gamanistigoya." Ascending this river, through Lake Des Chiens, Takamamiouen would be reached. Curiously enough, Bobé says nothing whatever of De Noyon's journey over this very route some thirty-two years before, nor of La Noüe, who had established posts at the mouth of the Kaministikwia and on Rainy Lake, but his mention of Lake Des Chiens shows that he must have known of De Noyon's discoveries. Jérémie, who probably got his information from Crees visiting Hudson Bay from the Lake Superior country, seems to have been Bobé's main authority for these waterways. He quotes Jérémie to the effect that a great river, called the Cerf, entered Lake Takamamiouen from the north. Ascending this river, a portage would lead to another great river having its source toward the north-east, and flowing westward to Cape Blanc, or perhaps a little higher on the Bourbonnie Sea. This route was strongly recommended because it presented only three portages in the entire distance from Quebec to the Western Sea: the first at Niagara; the second from the Kaministikwia to Lake Des Chiens; and the third from the Cerf River to the River of the West. Quite a simple matter to reach the Western Sea by this route!

The sixth was essentially an overland route. The expedition would take the Assinipoels country as a base, and set out thence to the westward, through vast and beautiful plains. After a few hundred leagues rivers would be met with flowing from the north of Bourbonnie, and which would lead to the sea south of that country. This last route Bobé did not very strongly recommend. It was practicable for the Indians, but would be difficult for the French.

Bobé's memorandum, elaborate and comprehensive though it was, apparently did not satisfy the French Government, for a few years later the celebrated Jesuit father, Charlevoix, was entrusted with a special mission "to proceed to the principal posts of the upper country in order to make inquiries there respecting the Western Sea." Father Charlevoix carried out his instructions with exemplary thoroughness. He visited the western posts, questioned every one he met there—officers, traders, *voyageurs, coureurs de bois*, and Indians—as to ways and means of reaching the sea, and embodied the results of his investigations in a memoir, addressed in 1723 to the Comte de Toulouse.

The Canadians whom Charlevoix met in the west

seem to have regarded him as their natural prey, for the learned historian complains that "they make no diffi-culty of substituting some romance which they had pretty well digested in place of the truth which they do not know." Probably Bobé and others had been vic-timized in much the same way. However, despite the puzzling and contradictory reports he received, Charle-voix returned to France with a fairly clear idea of the difficulties of the project. He suggested two plans. One was to ascend the Missouri, which he believed would be found to take its rise very near the Western Sea. The other, a slow and very problematical method, was to establish a mission among the Sioux, and obtain from them such information as might be of value in indicating the best and most feasible route. Charlevoix himself rather discredited the second plan, and favoured the Missouri route. The latter, however, meant a direct outlay of money on the part of the King—a mischievous precedent to establish. The Sioux plan was therefore adopted. It would cost nothing, and then there was the pious incentive of savage souls to be saved. A mission was to be established among the Sioux, and to support the mission, a fur-trading company, endowed with the usual monopoly.

The expedition left Montreal on the 16th of June, 1727, reached Michilimakinac about the end of July, crossed Lake Michigan to Green Bay, and by way of Fox River and the Wisconsin reached the Mississippi. Ascending that river, the canoes arrived on the 17th of September at a lake or enlargement of the river, which

was named Pepin after a connection of De Boucher-
ville's, Madeleine Loiseau, wife of Jean Pepin. Here
Fort Beauharnois was built, its completion on the 14th
of November being celebrated with fireworks, to the
astonishment and delight of the Sioux. The fort was
maintained for some years, but finally had to be abandoned. As a missionary and trading outpost it was
moderately successful, but there is no evidence that it
served any useful purpose so far as western exploration
was concerned.

Up to this time it is apparent that no serious attempt
had been made to reach the Western Sea overland.
There had been much talk, the preparation of elaborate
memoirs, and the establishment of several posts in the
west. The talk led to the memoirs, and the memoirs
gave rise to the posts. The posts began and ended in
the fur trade, and the great project was as far away as
ever. As a matter of fact, no one in New France had
any conception of the actual distance that must be
traversed, or of the difficulties that would have to be
encountered.

The search for the Western Sea demanded a man of
very different calibre from any hitherto connected with
the project. He must be a man of indomitable energy,
a man of resourcefulness, one undismayed by obstacles
animate or inanimate, finally, a man of the broadest and
most unselfish patriotism. In the words of Bougaln-
ville, those who sought the Western Sea must give up
all views of personal interest. As fortunately sometimes
happens, the crisis produced the man.

CHAPTER II

LINKING THE NORTH AND THE SOUTH

BEFORE proceeding with the story of French exploration westward toward the Rocky Mountains, it will be appropriate to give an account of two efforts to connect the French inland explorations to the head of Lake Superior with British explorations into Hudson Bay. The first of these overland journeys was made, or, at any rate, is believed by some historians to have been made, by two French-Canadians, Radisson and Chouart, whose later connection with expeditions by sea into Hudson Bay has already been described. The second journey was made by an Indian, or rather half-breed, Joseph La France, whose narrative is contained in Arthur Dobbs's *Account of the Countries adjoining Hudson's Bay*.[1]

The too brief narrative of Radisson's journey is found in what is known as his Fourth Voyage.[2] Radisson and Chouart returned in 1660 from their expedition to the Mississippi, and in the spring of 1661 journeyed west again by way of the Ottawa River, Lake Nipissing, French River, and Lake Huron, to Sault Ste. Marie.

[1] Pages 29 *et seq.* See also Papers presented to Hudson Bay Committee, Appendix, 1749, pp. 243 *et seq.*
[2] *Voyages of Peter Esprit Radisson.* Boston, 1885.

From thence they paddled along the south shore of Lake Superior to Chagouamigon Bay, and travelled inland to Mille Lacs, in what is now the state of Minnesota, where they wintered among the Sioux, making extensive excursions into the surrounding country.

In the spring of 1662 they returned to the south-western shores of Lake Superior, crossed the foot of the lake, and coasted along the north or north-western shore to a point where they met a party of "Christinos" or Crees. With these Crees they set out on a voyage of discovery. Where they went remains to be seen. An interesting historical controversy has circled around Radisson's Fourth Voyage for years, with the result that historians are divided into three fairly well-defined groups: those who believe that on this journey Radisson and Chouart reached the shores of James Bay; those who maintain that they travelled not to James Bay, but to Lake Winnipeg; those who treat the narrative as a deliberate fabrication.

Radisson's narrative, unfortunately, is exceedingly brief for such an important expedition, and to make matters worse it is written in the execrable English of one possessing scarcely even an elementary knowledge of the language. Almost any interpretation might be put upon such a narrative. To get at the truth, all the surrounding circumstances must be taken into account, and as it involves a claim to the first overland expedition from Lake Superior to James Bay, the narrative is worthy of careful consideration. To make the situation

clear, Radisson's narrative is quoted, in his own extraordinary English, from the time. of his departure from
the south-western shores of Lake Superior :—

"We thwarted a place of 15 leagues. We arrived on
the other side att night. When we came there we
knewed not where to goe, on the right or left hand, ffor
we saw no body. Att last, as we wth full sayle came
from a deepe Bay, we perceived smoake and tents.
Then many boats from thence came to meete us. We
are received wth much Joy by those poore Christinos.
They suffered not that we trod on ground ; they leade
us into the midle of their cottages in our own boats,
like a couple of cocks in a Banquett. There weare
some wildmen that followed us but late. We went
away wth all hast possible to arrive the sooner att y^e
great river. We came to the seaside, where we finde
an old howse all demollished and battered wth boulletts.
We weare told yt those that came there weare of two
nations, one of the wolf, the other of the long-horned
beast. All those nations are distinguished by the representation of the beasts or animals. They tell us
particularities of the Europians. We know ourselves,
and what Europ is, therefore in vaine they tell us as
for that.

"We went from Isle to Isle all that summer. We
pluckt abundance of Ducks, as of all other sort of
fowles ; we wanted nor fish nor fresh meate. We weare
well beloved, and weare overjoyed that we promised
them to come wth such shipps as we invented. This
place hath a great store of cows. The wildmen kill

them not except for necessary use. We went further in the bay to see ye place that they weare to passe that summer. That river comes from the lake and empties itselfe in ye river of Sagnes, called Tadousack, wch is a hundred leagues in the great river of Canada, as where we weare in ye Bay of ye north. We left in this place our marks and rendezvous. The wildmen yt brought us defended us above all things, if we would come directly to them, that we should by no means land, and so goe to the river to the other sid, that is, to the north, towards ye sea, telling us that those people weare very treacherous. Now, whether they told us this out of pollicy, least we should not come to them ffirst, & so be deprived of what they thought to gett from us [I know not]. In that you may see that ye envy and envy raigns every where amongst poore barbarous wild people as att Courts. They made us a mapp of what we could not see, because the time was nigh to reape among ye bustards and Ducks. As we came to the place where these oats growes [they grow in many places], you would think is strang to see the great number of ffowles, that are so fatt by eating of this graine that heardly they will move from it. I have seene a wildman killing 3 ducks at once wth one arrow. It is an ordinary thing to see five [or] six hundred swans together. I must professe I wondered that the winter there was so cold, when the sand boyles att the watter side for the extreame heate of the sun. I putt some eggs in that sand, and leave them half an houre ; the eggs weare as hard as stones. We passed that

summer quietly, coasting the seaside, and as the cold
began we prevented the Ice. We have the commoditie
of the river to carry our things in our boats to the best
place, where weare most bests.

" This is a wandering nation, and containeth a vaste
countrey. In winter they live in ye land for the hunting
sake, and in summer by the watter for fishing. They
never are many together, ffor feare of wronging one
another. They are of a good nature, & not great
whore masters, having but one wife, and are [more]
satisfied then any others that I knewed. They cloath
themselves all over with castors' skins in winter, in
summer of staggs' skins. They are the best huntsmen
of all America, and scorns to catch a castor in a trappe.
The circumjacent nations goe all naked when the season
permitts it. But this have more modestie, ffor they put
a piece of copper made like a finger of a glove, wch
they use before their nature. They have the same
tenents as the nation of the beefe, and their apparell
from topp to toe. The women are tender and delicat,
and takes as much paines as slaves. They are of more
acute wits then the men, ffor the men are fools, but
diligent about their worke. They kill not the young
castors, but leave them in the watter, being that they
are sure that they will take him againe, wch no other
nation doth. They burne not their prisoners, but knock
them in the head, or slain them with arrows, saying it's
not decent for men to be so cruell. They have a stone
of Turquois from the nation of the buff and beefe, with
whome they had warrs. They pollish them, and give

them the forme of pearle, long, flatt, round, and [hang] them at their nose. They [find] greene stones, very fine, att the side of the same bay of the sea to ye norwest. There is a nation called among themselves neuter. They speake the beefe and Christinos' speech, being friends to both. Those poore people could not tell us what to give us. They weare overjoyed when we sayd we should bring them commodities. We went up on another river, to ye upper lake."

The crucial statement is, of course, "We went away with all hast possible to arrive the sooner att ye great river. We came to the seaside, where we finde an old howse all demolished and battered wth boulletts." One of the main arguments against the theory that Radisson and Chouart reached James Bay on this journey is based on the extreme brevity of this statement. It does not seem possible that such an important journey could be dismissed in so few words. Any one, however, who has carefully read Radisson's voyages must have noticed the fact that he pays little or no attention to the character of the country through which he travels. The French with their Cree companions were travelling at top speed ; the voyage was perhaps eventless, except for the ordinary incidents of such a journey through the wilderness. Radisson would have little to say of it beyond the bare fact that they left their starting-point and arrived at their destination. Add to this the fact that the explorer wrote his narrative some years after the events described, when only crucial incidents would remain in his memory ; and that he wrote it for the entertainment and information of King Charles the Second, with the shrewd object of interesting that monarch in the prospective fur trade of Hudson Bay; and the absence of topographical detail in the narrative becomes more explicable.

Another argument against the James Bay theory is based on Radisson's reference to "an old howse all demolished and battered with boulletts." How, it is argued, could he have found any such house, or any house of any description, on the shores of James Bay? First it may be premised that, however this statement affects the James Bay theory, it is absolutely fatal to the theory that Radisson's journey took him to Lake Winnipeg, for there is not a particle of evidence pointing to the presence of white men on Lake Winnipeg previous to 1662, or for the matter of that, for many years afterward. Then as to James Bay, there is unquestionable evidence, in Prickett's narrative, that Hudson built a house on James Bay in 1611. The text is quoted in the chapter on Hudson, as is also the significant statement in the 1699 memorial of the Hudson's Bay Company, that Gillam built Fort Charles "upon the ruins of a House which had been built there about 60 Yeares before by the English." It remains to be seen whether Hudson's house could have been standing in 1662, or rather the ruins of it, for Radisson's narrative describes it as "demolished." Fortunately there is strong corroborative evidence on this point. In a letter from Father Allouez to Father Jacques Cordier in 1667, printed in the Relations des Jésuites, 1666–7, it is said:

"The Kilistinouc [Crees] have their usual abode on the shores of the North Sea, and their canoes ply along a river emptying into a great Bay, which we think is, in all probability, the one designated on the Map by the name of Hutson [now James Bay]. For those whom I have seen from that country have told me that-they had known of a Ship; and one of their old men declared to me that he had himself seen, at the mouth of the River of the Assinipoualac, some peoples allied to the Kilistinouc, whose country is still farther northward. He told me further that he had also seen a House which the Europeans had built on the mainland, out of boards and pieces of wood."[1] Among the colonial archives at Paris is a deposition made at Quebec in November, 1688, by Paul Denis, Sieur de Saint Simon, who had made an overland journey to the shores of James Bay with Father Albanel in 1671. In his deposition Saint Simon says that he descended a great river to the shores of the bay, and that on the banks of the river, near the bay, he found "deux maisons qu'il a appris depuis avoir este faittes par les Anglois lesquelles estoient abandonnees." The houses were in a very dilapidated condition, both doors and windows being gone.[2] The statement that there were "two houses" is somewhat puzzling in view of the previous evidence, but at any rate the fact is established that within a few years of the date of Radisson's journey the ruins of one

---

[1] *Jesuit Relations and Allied Documents.* Edited by Reuben Gold Thwaites. Cleveland, 1899. Vol. LI, p. 57.

[2] A copy of this deposition is in the Dominion Archives at Ottawa.

or more houses were still to be seen on the borders of
James Bay.

"This place hath a great store of cows," says Radisson. This, too, has been seized upon as evidence against
a journey to James Bay, on the ground that buffalo could
not possibly have been seen around the shores of James
Bay.   Assuming that Radisson meant buffalo, and that
is not altogether certain, there is no particular reason
why he should not have found buffalo in the wooded
country south or south-west of James Bay.   Dr. A.
P. Low, Director of the Canadian Geological Survey,
who is thoroughly familiar with the region, says that
wood buffalo may easily have ranged throughout that
country at the time of Radisson's journey.   In any case,
Radisson constantly refers to the buffalo in earlier parts
of his voyages as "Buff," and may have meant one
of the deer family by "cows."   An ingenious explanation that has been advanced is that Radisson's "cows"
were porpoises, commonly known to the French on the
St. Lawrence—Radisson's boyhood home—as sea-cows
or cows.   Porpoises are known to have ascended the
St. Lawrence to Montreal, and are even said to have
gone up the Ottawa as far as the Chaudière Falls,
where the city of Ottawa now stands.

Another stumbling-block is Radisson's reference to
the Saguenay, though why any one should find it difficult to reconcile this statement with Radisson's presence
on the shores of James Bay it is hard to imagine.
As a matter of fact, what Radisson says with regard to
the Saguenay furnishes strong proof of his presence on

James Bay. His language requires a certain amount of straightening out because of its peculiar construction, but his meaning is obvious. "We went," he says, " further in the bay to see ye place that they [the Crees] were to passe that summer. That river [presumably Rupert River] comes from the lake [Mistassini] and empties itselfe [that is, the lake empties itself] in ye river of Sagnes [Saguenay] called Tadousack, wch is a hundred leagues in the great river of Canada [the St. Lawrence] as where we weare in ye Bay of ye north." The last statement is obscure, but he apparently means that it is a hundred leagues from Lake Mistassini to the St. Lawrence, and an equal distance from the lake to where he was on James Bay. This information he had, of course, from the Indians. All this is substantially correct. Parties of Indians had already gone down to the French settlements on the St. Lawrence from James Bay, either by way of Rupert River, Lake Mistassini, the Ashwapmuchuan, and the Saguenay; or by way of the Nottaway and a string of small lakes and rivers to the Saguenay; or again by way of the Nottaway and the St. Maurice; and within a few years adventurous French-Canadians were to reach James Bay from Quebec by way of the Saguenay and Lake Mistassini. From the standpoint of James Bay, Radisson's statement is perfectly clear. Upon any other assumption it is inexplicable.

Returning, then, to the original proposition. The evidence against the probability of Radisson's having reached James Bay on his fourth voyage being, to say the least, inconclusive, it remains to be seen whether he himself set up such a claim ;. and, if so, whether his word is worthy of credence. As to the former, what he says is surely clear enough : "We came to the seaside." That he knew of an overland route to James Bay before the date of the fourth voyage, his narratives bear ample proof. It is equally certain that he knew the Crees were accustomed to spend their summers around James Bay. And, finally, there is clear evidence that he had planned a journey to the bay some time before 1662. All these statements could be substantiated by quotations from Radisson's narrative, but there is no space for it here, and the facts are patent to any one who will take the trouble to read the Voyages.

As to Radisson's credibility, assuming that he meant it to be understood that on his fourth voyage he had reached the Bay of the North or James Bay, what object could he have had in inventing such a statement? In the narrative of his third voyage, to the Mississippi, he says, speaking of the possibility of a route to the bay : "Because we had not a full and whole discovery, wch was that we have not ben in the bay of the north, not knowing anything but by report of ye wild Christinos, we would make no mention of it for feare that those wild men should tell or have told us a fibbe. We would have made a discovery of it ourselves, and have an assurance, before we could discover anything of it." This is not the language of a man who would deliberately invent the story of the fourth voyage. And, in fact, if he invented such a voyage in 1662, why should he not have done so in 1660? On the contrary, he says: "We have not ben in the bay of the north," but clearly intimates his intention of making such a journey. That Radisson and Chouart with a party of Crees did actually travel from Lake Superior to James Bay, by way of Lake Nipigon and the Albany, or the Michipocoton and Moose River, or one of the other routes familiar to the Crees in the seventeenth century, does not seem to be subject to reasonable doubt; and these two French-Canadians are therefore entitled to the credit of connecting Lake Superior with the waters of Hudson Bay by an overland expedition.

Joseph La France was born at Michilimakinac about the year 1707. His father was a French trader, and his mother of the tribe of the Saulteurs. When he was five years old his mother died, and his father took him down to Quebec to learn French. He remained at Quebec about six months, when his father brought him back to Michilimakinac. They remained there together until the father died. When Joseph La France was about sixteen years of age he went down to Montreal with a cargo of furs to trade, and after his return made a trip to the Mississippi, descending as far as the mouth of the Missouri. In 1735 he went down by way of Niagara to Oswego, where he sold a quantity of furs, through the Iroquois, to the English. A couple of years afterward he made a second trip to Montreal, where he tried to purchase from the governor a *congé* or licence to trade. The governor accepted the furs and money he offered, but in the spring refused the licence, on the ground that La France had been guilty of selling brandy to the Indians, which the Government of New France had made a punishable offence. La France slipped out of the fort at night with two Indian companions and managed to make his escape, taking with him the goods he had got in exchange for his furs. Having traded these at Michilimakinac for furs, he resolved to go down once more to Montreal, make his peace with the governor, and perhaps obtain a licence.

Crossing Lake Huron, he entered French River where he unexpectedly encountered a large party of French, under a brother-in-law of the governor, who seized him and his furs, and would have carried him to Montreal, but La France made his escape to the woods while they slept, with only his gun and five charges of powder and ball, and travelling along the north shore of Lake Huron, made his way back to Sault Ste. Marie. Having lost all his furs, and being hopelessly out of favour with the French authorities, he determined to make his way to one of the forts of the Hudson's Bay Company on the bay.

He set out in the beginning of 1739, travelling overland along the north shore of Lake Superior. Part of the winter he spent with Indians on the Michipicoton. Continuing his way to the westward, he reached Pic River in March, crossing the river on the ice. About the middle of April, 1740, he reached Grand Portage, and turning west over the route which was already familiar ground to both Indians and French traders, reached " Du Pluis," or Rainy Lake, about the end of the month. He stayed ten days at the falls from which the lake derived its name, fishing with the Monsoni, who had two great villages, one on the north and the other on the south side of the falls. La France took ten days paddling down Rainy River, and reached the Lake of the Woods toward the end of May. Upon an island in the lake he met a party of Monsoni and Sturgeon Indians, with whom he remained for a month, and then continued his leisurely way down the Ouinipique to the great lake.

Considering that the narrative of La France's journey was communicated verbally to Arthur Dobbs, it furnishes a remarkably full and accurate account of the country between Lake Superior and Lake Winnipeg, as well as of the tribes that inhabited that country. It is interesting to note that, if La France was correctly reported by Dobbs, he found buffalo along Rainy River, and even as far east as Grand Portage, in 1740. Curiously enough, although La Vérendrye and his sons had built forts on both Rainy Lake and Lake of the Woods nearly ten years before, as will be seen in the next chapter, and by this time must have been well known to all the surrounding tribes, La France says not a word either of the explorers or their forts. So far as his evidence goes both might be mythical.

He reached Lake Winnipeg in September, and coasting a little way up the east side fell in with a party of Crees, with whom he remained hunting throughout the autumn. He mentions two islands in the lake. One was full of wood, about three leagues long by two broad. He called it Isle du Biche, because of several deer that he saw upon it. This was no doubt present Elk Island, at the mouth of Traverse Bay. The other island is described as sandy, treeless, full of geese and other water-fowl. He called it Goose Isle, but says that the natives called it Sandy Isle. This may well have been the sandy point south of Elk Island. On Hind's 1858 map there is a note opposite the neck of land south of the point, " Canoes can pass thro' during high w^r."

La France learnt from the Indians of a river entering the west side of the lake. It was said to be navigable for canoes, and descended from Lac Rouge or Red Lake, so called from the colour of the sand. Two other rivers ran out of the lake, one into the Mississippi, the other westward into a marshy country full of beaver. The lake was evidently the one in Northern Minnesota still known as Red Lake. It is the source of a branch of the Red River, and though it has no direct communication with the Mississippi, is not very far north of the head-waters of that river.

" The great Ouinipique lake was frozen over in winter," continues the narrative. " The winter there was severe, it lasted about 3 months and a half, the frost breaking up in March. This lake is discharged into the little Ouinipique by a river he [La France] calls the Red River, or Little Ouinipique, after a course northward of 60 leagues. This river runs through the like woody country as the others ; but the west side is more temperate than the east, upon account of the

Q

mountains to eastward of it, from whence a river descends into it through a marshy country full of beavers. He made his canoe in the spring, at the north end of this lake, and went down to the little Ouinipique in the beginning of summer. This last lake is about 35 leagues long and 6 broad; there is but one small island in it, almost upon a water level. The Indians call it Mini Sabique. The course of this lake is from south to north, through a woody, low country. In all these countries are many kinds of wild fruit, as cherries, plums, strawberries, nuts, walnuts, &c. The winters here are from 3 to 4 months. He passed this lake and the River which runs into the Lake Du Siens, in summer and autumn. This is about 100 leagues from the other. He says there is a Fork in the River Du Siens by which one branch discharges itself more westerly and runs into the country where is the nation of Vieux Hommes. . . . The Lake Du Siens is but small being not above 3 leagues in circuit; but all around its banks in the shallow water and marshes grows a kind of wild oak of the nature of rice; the outward husk is black, but the grain within is white and clear like rice. . . . All the country adjoining this river is full of beavers."

All this is sufficiently puzzling, and but for one or two points that furnish possible clues it would be idle to attempt to interpret it. It must, of course, be remembered that Dobbs is reporting a conversation with an uneducated half-breed; that he himself knew literally nothing of the country described by La France; and

that he had every opportunity of confusing the narrative. That he did confuse it, to an almost ludicrous
extent, will be clear by a reference to his map. On this
extraordinary map, which accompanies his *Account of
the Countries adjoining Hudson's Bay*, the several lakes
and rivers described by La France are strung out like a
chain of beads from Lake Superior around to Hudson
Bay. From Lake Winnipeg, or the Great Ouinipique
Lake, the Little Ouinipique leads north to Little Ouinipique Lake. From thence the course is still north by
the River Du Siens to Du Siens Lake ; then north-east
to Lake Cariboux and an immense lake named Pachegoia, which empties by the Nelson into Hudson Bay.
Henry Ellis repeated the same errors in the map
appended to his *Voyage to Hudson's Bay, 1746-7*.

Evidently it is worse than useless to build any theory
based upon the accuracy of Dobbs's report of the
journey. Dobbs's map is a literal interpretation of the
narrative, and it is therefore clear that he got an entirely
erroneous idea of the topography of the Winnipeg
country from La France's description—which is not
altogether to be wondered at. Broadly speaking, of
course, La France's journey presents no serious difficulties. He followed the well-known route from Grand
Portage to Lake Winnipeg, and it is equally certain
that he reached York Factory by the Hayes route from
Lake Winnipeg ; but where was he during the intervening nineteen months? Where did he winter in 1740-1
and 1741-2?

There does not appear to be any good ground for

assuming that he went south of Lake Winnipeg. It is true that he describes the Red River and Red Lake, but it is definitely stated that he got this information from the Indians. His circumstantial account of wild rice growing around Lake Du Siens is important, as *Zizania aquatica* grows nowhere in Manitoba, while it is found in the lakes of Minnesota. But this alone is scarcely sufficient proof that La France went down into Minnesota. Remembering the character of the narrative, it is quite possible that Dobbs got his facts mixed. La France might very well have spoken of wild rice on the route from Grand Portage to Lake of the Woods. There is hardly an explorer who has gone over this route, from La Vérendrye to S. J. Dawson, who does not mention it.

It may be taken for granted, from the terms of the narrative, that La France wintered with the Crees on Lake Winnipeg. Then it is said that La France "made his canoe in the spring [of 1741] at the north end of this lake, and went down to the little Ouinipique in the beginning of summer; this last lake is about 35 leagues long and 6 broad." If one could assume that La France wintered in Minnesota, the Little Ouinipique might well be identified with Lake Winnibigashish, but taking all the circumstances into account, it seems more probable that after wintering on Lake Winnipeg, he built his canoe and paddled up Dauphin River to Lake Manitoba, and by way of Meadow Portage reached Lake Winnipegosis—his Little Ouinipique. It may be noted that Winnipegosis is Cree for Little Winnipeg.

The course of this lake is described as from south to north through a woody, low country.

La France "passed this lake, and the river which runs into the Lake Du Siens, in summer and autumn." Lake Du Siens is described as being one hundred leagues (270 miles) from Little Ouinipique. This probably means that he spent the summer and autumn of 1741 around Lake Winnipegosis and in the country to the westward, hunting with the Indians. The winter overtook him, and he "travelled and hunted through the country for six months," gradually working northward. He was on or near a river called Du Siens, flowing into a lake of the same name. There was a fork in the River Du Siens, "by which one branch discharges itself more westerly, and runs into the country where is the Nation of Vieux Hommes." Reversing the course of the river, does it not seem probable that the River Du Siens was Carrot River; Lake Du Siens, Saskeram Lake; and the branch discharging *from* the westward, the Saskatchewan? Of the nation of Vieux Hommes it is said "this Nation is not called so from the age of the inhabitants, but from a number of old men who separated from some others, under a Chief or Leader of their own, and from that time were so called." From this description the Vieux Hommes may be identified as Assiniboines, who broke away from the Sioux confederacy long before the advent of white men in the west, as mentioned by Carver, Umfreville, and other early western travellers. In Saint-Pierre's journal it is said that the Assiniboines were at Fort La Jonquière, on the upper waters of the Saskatchewan, in 1751—ten years after La France's journey. Their country was in fact the great plains, from Lake Winnipeg to the Rocky Mountains, and from the Missouri to the Saskatchewan.

La France hunted with the Crees throughout the winter of 1741-2, between Carrot River and Lake Winnipegosis, working north until he reached the Saskatchewan, probably at The Pas. He crossed the river on the ice, and at the beginning of March, 1742, reached a lake ten leagues long by five broad, which he calls Lake Cariboux. This was connected by a river of the same name with Lake Pachegoia. Pachegoia is described as "the lake where all the Indians assemble in the latter end of March every year to cut the birch trees, and make their canoes of the bark, which then begins to run, in order to pass down the river to York Fort on Nelson River with their furs. . . . The Lake Pachegoia was surrounded with fine woods of oak, cedar, pine, poplar, birch, &c." Into this lake emptied the River De Vieux Hommes, after a course of two hundred leagues from the west. It had a strong current, was always muddy, and there were no falls upon it. The River De Vieux Hommes and the branch of the River Du Siens are evidently one and the same river—the Saskatchewan; Lake Pachegoia is Cedar Lake; and Lake Cariboux is Moose Lake, north of Cedar Lake. Pachegoia has a suggestive resemblance to Pasquia, once applied to the Saskatchewan, and now to the small stream which empties into the Saskat-

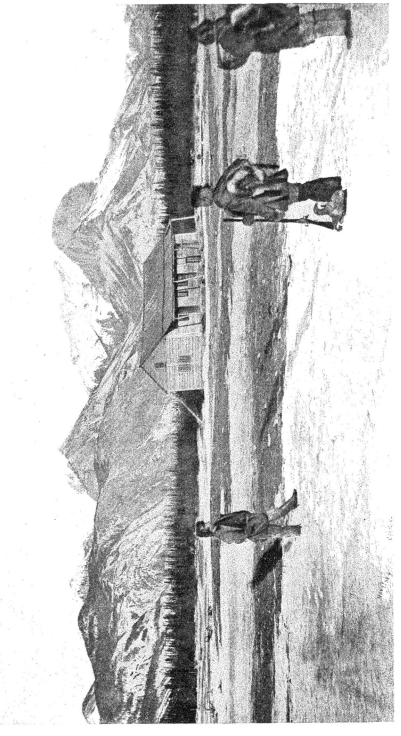

JASPER HOUSE, ROCKY MOUNTAINS

Face p. 230

chewan at The Pas. The reference to cedar is also significant. Cedar grows from Long Point on Lake Winnipeg westward to the south shore of Cedar Lake, but it is not found west of that lake, nor south of it until you come to the southern end of Lake Winnipeg. The fact that La France found cedar growing on the shores of Lac Pachegoia practically settles its identity as Cedar Lake. He refers to the River Manoutisibi or Churchill, and says that there is a passage or short land-carriage to that river, presumably from the River De Vieux Hommes. He means, no doubt, the since familiar route from Cumberland Lake to the Churchill by way of Frog Portage.

La France reached Lake Pachegoia about the end of March, 1742, and immediately began to make preparations for the voyage down to York Factory. He and the Indians cut bark for the canoes, and gathered a supply of provisions. April 4th everything was ready, and they set out for the bay. It was an imposing company, some two hundred Indians in one hundred canoes. No mention is made of Grand Rapids, but they evidently went that way, as the description which follows applies definitely to Lake Winnipeg. "They were three weeks in passing along the west side of the lake before they came to the place it is discharged by the River Savanne or Epinette, for they were obliged to coast the west side of the lake in their little canoes and keep along the bottom of each bay, for these small canoes can bear no surge or waves when the wind blows, and when they came to any point on the lake, if there was any wind, they were obliged to carry their furs and canoes over the land to the next bay, which, with hunting for provisions, delayed them greatly."

About the beginning of May they reached the mouth of the River Savanne. This was of course the Nelson. The name is not found in any other of the early narratives, or on any maps of that part of the country. It may have been applied to what is now known as East River, connecting Little Playgreen Lake with Pipestone Lake. From here they ascended the Echimamish, traversed Oxford and Knee lakes, and at the beginning of June reached the Great Fork "where the river is divided by a Rock, upon which a convenient fort might be built." This is the rock from which Painted Stone Portage took its name. The Great Fork is the point where Fox River joins the Hayes. It had taken them a month to come this far from Lake Winnipeg, which La France, or Dobbs, credits to the laziness of the Indians, "who would not stir or exercise in the heat of the day, it being then very warm." Time was also lost in hunting to supply the large party, and in getting over the many portages. The distance from the lake to the Forks is given as eighty or ninety leagues; and from the Forks to York Factory, sixty leagues. The latter figures are very much over the mark. Mention is made of another party of one hundred canoes that had gone down the Western Branch, meaning, no doubt, that they had descended the Nelson to Split Lake, and thence by way of Fox River to the Hayes.

La France says that from the Forks to York Factory

the river was known in his day as the River de Terre
Rouge, from the colour of its banks.   He reached York
Factory on June 29th, 1742, having been three and a
half years on his very roundabout journey from Sault
Ste. Marie.

CHAPTER III

LA VÉRENDRYE DISCOVERS THE GREAT NORTH-WEST

NEW FRANCE gave to the world many remarkable men; for the most part men of action; men who did things. Few won renown in the more peaceful paths of life; the times were not propitious. Many won it on the field of battle. But above all these sons of the old colony were explorers. The same spirit of adventure, the same mysterious influence—give it what name you will—which drew their fathers to the eastern shores of the new world, impelled the sons to win a way overland toward its western coasts. The cause of North American exploration owes much to the men of New France, and to none does it owe more than to Pierre Gaultier de La Vérendrye. No explorer ever accomplished so much under such extraordinary difficulties. His story is the story of a man who having set himself a gigantic task, not for his own profit but for the glory of his native land, followed it unflinchingly in spite of obstacles of every kind, in spite of wearing discouragements, in spite of misrepresentation and calumny, until at last death intervened, the task incomplete, but notable in its incompleteness. His name must always

234

remain one of the most honoured names in Canadian exploration.

La Vérendrye was born in 1685 at the little town of Three Rivers, from whence so many notable explorers have gone forth. His father, René Gaultier, Sieur de Varennes, was Governor of Three Rivers at the time of his birth. Pierre became a cadet at the age of twelve, and he is mentioned as having taken part in the 1704 expedition against New England. The following year he saw service in Newfoundland; and in 1706 sailed for France, where he spent a year or more in Flanders as an ensign of the Bretagne regiment of the Grenadiers. His eldest brother, afterward killed in Italy, was at this time a captain in the same regiment. At the battle of Malplaquet, Pierre won the rank of lieutenant as a reward for distinguished services. He received nine wounds, and was left for dead upon the field. His splendid constitution, however, stood him in good stead. He escaped, to render his country greater services in after years.

Unable to avail himself of the offered lieutenancy, Pierre returned to Canada, where through the interest of the then Governor, the Marquis de Vaudreuil, he was given the rank of ensign in one of the colonial regiments. A young man of keen ambition and untiring energy, La Vérendrye chafed under the burden of inaction now imposed upon him. A period of peace had succeeded to the stirring years of war, and there was little of moment to occupy the armies of France either in the motherland or in Canada. Seeing no immediate prospect of active service, he turned his eyes toward the west, that unknown west which held such limitless possibilities to the man of courage, resource, and determination.

In 1726 he was appointed commandant of the trading post of Nipigon, to the north of Lake Superior. He was now at the gateway of that land which was to be the scene of his labours for the remainder of his life. At Nipigon he devoted himself to the fur trade with the same fidelity and thoroughness which characterized all that he did, but never lost sight of the great object of his ambition—the discovery of the Western Sea. In 1728 there came to him from Kaministikwia an Indian named Ochagach, who told him of a great lake beyond Lake Superior, out of which flowed a river toward the west. Ochagach, according to his own account, had paddled down this river until he found water that ebbed and flowed. He said he had gone no farther through fear of the western tribes, but had been told that the river discharged itself into a great salt lake, upon the shores of which were many villages. Ochagach, with native prodigality, added many fabulous particulars. Shorn of these, there seems reason to believe that Ochagach's story amounted simply to this : He had followed the Kaministikwia route to the Lake of Woods, which was his first great lake. The river which flowed toward the westward was the Winnipeg, and the great salt lake was Lake Winnipeg. This is borne out by contemporary maps. In fact, twenty years later, in d'Anville's map of 1746, the following inscription is found on a

river flowing out of Lac des Bois toward the west:
"Grand Rivière qui court a l'Ouest, decouverte depuis
peu de tems par le Sauvage Ochagac."

Ochagach says that he paddled down this river—that
is, the Winnipeg—until he came to water that ebbed
and flowed. This raises an interesting point. Several
travellers who have visited Lake Winnipeg at different
periods have noticed the curious phenomena of an apparently regular rise and fall of the water. Keating, for
instance, in his expedition to the source of St. Peter's
River, says that while he was at Fort Alexander, near
the mouth of the Winnipeg River, the water rose rapidly
in the afternoon, until it had overflowed the wharf and
obliged them to remove their tents back from the river.
The following morning the river had returned to its
usual level. Keating explains the phenomena as merely
the result of a high wind blowing the waters of Lake
Winnipeg into Traverse Bay and piling them up the
river. Had he not been aware of the accidental cause
of this local rise, he confesses that he might probably
have mistaken it for the effect of a regular or periodical
rise, which it resembled very much. During the great
storm of September 21st, 1872, the waters at the
southern end of Lake Winnipeg rose nearly twenty
feet. At Lower Fort Garry, on the Red River, the
water rose fourteen feet, caused by the backing up at
the mouth of the river. The lake always rises and falls
in a change from northerly to southerly winds.

Ochagach's visit had put the torch to La Vérendrye's
enthusiasm, and he was now determined at all costs to

follow the search which he had so much at heart. He sent to Quebec by Father Gonor, who happened to be at Michilimakinac at the time, a report of his interviews with Ochagach, and a map which Ochagach had drawn for him of the western country. Father Gonor, who had lately come from Lake Pepin, was convinced that nothing was to be gained from the Sioux in regard to the Western Sea, and agreed with La Vérendrye in thinking that there was a better prospect of success if a more northerly route were adopted, through the lands of the Christinaux and Assiniboines, or what is now the province of Manitoba. La Vérendrye himself, after making further inquiries among the western Indians, followed Gonor down to Quebec, where he had an opportunity of discussing his plans with the Marquis de Beauharnois, his friend and patron, then Governor of New France. De Beauharnois entered into the scheme with interest and even enthusiasm. Himself a man of energy and broad sympathies, he could thoroughly appreciate La Vérendrye's devotion to the cause of western discovery. La Vérendrye had offered to lead an expedition to the Western Sea, if the King would pay and equip one hundred men. De Beauharnois did what he could for him with the home authorities, but Louis XV and his ministers had no money to waste upon projects that promised no very definite return. La Vérendrye, however, was not the man to give up in despair because fortune did not smile upon him. If the King would not equip the expedition, he would try elsewhere. The Governor finally secured for him a monopoly of the fur trade in the country he proposed to explore, and it was decided that he should make his way to Lake Ouinipigon and establish a post there, which would serve as a base for further explorations toward the Western Sea.

Armed with his fur-trading monopoly, La Vérendrye went to Montreal, where he succeeded in enlisting the support of several of the leading merchants. They cared nothing for his project of exploring the far west, but were willing to equip him with the necessary goods and provisions for the expedition on the strength of the enormous prospective profits of the western fur trade.

In the summer of 1731 La Vérendrye turned his face again to the west, determined, if possible, to solve one of the most formidable geographical problems of his age. With him went three of his sons, Jean-Baptiste, Pierre, and François, his nephew La Jemeraye, who had already seen service in the west, and a party of soldiers and *voyageurs*, about fifty in all. A Jesuit missionary, Father Messager, joined the expedition at Michili-makinac. Ochagach was to act as guide.

On August 26th they reached Grand Portage, near the mouth of Pigeon River, fifteen leagues south-west of Kaministikwia. La Vérendrye would have gone on at once to Lac La Pluie, where he proposed to construct the first of his western posts, but when he ordered his men to make the portage they openly rebelled. Two or three of the *voyageurs*, bribed by La Vérendrye's enemies at Montreal, had so played upon the fears of their superstitious comrades that they flatly refused to follow him into the unhallowed and fiend-infested regions that lay beyond. Even apart from this, what was known of the long and difficult series of portages that must be surmounted before Lac La Pluie would be reached was sufficient to dishearten men already ex- hausted by the arduous voyage from Montreal. For- tunately some of the men had been with La Jemeraye at Lake Pepin, and by exercising all his powers of persuasion he managed to induce these to continue the journey. The others weakened, and at last it was agreed that La Jemeraye should go on to Lac La Pluie with half the men, and build a fort there, while La Vérendrye would winter at Kaministikwia with the other half.

Late in May of the following year La Jemeraye returned from La Pluie, his canoes loaded with a rich cargo of furs, the result of the winter's traffic with the Indians. These furs were immediately sent down to Michilimackinac, for shipment to the partners at Mont- real. La Jemeraye reported that he had built a fort at the foot of a series of rapids, near the place where Rainy Lake discharges into the river of the same name. The lake teemed with fish, and the woods with game, so that there was no lack of provisions for the expedition.

On June 8th La Vérendrye with his entire party set out for Fort St. Pierre, as the new establishment had been named by La Jemeraye in honour of the leader of the expedition. It took them over a month to traverse the intricate chain of small lakes and streams, with their numerous portages, connecting Lake Superior and

Rainy Lake, but at length they reached their destination. Fort St. Pierre stood in a meadow, surrounded by a grove of oaks, altogether a delightful spot.

After a short rest at Fort St. Pierre, La Vérendrye pushed on rapidly, escorted in state by fifty canoes of Indians, to Lac Du Bois, or Lake of the Woods, where Fort St. Charles was built on a peninsula running far out into the lake, ideally situated both for trading purposes and defence. This fort consisted, according to Father Aulneau, who was stationed there a few years later, of an enclosure made with four rows of posts from twelve to fifteen feet in height in the form of an oblong square, within which were several rough cabins constructed of logs and clay and covered with bark.

La Vérendrye made this his head-quarters for a time, while his eldest son, Jean-Baptiste, descended the Winnipeg River to its mouth, where he built Fort Maurepas. The journey was made in winter on snow-shoes, along the ice-bound river and through the frozen forest, one hundred and fifty leagues as they computed it, in reality about one hundred and sixty miles; through a country never before traversed by white man. It has been supposed by some historians, as already mentioned, that Radisson and Chouart reached Lake Winnipeg on their fourth voyage, but the grounds for such a belief are very frail. The argument that De Noyon preceded La Vérendrye over this route has been dealt with in the preceding chapter. All the probabilities point to this journey of Jean-Baptiste de La Vérendrye being the first from Lake of the

R

Woods to Lake Winnipeg. An admirable site for the fort was found near the mouth of the river, and before the spring Jean-Baptiste and his men had felled trees, driven stout stakes into the frozen ground for a stockade, and put up a rough shelter inside. The mouth of the Winnipeg has always been a favourite point for the establishments of the fur traders. For years the North West Company had a fort here; and a Hudson's Bay Company's post, Fort Alexander, still stands not far from the site of Fort Maurepas.

In the spring of 1733 La Jemeraye with Father Messager went down from Fort St. Charles to Montreal to report the progress already made, and endeavour to obtain some financial assistance from the Government, but without success. Beauharnois appealed to the Court, pointing out that La Vérendrye had established posts as far as Lake Winnipeg, and that it was unreasonable to expect him to attempt to penetrate the unknown wilderness that lay beyond without some assistance from the King. The distance to be traversed, the difficulties of the way, and the consequent expense, had been far in excess of what had been anticipated, and he was already heavily in debt, having lost more than 43,000 livres on the expedition. The *voyageurs* were clamouring for their wages, and refused to go any farther until they had been paid. The Montreal partners would not send up any further supplies. Altogether La Vérendrye's situation was desperate. Beauharnois urged that the expenditure asked of the King would not be considerable; the cost of the *engagés* for three

FORT PELLY, ASSINIBOINE RIVER

Face p. 242

years, which was the period suggested by La Vérendrye for the completion of the discovery of the Western Sea, and the necessary supplies and equipment, most of which could be furnished from the King's stores, would amount at most to 30,000 livres. But the Court was obdurate. It was all very well to ask for a monopoly of the fur trade, but money was quite another matter.

La Vérendrye seemed now to have really reached the limit of his resources and endurance. In front was a stone wall. Should he turn back? His men were more than willing. Every step, every stroke of the paddle, to the eastward would bring them nearer their homes, their families, and the pleasures and dissipations of Canadian towns on the far-off St. Lawrence. To turn back was much the easiest solution of the problem, but it was not for a man like La Vérendrye. To return spelt failure, and failure was not in his vocabulary while health and strength endured.

Nevertheless, the situation was very critical. His own slender means were long since exhausted. True he possessed a monopoly of the fur trade, but what did it profit him? There was difficulty enough in getting the peltries down to Montreal, and whatever profit there might be went into the pockets of the Montreal partners. The shrewd merchants had seen well to that. In fact, to La Vérendrye the monopoly was simply a millstone added to the burdens he already must bear. It added nothing to his resources, delayed his great enterprise, and put an effective weapon in the hands of his enemies which they were neither slow nor scrupulous in using. Little cause had he to be grateful for the royal monopoly. He would have infinitely preferred even a score of capable, seasoned men, equipped and maintained at the King's expense, whom he might lead at once by the quickest route to the Western Sea.

Nothing was to be accomplished at Fort St. Charles. La Vérendrye must himself go down to Montreal and Quebec, and do his utmost to get further assistance for the enterprise. At Montreal he met his partners, explained to them the situation, assured them that the Assiniboines and Christinaux had promised to bring large quantities of beaver-skins to the forts, that the northern tribes were already turning from the Hudson Bay posts in the far north to the more accessible posts of the French, that this western country abounded in every description of fur-bearing animal. The prospect of hundred per cent profits appealed to the cupidity of the merchants. What they would not dream of doing for the glory of their country, they were more than willing to do for their own pockets. They agreed to equip the expedition again. La Vérendrye loaded his canoes with the new supplies, and lost no time in getting back to his western posts. He was deeper in debt than ever, but full of enthusiasm for his task. While in the east he had made arrangements for his youngest son Louis, a boy of eighteen, to be taught the making of maps and plans, so that when he joined the expedition the following year he would be of material assistance to the party. La Vérendrye would then have four sons engaged with him in western exploration.

Shortly after his return to Fort St. Charles his son Jean arrived from Maurepas with disastrous news. La Jemeraye, his right-hand man, whose knowledge of the western tribes was invaluable, and whose patience and resourcefulness had already helped the expedition out of many a tight corner, had died after a brief illness brought on by overwork and exposure. They had buried him in the wilderness.

Meanwhile the little garrison at Fort St. Charles was almost at the point of starvation. La Vérendrye had travelled ahead of his party in a light canoe, and the supplies and provisions were still a long way behind when he reached the fort. It was decided to send Jean down to meet the heavily laden canoes, and hurry back at utmost speed with what was urgently required. With him went the most active of the *voyageurs*, in several light canoes. Father Aulneau, who had replaced Father Messager at this western post, went down with Jean on his way to Montreal.

An early start was made from the fort, and when they stopped for breakfast they had reached an island off what is now known as Oak Point, a long, narrow peninsula running out into the lake and guarding the entrance to Rainy River. What actually happened after they had landed upon the island will never be known. All that is certain is that they were massacred to a man by the Sioux. How the Sioux managed to surprise such a comparatively large party of experienced *voyageurs* can only be conjectured.

A day or two after the ill-fated expedition left Fort

St. Charles for Kaministikwia, Sieur Legras arrived with the supplies from Michilimakinac. He had seen nothing of Jean and his men. La Vérendrye, fearing the worst, sent Legras back to the mouth of the river to search for any traces of the missing men. He returned the same day reporting that the entire party had been massacred. He had found them lying in a circle on the beach, most of them decapitated, and the heads wrapped in beaver skins. Jean de La Vérendrye was stretched on the ground, his back hacked with a knife, and his headless trunk decorated derisively with garters and bracelets of porcupine quills. The missionary, from his position, seemed to have been struck down by an arrow.

For some time it was not known why the Sioux had made such an apparently unprovoked attack on the French. Gradually, however, it leaked out that during La Vérendrye's absence a party of Sioux had visited Fort St. Charles. Some Christinaux (Crees) who were in the fort at the time, fired on the Sioux. The Sioux indignantly demanded, "Who fire on us?" The Crees, with grim humour, replied, "The French." The Sioux withdrew, vowing a terrible vengeance upon the treacherous White Men. They were only too successful in finding an opportunity to fulfil their vow.

This was the severest blow that had yet fallen upon La Vérendrye. The friendly Christinaux and Assiniboines urged him to lead a war party against the Sioux, which he was at first inclined to do, but upon consideration abandoned the idea as fatal to the success of western exploration.

Meanwhile his sons had not remained inactive at Fort Maurepas. They had explored Traverse Bay, and passing beyond Elk Island had seen for the first time the immense expanse of Lake Winnipeg. From the Indians they gained some idea of the extent of the lake to the northward, and also learned of a river flowing in from the south or south-west. This they determined to explore. Skirting the south-east shore of the lake, they reached the delta of the Red River, and picking their way through a labyrinth of muddy and rush-lined channels, emerged upon the main stream. Paddling up the river, they finally reached the mouth of the Assiniboine, where the city of Winnipeg now stands. Between the forks a rough fort was built. They then explored the Assiniboine to a point near the present town of Portage La Prairie, where they constructed another fort. This fort was first known as Maurepas, but the name was afterwards changed to La Reine. From a map prepared by La Vérendrye, and forwarded to the Court by Beauharnois in October, 1737, it appears that about this time a fort was also built some distance up the Red River, possibly in what is now United States territory. The fort is marked on the 1737 map as Pointe de Bois. Neither this post, nor that at the mouth of the Assiniboine, "Fort Rouge," seem to have had anything more than a very temporary existence. Fort Pointe de Bois appears nowhere but on the 1737 map. Fort Rouge is already labelled "abandoned" on the same map. On a later map of La Vérendrye's, or rather one based on his memoirs and dated 1750, it is marked " Ancien Fort."

In the spring of 1737 La Vérendrye once more went down to Montreal. This time he was able to take with him fourteen canoes laden with valuable furs, the proceeds of a successful winter's operations with the Indians. These went some way to satisfy the hungry creditors, and he was provided with an ample supply of provisions and goods suitable for trading and presents, to take back with him to his posts in the interior.

For some time he had been maturing a project of an overland expedition from Fort La Reine to the home of a remarkable sedentary tribe of Indians, who lived on the banks of a great river toward the south-west. These were the Mandans, and the river upon whose banks their villages were built was the Missouri, though it was not recognized as such for many years. Several maps both in La Vérendrye's day and later show the Upper Missouri as a distinct river, laid down very indefinitely, and sometimes connected with the River of the West. The Missouri had already been explored in its lower waters by several enterprising Frenchmen from both Canada and Louisiana, and Parkman even carries one of these explorations as far up as the Mandan villages, but there does not seem to be any substantial ground for such a belief, or for withholding from La Vérendrye and his sons the honour of first reaching the upper waters of the Missouri and the Mandan villages, an account of which will now be given.

On October 16th, 1738, La Vérendrye had the drummer at Fort La Reine beat to arms, reviewed his entire available force, and selected twenty of his best men for an overland journey to the Mandan country. Each man was provided with an ample supply of powder and balls, an axe and kettle, and two fathoms of tobacco. Leaving one of his petty officers, Sergeant Sanschagrin, in command of Fort La Reine, La Vérendrye set out for the Mandan country, taking with him his sons François and Pierre, a trader named De La Marque and his brother, the twenty soldiers and *voyageurs* and some twenty-five Assiniboines.

Their course lay approximately south-west from Fort La Reine, which, it will be remembered, stood on the north bank of the Assiniboine River, south of Lake Manitoba, and somewhere near the present town of Portage La Prairie. Unlike most expeditions in the west, whether for exploration or trade, this was strictly an overland journey. The waters of the Souris, which lay approximately along their route, were too shallow to admit even of light canoes ascending the river. La Vérendrye and his men therefore went on foot across the prairie, along what was then and for many years afterward the recognized Indian highway between the Upper Missouri and the Red River country. Indeed, Dr. George Bryce says that the old Indian trail may still be traced without difficulty.

At a distance of about seventy-eight miles they passed a mountain, probably Turtle Mountain, and another smaller mountain at one hundred and fifty miles from the fort. From this latter mountain or hill, by holding to the same course, they would before long reach the Mandans. But they were not permitted to travel the direct road. Like many travellers before and since, La Vérendrye suffered from the perversity of Indian guides. "The distance may have been," says he, "a hundred and twenty leagues, but our guide lengthened the road by from fifty to sixty leagues, and a number of stops to which we are obliged to agree, making us spend the finest autumn weather in inactivity. We took forty-six days to go a distance we should have done easily in sixteen or twenty days at the most." They must turn aside to visit a village of the Assiniboines, and the entire village came forth to escort the travellers to the Mandans.

La Vérendrye, though not altogether relishing this wholesale addition to his party, was impressed by the orderly formation adopted by the Assiniboines on the march, a formation adopted to prevent surprise. "They march," he says, "in three columns, with skirmishers in front, and a good rear guard, the old and lame marching in the centre and forming the central column. If the skirmishers discover herds of buffaloes they raise a cry which is returned by the rear guard, and all the most active men in the column join the vanguard to hem in the buffaloes, of which they secure a number, and each takes what flesh he wants. The women and dogs carried all the baggage, the men being only burdened with their arms." At this period the horse had not been adopted by the Assiniboines.

On the morning of the 28th, when they were approaching the Missouri, they were met by a Mandan chief
with thirty warriors, who presented La Vérendrye with
corn in the ear and native tobacco, emblems of peace
and friendship.   He had been prepared by the accounts
he had had from the Assiniboines to find the Mandans
white like himself, and was surprised to discover them
in no material respect differing in appearance from the
Assiniboines and other tribes.   " I knew," says he, " that
from that time we had to make an allowance for all
we had been told."   He was late in making that discovery.   The Mandan chief informed La Vérendrye
that his people lived in six forts or villages, of which
his own was the nearest to the river.   He invited the
French leader to make his lodge his own, and placed
everything that he had at his disposal.

Continuing their journey, the party arrived at the
Mandan village on December 3rd.   La Vérendrye made
an imposing entry into the village, with the French flag
flying in front.   Before entering, he drew his men up in
the open and had them fire a salute of three volleys
with all the available muskets.   He thoroughly understood, as did all the French explorers, the effect of
ceremony, especially unfamiliar ceremony, upon the
Indian mind.   The Mandans crowded out to meet the
French and their Assiniboine allies, and the walls and
trenches of the village were filled with curious squaws
and children.

La Vérendrye was led to the lodge of the chief,
followed by the other leaders of the party and a crowd

of Mandans. Arrived there, he discovered to his consternation that his bag of presents had been stolen. Search was made for it, but without avail. The Assiniboines charged the Mandans with the theft, and the Mandans returned the compliment. La Vérendrye and his men remained for several days at the village, where they were hospitably entertained by the Mandans. The latter, however, began to find six hundred Assiniboines something of a burden. The laws of hospitality forbade that they should be driven forth, and they would take no ordinary hint. The Mandans, however, thought of an effective expedient. They set afloat a rumour that the Sioux were approaching. The Assiniboines, who held the Sioux in particular dread, fell readily into the trap, and precipitately departed for their own country, to the amusement and satisfaction of their unwilling hosts. Unfortunately La Vérendrye's interpreter made off with the others, and he was reduced to the clumsy expedient of signs as the only means of communicating with the Mandans. As he could not question them, as he had hoped, with regard to the Missouri country and the prospects of reaching the Western Sea by that route, he decided to return to Fort La Reine without further delay, leaving two men behind to pick up the language and secure all the information possible from the Mandans against his return.

Before leaving, however, he examined with interest the Mandan village in which they were quartered. It was built in a commanding position, admirably suited to defence, and was surrounded by a ditch fifteen feet deep by from fifteen to eighteen wide. It consisted altogether of one hundred and thirty lodges or houses, built much more substantially than was customary among any of the tribes with which the French were acquainted. The streets and squares were clean and well kept; the ramparts level and broad. The palisades were supported on cross-pieces mortised into fifteen-foot posts. The houses were ingeniously constructed and commodious, with many conveniences not usually found among the Indian tribes. Everything was of native design and workmanship, as up to this time the Mandans had had no intercourse with Europeans, and little or nothing had filtered through the neighbouring tribes. Altogether La Vérendrye was struck with the comparatively high degree of intelligence displayed by the Mandans. His description of their appearance, dress, manners and customs, ceremonies, games, etc., closely resembles the accounts of later visitors, such as Lewis and Clark, Alexander Henry, David Thompson, Prince Maximilian of Wied, and Catlin.

La Vérendrye now made ready for the severe journey over the wind-swept plains to the banks of the Assiniboine. Before leaving he assembled the Mandan chiefs and the principal warriors, and made them presents of such small trifles as could be raked up among the party. To the head chief he gave a flag and a leaden plate, to be kept in perpetuity as a record of the taking possession of the Mandan country in the name of the great White Father, the French King. It is questionable whether the chief was much the wiser. Had he

thoroughly understood the significance of the ceremony he would doubtless have declined to become the
custodian of these evidences of white domination.

Upon the eve of their departure La Vérendrye was
taken violently ill. It was now late in the year; the
prairies were swept by fierce and biting winds-; fuel was
unobtainable. They would have to fight their way back
at top speed. Yet La Vérendrye insisted on going forward. With misgivings the men set forth. Their way
lay to the north-east, in the teeth of an ice-laden north
wind. Day after day they struggled on, camping at
night in the bottom of some deep *coulée* or gully, and
digging away the snow until they had cleared a space
sufficient for the entire party. Cold, hungry, dispirited,
many a time the men would have turned back if
La Vérendrye had consented. He alone was determined to go on. With grim, pain-racked face and
shaking limbs, he urged them forward. The indomitable spirit of the man rose superior to all physical pain.

At last the Assiniboine village appeared on the
horizon, and the French travellers dragged themselves
wearily to the lodges. La Vérendrye was too far gone
to attempt to reach the fort, but after his men had
rested he sent them on under the direction of his sons
to Fort La Reine, from whence they were to send him
assistance. On February 19th he himself reached the
fort.

In the autumn of 1739 the two men left with the
Mandans returned, bringing encouraging news. In the
early summer a number of strange Indians had arrived

at the Mandan villages from the far south-west. They told the French of bearded white men who lived in houses and prayed to the Master of Life. The home of these bearded white men was by the borders of the great lake whose waters were unfit to drink. The Indians offered to conduct the French to the sea, which they said could be reached before the winter.

La Vérendrye at once determined to avail himself of this promising opportunity. Not having yet recovered from the effects of his illness on the former journey, he did not feel able to lead an exploratory expedition in person, but sent his son Pierre with two men, directing him to secure guides among the Mandans, and seek out a path to the Western Sea. Pierre got as far as the Mandan villages, but failing to secure guides, returned to Fort La Reine.

In the spring of 1742 Pierre set out again, this time accompanied by his younger brother. They spent the months of May, June, and July among the Mandans, waiting impatiently for the arrival of certain Indians known as the Gens des Chevaux, who were to act as guides. The Gens des Chevaux—probably the same tribe known afterward as the Cheyennes—failed to make their appearance, and Pierre finally induced a couple of Mandans to lead them to their country.

For twenty days they journeyed, generally in a west-south-westerly direction. One of the Mandans deserted them, but the other, fortunately, remained true. Their course lay over the rolling prairie, among alkaline streams, and through the Bad Lands of the Little Missouri, where the Chevalier de La Vérendrye noticed the "earths of different colours, blue, green, red, or black, white as chalk, or yellowish like ochre," which are so characteristic of this region.

On the 18th September they arrived at a village of the Beaux Hommes (Crows, probably), where they were treated with every friendliness. Here the second Mandan left them, to return to his own people. They remained at the village for the better part of two months, leaving on the 9th November for a village of the Gens de Chevaux. Still journeying in a south-west direction, they reached, on the twelfth day, a tribe known as the Petits Renards, and continuing on the same course, they came to a village of the Pioya. Turning more to the south, they again encountered their friends the Gens des Chevaux, who were in a state of panic, having been attacked and defeated by a war party of the Snake Indians (Shoshones). From the Gens des Chevaux they learned of a tribe known as the Gens de l'Arc or Bowmen, who traded with the Spanish settlements on the Gulf of California.

On the 21st November they arrived at one of the Bow villages, and found the warriors about to set out on an expedition against the Snakes. The latter seem to have been the scourge of the western prairies, as the Sioux were in the middle west, and the Iroquois in the east. Their hand was against every man, and every man's hand was against them. At the urgent invitation of the Bows, La Vérendrye and his brother consented to accompany the war party, the more so as they found that their course would bring them within reach of a great range of mountains lying to the westward.

On the first day of the new year, 1743, the brothers saw upon the horizon a jagged outline. Day by day the mountains grew more distinct. The Frenchmen looked with amazement upon their towering, snow-capped peaks, glittering in the sun—the Mountains of Bright Stones—rumours of which they had heard in their far-off Canadian homes many years before. As they drew nearer, the slopes of the mountains were seen to be thickly clothed with pine and fir. Finally, on the 12th of the month, they had reached their very foot, but as ill luck would have it, the war party here came un-expectedly upon a camp of Snakes, which they found deserted and in the utmost confusion. The Snakes, evidently learning through their scouts of the approach of this formidable war party, had precipitately fled, but the Bowmen, with Indian perversity, jumped to the con-clusion that they had executed a flank movement, with the purpose of falling upon their defenceless camp, where were all the women and children. Turning back therefore, despite the remonstrances of their chiefs and the Frenchmen, they never paused until the camp was reached. The squaws had seen nothing of the Snakes, and were in perfect security.

Under the circumstances the Chevalier could do nothing but make the best of his way to the camp of the Bowmen, which he only reached with the greatest difficulty, having become separated from all the rest of the party. One can readily conceive the bitterness of his disappointment in being compelled to turn back when the prize for which he and his father had so long striven seemed almost within his grasp, for he confidently believed, and the Indians had led him to expect, that the Western Sea lay on the other side of these mountains, and that he had but to climb them to behold the long-sought object of his ambitions. La Vérendrye never dreamed that hundreds of miles of mountain and forest and plain still lay between him and that elusive Western Sea.

There was now nothing for the Frenchmen to do but retrace their steps. Between them and the mountains were the fierce and implacable tribe of the Shoshones, and none of the Gens de l'Arc could be persuaded to act as guide upon such a perilous journey. Young La Vérendrye and his brother therefore reluctantly returned to the Missouri, where they erected a pyramid of stones on the summit of a hill overlooking the river, buried a leaden plate bearing the arms of France, and formally took possession of the country in the King's name. They were now some distance down the Missouri, their journey having brought them around in a wide circle. Slowly they made their way up the banks of the river to the Mandan villages, where they were welcomed as men returned from the dead. On the 2nd of July, 1743, they returned to Fort La Reine, to the great joy of their father, who had become anxious on account of their prolonged absence.

The original intention of Pierre and his brother had been to turn west from the Mandan villages, and follow the Missouri to its source, which, according to current belief, would be found to rise within a comparatively short distance of the Western Ocean. Had they been able to bring with them such an effective and thoroughly equipped force as made up the Lewis and Clark expedition some sixty-two years later, they would probably have accomplished their design, though they certainly would have found when they reached the head-waters of the Missouri that the worst part of the journey still lay before them. But standing alone in the midst of numerous tribes, some at least sure to prove hostile, they were compelled to move with caution, relying on Indian guides to conduct them from tribe to tribe, and hoping that fortune would so favour them that they might in time get within reach of the sea. Under the circumstances, the marvel is not that they failed to reach the Pacific, but that they should have accomplished as much as they did.

There has been much difference of opinion as to the route followed by the younger La Vérendryes on this journey, and as to whether they did or did not actually reach the Rocky Mountains. Parkman, in his *Half Century of Conflict*, makes the Bighorn range of the Rockies their farthest point to the westward. He traces their route from the Mandan villages on the banks of the Missouri, between Heart and Cannonball rivers, west to the Little Missouri. They crossed the eastern branch of the Little Missouri, the Powder River Mountains, and then the west branch of the Little Missouri. They turned to the southward, following the east bank of Tongue River, a tributary of the Yellowstone, and finally crossing the Tongue River, reached the Bighorn Mountains. Their homeward route, as Parkman traces it, was almost due east, re-crossing Tongue River, traversing the Black Hills, and so to the banks of the Missouri, which they reached some distance below the Mandan villages.

Mr. Granville Stuart, in the first volume of the *Contributions to the Historical Society of Montana*, traces quite a different route for the explorers; one, too, which credits them with having reached a point considerably farther to the westward than that indicated by Parkman. Mr. Stuart believes that, starting from the Mandan villages, they ascended the Missouri as far as the Gates of the Mountains, where the river breaks through the Belt range near the present city of Helena, Montana. These, he maintains, were the mountains reached by young La Vérendrye on January 1st, 1743. This, it will be seen, carries the explorers several hundred miles farther to the westward than Parkman thought probable.

Leaving the Belt range, Mr. Stuart supposes that they passed up Deep or Smith's River, and over to the head of the Musselshell, an important branch of the Missouri, and from there they went south to the Yellowstone, crossing which they went up Pryor's Fork, and through Pryor's Gap to Stinking River, which they crossed, and continuing on south came among the Snake Indians on Wind River, who told them that on the south side of the Wind River Mountains was the

River Karoskiou (Kanaraogwa, in the modern Snake tongue), now called Green River. The Snakes also told them they would be killed if they tried to go any farther south, because war parties of the San Arcs band of Sioux, hereditary enemies of the Snakes, were always watching about the south pass, to kill and plunder them as they passed to and from Green River, where lived another band of the Snake tribe. Here the party turned back to the Missouri, which, according to Stuart, they would have reached some distance above, instead of below, the Mandan villages. This interpretation is based partly on La Vérendrye's narrative and partly upon two contemporary documents— one a letter of Father Coquard, who had been associated with La Vérendrye in their western explorations; the other a memoir prepared by Louis Antoine de Bougainville on the French Posts in 1757. Both these documents are among the French archives in Paris. The former was first quoted by Pierre Margry, for many years Keeper of the Archives in the Department of Marine and the Colonies at Paris, in a letter dated July 5th, 1875. The latter was published by Margry in his *Relations et Mémoires Inédits*, etc., 1867.

Coquard, after mentioning the different tribes met with by the La Vérendryes on their journey, indicates that the explorers followed the Missouri not only up to the falls, but thirty leagues beyond the falls, where they "found the passes of the Missouri between some mountains, and the Missouri is the discharge of the lake of which they know not the extent." This idea of the

Missouri being the outlet of a large lake Stuart supposes arose from the fact that the Flathead tribe, whom
the La Vérendryes met lower down the river, had told
them that they went up the river when returning to
their country, and that in their country was a very large
lake. It might also be noted that this supposititious lake
appeared repeatedly, before La Vérendrye's explorations, both in narratives and on French maps, sometimes alone, sometimes in conjunction with the "Shining
Mountains" or the "Mountains of Bright Stones." Its
proportions vary according to the imagination of the
writer or map-maker, from quite a small lake to a
boundless sea. Bougainville in his memoir also describes the route followed by La Vérendrye and his
brother, and mentions the tribes they encountered along
their route.

Mr. Stuart shows a great deal of ingenuity in identifying the tribes mentioned by La Vérendrye, by
Coquard, and by Bougainville, with those of more
recent times, and from the known habitat of these
tribes toward the latter end of the eighteenth century
he draws some interesting conclusions as to the regions
traversed by the La Vérendryes on their western
journey. It is important to add that Mr. Stuart was
himself thoroughly familiar with all this western country,
and with the tribes who inhabited it during the last
century. His identification of the route of the French
explorers is therefore entitled to a good deal of weight.
Much depends, however, on the authority that may
properly be attached to the evidence of Coquard and

Bougainville. Coquard is known to have been personally acquainted with La Vérendrye and his sons, and it is probable that Bougainville was also. It is therefore not unreasonable to assume that the information which they give, and which in a measure is supplementary to the original narrative of La Vérendrye, may have been obtained at first hand from the explorers themselves. In any event, whether we may or may not concede to the sons of La Vérendrye the honour of having traced the Missouri into the very heart of the Rocky Mountains, they may at least be credited with having reached a spur of the mountains ; and that, in view of their very small party and the difficulties they had to surmount, was no ordinary achievement.

Upon the return of the two brothers to Fort La Reine, they had an opportunity of discussing with their father the possibilities of the Missouri as a route to the sea. The hostility of some of the western tribes, however, and the danger, as they thought, of getting within territory claimed and controlled by the Spaniards, deterred them from making any further attempt in this direction. They therefore abandoned the south-western route, and turned their attention to the north-west, where another great river offered a tempting passage to the Western Sea. The history of this new project will be more conveniently dealt with in another chapter.

CHAPTER IV

FRENCH EXPLORERS ON THE SASKATCHEWAN

IN the last chapter the explorations of La Vérendrye and his sons have been traced from Lake of the Woods down the Winnipeg River to Lake Winnipeg, thence up the Red River, and its tributary the Assiniboine, and overland to the upper waters of the Missouri, and finally to the eastern slope of the Rocky Mountains. These explorations covered the years 1732 to 1743. At some time during the latter part of this decade one of La Vérendrye's sons discovered the Saskatchewan. Some of the journals are missing for this period, so that it is impossible to fix the exact year of the discovery or the circumstances which attended it. All that is known is what is contained in a later memoir giving a brief account of the discoveries made by La Vérendrye and his sons in the west. From this, and from their maps of the western country, it appears that before the year 1738 they had discovered not only Lake Winnipeg, but also Lake Manitoba, which La Vérendrye called Lac des Prairies. About the year 1741 they had established a post, Fort Dauphin, on the western side of this lake. About this time they seem

A NORTH-WEST VIEW OF PRINCE OF WALES'S FORT IN HUDSON BAY, NORTH AMERICA,
BY SAMUEL HEARNE, 1777

also to have explored the northern part of Lake Winnipeg, and knew from the Indians of its connection with Hudson Bay by way of the Nelson River.

Whether the Saskatchewan was first discovered by way of Lake Winnipeg, or by way of Lake Manitoba and Lake Winnipegosis, is not very clear. At any rate, it had been discovered, and explored up to the Forks between 1740 and 1750. In a map of the latter year prepared from information supplied by La Vérendrye, the Saskatchewan is shown under the name Poskaiao, and branching off from the Poskaiao is another river called the Rivière des Cristinaux flowing into Hudson Bay, an English fort being shown at its mouth. The river is evidently intended to represent the Churchill and the waterways connecting it with the Saskatchewan, while the English fort is Prince of Wales. Near the mouth of the Saskatchewan is shown a French post, Fort Bourbon. The sites of both Fort Bourbon and Fort Dauphin were known to the Canadian traders who traversed this part of the country immediately after the cession of Canada to England. Alexander Henry the elder says, in his *Travels*, that Fort Bourbon was situated at the north end of Lake de Bourbon, now Cedar Lake. Elsewhere he says : " We passed old Fort Bourbon, near which we entered one of the channels of the Saskatchewan."

Henry speaks in his narrative of several other French forts, traces of which were still to be seen when he ascended the Saskatchewan in 1808. At the mouth of the Montagne du Pas or Pasquia River, where a post of the Hudson's Bay Company was established many years later, he found the remains of an old French fort, and the trails leading to it were still visible. This was the Fort Poskoia built by the Chevalier de La Vérendrye over half a century before. It was a general rendez-vous for the Indians before small-pox decimated the tribes.

Farther up the river Henry passed the site of another French post, on the south side of the Saskatchewan, known as Nepawee or Nipawi. James Finlay, first of the Montreal traders to reach the Saskatchewan, wintered a little above Nipawi in 1767. Sir Alexander Mackenzie refers to this old French fort, and writes as if it were still in operation at the time of the cession of Canada in 1763.

Henry again speaks of another French post above Nipawi, which he calls Fort St. Louis. " It stands," he says, "in a low bottom, south side. At this place, some years ago, were to be seen agricultural instruments and remains of carriage wheels. Their road to the open plains is still to be seen, winding up a valley on the south side." Mackenzie also speaks of the marks of agricultural instruments and wheel carriages, but in connection with the Nipawi post. There is no record of such a fort having been built by any of the La Vérendryes. Mr. C. N. Bell, of the Manitoba Historical and Scientific Society, says that it was built by De La Corne, who commanded the western posts after Saint-Pierre. This fort, according to Dr. Elliott Coues, was situated about twelve miles in an air line below the

Forks of the Saskatchewan.   The Hudson's Bay Company afterward built a fort on the same spot.   It was named Fort à la Corne.   Probably the name had been applied by the French to the earlier establishment, and was transferred by the English traders to their own post.   It is said to have been in operation in 1858, and in fact is marked on recent maps of the Canadian Geological Survey.

Now as to the location of these two French posts.

First, as to Nipawi.   Mackenzie places it in long. 103°. Dr. James Bain, the editor of Alexander Henry's Journal, makes it a little west of 104°.   Mathew Cocking, of the Hudson's Bay Company, ascending the Saskatchewan in 1772, passed an old trading house "belonging to the French pedlars before the conquest of Quebec."   This fort, evidently Nipawi, was about one hundred miles above The Pas, or the site of Fort Poskoia.   This would make its position about where Mackenzie has it. Cocking passed Finley's, or Finlay's, House about ten miles above Nipawi.

Then as to the upper French post, Fort St. Louis, des Prairies, or La Corne.   As already mentioned, Dr. Coues estimated that this fort must have been about twelve miles in an air line below the Forks.   It so appears, or rather its modern equivalent, on several recent official maps.   According to Alexander Henry, Fort des Prairies was almost immediately below the Forks.   Cocking makes it one hundred and fifty miles above The Pas, or about fifty miles above Nipawi.   This brings it considerably below the position as given by

Henry and Dr. Coues. Either the French post passed by Cocking must have been one of which no mention is elsewhere made, or else Fort St. Louis was lower down the river than has hitherto been supposed. But to return.

The elder La Vérendrye, having ascertained through his son the course of the Saskatchewan, and realizing its importance as a route to the Western Sea, returned to Quebec to make one final appeal to the Government for financial assistance. He lingered on, month after month, hoping against hope that a generous impulse might visit those in authority. Finally he made up his mind to return to the west, with such supplies as he could beg or borrow, and complete the object of his life's work, trusting to a kind Providence to see him through.

One ray of sunshine now appeared, to brighten what proved to be the closing days of his life; one tardy act of justice in a lifetime of injustice, calumny, and mis-representation. The King and his ministers had at last been brought to see the purity of his motives and the genuineness of his patriotism. La Vérendrye was given the rank of captain, and decorated with the coveted Cross of St. Louis. At the same time he was authorized by Galissonière, who had succeeded Beau-harnois as Governor, to resume his explorations—at his own expense.

La Vérendrye needed no urging. The King's belated recognition was better far than gold. He would find the Western Sea now at all hazards. But he reckoned without the one insurmountable obstacle. His iron constitution, overtaxed for years to meet the demands of an indomitable spirit, at last rebelled. His health was breaking down, irretrievably, as the result of years of exposure and hardship.

In September, 1749, he writes this characteristic letter to Maurepas—the last public act of the great explorer :—

" I take the liberty of tendering you my very humble thanks for having been pleased to procure for me from His Majesty the Cross of St. Louis, and for two of my children their promotion. My ambition, coupled with my gratitude, induces me to set out next spring, honoured with the orders of Monsieur the Marquis de la Jonquière our general, to look after the posts and explorations in the west, which have been suspended for several years. I have sent to Monsieur the Marquis de la Jonquière a map and memorandum of the course I must follow for the present. Monsieur the Comte de la Galissonière has like ones. I will keep a very exact account of the course from the entrance of the territories unto the boundaries unto which I and my children may attain. I cannot leave Montreal except during the month of May next, at which season navigation is open to the upper countries. I intend making all haste possible so as to winter at Fort Bourbon, which is the last on the lower part of *Rivière aux Biches* of all the forts I have established ; most happy if, as the outcome of all the trials, fatigues, and risks I have undergone in this protracted exploration, I could succeed in proving to you my unselfishness, my great ambition, as well as that of my children, for the glory of the King and the welfare of the Colony."

Three months after this letter was written La Vérendrye died. First and always a man of action, while others talked of the Western Sea and wrote learned memoirs as to the best means of reaching it overland, he set out to find a way, devoting to the task not one or two years, but his lifetime. In his singleness of purpose, his devotion to duty, his resourcefulness, his power of rising superior to all obstacles, and his extraordinary perseverance, he bore a striking resemblance to that other great explorer Vitus Bering, who almost at the same time was toiling slowly and painfully across the vast, dreary wastes of Siberia, toward the same goal. That La Vérendrye left his work unfinished is no cloud upon his fame. Had he lived, and especially had his Government given him even the most moderate support, he and his intrepid sons would without doubt have forced their way across the continent to the shores of the far-off Pacific.

After the death of their father, the younger La Vérendryes sought permission to return to the west and take up their father's unfinished task. They appealed earnestly to the Governor, La Jonquière, but without avail. La Jonquière, who had not dared to thwart the father in his hour of triumph, had no hesitation in denying the sons. He already had his greedy eye on the profits of the fur trade, and had determined to send friends of his own to the west to reap where the La Vérendryes had sown; ostensibly to continue the search for the Western Sea, but in reality chiefly to exploit the fur trade. The La Vérendryes were not merely refused permission to continue their explorations, but were not even given an opportunity of securing their personal property and supplies in the forts which they had themselves constructed. These forts, with all they contained, were now turned over to Captain Jacques Repentigny Legardeur de Saint-Pierre, a brave but not over-scrupulous officer, who was directed to use them as bases of supply for his explorations toward the Western Sea.

It would be unjust to Legardeur de Saint-Pierre to say that he went to the west with no serious thought of exploration. He was a better man than the Governor who had sent him, and in spite of his gross injustice to the La Vérendryes there is reason to believe that he had every intention of finding a way across the continent. He knew, however, little or nothing of the difficulties to be overcome; he had no knowledge of the geography of the west, and scorned to accept the guidance of those who alone could have set him right; and he showed himself quite incapable of handling the western tribes. As a result he himself added nothing to what was already known of the western country.

Under instructions from La Jonquière, Saint-Pierre left Montreal in 1750 and proceeded to Michilimakinac. The manuscript of his journal is very much defaced, and many of the dates are undecipherable. After a short stay at Michilimakinac to give his men a rest, he pushed on to Grand Portage, and Fort St. Pierre on Rainy Lake. "This," he says, "is the first of the western posts." He found the route from Lake Superior to Rainy Lake very difficult. "Bad as I had imagined the roads, I was surprised at the reality. There are thirty-eight carrying-places; the first of these is four leagues [that is, the Grand Portage], and the least of all the others is a quarter of a league. The remainder of the road [before him] was not more attractive; on the contrary, I was assured it was infinitely worse, besides being dangerous. In fact, I had time to feel that there was the constant risk of not only losing goods and provisions, but even life itself." La Vérendrye had been over this same route time and again, but there is not one word in his narratives about the dangers and difficulties of the way. He cared nothing for natural obstacles; it was the opposition of those who should have supported him that embittered the great explorer.

At Fort St. Pierre, Saint-Pierre gathered all the surrounding Indians together and harangued them on the iniquity of their conduct in waging war against the Sioux. The Crees listened to him patiently, but it was not long before he noticed that they were becoming unsettled and impertinent, which he attributed to "the too great indulgence with which they had been treated." Continuing his journey, he reached Fort St. Charles on the Lake of the Wood, and descended Winnipeg River to Fort Maurepas. Provisions were so scarce at both these posts that the whole party suffered great privations. Saint-Pierre spent the winter probably at Fort Maurepas, and in 1751 went on to Fort La Reine on the Assiniboine, which he made his head-quarters.

Meanwhile he had sent the Chevalier de Niverville to the Saskatchewan with instructions to push his discoveries up that river beyond the farthest point reached by the La Vérendryes. Winter had set in before De Niverville set forth on his journey, and he travelled over the snow and ice with toboggans. He was obliged to cache part of his provisions in the woods, and before reaching Fort Pascoya he and his men were at the point of starvation, their only resource having been a few fish caught through the ice. De Niverville was taken ill and had to remain behind at Fort Paskoya, while ten of his men went forward in the spring of 1751, in two canoes.

These men, it is said, ascended the river as far as the Rocky Mountains, where they built a stockaded fort, named Fort La Jonquière after the Governor of that name. De Niverville was to have followed in a few weeks, but his illness proved too serious. Apparently he did finally reach the fort, for toward the end of Saint-Pierre's memoir, from which these particulars are taken, it is said: " M. de Niverville . . . gave me an account of what he had learned at the settlement he had made near the Rocky Mountains."

The exact whereabouts of Fort La Jonquière has been the subject of some speculation. All that Saint-Pierre tells us is that the fort was on the Paskoya or Saskatchewan River, three hundred leagues above Fort Paskoya, and at or near the Rocky Mountains. There is nothing in his memoir to indicate whether it was built on the North or the South Saskatchewan ; nothing,

274 THE SEARCH FOR THE WESTERN SEA

that is to say, except a random word or two, which
may, however, have a good deal of significance. Speaking of his projected discoveries in the west, and of the
courses to be followed in pursuing these explorations,
he says: "I had only to fear landing at Hudson Bay,
which I had fully determined to avoid by turning to the
west, in order to find the sources of the Missouri River,
in the hope that they would lead me to some rivers
having their course in the part to which I sought to
penetrate." Presuming that De Niverville was instructed to this effect, what course would he follow
when he came to the parting of the ways at the forks of
the Saskatchewan? Obviously the south branch, which
would lead him away from Hudson Bay, and toward
the sources of the Missouri. In Bougainville's Memoir
on the French Posts, Fort Lajonquière appears under
the name "Des Prairies." This would be a more
appropriate title for a fort situated on the South Saskatchewan than for one on the North Saskatchewan,
which flows not through level plains, but through a
partially wooded country; though it must be admitted
that in the west the term "prairie" was loosely applied
to all the open country between Lake Winnipeg and
the mountains.

Dr. Coues suggests the south branch, but very
cautiously: "The French are said to have ascended the
South Branch in 1752 [St. Pierre's memoir shows clearly
that it was in 1751], when Fort Jonquière is supposed to
have been built by St. Pierre at the foot of the Rocky
Mountains, perhaps at or near present Calgary on Bow

river." This was the view also taken by Masson, who says: "En 1752, quelques années seulement avant la conquête, un parent de M. de La Vérandrye, M. de Niverville, établissait le fort Jonquière au pied des montagnes, à l'endroit même où, plus d'un siècle après, le capitaine Brisebois, de la police à cheval, fondait un poste qui porta, pendant quelques mois, le nom de son fondateur, et se nomme aujourd'hui Calgary." Brisebois told Benjamin Sulte, the Canadian historian, some years ago, that he had found traces of the spot mentioned of what he believed to be Fort Lajonquière.

On the other hand, J. B. Tyrrell, of the Geological Survey, and James White, Geographer of the Department of the Interior, incline to the north branch, on the ground that the Indians along that branch were known to be friendly to the French, while the tribes on the plains to the south-west about the head-waters of the South Saskatchewan, notably the Blackfeet, were fierce and hostile. Against this view there is the decisive fact that in 1754–5, within three or four years of the date of De Niverville's expedition, Anthony Hendry, of the Hudson's Bay Company, travelled from York Factory to the Saskatchewan, and thence to the country south-west of Red Deer River, where he was received in a very friendly manner by the Blackfeet, and remained there throughout the winter. On the whole, although positive evidence one way or the other is lacking, the balance tends toward the South Saskatchewan. Nevertheless it is, to say the least, extraordinary that when Hendry was among the Blackfeet they should have told him nothing of such an important event. Certainly there is not a word in his journal to indicate the existence of a French fort anywhere on the South Saskatchewan, or even the presence of French explorers in the Blackfeet country.

Difficult as it is to determine upon which branch Fort La Jonquière was built, it is even more difficult to say how near, or far, from the Rocky Mountains it stood. Saint-Pierre says that he sent De Niverville to make an establishment at three hundred leagues higher than that of Paskoya; and later he says: "The order which I gave to the Chevalier de Niverville to establish a post three hundred leagues above that of Paskoya was executed on the 29th May, 1751"; and he adds the significant bit of information that the men who had been sent "ascended the river Paskoya as far as the Rocky Mountains." The fact that in his instructions to De Niverville Saint-Pierre says nothing of the mountains, and seems to have contemplated merely the establishment of a post far out on the plains which would serve as a convenient base for further discoveries toward the west, and incidentally, no doubt, as a centre of the fur trade, lends importance to the subsequent statement that in carrying out his instructions the men had ascended the river as far as the Rocky Mountains. There is, however, another point to consider. Saint-Pierre says that the new fort was built three hundred leagues above Paskoya. The French league was about equal to two and a half English miles. Fort La Jonquière was consequently seven hundred and fifty miles from Paskoya, and eight hundred and sixty miles from the mouth of the Saskatchewan, assuming Saint-Pierre's three hundred leagues to be approximately correct. This would put the fort not much above the confluence of the Bow and Belly rivers. This is on the assumption that the explorers ascended the south branch. If, on the other hand, they ascended the North Saskatchewan, Fort La Jonquière would be some distance below the town of Edmonton. All this, however, is hypothetical.

Saint-Pierre brings up an interesting point, in the course of his narrative. " I set myself," he says, " to obtain as much knowledge as possible from the most experienced Indians, to find out if there were not some river which led elsewhere than to Hudson Bay. At first they said they knew of none. However, an old Indian of the nation of the Kinougeouilini assured me that a short time before an establishment had been made at a great distance from them, where they go to trade ; that the merchandise brought there is almost similar to that of Canada ; that they are not absolute English ; he rather thinks they are French, but they are not altogether so white as we are ; that the road they take to go to them is directly towards where the sun sets in the month of June, which I have estimated to be West-North-West." Again, Saint-Pierre says that De Niverville confirmed this story of the old Indian. De Niverville learned at Fort Lajonquière that a war party had met with a party of Indians of another tribe, loaded with beaver skins. These strange Indians told them that they were on their way, by a river which issued from the Rocky Mountains, to trade with white men—French, as they supposed—who had their first establishment on an island at a small distance from the land, where there was a large storehouse. They said that when they arrived at their destination, they made signals, and the people came to them to trade. In exchange for their beaver skins they gave them knives, a few lances, but no fire-arms. They also sold them horses and saddles. These Indians positively asserted that the white traders were not English, and, adds Saint-Pierre, as the establishment is by compass west-by-west (he probably meant to say, west-by-north), it cannot possibly belong to them.

Parkman characterizes these as idle stories, but it is quite possible that they had some foundation in fact. They point to a trading post somewhere on the Pacific coast, reached by a river flowing west from the Rocky Mountains. In one case Saint-Pierre gives the direction as west-north-west, and in the other as "west-by-west" or, as suggested, west-by-north. This would seem to indicate a Russian establishment on the north-west coast. The reference to horses and saddles, however, suggests one of the Spanish settlements toward the south-west.

Saint-Pierre's experience with the western tribes was in striking contrast with that of the La Vérendryes, and in itself marked him as incapable of successfully prosecuting any explorations through their lands. La Vérendrye and his sons possessed that faculty, so strikingly revealed by nearly all French explorers in the New World, of winning the confidence of the Indians, and as a result their long residence in the west was marked by but one act of treachery on the part of the Indians, and that clearly arose from a misunderstanding. Saint-Pierre, on the other hand, treated the Indians with a high - handedness which defeated all his plans for western discovery. His difficulties finally culminated in an incident which very nearly cost him his life. The story cannot be better told than in his own words.

"On the 22nd of February, 1752, about nine o'clock in the morning, I was at this post [Fort La Reine] with five Frenchmen. I had sent the rest of my people, consisting of fourteen persons, to look for provisions, of which I had been in need for several days. I was sitting quietly in my room, when two hundred Assinipoels entered the fort, all of them being armed. These Indians scattered immediately all through the house ; several of them entered my room, unarmed ; others remained in the fort. My people came to warn me of the behaviour of these Indians. I ran to them and told them sharply that they were very forward to come to my house in a crowd, and armed. One of them answered in Christinaux, that they came to smoke. I told them that that was not the proper way to take, and that they must retire at once. I believe that the firmness with which I spoke somewhat intimidated them, especially as I had put four of the most resolute out of the door, without them saying a word. I went at once to my room, but at that very moment a soldier came to tell me that the guard-house was full of these Indians, who had taken possession of the arms. I ran to the guard-house and demanded from them, through a Christinaux, who was in my service as interpreter, what were their views. During this time I was preparing to fight them with my weak force. My interpreter, who betrayed me, said that these Indians had no bad intentions, at the very time an Assinipoel orator, who had been constantly making fine speeches to me, had told the interpreter that in spite of him his nation would kill and rob me. I had scarcely made out their intentions than I forgot it was necessary to take the arms from them. I seized hold of a blazing brand, broke in the door of the powder magazine, knocked down a barrel of powder, over which I passed the brand, telling the Indians in an assured tone that I expected nothing at their hands, and that in dying I would have the glory of subjecting them to the same fate. No sooner had the·Indians seen my lighted brand and my barrel of powder with its head staved in, and heard my interpreter, than they all fled out of the gate of the fort, which they damaged considerably in their hurried flight. I soon gave up my brand, and had nothing more urgent to do than to close the gate of the fort."

Saint-Pierre finally came to the conclusion that it was not possible to make any further discoveries toward the Western Sea on account of the hostility of the Indians. He complains that all the tribes were engaged in war, and that they were incited thereto by the English. "It is evident," says he, "that so long as these Indians trade with the English, there is no ground for the hope of succeeding in the discovery of the Western Sea. I believe I may even say, without risking too much, that they were the indirect authors of the ill-feeling of the Indians, and chiefly of my adventure." He thinks that if there were no English establishments at Hudson Bay, it would be an easy matter to discover a way to the Western Sea; but so long as the English were entrenched on the bay, and were in a position to incite the Indians against the French, it was useless to attempt any further explorations. He hints gently that in the event of an expedition being sent north to capture the Hudson Bay posts, his knowledge would be of great service should he be placed in charge of the expedition.

Saint-Pierre had been over three years in the west, and yet in all that time never got farther than Fort La Reine. Yet La Jonquière had ignored the claims of the sons of La Vérendrye, and recommended Saint-Pierre to the French minister as one who knew the west " better than any officer in all the colony."

In August, 1763, Saint-Pierre handed over the command of the western posts to De La Corne, in accordance with the instructions of the Marquis Du Quesne, who had succeeded La Jonquière as Governor of the colony. De La Corne seems to have done even less than Saint-Pierre for the cause of western exploration. Nothing in fact except the fort which he is credited with having built on the Saskatchewan in 1753.

It will be convenient here to sum up the results of

French exploration west of Lake Superior, up to the close of the French regime in Canada. Within this period French explorers had ascended the Kaministikwia River and discovered Rainy Lake and Lake of the Woods. They had discovered the Grand Portage route. They had descended the Winnipeg River to Lake Winnipeg. From there they had explored the Red River up to the mouth of the Assiniboine, and possibly as far south as the international boundary. They had ascended the Assiniboine, and crossed the open prairies to the Missouri. They had explored the valley of the Missouri westward to the Rocky Mountains, or at any rate to the eastern spur of those mountains. From the Assiniboine, or from Lake Winnipeg, they had discovered lakes Manitoba, Winnipegosis, and Dauphin. Finally, they had discovered the Saskatchewan, and followed one of the branches of that great river, if not to the Rocky Mountains, at least to a point far out on the western plains. In the group of French explorers who devoted themselves to this great task, La Vérendrye and his sons stand unquestionably first from every point of view. They must always be regarded as the true discoverers of the great north-west. Their hard-won achievements made possible the further discoveries toward the Western Sea under the British regime in Canada, the story of which is now to be told.

We get one last fleeting glimpse of the French posts in the far west in a dispatch from Sir Guy Carleton to Lord Shelburne, dated at Quebec, 2nd March, 1768. This dispatch was accompanied by a map showing the western posts occupied by the French at the time of the conquest, but unfortunately the map, which from an historical point of view would have been both interesting and valuable, has been lost. It was apparently based on the maps, memoirs, and relations of La Vérendrye, Saint-Pierre, and other western explorers. Carleton questions the accuracy of the distances as mentioned or laid down in these documents, as, so far as his knowledge went, none of the French officers engaged in western exploration understood the use of any mathematical instrument. But, he says, they all agree that Fort Pascoyat (as he spells it) is two and a half or three months' journey beyond Michilimakinac, and reckon the distance about nine hundred leagues, which seemed to Carleton probably far beyond the true distance, as the explorers followed the serpentine course of lakes and rivers. He reports that the river on which Pascoyat stands is said to be five hundred leagues long, or about twelve hundred and fifty miles. Here at least the French explorers, if they were not merely guessing, showed remarkable accuracy, the actual length of the Saskatchewan being, as already mentioned, about twelve hundred and five miles. Carleton speaks of a fort that had been built one hundred leagues beyond Pascoyat. This is apparently Fort Lajonquière, and if the distance is correct, that fort could not have been anywhere near the Rocky Mountains. It would not, in fact, have been west of the province of Saskatchewan, which would fit in with Saint-Pierre's statement that the Christinaux and

Assinipoels were to meet him at this post, and accompany him in further explorations toward the west.

Carleton annexes to his dispatch a return of the French posts in the west, with the troops employed for the protection of trade, and the number of canoes sent up in the year 1754. The posts west of Lake Superior are grouped together, as in Bougainville's memoir, under the general name of *Mer l'Ouest.*

CHAPTER V

JONATHAN CARVER POINTS THE WAY

IN actual exploration Jonathan Carver accomplished comparatively little, but his ambitious project of an overland journey to the Pacific is of interest as the first attempt on the part of the new proprietors of Canada to realize the dream of French explorers, and it may be conveniently considered here as it immediately preceded, and foreshadowed, the long story of the exploration of the west by British fur traders. Carver's *Travels* is an entertaining though untrustworthy narrative, worthy to take its place between the equally entertaining and untrustworthy narratives of the Baron de Lahontan and Father Hennepin.

Jonathan Carver was born at Canterbury, Connecticut. The date of his birth is not known,[1] but he married Abigail Robbins in 1746, by whom he had

---

[1] The place and date of Carver's birth have been the subject of much speculation. In the preface to the third edition (1781) of the *Travels*, he is said to have been born at Stillwater, Connecticut, in the year 1732, and to have been the grandson of the first Royal Governor of the Colony of Connecticut. In Appleton's *Cyclopædia of American Biography* the place of his birth is given as Stillwater, New York. Rev. Samuel Peters, the Connecticut historian, in a deposition made in 1824, states positively that Carver was born at Canterbury, Connecticut. Dr. Peters himself was born near the same town. Later investigations by Prof. E. G. Bourne disclose the interesting facts that there is no Stillwater in Connecticut; and that Stillwater, New York, was not settled until 1750.

seven children. He commanded a company of provincial troops in the expedition against Quebec. Upon the establishment of peace by the Treaty of Paris in 1763, Carver determined to turn his energies into another channel. Having, as he modestly puts it, rendered his country some service during the war, he bethought that he might add an even more signal service by contributing, as much as lay in his power, to make that vast acquisition of territory gained by Great Britain in North America advantageous to the nation.

In the Introduction to his *Travels through the Interior Parts of North America* he says that what he chiefly had in view, after gaining a knowledge of the manners, customs, languages, soil, and natural productions of the different nations that inhabited the "back of the Mississippi," was to ascertain the breadth of that vast continent which extends from the Atlantic to the Pacific, in its broadest part between 43° and 46° northern latitude. Had he been successful in this exploration, he intended to have proposed to Government the establishment of a post in some of those parts about the Straits of Anian, which, having been discovered by Sir Francis Drake, of course belonged to the English. So Carver thought, at any rate. The mythical Straits of Anian still figured prominently in the supposititious geography of North America; and the discovery of a north-west passage was the dream of many explorers and geographers. Carver was convinced that if his plan could have been carried out it would greatly have facilitated the discovery of a north-west passage, which had been so often sought without success. He adds, with a good deal of sound common sense, that the establishment of a British settlement on the north-west coast of North America would not only disclose new sources of trade and promote many useful discoveries, but would open a passage for conveying intelligence to China and the English settlements in the East Indies, with greater expedition than a tedious voyage by the Cape of Good Hope or the Straits of Magellan. Could Carver have lifted the veil of the future, he would have seen his dream amply fulfilled.

Carver complains, with *naïveté*, of the artfulness of the French in keeping other nations in ignorance of the geography and resources of the western country which they had explored and taken possession of. To accomplish their design, he says (though it is difficult to suppose on what authority) that the French published inaccurate maps and false accounts. The French maps were scarcely more inaccurate than his own, and it is altogether probable that in both cases the inaccuracy proceeded from the same cause—lack of information, or perhaps a too ready and literal interpretation of Indian exaggerations. However, they seemed to Carver obstacles maliciously raised by the French in the path of his projected exploration. He makes much of these imaginary difficulties, but it is abundantly clear from his map that he had no conception of the very real difficulties that he would have to surmount before he could hope to stand upon the shores of the Pacific.

Leaving Boston in 1766, he proceeded by way of Michilimakinac, Green Bay, the Fox and Wisconsin rivers, to the Mississippi, then up the Mississippi to the mouth of the St. Pierre. He asserts that he ascended the St. Pierre for two hundred miles to the country of the Naudowessies of the Plains or Sioux, but his statement has not been received without question. William H. Keating, in his account of Long's expedition to the source of St. Peter's River in 1823, challenges the accuracy of the above statement, as well as of Carver's further assertion that he resided five months among this tribe. Keating believes that he ascended the Mississippi to the Falls of St. Anthony, that he saw the St. Peter, and may even perhaps have entered it, but "had he resided five months in the country, and become acquainted with their language, it is not probable that he would have uniformly applied to them the term of Naudowessies, and omitted calling them the Dakota Indians, as they styled themselves." One might as well say that Champlain could never have been in the Iroquois country, or come into contact with members of that remarkable confederacy, because he calls them the Iroquois, while they called themselves the Ho-de-no-sau-nee. Similarly it would be clear that Franklin or Richardson could not have had any first-hand knowledge of the Eskimo, or they would have called them Innuits. The same thing applies to many other tribes. Keating's argument is extraordinary. It does not seem to have occurred to him that a remote tribe is first known to the outside world not by the name adopted by the tribe, but by the name current among the neighbouring tribes; and that a traveller visiting this tribe for the first time is much more likely to use the name with which he is already familiar than what may be called the domestic name. Keating suggests a number of other reasons for discrediting Carver's account of his journey up St. Peter's River to the land of the Sioux. Carver exaggerated the width and depth of the river, but Keating admits that he may have seen the river at a time when it was unusually high. He admits also that Carver's vocabulary was taken from the Dakota language, and yet goes out of his way to suggest that " it may have been obtained from the Indians along the banks of the Mississippi," or " more probably copied from some former traveller." There are many points about Carver's narrative that are open to question, but there does not seem to be any substantial reason for doubting his statement that he ascended St. Peter's River to the Sioux country, though he may have exaggerated the distance.

Carver's plan was to continue up the St. Pierre to its head-waters, where, according to Indian report, a short portage would bring him to the head-waters of another river flowing westward to the Pacific. The route was a delightfully simple one, on paper, and it is unfortunate that Carver found no opportunity of testing it. While at Michilimakinac he had obtained from Mr. Rogers, the officer in charge, a scanty supply of goods to use as presents to the Indians in his proposed journey, and a further supply was to be sent on to him

U

at the Falls of St. Anthony on the Mississippi. These goods, however, did not arrive, and he was reluctantly compelled to abandon the St. Pierre route, so inviting in its simplicity.

Being disappointed here, he determined to try another road. Returning to Prairie du Chien, he ascended the Mississippi and made his way to Lake Superior, through what was practically unknown territory, hoping at the Grand Portage to find traders who would supply him with the needed goods. If he could have secured these, it was his purpose to attempt the northern route by way of Rainy Lake, Lake of the Woods, and Lake Winnipeg. From the latter he expected to ascend the Assiniboine to its head-waters, which, like those of the St. Pierre, he believed approached the westward-flowing river; and crossing over to this convenient stream, he anticipated no serious difficulty in completing his journey to the Pacific. The traders at Grand Portage unfortunately had no goods to spare, and as it would be madness to attempt a journey through unknown tribes without them, Carver reluctantly turned his steps homeward, paddling around the north shore of Lake Superior, and studying its peculiarities with a good deal of intelligence and accuracy.

He reached Michilimakinac in November, 1767, and spent the winter there, very agreeably as he says. He seems in fact to have thoroughly enjoyed himself, and found the traders congenial company. One wonders whom he met there. One of the leaders among the fur traders, Alexander Henry the elder, of whom a good deal will be heard presently, was at Michipicoten on the north shore of Lake Superior at the time Carver passed, and as Henry returned to Michilimakinac in the spring, while Carver says he did not leave that post until June, 1768, it is probable that they met. Unfortunately neither seems to have been sufficiently impressed with the other to mention him in his journal. It would have been interesting to compare Alexander Henry's impressions of Carver with Carver's impressions of Henry. Carver returned to Boston in October, 1768, having travelled, as he says, nearly seven thousand miles during his absence. From Boston he sailed to England the following year "to announce his discoveries." He did not entirely abandon the idea of crossing the continent after his unsuccessful attempts by way of the St. Pierre and Grand Portage. He mentions, toward the end of his book, that in the year 1774 Richard Whitworth, M.P. for Stafford, who is described as of an active, enterprising character, and possessing an extensive knowledge of geography, was so impressed with the feasibility of Carver's route to the Pacific, and the advantages to be derived from the establishment of a settlement on the north-west coast, that he had determined to make the attempt.

"He intended," says Carver, "to have pursued nearly the same route that I did; and after having built a fort at Lake Pepin, to have proceeded up the River St. Pierre, and from thence up a branch of the River Messorie, till having discovered the source of the Oregan, or River of the West, on the other side of the summit of the lands that divide the waters which run into the Gulf of Mexico from those that fall into the Pacific Ocean, he would have sailed down that river to the place where it is said to empty itself near the Straits of Anian.

" Having there established another settlement on some spot that appeared best calculated for the support of his people, in the neighbourhood of some of the inlets that trend toward the north-east, he would from thence have begun his researches. This gentleman was to have been attended in the expedition by Colonel Rogers, myself, and others, and to have taken out with him a sufficient number of artificers and mariners for building the forts and vessels necessary for the occasion, and for navigating the latter; in all not less than fifty or sixty men. The grants and other requisites for this purpose were even nearly completed when the present troubles in America began, which put a stop to an enterprise that promised to be of inconceivable advantage to the British dominions."

Convinced at last that Fate did not intend him to explore the great north-west, Carver abandoned the project to others. So sure was he that what he had planned would some day be accomplished, that he begs the future explorers not to forget him in their hour of triumph. "Whilst their spirits are elated with their success, perhaps they may bestow some commendations and blessings on the person who first pointed out to them the way. These, though but shadowy recompense for all my toil, I shall receive with pleasure."

Professor Bourne notes that when Carver sailed for

England in 1769 he carried with him a letter of introduction from Samuel Cooper, of Boston, to Benjamin
Franklin, who thanked his correspondent "for giving
me the opportunity of being acquainted with so great a
traveller." Oliver Wolcott, at that time Auditor of the
Treasury of the United States, in a letter to Jedediah
Morse, the geographer, dated 1792, expresses grave
doubts as to Carver's authorship of the *Travels*. "He
doubtless resided a number of years in the western
country, but was an ignorant man, utterly incapable of
writing such a book. When in England he was in
needy circumstances, and he applied to the government, stating that he had made important discoveries,
for which he was entitled to receive compensation. His
notes were inspected by a board, who pronounced them
to be unimportant. A sum of money was, however,
given him, more in charity to relieve his wants than as
a reward for important services. When his money was
expended he renewed his application, but was refused.
He then abused the administration for having obtained
of him his work without having paid a proper compensation. To silence his clamor, the notes which had
been deposited with the officers of the government
were restored, which were soon after pawned by Carver
with a bookseller. There is reason to suspect that the
book styled *Carver's Travels* is a mere compilation
from other books and common reports, supported by
some new remarks which Carver may possibly have
made."

Professor Bourne quotes Greenhow (*History of Oregon*)

stretch a point and call the redoubtable Arthur Dobbs a contemporary of Carver's.

Carver professes to have discovered a great geographical fact. Four great rivers, he says, take their rise within a few leagues of each other, nearly about the centre of the North American continent. These are: the River Bourbon or Nelson, which empties itself into Hudson Bay; the waters of the St. Lawrence, which find their way to the Atlantic; the Mississippi, which finally reaches the Gulf of Mexico; and the River Oregan or River of the West, that falls into the Pacific Ocean at the Straits of Anian.

Unfortunately for Carver, although there was a germ of truth in his theory, he was hopelessly at sea on a number of vital points, and in any event he had not even the merit of first putting it forth, for it had already been propounded, more than once, by French geographers and explorers. Like a good many other ingenious theories touching the geography of Western America, this one of the four great river systems probably grew out of the highly coloured and imperfectly understood yarns of the natives.

Examining Carver's map, with the help of his narrative, one can make a fairly close guess at his conception of the geography of North-Western America. Curiously enough, although he crowds on to his map nearly every erroneous idea that had so far been formulated as to the geographical features of the far west, he stumbled upon the truth in at least one important instance, for he shows an almost continuous water communication from the Mississippi on one side, and Lake Superior on the other, to the Pacific Ocean. He carries the Missouri only to a point south of Lake Winnipeg. Near the head-waters of the Missouri another river, which he calls the Mantons River (evidently he had heard of the Mandan tribe, or Mantannes, as La Vérendrye spelt the name), takes its source, and flows west into Pikes Lake. From this same lake, the River of the West flows through the heart of an immense valley, until finally it empties into the Pacific, at or near the Straits of Anian, a few miles north of Cape Blanco. The mouth of the River of the West, or the Strait of Anian—it is not quite clear which—is marked as discovered by Aguilar. In the text these parts are said to have been discovered by Drake. A little farther up the coast appears another entrance or strait, perhaps also part of the Strait of Anian, leading into the mythical Western Sea. As sometimes happens, to the confusion of historians, Carver's more or less imaginary coast-line corresponds quite closely with actual conditions. The last-mentioned strait, credited by Carver to Juan de Fuca, might easily be taken for that which now bears Juan de Fuca's name, and the more southerly entrance might be identified as the mouth of the Columbia. It is quite characteristic of Carver's credulity in geographical matters that he goes out of his way to replace on the map the discredited myth of a great inland Western Sea.

North of the Mississippi the map shows clearly enough the communication between Lakes Superior and Winni-

peg, although the distance is exaggerated. The Red
River is approximately correct, and the Assiniboine is
laid down as rising in the "Mountains of Bright Stones,"
and joining the Red River a few miles south of Lake
Winnipeg. These "Mountains of Bright Stones" form
one of the many versions of the Rocky Mountains,
as they were described to European travellers by the
western Indians. It is not to be wondered at that being
described to so many different travellers, by Indians of
various tribes, inhabiting widely separated regions, and
generally getting their information of the mountains
from the remote western tribes, very confused ideas
were entertained as to the character of the Rockies, and
they were for a long time conceived to be not one great
continental chain, but a number of distinct and more or
less remote mountains.

Following Lake Winnipeg to its northern end, the
Saskatchewan appears on the map in a rudimentary
form, under the name of White River, with the French
Fort Bourbon at its mouth. The Nelson is laid down
with approximate accuracy from Lake Winnipeg to
Hudson Bay. The Churchill appears farther north as
an insignificant stream; and some distance to the north-
westward of Lake Winnipeg is another large lake, unnamed, but probably representing Indian accounts of
Lake Athabaska, or possibly Reindeer Lake. From
this lake a river, called Rapid River, flows south-east
into Lake of the Forts (Split Lake) on the Nelson
River.

Carver here falls into the curious error, repeated on

one or two later maps, of crediting the upper waters of the Churchill to the Nelson, and emasculating the former. The error is readily explained. In Carver's day Lake Athabaska and its connecting rivers and lakes were known only by Indian report. The Indians of the Athabaska district on their way down to York Factory followed the waterways which connect the Upper Churchill with Split Lake, and in describing their route they would very readily give the impression that it constituted a branch of the Nelson. At the same time, as they did not use the Churchill to anything like the same extent as a route to the bay, they would ignore its communication with the great lakes of the far northwest. This false impression would not be weakened by passing through several Indian tribes before it reached Carver's ears.

Carver's treatment of the Rocky Mountains is in some ways the most interesting feature of his map. The " Mountains of Bright Stones," already mentioned, appear to the northward of the River of the West, while well to the south of that mighty but rather apocryphal stream are the "Snowy Mountains," lying, for some unexplained reason, east and west, parallel with the river. Another range is shown to the eastward of the "Snowy Mountains" in about the position of the Rockies. Through the vast valley of plain between the " Mountains of Bright Stones " and the " Snowy Mountains" flows the River of the West. Here, however, Carver's narrative corrects the map, for he says: " This extraordinary range of mountains is calculated to be more than three thousand miles in length, without any very considerable intervals, which I believe surpasses anything of the kind in the other quarters of the globe." Filled with the magnitude of his theme Carver rises to the heights of prophecy, and curiously enough his bombastic predictions, though nothing but guesswork, have been in a large measure fulfilled. "Probably in future ages," he exclaims, these mountains "may be found to contain more riches in their bowels than those of Indostan and Malabar, or that are produced on the golden coast of Guinea; nor will I except even the Peruvian mines. To the west of these mountains, when explored by future Columbuses or Raleighs, may be found other lakes, rivers, and countries, fraught with all the necessaries or luxuries of life; and where future generations may find an asylum, whether driven from their country by the ravages of lawless tyrants, or by religious persecutions, or reluctantly leaving it to remedy the inconveniences arising from a superabundant increase of inhabitants; whether, I say, impelled by these, or allured by hopes of commercial advantages, there is little doubt but their expectations will be fully gratified in these rich and unexhausted claimes." It is characteristic of the man and his point of view that he must look beyond the mountains for this wonderful land of promise, although he had himself travelled far and wide through a country of illimitable possibilities.

In Sir Guy Carleton's dispatch, referred to in the preceding chapter, an interesting project is outlined for an overland expedition to the Pacific—the first official suggestion of such an undertaking on the part of the English.

"I shall easily find in the troops here," he writes, "many officers and men very ready to undertake to explore any part of this continent, who require no other encouragement than to be told such service will be acceptable to the King, and if properly executed will recommend them to his favour; but as they are un-acquainted with the country, the Indian language and manners, 'tis necessary to join with them some Canadians, to serve as guides and interpreters. The gentlemen here are mostly poor and have families; in order to induce them to attach themselves thoroughly to the King's interests 'tis necessary they should be assured of their being taken into his Service for life, and in case they perish on these expeditions, that their widows will enjoy their pay, to support and educate their children.

"Should His Majesty think proper to allow the traders to go up to the western Lakes, as formerly, I think a party might winter in one of those posts, set out early in spring for the Pacific Ocean, find out a good port, take its latitude, longitude, and describe it so accurately as to enable our ships from the East Indies to find it out with ease, and then return the year follow-ing. Your Lordship will readily perceive the advantage of such discoveries, and how difficult attempts to explore unknown parts must prove to the English, unless we avail ourselves of the knowledge of the Canadians, who are well acquainted with the country, the language, and manner of the Natives."

Nothing apparently came of Carleton's proposal. Had the exploration been carried out, the political geography of North America might have been somewhat different from what subsequent events made it. The exploration was eventually accomplished, but not by British officers acting under official instructions. It was accomplished by fur traders, acting on their own responsibility, and with little or no encouragement from the Government.

CHAPTER VI

BRITISH TRADERS INVADE THE WEST

CANADA had scarcely been handed over to England before British traders began to make their way into the west by way of the Great Lakes, to reap the harvest of peltries for which French explorers and traders had sown the seed. Alexander Henry (the elder) reached Fort Michilimakinac on a trading expedition as early as 1761, and remained there long enough to narrowly escape death in the massacre of 1763. He tells the story of his dramatic escape and subsequent adventures in his *Travels*, and Parkman relates the same story, in his own inimitable way, in the *Conspiracy of Pontiac*. As Michilimakinac does not come within the scope of this book, however, it would be unnecessary to repeat the story here, even if it were not already so familiar. Some years later Alexander Henry will again be met with on the Saskatchewan, but before he reached the banks of that then remote river, other English traders had already penetrated beyond Lake Winnipeg.

Who the first British traders were that reached Lake Winnipeg from Lake Superior there is no certain means now of knowing. In a letter from Benjamin and Joseph Frobisher to General Haldimand—which will be referred to again—it is stated that the first adventurer went from Michilimakinac in the year 1765; that the Indians of Lake La Pluye or Rainy Lake, having been long destitute of goods, owing to the disorganization of French trade in the west after the surrender of Canada, stopped this adventurer and plundered his canoes, and would not suffer him to proceed further; that he attempted it again the year following, and met with the same bad fortune; that another attempt was made in 1767, goods being left at Rainy Lake to be traded with the natives, who permitted the adventurers to proceed with the remainder; and that the canoes on this occasion penetrated beyond Lake Winnipeg—how far, or in what direction, or who the traders were, the Frobishers do not say. Carver says that he met the traders at Grand Portage in the summer of 1767, and that these traders had already penetrated as far as Fort La Reine on the Assiniboine, where they traded with the Assiniboines and Crees.

Hitherto it has been supposed that none of the British traders from Montreal penetrated to the Saskatchewan before 1770, when Thomas Curry is said to have wintered on the shores of Cedar Lake, somewhere in the vicinity of La Vérendrye's Fort Bourbon. Mathew Cocking's journal of 1772, however, throws new light on the subject. In his journey of that year from York Factory to the Saskatchewan and the western plains, Cocking says under date of August 9th: "One Mr. Finley from Montreal resided in it [an old trading post on the banks of the Saskatchewan which he had passed that day] five years ago." This is no doubt the James

Finlay mentioned by Mackenzie in his *Account of the Rise, Progress, and Present State of the Fur Trade;* but Mackenzie makes Curry the pioneer on the Saskatchewan, and dates Finlay's arrival the following year. "Mr. James Finlay," he says, "was the first who followed Mr. Curry's example, and, with the same number of canoes, arrived, in the course of the next season, at Nipawee, the last of the French settlements on the bank of the Saskatchiwine River, in latitude nearly 43½° north [evidently a misprint for 53½°] and longitude 103° west; he found the good fortune, as he followed in every respect the example of, his predecessor." If Cocking is correct, and there is no reason for doubting his statement, James Finlay reached the Saskatchewan not later than 1767. Taken in conjunction with the statements of the Frobishers and Carver, it is evident that one at least of the unnamed adventurers who are said to have "penetrated beyond Lake Winnipeg" was James Finlay. It is quite possible that Thomas Curry accompanied Finlay on this expedition, as the Frobishers' letter speaks of more than one adventurer. These men, with the courage and enterprise that made Montreal traders such formidable competitors of the Hudson's Bay Company, broke down the barriers of native hostility, and made their way not only to the Assiniboine but also to the banks of the Saskatchewan. How formidable their competition became may be seen from a note appended to Cocking's journal, by Andrew Graham, at that time factor at York Factory. "Mr. Currie's encroachments," he says, "was the reason I sent Mr. Cocking inland." When Cocking reached the Saskatchewan, by way of Moose Lake, July 23rd, 1772, he notes in his journal: "The Pedlar Mr. Currie, who intercepted great part of York Fort trade this year, is one day's paddling below this river, at Cedar Lake." It was the amiable custom of the officers of the Hudson's Bay Company to refer to the Montreal traders as "pedlars."

As to the whereabouts of Finlay's trading establishment, Arrowsmith in his 1850 map shows Finlay's house a few miles below the Forks. Dr. James Bain says that Finlay's house was two or three miles west of the 104th degree west, at the site of the old French fort of Nipawi. Alexander Henry passed the site of Finlay's fort in 1776, and mentions in his narrative that Finlay was now stationed at Fort des Prairies, immediately below the Forks. Finlay is reputed to have made a small fortune in the fur trade, and finally returned to Montreal about 1785, to enjoy the fruits of his labours.

In June, 1775, Alexander Henry the elder (as he is generally called, to distinguish him from his nephew of the same name, whose voluminous journals the late Dr. Coues edited with such painstaking skill) reached Grand Portage. It is regrettable that neither Carver nor Henry has left any description of this famous rendezvous of the fur traders as it was in their day. Carver, in fact, applies the name only to the formidable nine-mile portage, and to all appearances no permanent establishment had been made at the landing-place until

x

ALEXANDER HENRY, ESQ.

Face p. 306

A clerk, a guide and four men are considered watch enough. These are Montreal *engagés* (known to the western traders as 'pork-eaters'). The North men— that is, the men engaged in the interior trade—while here live in tents of different sizes, pitched at random, the people of each post having a camp to themselves. Within the fort are sixteen buildings, with cedar and white spruce floors, squared timber frames, and shingle roofs. Six of these buildings are store-houses for merchandize and furs, etc. The rest are dwelling-houses, shops, compting-house, and mess-house. They have also a wharf for their vessel to load and unlode." This vessel, the first on Lake Superior, was built this same year, 1793.

Rev. George Bryce, in his *Mackenzie, Selkirk, Simpson*, gives a graphic picture of the site of Grand Portage as it appears to-day: " A few sunken timbers only are left in the water to represent the warehouses and wharves of this once thronged and important place." A solitary French fisherman is the only white inhabitant.

But to return to Henry and his western travels. In 1775 he entered what is now the Canadian North-West, crossing the height of land between Lake Superior and the Lake of the Woods by way of Grand Portage and the River au Groseilles,[1] as he calls it—now known as Pigeon River. The difficulties of the Grand Portage may be gathered from the fact that it took seven days of severe and unremitting toil to transport Henry's trading

---

[1] This name is supposed to have been given after Medart Chouart, the Sieur des Groseilliers, whose explorations with his brother-in-law Pierre Esprit Radisson are elsewhere mentioned.

goods and canoes from Lake Superior across the portage
to Pigeon River, the portage being designed to overcome
the formidable series of rapids which mark the lower
waters of that river. From Pigeon River their way lay
through numerous small lakes, over the height of land,
to Rainy Lake; thence by way of Rainy River to the
Lake of the Woods. Fort St. Charles, built by La
Vérendrye in 1732, seems to have been still standing
when Henry passed, or at least some portion of it, as he
speaks of an old French fort or trading house on the
west side of the lake.

Leaving Lake of the Woods, Henry descended the
Winnipeg River for about one hundred miles, where
the canoe route turns into the Pinawa River to avoid
the series of rapids that break this portion of the
Winnipeg. At Bonnet Lake he rejoined the main
stream, and followed it to its outlet into Lake Winnipeg.
Henry must have passed the site of La Vérendrye's
post, Fort Maurepas, shortly before entering the lake,
but makes no mention of it. The anonymous writer
quoted above was more observant. On the 30th
August, 1793, he notes in his journal that upon a high
round knoll near the last rapid and on the north-east
shore of the river stood a French fort, of which there
was now (1793) not a vestige remaining except the
clearing.[1]

---

[1] Thomas Jefferys, in his *Natural and Civil History of the French
Dominions*, gives a list of the French posts in the west at the time of the
conquest. Fort Maurepas is described as one hundred leagues distant from
Fort St. Charles, on Lake of the Woods, and near the head of the Lake
of Quinipigon.

Coasting along the east side of Lake Winnipeg, Henry reached the mouth of the Saskatchewan on the 1st of October. On the way north he had been overtaken by Peter Pond, and later by Joseph and Thomas Frobisher, all notable fur traders, of whom more will be heard presently. Pond had preceded Henry into the west. He was already in fact, in Henry's words, "a trader of celebrity in the north-west." It is clear from one of his maps that he had been on St. Peter's (Minnesota) River in 1774; and it appears from a statement of St. John de Crèvecoeur, who made a copy of this map for La Rochefoucauld, that Pond had gone into the west as early as 1768. The Frobishers too were no new-comers, Joseph having spent the previous year in a trading and exploring expedition north of the Saskatchewan. He had penetrated to the banks of the Churchill, by way of Sturgeon or Cumberland Lake, Sturgeon-Weir River, and Frog Portage, or as it was called in the early days of the fur trade, Portage de Traite. Near the portage he built a temporary post, *Frog Por* and had been extraordinarily successful in intercepting the Indians on their way down to the bay, and persuading them to exchange their peltries for his goods.

On the 26th October Henry reached Cumberland *Cumberland* House, built, as he says, by Samuel Hearne, in the previous year. Hearne "was now absent on his well-known journey of discovery"—which of course was entirely a mistake on Henry's part, Hearne having returned from his third and last journey to the far north in June, 1772, three years and more before Henry reached Cumberland House. It is rather singular that Dr. Coues, usually extremely accurate, should not only have allowed this statement to pass unchallenged, but should have repeated it, in his edition of the Henry and Thompson Journals. Henry found Cumberland House garrisoned by Scotchmen from the Orkney Islands, under the command of a Mr. Cockings,[1] by whom, though unwelcome guests, he and his men were treated with every civility.

On their way up the Saskatchewan the fur traders had stopped at a Cree encampment, at the mouth of the Pasquia River. The village consisted of thirty families, lodged in conical teepees of buffalo hide stretched upon poles twelve feet in length. On their arrival the chief, Chatique, came down to the shore attended by thirty followers, all armed with bows and arrows and spears. Chatique is described as a man of striking appearance, over six feet tall, somewhat corpulent, and, as Henry naively puts it, "of a very doubtful physiognomy." He invited the traders to his tent, and it was observed that he seemed particularly anxious to bestow his hospitalities on those who were the owners of goods. Henry suspected some evil design, but thought it wiser to go forward than to discover fear. They entered the lodge accordingly, where they were almost immediately surrounded by armed warriors.

Chatique arose with the gravity and dignity of his race. He was glad, he said, to see the white men. The

---

[1] No doubt the Mathew Cocking whose 1772 journey has been previously mentioned.

young men of his village, as well as himself, had long
been in want of many things of which he perceived the
traders were possessed in abundance. He was sure they
must be well aware of his power to prevent their going
further; that if they passed now, he could in any event
put them to death on their return; and under all the
circumstances, he expected them to be exceedingly
liberal in their presents. He added, to avoid any misunderstanding, that the presents must consist of three
casks of gunpowder, four bags of shot and ball, two
bales of tobacco, three kegs of rum, and three guns,
together with knives, flints, and some smaller articles.
He went on to say that he had met white men before,
and knew that they promised more than they performed; that with the number of men he had, he could
take the whole traders' property without their consent,
and that therefore his demands ought to be regarded as
very reasonable. He was, he said, a peaceable man,
and one of moderate views. He always preferred to
avoid quarrels. Finally he told the traders that they
must agree to his terms before they quitted their places.

With Henry in the lodge were the Frobishers, Peter
Pond, a trader named Cadotte, and one or two others.
They were hopelessly outnumbered, and there was
nothing for it but to comply with Chatique's demands.
As soon as the Indians had been assured that the
"presents" would be forthcoming the ceremonial pipe
was produced and handed round. The omission of this
ceremony when the traders first entered the lodge had
indeed, as Henry observes, been sufficient proof that

Chatique's intentions were not friendly, for according to the Indian code of honour nothing would be more unforgivable than treachery to a guest who had smoked the pipe of peace.

Having handed over the tribute demanded by Chatique, the traders departed. They had made but two miles, however, when they saw a canoe rapidly approaching from the village. It proved to be the insatiable Chatique. Pushing his canoe into the midst of the traders' fleet, he boarded one of the canoes, spear in hand, and demanded another keg of rum, threatening to put to death the first that opposed him. "We saw," says Henry, "that the only alternative was to kill this daring robber, or to submit to his exaction. The former part would have been attended by very mischievous consequences; and we therefore curbed our indignation, and chose the latter." On receiving the rum Chatique saluted them with the Indian cry, derisive enough as one may imagine, and departed.

On the face of it it seems monstrous that a party of white men should tamely submit to such an outrageous piece of extortion. It must not, however, be forgotten that the traders were but a handful of men in the midst of thousands of Indians, who only tolerated them for the sake of their tempting commodities. Had they killed a prominent chief like Chatique, it is doubtful whether any of their number would have got out of the country alive.

At Cumberland House the traders separated, Cadotte proceeding up the Saskatchewan to Fort des Prairies;

Peter Pond returning down the river on his way to Fort *Fort*
Dauphin, on the lake of the same name, where he
proposed to winter; and Henry with the Frobishers
and forty men in ten canoes paddling across Cumberland
Lake and up the Sturgeon-Weir River to Beaver Lake, *Bear*
where they decided to build a fort and spend the winter.
It seems extraordinary that Pond, after travelling all
the way from the lower end of Lake Winnipeg to
Cumberland House, should immediately retrace his
steps. To reach Lake Dauphin he would have to
return down the Saskatchewan to Cedar Lake, cross
what was afterwards known as Mossy Portage to Lake
Winnipegosis, and ascend Mossy River to Dauphin
Lake. Whatever the reason, there can be no doubt
that Pond did go from Cumberland House to Lake
Dauphin. Henry explicitly says that he did, and Pond's
own map shows that he wintered there in 1775. One
wonders what further tribute the insatiable Chatique
imposed on the way down.

On the first day of the new year, 1776, Henry set out
on a hunting and exploratory trip to the western
prairies. His way lay down to Cumberland House, and
thence up the Saskatchewan to Fort des Prairies. At
Fort des Prairies he found James Finlay, the pioneer *Fit a*
trader in this part of the west. Finlay and his men
were living on the fat of the land, or, to be more literal,
on the fat of the cattle that lived on the land. The
buffalo roamed in countless herds up and down the
vast continental plain, extending north and south for
several thousand miles, and the table at Fort des

Prairies was loaded every day with the tongues and marrows of " wild bulls," as the buffaloes were called in Henry's day. Henry was amazed at the quantity of provisions which he found collected here. It exceeded everything of which he had previously formed a notion. " In one heap," he writes, " I saw fifty tons of beef, so fat that the men could scarcely find a sufficiency of lean." Henry's astonishment was accentuated by the fact that he had lately left Cumberland House, where the traders were living on a meagre diet of fish, and he and his men had narrowly escaped starvation on their journey up the river.

At Fort des Prairies Henry joined a party of Assiniboines who were setting out across the plains to their winter camp. The Indians travelled swiftly on snowshoes, and Henry had no little difficulty in keeping up with them. The baggage was drawn by dogs, and these with the women broke the trail in front. At night they encamped in one of the numerous clumps of trees— " bluffs " as they are now called in the west—which everywhere dot the plains. The women cleared away the snow, put up the tents, and prepared the evening meal. They feasted royally on buffalo tongues, boiled in Henry's kettle, which was the only one in the camp.

Before daybreak the camp was astir, tents struck and loaded on the dog-sleds, and the whole party off again on their journey. Day after day they travelled at the same rapid pace. One morning Henry awoke to find the prairie covered with an immense herd of buffalo. The herd extended for a mile and a half—a

dense mass, too numerous to be counted. They travelled, not one after the other, as in the snow other
animals do, but in a broad phalanx, slowly, and stopping
occasionally to feed on the coarse grass uncovered by
their hoofs.

A few days later the Assiniboine village was reached.
Messengers from the great chief of the tribe had met
them on their way, and they were escorted to the
village by a guard of Indians, who formed themselves
in regular file on either side, keeping the curious on-
lookers at a distance. They were taken to a large
lodge set apart for their use, and after resting a mes-
senger invited them to the tent of the great chief,
where a feast had been provided.

The following day the traders were invited to a
buffalo hunt. Buffalo massacre would perhaps more
correctly describe the method adopted. It consisted
of an enclosure or pound, formed of birch stakes four
feet high, wattled with small branches. From the
entrance to the pound two lines of stakes extended
out diagonally for a considerable distance, so as to
form an immense funnel. The hunters, dressed in
buffalo skins, with head and horns, and so cleverly
imitating the motions and bellowing of the animals
that Henry confesses he could hardly distinguish the
imitation from the real animal, decoyed the herd to
the mouth of the funnel, and down to the pound,
where they were shut in and slaughtered. This method
of hunting buffalo seems to have been practised by
all the tribes of the western plains, from the earliest

times. It has been described, with minor variations, by many travellers since Henry's day.[1] Hearne describes a similar pound or park utilized by the Chipewyans in the Barren Grounds in hunting the caribou.

Henry returned to Fort des Prairies, and from thence down to Cumberland House, and north to his own fort on Beaver Lake. The following April (1776) Thomas Frobisher went with several men north to the Churchill, by way of Frog Portage, erected a fort on the Churchill, and made preparations for intercepting the western Indians on their way down to Hudson Bay. In June Henry joined Frobisher at the new post. Pond has on his map at this place a Fort de Trait, said to have been erected in 1774, but this must have been the temporary post built by Joseph Frobisher, not the more permanent establishment erected by Thomas Frobisher two years later.

The adventurous Canadians had now reached a place of strategical importance, from the point of view of either trade or exploration. Their way thither from Cumberland House had been through Cumberland Lake and its north-eastern extension Namew Lake, thence up the Sturgeon-Weir River to Amisk Lake, or Beaver Lake as it was then called, where they wintered. From Amisk Lake they continued up the Sturgeon-Weir River to the long lake or series of lakes now known as Heron, Pelican, and Woody lakes, but which in Henry's day were grouped together under the general name Lake Mineront. From the northern

---

[1] See description and illustration in Umfreville's *Hudson's Bay*, p. 160.

1776

extremity of this lake Frog Portage carried them to the waters of the Churchill.

Frog Portage was the doorway that led from the Saskatchewan and the known east, to the unknown west, to that limitless land of forest and plain, mountain, lake, and stream, that lies beyond the Saskatchewan. The explorer crossing this portage had before him the whole vast field of the north-west. The Churchill would lead him to Ile à la Crosse Lake, Buffalo Lake, and Lake La Loche, and from this latter lake Methye Portage would carry him over the height of land dividing the waters that flow into Hudson Bay from those flowing into the Arctic Ocean, and into the Clearwater River, a branch of the Athabaska. By the Clearwater and the Athabaska a road lay to Athabaska Lake. From this lake the Peace River offered an ideal route, not only to the mountains, but beyond the mountains; and the Slave River invited the explorer to discover the gigantic lakes and rivers of the far north. All this great field, at least in its broad features, was in time to be explored, but it was not done in a single year, neither was the work confined to a single explorer.

The first step in opening up this field was taken by Alexander Henry and the Frobishers, when they turned up the Churchill in search of a certain band of Indians whose home was said to lie about Lake Arabuthcow, or Athapuscow, or Athabaska. They purposed exploring the country as far as Lake Athabaska, should the Indians not turn up; and actually got as far as Ile à la Crosse Lake, when they encountered the Indians, who proved to be Chipewyans. Henry gives an interesting account of the Chipewyans, which, however, differs in no important particular from that written by Hearne a few years earlier.

The Chipewyans were, generally speaking, a peaceable, simple, inoffensive tribe. A little incident described by Henry throws an instructive light on their character. The chiefs of the Chipewyans visited the traders' camp, and inquired whether or not they had any rum. Being answered in the affirmative, they observed that several of their young men had never tasted the liquor, and that if it was too strong it would affect their heads. The rum was in consequence submitted to their judgment, and after tasting it several times, they pronounced it too strong, and requested that Henry would *order a part of the spirit to evaporate.* This was done, by adding more water to the already weak mixture, when the chiefs expressed themselves as satisfied.

From the Chipewyans Henry secured a good deal of information as to the topography of their country. They told him of a river, which apparently then bore the name it has ever since been known by—Peace River. This stream, they said, descended from the Stony or Rocky Mountains. From these mountains the distance to the Salt Lake (Pacific Ocean) was not great. They told Henry that Lake Athabaska emptied itself by a river running to the northward which they called Kiratchinini Sibi, Slave River. This name also remains to the present day, although, as before mentioned, the

PEACE RIVER, NEAR FORT DUNVEGAN

FORT ST. JOHN, PEACE RIVER, 1875

Face p. 318

river bore for a short time the name given it by Hearne of Great Athapuscow. The Indians said that Slave River flowed into another lake called by the same name; all of which was strictly accurate. They were somewhat hazy as to what lay beyond Great Slave Lake. They were not sure whether this might not itself be the sea; or if not, whether it did or did not empty into the sea. All these points were eventually to be made clear, though not by Alexander Henry, who now turned back to the civilized east after an absence of fifteen years and two months. With him went Joseph Frobisher.

Meanwhile Thomas Frobisher had packed his merchandise in canoes and was making a second attempt to reach Lake Athabaska. He got only as far as Ile à la Crosse Lake, and spent the winter of 1776–77 on a peninsula on the western side of the lake, where Ile à la Crosse House was afterward built. In the spring he returned, his canoes riding deep with their rich cargo of furs. He had intercepted the western Indians on their way down to York Factory, and found them willing enough to trade with him in their own country in preference to making the long, hazardous voyage down to the bay. Frobisher's wintering-place is clearly shown on Peter Pond's map. The fur traders from Montreal had now gained another strategic point, and from the time that Thomas Frobisher intercepted the Indians on their way down to York Factory from the Athabaska country, and built the first rude post on the long point that runs out into the middle of Ile à la Crosse Lake and commands so effectively the approaches from every direction, numerous trading forts were built here both by the North West Company and by their rivals of the Hudson's Bay Company.

Henry left Frobisher at Grand Portage, and went on to Montreal, where he arrived on October 15th, 1776. He sailed for Europe the same year, returning in-the spring of 1777. Both in England and France he made many friends, notable among whom were Sir Joseph Banks,[1] President of the Royal Society, to whom he afterward dedicated his book, and Abbé La Corne, through whose influence he was introduced to the French Court, and found an interested listener in Marie Antoinette to his tales of the far west. There is extant a letter or memoir of Henry's addressed to Sir Joseph Banks, dated October 18th, 1781, and bearing the title: "A proper Rout, by land, to cross the Great Continent of America, from Quebec to the Westernmost extremity, by Alex. Henry, founded on his observations and experience during the space of sixteen years' travelling with the natives, in least known, and before unknown parts of that extensive country."

Before his departure for England he had prepared for Lord Dorchester, then Governor of Canada, a chart of the western country so far as he was familiar with it. Unfortunately no trace can now be found of this chart, but one who was apparently familiar with it praised its accuracy, which he said had been confirmed in nearly every particular by subsequent surveys. After his

[1] It is a curious fact that both Alexander Henry and Jonathan Carver dedicated their books to Sir Joseph Banks.

return to Canada Henry went west on a brief visit, and returning to Montreal, sailed again for England the same year. He crossed once more in 1780, and upon his return to Montreal settled down there to a quiet life of business. He died at Montreal, April 4th, 1824, in his eighty-fifth year, having some time before disposed of his share in the North West Company to his nephew, Alexander Henry the younger.

CHAPTER VII

PETER POND AND HIS MAPS See p. 182

THE meagre details of Peter Pond's life in the west from 1768 to 1775 have been given in the preceding chapter. He was left on his way down to Fort Dauphin, near the north-west angle of Dauphin Lake, where he spent the winter of 1775. Pond was one of the most singular of the many remarkable men engaged in the western fur trade, and incidentally in the exploration of the immense region that now constitutes Western Canada. Born at Milford,[1] in the State of

---

[1] This is on the authority of Dr. Kohl. Mr. P. Lee Phillips, Chief of the Division of Maps and Charts in the Library of Congress, says that " one Peter Pond, of whom it is stated no trace could be found, was born at Milford in 1741."

Since writing the above my attention has been called to an exceedingly interesting manuscript Journal of Peter Pond, discovered in Connecticut by the wife of Pond's great-grand-nephew some years ago, and now published for the first time in the *Journal of American History*. The Journal opens with this important statement : " I was born in Milford in the countey of New Haven in Conn the 18 day of Jany 1740 and lived there under the Government and protection of my parans til the year 56." This fixes conclusively the date of Pond's birth. It is a matter of deep regret to me that I am unable to avail myself of the evidence doubtless afforded by this Journal as to the extent of Pond's western explorations. Unfortunately the portion already published carries Pond only to the upper waters of the Mississippi, and I have been unable to secure either from Mrs. Nathan, Gillet Pond, who edits the Journal, or from the editor of the *Journal of American History*, any particulars of the later portions of the Journal, which, so far as the field of north-western exploration is concerned, are the vital portions.

Connecticut, he came north into Canada very soon after the French colony passed into English hands, and identified himself with Alexander Henry, the Frobishers, and others who saw the possibilities of the western fur trade and had made up their minds to exploit it at all hazards. That the hazards were not imaginary the history of the fur trade bears ample evidence. Pond was in many ways admirably fitted for the arduous work of a trader in the wilderness, and it may also be said of him that he was, in a truer sense than many of his contemporaries, an explorer. The Frobishers and Henry looked upon exploration solely as a means to an end. First and always they were fur traders. They penetrated the unknown west, paddled over unexplored waterways, discovered portages that led them into new river systems, but all with an eye to the possibilities that each new field offered in the way of peltries. Pond, too, was a fur trader, but he seems to have been equally, or even more, a pathfinder. He was possessed by that *Wanderlust* that after all has been at the bottom of most of the world's exploration—the passion for discovering what may lie beyond the uttermost bounds of the known, that has carried men across untravelled seas to the shores of unknown lands, to the heart of great continents ; and that neither arctic cold nor tropic heat could dampen. Pond lacked the finer courage, the resourcefulness, the steadfast purpose of an Alexander Mackenzie, and he therefore achieved comparatively little as an explorer, but that he did accomplish something, and enough to entitle him to a place in the history of western exploration, will be seen from the following pages.

Pond having wintered at Fort Dauphin, set out in the spring of 1776 for the Saskatchewan, by way of Lake Winnipegosis, or Little Lake Winipique as he calls it on his map, and portaged from thence into what is now Cedar Lake, but which in Pond's day was known as Lake Bourbon. Here he passed the site of La Vérendrye's Fort Bourbon, long since fallen into decay, and ascended the Saskatchewan, which he says the natives called the Pasquia, to the forks, where he remained until the following spring. The year 1777 was spent in trading along the Saskatchewan, and Pond again wintered at the forks. In the spring of 1778 he descended the river to Sturgeon Lake, where a number of the traders had gathered to plan future operations.

As a good deal of misunderstanding has arisen owing to the fact that both the North West Company and the Hudson's Bay Company had forts on Cumberland Lake, a few words may not be out of place. The first trading establishment here was that made by Joseph Frobisher about 1772. In 1774 Hearne built Fort Cumberland for the Hudson's Bay Company. While the Canadian traders could therefore claim priority, it seems clear that Frobisher's house must have been a very temporary structure, for when the elder Henry reached Cumberland Lake on the 26th October, 1775, he makes no mention of Frobisher's post, but states explicitly that the house at which they stopped was Cumberland House of the Hudson's Bay Company. It

FORT McPHERSON, THE MOST NORTHERLY POST OF THE H. B. CO.

does not appear that anything like a permanent establishment was built here by the Canadian traders until several years later. Pond shows a Cumberland House on his map, but does not say whether it was the Hudson's Bay post, or an establishment of the Canadian traders.

Hereabouts, at any rate, the fur traders forgathered in the spring of 1778, and finding that they had a quantity of goods to spare, as Mackenzie tells in his *Account of the Rise, Progress, and Present State of the Fur Trade*, agreed to pool their stock, and placed it in the hands of Peter Pond, who was to make his way into the heart of the Athabaska country, and establish a post there in the most advantageous place he could find.

Pond loaded his venture in four canoes, and, following the waterways already explored by the Frobishers and Alexander Henry, reached the Churchill and ascended it to Ile à la Crosse Lake. He had now gained the farthest point to the north-west yet reached by the fur traders, and was about to explore a country that had hitherto been known to Europeans only by the report of the Indians.

Pond's course from Ile à la Crosse Lake may be clearly traced by a reference to the map. It lay along a route which for generations had been used by the Indians of the Athabaska country, and which since Pond's day has always been the recognized road from the Winnipeg and the Saskatchewan country to the Athabaska country. Mackenzie, a contemporary of

Pond's, describes the route as it was known in his day. Following a north-westerly course, Pond and his men paddled for about twenty miles up a long arm of the lake to a point where it contracts into a waterway about two miles broad, which after a course of ten miles opens into Lake Clear. Rounding a narrow neck of land, the traders found themselves in what is now known as Buffalo Lake, running to the north-west for a distance of about thirty-six miles. Into the north-west end empties the shallow La Loche. Entering this stream, at the mouth of which a Hudson's Bay post now stands, or did not long ago, Pond dragged his heavily laden canoes with difficulty up its rock-encumbered channel for twenty-four miles, when he found himself in the long, narrow lake which bears the same name as the river just mentioned. Lake La Loche is only a few miles from the height of land, a high rocky ridge dividing the waters which flow into Hudson Bay from those which find their way into the Arctic Ocean. After leaving the lake the way lay up a small stream for about a mile and a half, when the canoes and their lading had to be carried for a distance of thirteen miles, over extremely difficult ground, to the Clearwater River, a tributary of the Athabaska.

This portage, variously known as Portage La Loche and Methye Portage, first crossed by Pond, was to be made famous in later years, not only as the gateway to the immense water systems of the far north-west, but as containing one of the most charming bits of scenery on the continent. One wonders whether the beauty of the scene made any particular appeal to Pond. It certainly has never lacked admirers among those who came after him. Alexander Mackenzie, Back, Harmon, Franklin, every man, in fact, who passed this way and left any account of his journey, has been loud in praise of the beautiful valley that lies at the foot of Methye Portage. The scene, so charmingly caught by Back in one of his illustrations to Franklin's *Polar Sea*, had been described many years before by Alexander Mackenzie. Standing at the summit of the portage, the valley of the Clearwater lay beneath him a thousand feet below. " The valley," he says, " is about three miles in breadth, and is confined by two lofty ridges, displaying a most beautiful intermixture of wood and lawn, and stretching on till the blue mist obscures the prospect." The twin heights were covered with stately forests, broken by patches of emerald lawn, on which herds of buffalo and elk were feeding. It was the month of September, the rutting season of the elk, whose whistling mingled with the cry of birds and the myriad voices of the wilderness.

Descending the precipice, Pond found himself on the banks of a stream, sometimes called the Pelican, sometimes Swan River, but now known as the Clearwater. For the first time in the history of exploration in North-Western America, that which had been talked of for so many years and been the subject of so many geographical theories, was discovered—a river flowing to the westward, toward the Western Sea. Pond was probably quite aware, from Indian report, that the

Clearwater did not itself empty into the Pacific, but he was not without hope that by following it he might find waterways which would lead to the long-sought ocean.

Paddling down the Clearwater, through the heart of the beautiful valley first seen from the heights above, for a distance of eight odd miles, the canoes at last swept out on to the waters of the Athabaska, at this point and for the remainder of its course a considerable river averaging three-quarters of a mile in width. Continuing down the Athabaska, Pond at length reached a spot about thirty miles above the mouth of the river, admirably suited to the requirements of a trading post. Unloading his canoes, therefore, he and his men set to work to build a rude fort, which was ready for occupation before winter set in. This post he made his headquarters for the next six years, during which time he wandered back and forth throughout all this western country, from the Saskatchewan to Lake Athabaska, and probably as far as the Peace River. That Pond was the first white man to stand on the shores of Lake Athabaska there can be no question. No record exists of the exact date of his discovery, but doubtless it was soon after the building of his fort on the Athabaska River.

In 1782 he is found encamped on the shores of Lake la Ronge, south of the Churchill, and west of Frog Portage. The following year he is back at Ile à la Crosse, and then again at his post on the Athabaska. This latter post is constantly mentioned in the narratives of later explorers and traders as "The Old Establishment,"

" Old Pond Fort," etc.   David Thompson, of the North
West Company, passed it in 1804 and found its position
to be in lat. 58° 25′ N., long 111° 23′ W.   We learn from
Mackenzie that Pond's fort was the only one in this
part of the country up to the year 1785.   It was the
father of Fort Chipewyan, built in 1788 on the south
side of Lake Athabaska, and for many years one of the
most important establishments of the North West Company.

Before considering some interesting points in connection with Peter Pond's maps, it may be well to give a
brief account of his stormy and not over-creditable
career subsequent to the establishment of the Athabaska fort.   It has already been mentioned that Pond
was at Lake la Ronge in 1782, as appears by his map,
but it is evident that this was not his first appearance at
the lake.   There were reasons, however, why he preferred to forget some of the incidents of his earlier
visit.   In 1779 one Wadin went to Lake la Ronge, and
the following year he was joined by Pond, the two
representing the joint interests of a number of partners
at Grand Portage.   In character the two men had
almost nothing in common, and sooner or later there
was bound to be trouble.   Pond was, in fact, a man
whom it was impossible to get along with, as we find
abundant evidence of in the narratives of his contemporaries among the fur traders.   He was a morose, un-
sociable man, suspicious, scenting offence where none
was intended.   He seems never to have found happiness
in the company of men of his race, but preferred the

wilderness and its savage inhabitants, with which and with whom he had a great deal in common. Finally, the ill-will and bickering at Lake la Ronge ended in a tragedy. Pond had been dining with Wadin and one of his clerks, and during the night Wadin was shot through the thigh. He died before morning. Pond and the clerk were tried for murder at Montreal and acquitted, mainly, it seems, through a technicality. "Nevertheless," dryly remarks Mackenzie, "their innocence was not so apparent as to extinguish the original suspicion." Pond was afterwards implicated in the death of another trader, John Ross.

Some time after his acquittal Pond is found at Quebec (18th April, 1785), joining with the Frobishers in an effort to secure from the Government a monopoly of the fur trade from Lake Superior to the interior country for ten years, in consideration of certain explorations which the petitioners allege to have been performed on behalf of the North West Company, and of other and much more ambitious explorations which they had in contemplation.

From the memorial of Benjamin and Joseph Frobisher it is learned that the North West Company, knowing that as a result of the stipulations of the Treaty of Peace with the United States, Grand Portage would fall in American territory, and fearing that they might thereby be deprived of their one and only route into the north-west, had at their own expense, and with the approval of Governor Haldimand, sent out two competent men to search for another water route from

Lake Superior to Lake Winnipeg entirely within British territory.

These two men were Edouard Umfreville, who had lately left the Hudson's Bay Company after a service of eleven years, and Venance St. Germain. They were accompanied by six or eight French-Canadians, and travelled in light canoes, equipped only with provisions. Umfreville's instructions were to proceed to Lake Alempigon (Nipigon), and from thence to search to the westward for a water route suitable to the requirements of the fur trade. From the journal of his voyage, found not in his *Hudson's Bay*, but in a manuscript among the Masson papers in the McGill University Library, it appears that he succeeded in his task, discovering and surveying a canoe route from Lake Superior by way of Lake Nipigon, Sturgeon Lake, and English River to Portage de l'Isle on the Winnipeg River. This route, however, was so difficult and inconvenient that it was never adopted by the traders, and as a matter of fact, owing to disputes between the British and United States Governments as to some of the terms of the treaty, Grand Portage remained in British hands for some time thereafter, and the traders continued to use the old route. When finally compelled to abandon it they found a more convenient substitute in the Kaministikwia route, only a few miles north of the international boundary.

That this Kaministikwia route should have remained so long unknown to the English fur traders from Canada, although discovered and used by the French traders before the conquest, is curious enough. One would have thought that among the many French-Canadians employed by the North West Company, and the independent traders who preceded the Company, some at least must have traversed or heard of the Kaministikwia route. Yet when Umfreville is sent to look for a new channel in 1784 there is no word, no suggestion even, of a thoroughfare by way of the Kaministikwia. He is sent direct to Lake Nipigon to search for a passage. It is not, in fact, until 1798 that we hear of this route. In that year it was rediscovered by one of the partners of the North West Company, Roderick McKenzie. On his way from Grand Portage to Rainy Lake, McKenzie accidentally learned from a party of Indians of the existence of a water communication a short distance north of the Grand Portage. Finding the entrance to this new route in Lake St. Croix, he followed it to the mouth of the Kaministikwia, and then made his way around to Grand Portage, with this very satisfactory news for the partners. As a result of his discovery, or rediscovery, of the Kaministikwia route, steps were taken by the North West Company for the removal of their establishment from Grand Portage to the mouth of the Kaministikwia, and in 1801 the post, afterward known as Fort William, was built there.

From the memorial of the Frobishers, already alluded to, it appears that in addition to the exploration conducted by Umfreville the North West Company had in view, or at any rate professed to have in view, a much more ambitious project. This was nothing less than the exploration at their own expense, and with their own men, of the country lying between the 55th and 65th degrees of latitude, from Hudson's Bay to the Pacific Ocean. Of this immense territory surveys were to be made as far as practicable, and such surveys, with remarks thereupon respecting the nature of the country and the rivers which should be found to discharge into the Pacific, together with such additional information as might be collected from the natives, were to be laid before the Governor, for transmission to the home Government. As already mentioned, the traders asked in return for these discoveries, the value and importance of which could not be disputed, that the Company should be granted " an exclusive right to the passage they may discover from the North side of Lake Superior to the River Ouinipique ; and also of the trade to the North-West either by that passage or by the present communication of the Grand Portage for ten years only."

In a further memorial, signed by Peter Pond, Lieutenant-Governor Hamilton is assured that the North West Company were able and willing to accomplish the important discoveries proposed by them, provided they met with due encouragement from the Government, having " men among them who have already given proof of their genius and unwearied industry, in exploring those unknown regions as far as the longitude of 128 degrees West of London, as will appear by a map with remarks upon the country therein laid down, which your Memorialist had lately the honour of laying before you, for the information of Government." Pond adds that he " has had positive information from the Natives, who have been on the coast of the North Pacific Ocean, that there is a trading Post already established by the Russians," and that he is " credibly informed that ships are now fitting out from the United States of America, under the command of experienced seamen (who aecom-panied Captain Cook in his last voyage), in order to establish a Fur trade upon the North-West Coast of North America, at or near to Prince William's Sound ; and that if the late Treaty of Peace is adhered to respecting the Cession of the Upper Posts, the United States will also have an easy access into the North-West by way of the Grand Portage." Pond finally urges the necessity of protection and encouragement being afforded the North West Company in the early prosecution of their proposed discoveries, in order that trading posts may be built, and connections made with the far western tribes, to the shores of the Pacific ; by which means "so firm a footing may be established as will preserve that valuable trade from falling into the hands of other Powers."

In a Memorandum, dated the same year (1785), from Haldimand to Lord Sydney, the granting of the ex-clusive privileges asked by the North West Company is recommended, in view of the advantages which would accrue to the nation from the explorations which the Company were prepared to undertake. The home Government seem to have taken a different view of the

matter. At any rate, there is no record of such ex-
clusive privileges ever having been granted to the North
West Company. The influence of the Hudson's Bay
Company would probably be sufficient to ensure the
rejection of the request. In the meantime, the discovery of the old Kaministikwia route removed the
immediate cause of anxiety, so far as the North West
Company was concerned, and they were probably content to let things rest as they were.

As to their ambitious project of exploring the far
north-west, that was, as we shall presently see, fully
carried out. How far the North West Company as a
company is entitled to the credit of these explorations
is a nice point. It is perhaps safe to say, however, that,
as the merit of Hearne's achievement and Hendry's is
due much more to their own courage and perseverance
than to any act of the Hudson's Bay Company, so the
credit for the explorations of Sir Alexander Mackenzie,
David Thompson, Simon Fraser, and other partners
or employees of the North West Company, belongs
primarily to the men themselves, and only in a very
secondary sense to the Company. There is no evidence
that these explorations were the result of any settled
policy on the part of the Company. The evidence, in
fact, points the other way. Mackenzie, for instance,
refers in one of his letters to the indifference shown by
the partners at Grand Portage toward his projected
journey to the Pacific. The explorations were, it may
be repeated, due rather to the enterprise and enthusiasm
of the individuals, who achieved such splendid and last-

ing results under most discouraging and difficult conditions, than to any initiative on the part of the North West Company.

Peter Pond returned to the west in 1785, and from contemporary evidence it appears that he remained there until 1788, when he again turns up at Quebec. In 1786 he is said to have sent Cuthbert Grant and one ·Laurent Leroux to establish a trading post on Great Slave Lake. Roderick McKenzie says that Pond retired from the North West Company in 1788. "He thought himself," says McKenzie, "a philosopher, and was odd in his manners. I understood he published something of the North-West." It is not clear whether McKenzie meant a book or a map. So far as is known, Pond never published one or the other. His manuscript maps will be described presently, but no narrative of his western explorations has ever come to light.[1] His memorial on behalf of the North West Company can hardly be so described. The following letter from Dorchester to Grenville, dated Quebec, 23 November, 1790, indicates that Pond did intend to publish both his map and a narrative of his explorations: "I transmit," writes Dorchester, "a sketch of the northwestern parts of this continent communicated by Peter Pond, an Indian Trader from this Province, showing his discoveries, the track pursued, and the stations occupied by him and his party during an excursion of several years, from which he returned in 1788 after

[1] This was written before the appearance of Pond's Journal in the *Journal of American History*, as mentioned in a previous note.

FORT RESOLUTION, GREAT SLAVE LAKE.

Face p. 336

having penetrated as far as the Great Slave Lake. Mr. Pond proposing some advantage to himself from publishing it hereafter with a detailed account has requested care may be taken to prevent its getting into other hands than those of the King's Ministers. I am told he has quitted this Province somewhat dissatisfied with the Trading Company whom he served and with a view of seeking employment in the United States, of which he is a native."

Pond returned to New England about the end of 1790, according to the late Dr. Douglas Brymner, Dominion Archivist. Charles Lindsey, in his *Investigation of the Unsettled Boundaries of Ontario*, gives the year as 1792, and adds that Pond himself was very useful to the United States Commissioners who were dealing with the boundary question. " The British Commissioners," says Lindsey, " were ignorant of the geography of the country beyond Lake Ontario ; and they had but wretched assistance for their guidance in the shape of maps ; one of them by Farren,[1] dated 1773, stopped short in any actual information at Toronto ; the whole country to the west being represented as alternations of rock and swamp, and uninhabitable. Mitchell's was somewhat better, and was the best to which they had access. The American Commissioners

---

[1] The map by Farren is not known at Ottawa ; neither is there any such map either in the British Museum or the Library of Congress. The name is probably a misprint for Faden. There are several maps by William Faden ; and the one dated 1777 in his *North American Atlas*, though it does not agree exactly with the description, and the date is different, is probably that to which Lindsey refers.

had Pond at their elbow; and though his knowledge of
the true position of places was extremely inaccurate, he
had much knowledge of the value of the interior
countries. Pond is said to have designated to the
American Commissioners a boundary line through the
middle of the Upper St. Lawrence and the lakes, and
through the interior countries to the north-west corner
of the Lake of the Woods, and thence west to the
Mississippi; a line that was accepted by the British
Commissioners."

Mr. Lindsey seems to have been at fault in one
particular. The ignorance of the British Commissioners
did not arise from the actual lack of suitable maps, so
much as from that supreme indifference to the territorial
interests of British North America which has been so
painfully apparent in all the boundary disputes with the
United States; for the British Commissioners must have
had at the time of the negotiations, and for some time
before, access to a map of the western country, with
remarks upon its character, prepared by Peter Pond
himself. No doubt this map was at the time it was
most needed tucked comfortably away in some pigeon-
hole in London.

Now as to Peter Pond's map, or rather maps, for
there were at least two distinct manuscript maps. In
a letter from Lieutenant-Governor Hamilton to Lord
Sydney, dated 9th of April, 1785, he writes: "This
gentleman [Pond] has communicated to me the map
on which his route is traced; he has also without
difficulty entrusted me with the remarks he has made."

In Pond's memorial, dated the same month and year, the map is referred to as having been submitted to Hamilton, "for the information of Government." The map was sent to Lord Sydney under cover of Hamilton's letter of the 6th June, 1785.

In the archives of the Hudson's Bay Company at London there is a map bearing the following inscription: "Copy of a map presented to the Congress by Peter Pond, a native of Milford in the State of Connecticut. This extraordinary man has resided seventeen years in those countries, and from his own discoveries as well as from the reports of the Indians, he assures himself of having at last discovered a passage to the North Sea. He is gone again to ascertain some important observations. New York, 1st March, 1785, copied by St. John de Crèvecoeur for his Grace of La Rochefoucault." This map is noted in the *Kohl Collection of Maps Relating to America*, edited by Justin Winsor.

There is reason to believe that St. John de Crèvecoeur's copy was made from the map submitted by Pond to Hamilton ; that the former met Pond, probably at Quebec, and obtained permission to copy the map for the duc de La Rochefoucauld-Liancourt, who, it will be remembered, travelled through the Eastern States, the Iroquois country, and Upper Canada in 1795–7 (an account of which he published in 1799); and that the original was subsequently sent by Hamilton to Lord Sydney.

In the Report on Canadian Archives for 1890 there is a reproduction of a map by Pond, which Dr.

Brymner refers to as the one presented to Hamilton. This can hardly be the case, if the assumption is correct that de Crèvecoeur's copy was taken from the Hamilton map. A comparison of the Kohl copy with the Canadian Archives reproduction makes it clear that they could not have come from the same original. It is said that Kohl's drawings frequently differ from the originals, and it has, of course, to be borne in mind that this particular drawing was taken not from the original, but from a copy of the original; but while this would account for many minor discrepancies, there are vital points of difference that will not bend to such a theory. The Kohl copy, for instance, shows that Pond was on St. Peter's River (the Minnesota) in 1774. The Canadian Archives map does not contain this information. The former dates Pond's post on the Athabaska 1782–3; according to the latter he wintered there 1778–84. The Archives map shows Great Bear Lake, under the name of Red Knife Lake; Kohl's copy carries the river from Slave Lake directly into the " Mer du Nord Ouest." The first carries the north-west coast up to Cook Inlet, which is shown as Cook's River; the other only vaguely indicates the coast to about the latitude of Cape Flattery, north of which is blank. There are many other serious differences : the same rivers or lakes appear under different names on the two maps; topographical features of one are omitted from the other; the dates of trading posts are not always similar. Altogether it does not seem possible to identify the Kohl map, or de Crèvecoeur's map, with the original of which the Canadian Archives map is a reproduction. So far as can at present be ascertained, the map which de Crèvecoeur saw and copied has disappeared, if it ever reached the Colonial Office.

It remains to identify the Canadian Archives map. There does not appear to be any reason for doubting that this was the map sent by Dorchester to Grenville in November, 1790. It bears strong internal evidence of being of later date than the original of the Kohl map, and several surrounding circumstances help to fix its date as 1789. In a letter dated February 24th, 1788, from Patrick Small,[1] of the North West Company, to Simon McTavish, Pond is said to be " preparing a fine map to lay before the Empress of Russia "—evidently Catherine II. Again, in a letter to David Ogden, of London, of November 7th, 1789, Isaac Ogden, of Quebec, says that he has " had an opportunity of seeing a map or chart of the western country made by a gentleman of observation and science [whom he identifies later as Pond] who has actually traversed it, and made his map in it, and with whom I have this week had several conversations, with the map before me." He adds that he could not get a copy of the map, but hopes to send it the following summer.

To briefly recapitulate, there is the 1785 map, with the de Crèvecoeur and Kohl copies; and there is the 1789 map, mentioned by Small in 1788 as in prepara-

[1] Roderick McKenzie, in one of his manuscript notes, says that Patrick Small was a nephew of General Small, of the 42nd Highlanders. Patrick Small was engaged in the western fur trade, and eventually retired to Montreal with a competency.

tion, seen and described by Ogden in 1789, and sent to the Colonial Office by Dorchester in 1790.

Ogden's letter is important not only in its bearing on the map, but still more because it records the substance of a conversation with Peter Pond in regard to western exploration and the character of the country which Pond had made so especially his own. It reveals a marked increase in knowledge of western topography since the 1785 map. It reveals, too, some curious anomalies, hard to explain on any other hypothesis than a deliberate attempt on Pond's part to mislead.

The map shown to Ogden begins at the upper end of Lake Superior, where "there is a portage of near nine miles before you enter the waters communicating to the North West." This was of course Grand Portage. In view of Roderick McKenzie's statement that the Kaministikwia route was unknown to British traders before his rediscovery of the old French water road in 1798, it is curious to note that that route, as well as the Grand Portage, is distinctly marked on Pond's 1789 map. As Small does not say that he actually saw the map, and as Pond was at the time on unfriendly terms with the partners of the North West Company, it is quite possible that the map was never actually examined by any of the western fur traders, and the knowledge of this route, so vitally important to their interests, was thus kept from them for another decade. Umfreville, it will be remembered, had been sent out by the North West Company in 1784 to hunt for a route to the westward by the roundabout and inconvenient way of Lake

Nipigon, but at that time Pond himself was apparently ignorant of the Kaministikwia route, as it does not appear on his 1785 map, or rather on the extant copies of that map.

To return to Ogden's letter. " From the end of the Portage at the Head of Lake Superior," he says, "all the lakes and waters as high up as Lat. 58 and Long. 124 set first to the North West and North, and then take a South-Easterly and South course, and empty into York River [Hudson's Bay]." The 1789 map shows the connecting waterways between Lake Superior and Lake Winnipeg with tolerable accuracy, but, as in Carver's map, the distance is greatly exaggerated, and, on the other hand, only a comparatively narrow neck of land separates Lake Superior from James Bay.

Ogden mentions a post of the Hudson's Bay Company—evidently Cumberland House—and continues: "A chain of lakes &c. continue from thence to the Lat. 58 and Long. 124 when with a small portage [Methye Portage] they enter into the rivers and lakes that run a north-west course and empty into other lakes and rivers, which all finally communicate and empty into a great lake called the Slave Lake, which lays between the Lat. of 63 and 65, being three degrees in width, and Long. from 125 to 135, and this lake is the last water before you come to the Great Northern Ocean, which lays in Lat. 68$\frac{1}{2}$ and in Long. 132 where the water ebbs and flows, of which the Gentleman [Pond] gave me indubitable proofs."

Although Pond is supposed to have reached Great

Slave Lake, and from Ogden's letter evidently had at least a general idea of its magnitude, he makes it comparatively small on both his maps. Pond, of course, was not a surveyor, and only a very amateurish cartographer, which explains the fact that on his 1789 map Great Slave Lake is shown as actually smaller than the Lake of the Woods ; even smaller than Split Lake ; the size of both these latter lakes being much exaggerated. Ogden's statement that Great Slave Lake was "the last water before you come to the Great Northern Ocean" is also hard to explain, on the assumption that he had before him Pond's 1789 map. As previously stated, that map shows a lake north of the Great Slave Lake, evidently intended to represent Great Bear Lake. To the eastward of Great Slave Lake a river is shown taking a north-westerly course and falling into the Ice Sea —apparently the Coppermine, which Hearne had discovered thirteen years before. Pond was evidently familiar with the general results of Hearne's great journey of 1771–2 ; or may have got his information from the Indians.

After describing the Athabaska and Slave rivers, Ogden says : "From out of the Great Slave Lake runs a very large river, which runs almost south-west, and has the largest falls on it in the known world ; it is at least two miles wide where the falls are, and an amazing body of water. This river leaves the lake in Lat. 64 and Long. 135, and the falls are in Long. 141. The great chain of mountains that extend from Mexico along the Western or Pacific Ocean, and

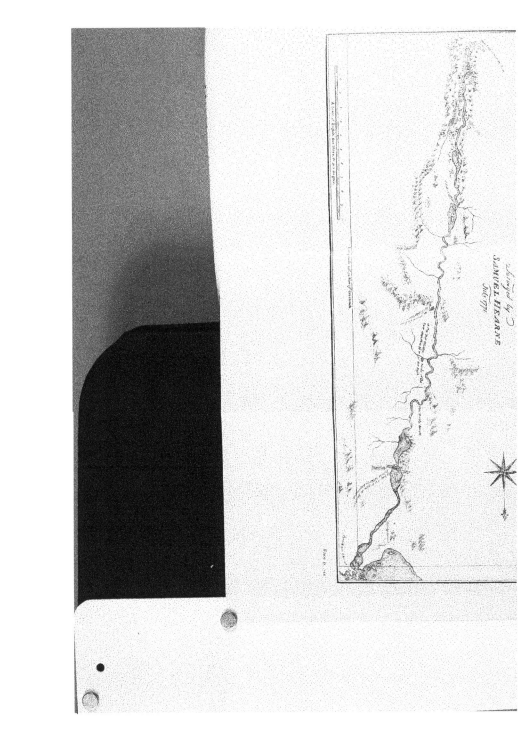

Surveyed by
SAMUEL HEARNE
July 1771

A Scale of English Sea Miles, 60 to a Degree.

Face p. 14

the Northern Pacific Ocean, terminates in Lat.
62½ and Long. 136, so that the Slave River runs to
the westward of them and empties into the Ocean by
its course in about the Lat. of 59." "When you have
proceeded thus far," he continues to his correspondent,
"and have looked over your map, you will readily conjecture what river the above Slave Lake River is known
by, when it empties into the Ocean. To save you much
trouble I will tell you it is Cook's River, which he
penetrated upwards of 70 leagues North Eastward,
as you will see by his chart."

Ogden—or is it Pond?—proceeds to build up an
elaborate argument, proving at least to his own satisfaction that the river emptying out of Great Slave Lake,
and Cook's River, are one, and that consequently a continuous waterway exists from Great Slave Lake to the
Pacific. Cook's River has been traversed, he says, for
seventy leagues north-easterly; the river out of Slave
Lake is known as far south-westerly. As Slave Lake,
according to Pond's map, is as far west as 134°, only
a short gap remains between the known limit of the
Slave Lake River and that of Cook's River. Further,
argues Ogden, there is no known vent for the river
setting out of Slave Lake, nor any other river in that
country to the north or south of Slave Lake to form
such a river as Cook's River. Cook, too, had found
a great quantity of driftwood on the coast, and this
wood is found only on the banks of the river that
empties into Slave Lake; or so Pond has told Ogden.
Pond professed also to have met two Indians, in 1787, at

Great Slave Lake, who had come up a river from the North Pacific Ocean. They brought him a blanket which they had received from vessels trading at the mouth of the river. They told him that the river was large to the place of discharge, and navigable.

From all of which Ogden draws the following conclusions :—

1st. That Lake Superior lies in the first range of high lands between the Atlantic and the Western oceans, in lat. 46° or 47°, and the waters from thence are discharged by the rivers St. Lawrence and Mississippi.

2nd. That the waters to the westward and northward of the lake up as high as lat. 58° and long. 124° discharge themselves by an easterly course into York River, which empties into Hudson Bay.

3rd. That in lat. 58° lies the great height of land from whence the waters divide and run easterly and westerly, the former into the Atlantic and the latter into the Pacific Ocean.

4th. That the Great Slave Lake is the most northerly large piece of water before you arrive at the Northern Ocean, and that the river which rises from that lake empties into the Northern Pacific Ocean, and is the river that Cook discovered.

5th. That an easy communication with, and an advantageous commerce, may be carried on by posts established on lakes Slave, Athabaska, Pelican, etc., and to deliver the fruits of their commerce at the mouth of Cook's River, to be then carried to China, etc., and that

ATHABASKA RIVER

Face p. 346

as Cook's River and the lands on Slave Lake, Arabaska, etc., are very fine, some advantageous settlements may be made there which may be beneficial to Government.

It is interesting to find this early vindication of the quality of the lands in the Canadian North-West, though curiously enough as recently as 1905 a fierce dispute raged at Ottawa as to whether or not the Peace River country was fit for settlement, a dispute in which not merely politicians, but men of science who had visited the country, were found ranged on opposite sides. Pond justified his faith in the excellent quality of these lands by planting a vegetable garden at his fort on the Athabaska, and abundantly supplying his table therefrom. But that is not much to the present purpose.

Ogden's theory (or Pond's) of a great river connecting Great Slave Lake with the Pacific is somewhat puzzling. It is susceptible of two different explanations. The large river running out of Great Slave Lake must have been either the Peace River or the Mackenzie. The latter would fit in with the very positive statement made in Ogden's letter that this river ran *out of* Great Slave Lake. Peace River assuredly does not; and it is certain that Pond knew it did not, for his map of 1789 clearly shows the river—under the name River of Peace—rising in the mountains, toward the south or south-south-west, and flowing *into* Great Slave Lake. At the same time Ogden describes the river as running almost south-west; which, reversing the course, applies to the Peace, but not to the Mackenzie. The 1789 map proves that Pond had then learned, approximately at least, the true course of the Mackenzie, which is shown flowing, not into the North Pacific Ocean as Ogden describes his great river, but into the Ice Sea, by a north-west and north course. It is a nicely balanced question whether Ogden's river was the Peace or the Mackenzie; but in either case Pond's reputation stands to suffer. If it is decided that the river was the Peace, it must be assumed that for purposes of his own Pond misrepresented the course of the river; while if preference is given to the Mackenzie, it is again evident that Pond must have deliberately deceived Ogden.

There is an interesting statement in the last paragraph of Ogden's letter. "Another man," he says, "by the name of McKenzie was left by Pond at Slave Lake with orders to go down the River, and from thence to Unalaska, and so to Kamskatsha, and thence to England through Russia, &c. If he meets with no accident you may have him with you next year." Is this another of Pond's ingenious inventions; or is he coolly taking credit for Alexander MacKenzie's expedition to the Arctic? Mackenzie, of course, was in no sense under Pond's orders, and although he had actually started on his famous voyage to the far north five months before Ogden's letter was written, there is nothing either in his book, or in his correspondence so far as we have it in Masson's *Bourgeois de la Compagnie du Nord-Ouest*, to indicate that he had the slightest idea of attempting the gigantic task of an expedition from the Mackenzie River across Alaska, thence to Kamschatka, and across Siberia and Russia to England. It is true, he says in a letter to Roderick McKenzie that he is taking money with him "to traffic with the Russians," but this only means that he expected to find Russian traders on the Pacific coast. Apparently the statement must be added to Pond's formidable list of misdeeds.

Pond finally left Canada, as already mentioned, some time between the years 1790 and 1792, having disposed of his share in the North West Company to Simon McGillivray for £800. According to Masson, he died in poverty at Boston some years later.

CHAPTER VIII

OVERLAND TO THE MISSOURI AND THE MANDAN VILLAGES

IN the preceding chapters the story of French exploration has been traced from Lake Superior to Lake Winnipeg; from Lake Superior and Lake Winnipeg north to Hudson Bay; and from Lake Winnipeg south-west to the Assiniboine, thence to the Missouri on the one hand and north-west to the Saskatchewan on the other. An attempt has also been made to trace the movements of the English traders who followed in the footsteps of the French to and up the Saskatchewan, and who broke entirely new ground north of that river as far as Great Slave Lake, where their explorations connected with the earlier discoveries of Samuel Hearne. The story now moves around to the south-west again, where a number of English traders and explorers are reopening the forgotten route to the Missouri, first discovered by La Vérendrye.

It is difficult, in the absence of journals or other original documents, to say just when the first English traders from Canada ascended the Red River from Lake Winnipeg and turned thence up the Assiniboine. John McDonnell, in his account of the Red River, 1797,[1]

---

[1] Masson's *Bourgeois de la Compagnie du Nord-Ouest*, I, 268.

speaks of a clearing on the banks of the Red River about three leagues below the Sault à la Biche, now St. Andrew's Rapids, as being the place where Joseph Frobisher had wintered, and adds that the place was called "Fort à M. Frobisher." He gives no date for this establishment, but there is reason to believe that it was earlier than 1774, for in that year Frobisher had reached the Saskatchewan and was devoting all his energies to the development of trade to the north-west of Lake Winnipeg. Frobisher's fort was only a temporary affair, but it appears to have been the first English settlement of any kind on the Red River. How far Frobisher ascended the Red River; whether he ascended or even reached the mouth of the Assiniboine; or who among the English traders did first ascend the Assiniboine, and when: these are all questions that with our present knowledge it is impossible to answer.

Curiously enough, the earliest English settlement of which there is any available record, in the Assiniboine country, was not on the main stream, but upon its tributary the Qu'Appelle. It was known as Fort Espérance, and according to John McDonnell was built by Robert Grant about 1783. It is described as being "two short days' march in canoes" up the Qu'Appelle from its junction with the Assiniboine. Rev. George Bryce locates it near the mouth of Cut Arm Creek, and according to David Thompson it was in lat. 50° 28′ 58″ and long. 101° 45′ 45″. Dr. Bryce says that the first English traders from Canada who occupied the valley of the Assiniboine reached that river not by way of the Red River, but from the north through Lake Winnipegosis, up Swan River, and thence by portage to the Assiniboine. This may be perfectly true, but it lacks confirmation, and the whole question is so shrouded in obscurity that it would be rash to make any very positive statement as to the route by which English traders first reached the Assiniboine. All that is known with any degree of certainty is that they did reach the Assiniboine some time about 1780, and not only explored that river as well as its tributaries the Qu'Appelle and Souris, but crossed the prairie to the Mandan villages on the Missouri.

Half a century elapsed between the expedition of La Vérendrye to the Mandans and the first recorded visit of English traders from the Assiniboine to the Missouri. In McDonnell's Journal, already referred to, mention is made of a party of free traders—that is, traders working on their own account, not attached to any of the existing companies—who left Fort Espérance in December, 1793, for the Missouri; and in May, 1795, McDonnell speaks of another party just returned from the Mandans. There is evidence that the Hudson's Bay Company had also sent men from the Assiniboine to the Missouri about this time, but neither names nor dates are now extant.

The first expedition of which there is any detailed account is that of David Thompson, astronomer, explorer, and fur trader—one of the most remarkable men

in the history of western exploration. Thompson set
out from McDonnell's House (also known as Stone
Indian River House) on the Assiniboine, a little above
the mouth of the Souris, on November 28th, 1797, with
a party of nine men. His guide and interpreter was
René Jussaume, a famous trader frequently mentioned
in contemporary and later journals from McDonnell to
Lewis and Clark. He had been an independent trader
on the Missouri for some years when Thompson first
met him, and was familiar with the Mandan language.
Alexander Henry the younger describes him in very
unflattering terms: "He retains the outward appearance of a Christian, but his principles, as far as I could
observe, are much worse than those of a Mandane; he
is possessed of every superstition natural to those
people, nor is he different in every mean, dirty trick
they have acquired from intercourse with the set of
scoundrels who visit these parts—some to trade and
others to screen themselves from justice." Other
travellers on the Missouri are almost equally severe on
this unprepossessing character. Yet he was useful as
an interpreter, and served Lewis and Clark as well
as David Thompson in that capacity. Another of
Thompson's party, Hugh McCraken, described as a
good-hearted Irishman, had also been to the Mandan
villages before. The rest of his party consisted of
French-Canadians. They were, however, only nominally
of his party; they were travelling to the Missouri as
free traders, having obtained at McDonnell's House an
equipment of trading goods on credit to the value of

2 A

forty or fifty skins apiece, to be paid for in kind on their return from the Missouri.

Everything being ready, the expedition set forth from McDonnell's House, Thompson with two horses, Jussaume with one, the goods and supplies being drawn on sleds by thirty dogs purchased from the Assiniboines. It took the party thirty-three days to cover the distance to their destination on the Missouri, two hundred and eighty miles as they travelled. Their course for various reasons was very roundabout, the actual distance in a straight line being only about one hundred and eighty-eight miles. On December 7th Ash House was reached, on Mouse River (the Souris); its position Thompson found to be 49° 27′ 32″ N. Leaving Ash House, Thompson struck boldly over the prairie to that familiar landmark in all the Mandan expeditions, Turtle Mountain; encountered a terrific snowstorm on the 20th; crossed the Souris and followed it for a few miles; then across country a distance of thirty-seven miles to the Missouri, which he reached on December 29th, at a point six miles above the uppermost of the Mandan villages. It was by no means easy travelling, the thermometer nearly always below zero, sometimes as much as 36° below, high winds and drifting snow, food scarce, fuel practically unobtainable, and always the menace of savage Sioux.

La Vérendrye found six villages on the Missouri when he visited the Mandans. Thompson now notes five, altogether of 318 houses and seven tents, and of these some were not Mandans, but Willow or Fall

Indians (the Gros Ventres of the French),[1] so that the Mandans would seem to have diminished in numbers in the interval between the two visits. When Lewis and Clark reached the Mandan villages in 1804 they found five villages, only two of which were occupied by Mandans, the others belonging to the Minnetarees and the Ahnahaways or Amahami. From the Mandans themselves, Lewis and Clark obtained an interesting account of their origin. "Within the recollection of living witnesses, the Mandans were settled forty years ago in nine villages, the ruins of which we passed about eighty miles below, and situated seven on the west and two on the east side of the Missouri. The two, finding themselves wasting away before the small-pox and the Sioux, united into one village and moved up the river opposite to the Ricaras. The same causes reduced the remaining seven to five villages, till at length they emigrated in a body to the Ricara nation, where they formed themselves into two villages and joined those of their countrymen who had gone before them. In their new residence they were still insecure, and at length the three villages ascended the Missouri to their present position. The two who had emigrated together still settled in the two villages on the north-west side of the Missouri, while the single village took a position on the south-east side. In this

---

[1] Some confusion here. Thompson evidently means the Minnetarees, who were neighbours of the Mandans. The Fall Indians, or Atsinas, were a Saskatchewan tribe, of entirely different stock. The opprobrious name of Gros Ventres was applied by the western traders to both tribes— for some unexplained reason.

situation they were found by those who visited them in
1796, since which the two villages have united into one.
They are now in two villages, one on the south-east of
the Missouri, the other on the opposite side and at the
distance of three miles across. The first, in an open
plain, contains about forty or fifty lodges, built in the
same way as those of the Ricaras; the second, the
same number ; and both may raise about three hundred
and fifty men."

Lewis and Clark say that the Ahnahaways occupied
a village at the mouth of Knife River; that these people
formerly lived about thirty miles farther down the
Missouri; that they had been attacked by the Assiniboines and Sioux and the greater number put to death,
the few survivors emigrating to the position where they
were found in 1804, in order to obtain an asylum near
the more powerful and numerous Minnetarees. The
Ahnahaways were known to the French as Soulier Noir,
and the Mandans called them Wattasoons. There were
only about fifty of them left when Lewis and Clark
visited the village. The Minnetaree villages were
situated on either bank of Knife River, the one on the
south side half a mile, and that on the north side a mile
and a half above the junction of Knife River with the
Missouri.

Thompson remained with the Mandans until January
10th, trying to induce them to come north to the Assiniboine to trade, but without much success. The tribe
was much less dependent upon the traders than any
other in the west. They had learned to till the soil, in

situation they were found by those who visited them in 1796, since which the two villages have united into one. They are now in two villages, one on the south-east of the Missouri, the other on the opposite side and at the distance of three miles across. The first, in an open plain, contains about forty or fifty lodges, built in the same way as those of the Ricaras; the second, the same number; and both may raise about three hundred and fifty men."

Lewis and Clark say that the Ahnahaways occupied a village at the mouth of Knife River, that these people formerly lived about thirty miles farther down the Missouri, that they had been attacked by the Assiniboines and Sioux and the greater number put to death, the few survivors emigrating to the position where they were found in 1804, in order to obtain an asylum near the more powerful and numerous Minnetarees. The Ahnahaways were known to the French as Soulier Noir. Lewis and Clark and the Mandans called them Wattasoons. There were only about fifty of them left when Lewis and Clark visited the village. The Minnetaree villages were situated on either bank of Knife River, the one on the south side half a mile, and that on the north side a mile and a half above the junction of Knife River with the Missouri.

Thompson remained with the Mandans until January roth, trying to induce them to come north to the Assiniboine to trade, but without much success. The tribe was much less dependent upon the traders than any other in the west. They had learned to till the soil, in

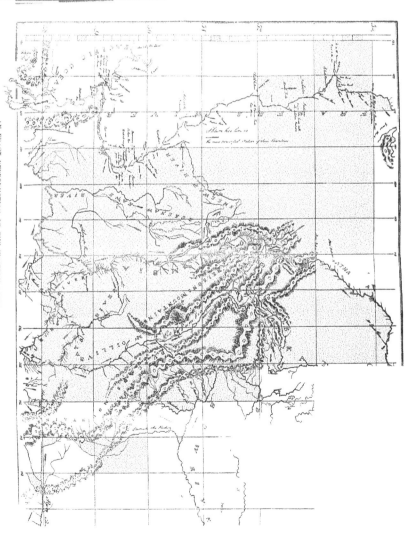

AN EXACT REPRODUCTION OF THE WESTERN PORTIO
OF NORTH-WESTERN

a rude fashion it is true, yet quite sufficient to supply all their wants and even to leave a considerable surplus for hospitality to strangers and purposes of trade. They were glad to have guns and ammunition, but could get on very well without them. Countless herds of buffalo came periodically to their very doors, and in hunting them bows and arrows were quite as serviceable as guns. On the whole, while willing enough to have the traders come to their villages, they saw no great necessity of going to their forts on the Assiniboine, and were by no means inclined to engage in the unfamiliar and degrading task of beaver hunting merely to satisfy the extraordinary demand of the white traders for these skins.

Thompson did his best to work up trade for the North West Company, but failing in this he turned, no doubt with considerable relief, to the much more congenial task of fixing the astronomical position of the several villages, estimating the distance and position of the source of the Missouri from such information as he could gather from the Indians, noting points of interest in connection with the Mandans and their neighbours, their manners, customs, and habitations, and preparing a vocabulary of the Mandan language said to contain about three hundred and seventy-five words. On January 10th he left the villages on his homeward journey. The lower village of the Mandans he found to be in lat. 47° 17′ 22″, long. 101° 14′ 24″, variation ten degrees east. Thompson's homeward course was practically identical with that followed on his way to the

Mandans. Leaving the Missouri, he travelled north, taking advantage of every little bit of woodland on his course for fuel and shelter. The weather was intensely cold and very stormy, and his progress was correspondingly slow. At fifty miles from the Missouri he reached Dog Tent Hill, passed on the outward journey. The distance from this hill to the elbow of the Souris River was twenty miles, and another fourteen miles brought him to the south end of Turtle Mountain. The distance from Turtle Mountain to Ash House he found to be twenty-four miles, and Ash House to McDonnell's House, forty-five miles. Thus he travelled one hundred and fifty-three miles from the Mandan villages on the Missouri to McDonnell's House on the Assiniboine. He arrived there on February 3rd, having been twenty-three days on his journey—not bad travelling in midwinter on the western plains. At McDonnell's House he remained for several weeks plotting his work and making preparations for an expedition on foot to the source of the Mississippi—a journey which he successfully accomplished in spite of the predictions of every one to the contrary. Before leaving McDonnell's house he determined its position by a series of observations to be lat. 49° 40′ 56″, long. 99° 27′ 15″, variation eleven degrees east.

The narratives of two subsequent expeditions to the Mandan villages are contained in Masson's *Bourgeois de la Compagnie du Nord-Ouest*. These are the Missouri Journal of F. A. Larocque, 1804-5, and the Missouri Indians of Charles Mackenzie, 1804-5-6. Both are of

interest. Larocque's journal and the narrative of Mackenzie's first expedition to the Missouri (he made four
altogether) describe the same journey. Mackenzie,
Larocque, and five men left Fort Assiniboine[1] in
November, 1804. Mackenzie's account of the way they
got away from the fort is instructive as to the rivalries
and jealousies of the fur traders. Chaboillez, the local
partner of the North West Company, had agreed with
his opponents that neither party should add to the existing outposts, within the limits of the district. Finding himself, however, with an inconvenient surplus both
of men and goods, he determined to send both to the
Mandan country, which lay without the bounds of the
agreement. It was necessary that the rival traders
should know nothing of this plan, lest they might adopt
the same expedient and perhaps get there first. Preparations were therefore made with the utmost secrecy,
and the party waited for an opportunity to steal away
without being noticed either by the rival traders or the
Assiniboines, who on account of their enmity to the
Missouri Indians would do all they could to prevent the
expedition. At length a fair opening presenting itself,
they took their departure. An independent trader
named La France, who had previously been to the

[1] This is the same establishment known in 1797–8, when David
Thompson visited it, as McDonnell's House or Stone Indian River House.
It was exceptionally well situated for the fur trade, affording easy communications in every direction. Dr. Coues notes the existence at this
place in the winter of 1794–5 of no less than five mutually opposing
trading houses. C. J. B. Chaboillez was in charge of Fort Assiniboine at
the time of Mackenkie and Larocque's journey to the Mandans, and corre-
sponded with Lewis and Clark, who were then at the Mandan villages.

Mandans, accompanied the party as guide and interpreter.

Larocque and Mackenzie had successfully eluded their opponents, but it was by no means certain that they were yet clear of the Assiniboines, who were encamped some distance south of the fort.- To avoid them the traders swung around on a south-westerly course until they should be clear of the Assiniboine country. But if this was not out of the frying-pan, it was literally into the fire, for as they got into the open country they found themselves almost surrounded by prairie fires. In the course of a few days they passed whole herds of buffaloes all singed with the flames, many maimed, some blind, while half-roasted carcasses strewed the way. Wood and water were unobtainable, and both the men and their horses were well-nigh exhausted by the time they reached the other side of the fire belt. Finally they came to a high hill known as Dog Lodge, between the Souris and the northern edge of the Coteau de Missouri. As this was a favourite stopping-place of the Sioux on their war expeditions, the traders advanced with caution, and not without reason, for as they reached the summit of the ridge they suddenly heard the signal cry of Indians in the valley below. As there was no possibility of escape, they went boldly on, determined to fight their way through if necessary. On approaching the Indians, however, they found them to be Assiniboines from one of the North West Company's posts on the Souris River. After smoking a pipe together, the traders mounted their horses and were about to proceed on their way, when one of the Assiniboines, who had stood moodily aside and refused to smoke with them, suddenly laid hold of the bridle of one of the horses. Larocque, without a moment's hesitation, snatched the bridle out of his hand. The Indian dropped his robe and put an arrow to his bow as if to shoot the horse, but dropped it hastily as one of the traders levelled his gun. The man would even then have shot the Assiniboine, had not Larocque interfered and compelled him to put up his gun.

After this disagreeable incident, which might have turned out much more seriously than it did, the party proceeded on its way. This was but an advance party of a large band of Assiniboines who were on their way back from a trading expedition to the Mandan villages, which accounted for the fact that they had not seriously opposed the passage of the white men. A peace had been patched up and the two tribes were, temporarily at least, on friendly terms.

That night they camped by the side of a small creek, and not only picketed their horses, but took turns in sentinel duty throughout the night. Notwithstanding all their precautions, however, the Assiniboines —the most skilful horse-thieves in the world—carried off two. The following morning they found the Assiniboine road leading to the Missouri, and travelled rapidly south ; passed an Indian encampment at noon and counted seventy-five fire-places ; passed two more encampments in the evening, and camped by the side of a small lake, the only spot they could find that afforded any grass for their horses.

Setting out at sunrise the next morning, they had not travelled two hours before they met a couple of Minnetarees out hunting. They smoked a pipe together and went their several ways. At midday they saw the smoke of one of the Minnetaree villages, and at two in the afternoon arrived at another, where, says Mackenzie, "the natives flew in crowds to meet us, wishing us joy, and congratulating themselves upon our appearance as traders amongst them." Here they found four Hudson's Bay Company men, also on a trading expedition, who, having lost their way a few days before and fallen in with a party of Assiniboines, the latter had made them pay handsomely for their liberty. They had reached the village with a very much diminished stock of goods, and expecting no opposition had endeavoured to recoup themselves by doubling the prices of the remainder. Hence the joy of the Minnetarees on the appearance of the rival traders.

Leaving Mackenzie here to secure all the furs that the Hudson's Bay men had not already purchased, Larocque went on to the Mandan villages, meeting on the way Captain Meriwether Lewis, of the Lewis and Clark expedition, who invited him to the fort which they had just completed and in which they were to pass the ensuing winter. A few days later Captain Lewis sent for Larocque, having heard that he was distributing flags and medals to the Indians, which he forbade him to do in the name of the United States.

"As I had neither flags nor medals," dryly remarks Làrocque, " I ran no risk of disobeying those orders." On another occasion Lewis, who was inclined to be overbearing in his attitude toward the Indians, har- angued them on the objects of his expedition, but Mac- kenzie thought the Indians did not seem to be very deeply impressed. "Had these Whites come among us," said one of the warriors, "with charitable views, they would have loaded their Great Boat with neces- saries. It is true they have ammunition, but they prefer throwing it away idly to sparing a shot of it to a poor Mandan." One of the chiefs of the Minne- tarees remarked contemptuously that if he had these white warriors on the upper plains, his young men on horseback would soon do for them as they would do for so many wolves, for, said he, there are only two sensible men among them, the worker of iron (black- smith) and the mender of guns.

The Mandan villages were revelling in plenty, buffalo having paused an unusually long time around the Missouri on their great annual migration to the south. The Indians, with characteristic prodigality and lack of foresight, surrounded whole herds, killing them all, old and young, and taking nothing but the tongues. Wolves feasted on the carcasses until they could no longer run, and became an easy prey to the hunters. Though beaver were plentiful along the Missouri, the Mandans and Minnetarees could not be induced to hunt them. "White people," said they, "do not know how to live. They leave their houses in small parties; they risk their lives on the great waters, among strange nations who will take them for enemies. What is the use of beaver? Do they make gunpowder of them? Do they preserve them from sickness? Do they serve them beyond the grave?"

Mackenzie remarked to one of the Missouri Indians that the Assiniboines and Crees were very industrious, and great friends to the white people. "We are no slaves!" he replied scornfully. "Our fathers were not slaves! In my young days there were no white men, and we knew no wants. We were successful in war ; our arrows were pointed with flint, our lances with stone, and their wounds were mortal. Our villages rejoiced when the men returned from war, for of the scalps of our enemies they brought many. The white people came; they brought with them some good, but they brought the small-pox, and they brought evil liquors. The Indians since diminish, and they are no longer happy." What an indictment to come from savagery to civilization!

Mackenzie has much to say as to the primitive agriculture of the Mandans, and his account is worth comparing with those of Lewis and Clark, Catlin, Alexander Henry, and Prince Maximilian. "In the spring," he says, "as soon as the weather and the state of the ground will permit, the women repair to the fields, when they cut the stalks of the Indian corn of the preceding year and drop new seed into the socket of the remaining roots. A small kind of pumpkins which are very productive they plant with a dibble, and raise the ground into hillocks the same as those about Indian corn. Their kidney beans they plant in the same manner.

" They cultivate a tall kind of sunflower, the seed of which is reckoned good eating, dry and pounded with fat and made into balls of three or four ounces. They are found excellent for long journeys. One of these balls, with the addition of a few roots gathered occasionally in their way, is considered sufficient for a whole day. Warriors who generally travel great distances in quest of an enemy, and who dare not raise a smoke or fire a shot for fear of discovery, find these balls useful, light, and convenient.

" The only implement used among the Mandans for the purpose of agriculture is a hoe made from the shoulder-blade of a buffalo, and which is ingrafted on a short crooked handle. With this crooked instrument they work very expeditiously, and soon do all that is required for their supplies.

" The men never trouble their heads about the labours of the field unless to reprimand the women for some noted neglect, and to sow a few squares of tobacco, which, being a sacred plant, the women, who are considered unclean, must not interfere with, except in preparing the ground for its reception. The tobacco squares are carefully kept clear of weeds. The blossoms are cautiously collected and, dried in the sun, are reckoned the very best of tobacco. The plants do not exceed a foot in height; they resemble spinage, and are dried the same as the flowers, then pounded and mixed with grease for use. This kind of tobacco is weak, tastes differently from ours, and the smell which the smoke emits is very disagreeable to strangers."

Larocque records the fact that the observations of Lewis and Clark for the longitude of the Mandan villages differed materially from those of David Thompson. Lewis and Clark asserted that Thompson had placed the villages and this part of the Missouri a great deal too far to the westward, and expressed the opinion that this was the case with all his observations for longitude. On the other hand, Dr. Elliott Coues has stated that Thompson's longitude was remarkably accurate, differing only slightly from the latest official observations.

On April 2nd, having spent the winter among the Mandans, Mackenzie and Larocque left the Missouri for Fort Assiniboine, which they reached after an uneventful journey on May 22nd, 1805. On June 3rd of the same year, accompanied by three men with thirteen horses, they again left Fort Assiniboine for the Mandan villages, intending to proceed from thence on a tour of discovery toward the Rocky Mountains, and if possible open up a trade with the Rocky Mountain Indians or Crows. Arrived at the Missouri, they found a number of the young men in one of the Minnetaree villages dressed in clothing which they recognized as that of Canadian *voyageurs*. They could get nothing but evasive answers to their questions, until at last the truth came out. A war party had been to the banks of the South Saskatchewan, and coming upon an encampment in the night, fired on what they supposed to be Blackfeet, but which turned out to be a party of white traders. The traders fled to their canoes, and the warriors plundered the tent and returned with the spoils. This at least was the tale the Indians told. The other side of the story is found in the Autobiographical Notes of John McDonald of Garth.[1] McDonald on his way down the Saskatchewan had ordered his guide Bouché with several men to camp at a certain place where buffalo were plentiful, while he went on to meet some Indians who had promised to bring him a quantity of furs. He told Bouché the day he was to leave camp, and when he would be expected at the next fort down the river. That night, while some of the party were sleeping under their canoes on the beach, and others in the tent some little distance back from the water at the foot of a high sloping bank, one of the men came to Bouché and told him that he had gone to the top of the bank and seen in the distance what looked like a band of horsemen, and he urged Bouché to break camp and move to a safer spot. Bouché, however, with rare fidelity, would not disobey his instructions. "My orders are to stay here," he replied; "the time will be out to-morrow morning, and then we shall all leave this; all is ready as ordered." Next morning at daybreak they were attacked by the Minnetarees; Bouché and two of his men were shot down in their tent; those on the shore managed to get out in their canoes and drove off the Indians.

[1] Masson, II, 33-4.

Some time before, while McDonald was at Chester-field House, at the confluence of Red Deer River with the South Saskatchewan, trading with the Blackfeet, a horseman was seen by the watch riding at full speed toward the fort. He was superbly mounted and dressed in a richly ornamented suit of deerskin; a very handsome man and a perfect rider. In an instant he was off his horse, which he gave in charge to one of the men standing by idle, and stalked into McDonald's tent. "I am of the Missouri Indians," he said to McDonald. "We have made peace with the whites, but we are at war with the Blackfeet; they surround you, and are also your friends. I come from a small band; we are but few; but if you receive us as friends, we will fight our way in, and trade or fall." McDonald smoked a pipe with him, and told him that he had nothing to do with their quarrel. With this he mounted his fiery steed, and made off at full gallop through the astonished Blackfeet. Next day about noon the band of Minne-tarees appeared and attacked the Blackfeet. The battle raged all the afternoon, when the remnant of the Minnetarees were surrounded and captured. During the night, however, in spite of the vigilance of the Blackfeet, they managed to escape, carrying their wounded and dead with them. It was no doubt this small party of Minnetarees that afterward attacked Bouché and his men. That they mistook the traders for Blackfeet is improbable. More likely the attack was premeditated in retaliation for McDonald's refusal to side with the Minnetarees against the Blackfeet. It

INDIAN TEEPEES, NEAR ELBOW OF SASKATCHEWAN

must be remembered that McDonald had left Chesterfield House with Bouché, and it was only by a mere
accident that he was not in camp when the Minnetarees made their attack.

Returning to Larocque and Mackenzie, when they
broached their project of an expedition to the Rocky
Mountains they found the Minnetarees bitterly opposed. The burden of their opposition was that if
the traders opened communications with the Crows
and other tribes toward the mountains they "not only
would lose all the benefit which they had hitherto
derived from their intercourse with these distant tribes,
but that in measure as these tribes obtained arms they
would become independent and insolent in the extreme."

This put the traders in a quandary, and they decided
to consult the head chief of the tribe, Le Borgne, a
man of very superior character, who wielded an extraordinary influence over his wild followers.   Le Borgne
was ill, but at once reassured them.   " The Chief of the
white people wishes you to visit the Rocky Mountains,"
said he, "and you shall visit them.   When I shall be
well, no one dare hinder you."   And he was as good as
his word.

About the middle of June a large party of Crows
arrived on the banks of the Missouri. " They consisted,"
says Mackenzie, " of more than three hundred tents,
and presented the handsomest sight that one could
imagine; all on horseback, children of small size were
lashed to the saddle, and those above the age of six

2 B

could manage a horse. The women had wooden saddles; most of the men had none. There were a great many horses for the baggage, and the whole, exceeding two thousand, covered a large space of ground and had the appearance of an army. They halted on a rising ground behind the village, and, having formed a circle, the chief addressed them. They then descended full speed, rode through the village exhibiting their dexterity in horsemanship in a thousand shapes. I was astonished to see their agility and address, and I do believe they are the best riders in the world."

The Crows remained for a few days trading, and then prepared to return to their homes. A dramatic scene followed. Le Borgne sent word to Larocque to make ready for the journey. The Minnetarees, "perceiving the intention of the preparations, crowded into our quarters and threatened Mr. Larocque with their displeasure should he persist in his design. At this moment the Great Chief entered with a battle-axe in his hand. Staring around him with an imperious air, he asked in a thundering tone why so many Indians were assembled there? They answered that they came to take their last farewell of the white men, who they expected never to see again.

"'Why,' asked the Chief, with a sneer, 'should you feel so much concern if the white men are inclined to risk their lives in a strange land? That is no business of yours. You have warned them sufficiently of the danger, yet they will go on.' By this time the Indians, one by one, went sneaking out of the way."

Larocque accompanied the Crows to their far western home, while Mackenzie remained with the Minnetarees and Mandans.   Mackenzie notes his return on the 18th November, in his journal, but adds : " It is not necessary that I should give the particulars of his journey, as Mr. Larocque himself has kept an account of it.   I shall merely observe that he was disappointed in his expedition [presumably so far as working up a trade with the Crows was concerned], suffered great hardships, and took no less than thirty-six days on his return to our establishment."

In 1806 Alexander Henry the younger made a journey to the Mandans.   He left Fort Assiniboine on July 14th.   His party consisted of seven men.   The guide was the same Hugh McCraken who had aecompanied Thompson.   From Henry's narrative it appears that he had formerly been in the artillery.   Ammunition, tobacco, knives, beads, etc., were taken to trade with the Mandans ; half a bag of pemmican and three pieces of dried meat formed all their stock of provisions.   They expected to encounter buffalo and antelope, and could always fall back on wild duck and other small game.   Each man rode on horseback, and the horses had to carry also fifty pounds of provisions and equipment, as well as arms, blankets, and ammunition —altogether a pretty heavy burden.   Their course was at first through a hilly country.   Herds of antelope were always in sight.   They had left the fort early in the morning, and by the middle of the afternoon crossed the Souris River at Plum Creek, where the town of Souris now stands. Keeping along the north side of the river, at sunset they reached the site of Ash House, where they camped. Fearing the Assiniboines, who were inveterate horse-thieves, they fettered their horses around the fire. A strong breeze kept the mosquitoes down in the grass, and the tired travellers sat around contentedly until eleven o'clock, when suddenly the wind came about from the north-west, bringing a terrible thunderstorm. The rain fell in torrents, the weather became excessively sultry, and the mosquitoes were upon them in clouds. They passed a miserable night, having but one small tent, into which was crowded all the baggage besides the seven members of the party.

In the morning they had much difficulty in saddling the horses, who were dancing mad with the mosquitoes. Finally they mounted, wet to the skin, and proceeded along the bank of the river, here very high. Antelope were still in sight, but so shy that they could not get a shot. From the top of a sand-hill on the Assiniboine trail they could see Turtle Mountain bearing south-east, distant about seven leagues. The heat was intolerable, without a breath of air, and the mosquitoes tormented them continually. They camped that night in comparative comfort on a high hill near the banks of the Souris. It was the rutting season, and the buffalo, who were in immense numbers to the westward, kept up a terrible bellowing all night long. They were now some distance to the westward of Turtle Mountain, having made a wide circuit to avoid the Assiniboines who were camped thereabout.

. At daybreak they saddled and continued their journey. The level plains were covered with buffalo, all in motion, bellowing and tearing up the ground as they went. They killed a bull, and took a few slices of the flesh for the noon meal. That day they made good progress, sometimes travelling at a gallop, never slower than a trot, and camped for the night out on the open prairie. The following day they again crossed the Souris and journeyed south toward the Coteau du Missouri, the tableland which separates the waters of the Missouri basin from those of the Assiniboine. This was Sioux territory, and a watch was kept each night to guard against surprise. Finally, ascending a range of high hills, they discerned through a spyglass the high red banks of the Missouri about six leagues distant. The question was, however, where were the Mandan villages? Some of the party were confident that they were many leagues below; others, including the guide, were equally sure that they were above the villages. The situation was rather critical. If they were below the Mandans, and persisted in following the river downward, they would fall in with the Pawnees and Tetons, both of whom were supposed to be at war with the Mandans, and would have no mercy on the traders. On the other hand, if they were too high up their situation would be equally dangerous, for they might travel as far as the south branch of the Saskatchewan, where they would be very likely to fall victim to the Blackfeet.

In this dilemma Henry thought it best to trust to

McCraken, the guide, who at least was more familiar
with the Missouri country than any one else in the
party. McCraken was convinced that they were some
distance above the Mandans, and so the sequel showed.
Under his guidance they made straight for the banks
of the river, and on ascending a high hill he pointed out
a prominent landmark then called the Loge de Serpent,
and still well known as the Snake's Den. This at once
fixed their position, for the Loge de Serpent was
familiar to every one who had visited the Missouri.
About noon they reached the banks of the river, and
descending the high banks at the mouth of Rivière
Bourbeuse, now Snake Creek, followed the river down
to the winter village of the Minnetarees. Leaving this
behind, they travelled for a few miles through a rough
country, and with much difficulty got their horses up a
steep bank, from which they obtained a delightful and
extensive prospect of the river in both directions. Its
borders were well lined with several varieties of trees,
and the valley of the river, about two miles wide, was
hemmed in on either side by stupendous banks on
which nothing grew but a short grass. They had now
a clear road before them with good travelling. About
the middle of the afternoon they descended a long
sloping hill, and arrived opposite the upper Minnetaree
village. They shouted to the natives to come and ferry
them across, but, no notice being taken of the request,
they mounted and rode down about five miles to the
Mandan village on the north side, having noticed as
they passed another Minnetaree village, as well as a

village of "Saulteurs," as Henry calls them, the small tribe which Lewis and Clark call Ahnahaways.

As they approached the village they met one of the Mandans armed with his gun guarding a party of women who were hoeing corn. On perceiving them he came forward in a friendly manner and requested by signs that they would put up at his village. As they neared the village the chief, Le Chat Noir, came out to meet them and bade them welcome. He conducted them to one of his lodges appropriated for the reception of strangers and sent one of his wives to wait on them. On going into the hut they found buffalo skins spread out on the ground, a good fire burning in the centre, and presently two large dishes of boiled corn and beans were brought in, with boiled venison.

When Henry and his party had satisfied their hunger, the Mandans brought buffalo robes, corn, beans, dried squashes, etc., to trade, but he informed them that he had come merely to visit them and see the country. They could not comprehend why he had come so far out of mere curiosity, and told him that all white people who came to their villages did so with a view to trade. Finally they went away disappointed and incredulous.

Henry, with that generous curiosity which makes his journal so extremely valuable as an exact record of native life on the western plains at the beginning of the nineteenth century, examined every nook and corner of the Mandan village, and recorded what he found there with a frankness that is sometimes rather startling. It is interesting to find that the habits and customs of this noteworthy tribe were practically the same as La Vérendrye had found them in 1738. Henry's description of the Mandan huts is exceptionally minute. " I examined," he says, " the one I lodged in, and found it ninety feet from the door to the opposite side. The whole space is first dug out about one and a half feet below the surface of the earth. In the centre is the square fireplace, about five feet on each side, dug out about two feet below the surface of the ground flat. The lower part of the hut is constructed by erecting strong posts about six feet out of the ground, at equal distances from each other, according to the proposed size of the hut, as they are not all of the same dimensions. Upon these are laid logs as large as the posts, reaching from post to post to form the circle. On the outer side are placed pieces of split wood seven feet long, in a slanting direction, one end resting on the ground, the other leaning against the cross-logs or beams. Upon these beams rest rafters about the thickness of a man's leg, and twelve to fifteen feet long, slanting enough to drain off the rain, and laid so close to each other as to touch. The upper ends of the rafters are supported upon stout pieces of squared timber, which last are supported by four thick posts about five feet in circumference, fifteen feet out of the ground and fifteen feet asunder, forming a square. Over these squared timbers others of equal size are laid, crossing them at right angles, leaving an opening about four feet square. This serves for chimney and windows, as there are no other openings to admit light, and when it rains even this hole is covered over with a canoe to prevent the rain from injuring their gammine [*sic*] and earthen pots. The whole roof is well thatched with the small willows in which the Missourie abounds, laid on to the thickness of six inches or more, fastened together in a very compact manner and well secured to the rafters. Over the whole is spread about one foot of earth, and around the wall, to the height of three or four feet, is commonly laid up earth to the thickness of three feet for security in case of an attack and to keep out the cold. The door is five feet broad and six high, and a covered way or porch on the outside of the same height as the door, seven feet broad and ten in length. The doors are made of raw buffalo hide stretched upon a frame and suspended by cords from one of the beams which form the circle. Every night the door is barricaded with a long piece of timber supported by two stout posts set in the ground in the inside of the hut, one on each side of the door.

"On entering the hut, the first thing that strikes the view is a kind of triangular apartment, always on the left hand and fronting the fire, leaving an open space on the right; this is to hold firewood in winter. . . . Between this partition and the fire is commonly a distance of about five feet which the master of the hut occupies during the day, seated on a mat made of small willows of equal size, fastened together by threads of their own manufacture passed through each stick about a foot apart. . . . Over the mat is spread a kind of buffalo skin. Some of these couches are raised a foot off the ground.

"Upon this a Mandane sits all day, receives his friends, smokes, and chats the time away with the greatest dignity. . . . At the bottom of the hut, fronting the master's seat, stands his medicine-stage, which may be called his chief treasure, as it contains everything he values most. The article of most consequence is a pair of bull's horns. . . . There are also laid, or rather hung up, his arms, shield, ammunition, scalps, and everything else he most values. Next this stage stands the mortar and pestle, fixed firmly in the ground. The rest of the hut, from this place to the door, is vacant during the day, but occupied at night by the horses."

One notable change that had taken place in the life of the Mandans since La Vérendrye's visit sixty-eight years before was the introduction of horses. In La Vérendrye's day they hunted and travelled and went to war on foot. In 1806 they did all this on horseback. Of their horses they were extravagantly fond; many owned from twenty to thirty, but could rarely be induced to part with even an inferior animal. For a trained war horse they demanded fabulous prices; in fact there was but one equivalent for such a horse—the sacred hide of a white buffalo. Henry gives an amusingly graphic account of the manner of offering such a hide for sale.

"The person who has brought it to the Missourie gives

out that on such a day he will expose it for sale in a certain hut. That morning he fixes two sticks in the ground with a crotch to support the ends of a pole, about four feet in length, over which he stretches the skin, raised about three feet from the ground, the tail hanging downward. When he takes his station near by, the sale commences by a native bringing a horse, which he ties in the hut. But as this is not a sufficient price, the owner of the hide casts a look at it, and, without saying a word, takes hold of the tail of the hide and gives it a gentle shake, which signifies 'not enough.' Soon another horse is brought, generally loaded with corn, beans, etc. The owner of the hide again gently shakes the tail, and continues to do so until they have brought in six or eight horses, loaded with corn, beans, robes, garnished leggings, shoes, smocks, etc. Not until he has secured an enormous payment does he cease to shake the tail at every article that the natives bring to add to the price. But when they imagine they have given enough for the hide, they then bring mere trifles, just to keep tally with the tail. The owner, who then perceives there is no prospect of getting anything more of consequence, rises from his seat, and shakes the tail no more, which is considered as the conclusion of the sale. The hide is then taken away, cut into strips, and distributed among those who gave anything towards the purchase, every one receiving according to the value of his contribution."

Henry notes a peculiarity of the Mandans that has attracted the attention of every traveller who has visited this tribe, from La Vérendrye to Maximilian of Wied; that is, the unusual colour of their hair. " These people in general," he says, " have not such strong, coarse hair as other natives of North America; they have it much finer, rather inclining to a dark brown, and I observed some whose hair was almost fair "; but what struck him as most singular was that several children about ten years of age had perfectly grey hair. Their eyes, too, were not jet black, as in most of the Indian tribes, but inclined to a dark brown, some few dark grey.

Toward the end of July Henry returned to the Assiniboine, following a more direct route than on his outward journey, but on the whole a more dangerous one. As he says, by the more westerly route they had nothing worse to fear than the stealing of their horses by the Assiniboines, while here they were within the borders of the Sioux country, and " should they fall in with us we could expect no mercy, as they have never been known to give any quarter to white people in this country." However, the whole party arrived safely at Fort Assiniboine without serious misadventure.

PART III

THE ROAD TO THE SEA

CHAPTER I

ALEXANDER HENRY, FUR TRADER AND TRAVELLER

ALEXANDER HENRY, nephew of the pioneer fur trader of the same name, entered the service of the North West Company about the year 1792, but there is no record of his movements until the autumn of 1799. In that year he went up, probably by the usual route from Montreal, which followed the Ottawa River, Lake Nipissing, French River, Lake Huron, and Lake Superior, to Grand Portage, and thence to Lake Winnipeg and the Assiniboine country to the westward of Lake Manitoba. His journal opens abruptly, in the autumn of 1799, at Rivière Terre Blanche (White Mud *White Mud* River), about thirty-five or forty miles west-north-west of Portage la Prairie, where he was building a trading post. Here he spent the winter, suffering seriously from lack of provisions. This was a lean year; game was scarce, and "hunger was the general cry at our establishments along the Assiniboine."

In the spring of 1800 Henry returned to Grand Portage with the results of his first winter's trade, and on the 19th July he is again found on his way west by way of Rainy Lake and the Lake of the Woods. From Lake Winnipeg he turned up Red River and reached the mouth of the Assiniboine on August 18th, where he found traces of an old French trading post, no doubt the Fort Rouge of La Vérendrye's day. Henry speaks feelingly of the clinging character of the black mud or clay along the river's edge, which "the last rain had turned into a kind of mortar that adheres to the foot like tar, so that at every step we raise several pounds of it." Those who knew the streets of Winnipeg a few years ago, before they had been paved, will recognize the picture presented by Henry, and conjure up as a companion to it the once familiar sight of a cart sunk to the axle in thick, black, tenacious clay, and successfully resisting the united efforts of horse, driver, and any number of bystanders to drag it out.

Henry continued his way up the Red River, part of the brigade having already been sent up the Assiniboine to Portage la Prairie. A few days' paddling brought the Red River brigade to the borders of the buffalo country, to the delight of all, for this meant an abundance of fresh meat. Henry's narrative gives one an idea of the amazing numbers of the buffalo in his day. "The beach," he says, "once a soft black mud into which a man would sink knee-deep, is now made hard as pavement by the numerous herds coming to drink. The willows are entirely trampled and torn to pieces; even the bark of the smaller trees is rubbed off in places. The grass on the first bank of the river is entirely worn away." The traders had reached the commencement of the great plains of Red River, "where the eye is lost in one continuous level westward." Again, farther up the river, Henry describes the buffalo as forming "one body commencing about half a mile from camp, whence the plain was covered on the west side of the river as far as the eye could reach. They were moving southward slowly, and the meadow seemed as if in motion."

Traders and Indians alike were in continual dread of the fierce Sioux, across whose war path the party was now travelling. Henry had the utmost difficulty in preventing his men from turning back. Scarcely a day passed but false alarms were raised: horsemen were seen far out on the plains, who gradually resolved themselves into a herd of buffalo; footprints were discovered on the river's bank, which were found to be those of some of their own party; and so the story goes from day to day. A detachment was left at the mouth of Red River to build a post, and Henry and the others continued up the river, crossing the present international boundary, and so on up to the mouth of Pembina River, where stood a fort built by Chaboillez of the North West Company in 1797, and on the other side of the Red River the remains of an old fort built by Peter Grant four or five years earlier, the first trading post on the upper waters of the Red River, if we except the somewhat doubtful French post attributed to La Vérendrye. Still making his way up the Red River, Henry at last reached the mouth of Park River, and about a quarter of a mile up the latter found a suitable place for a fort. All hands went energetically to work, by the end of September the stockade was completed,

2 C

and before cold weather set in they were under cover. Deadly fear of the Sioux still haunted the men, and this, from Henry's point of view, was not an unmixed evil. "Fear," he remarks dryly, "is an excellent overseer, and the work went on with expedition."

Henry wintered at his Park River post, spending the time trading with the Indians, hunting, and making short journeys into the surrounding country. In May, 1801, he abandoned Park River, and moved down to the Pembina, where he selected a site for a fort at the mouth of the river, on the north side, opposite the old Chaboillez establishment. Leaving some of his men to build the fort, Henry descended the Red River with the proceeds of his winter's trade; learned at the Forks that the people at Portage la Prairie were living on roots; went up on horseback to investigate, and found them at the point of starvation. He remained at Portage la Prairie until June 1st, when he embarked in a light canoe with eight men for Grand Portage.

On August 23rd he was back at the Pembina, where he found the stockades erected and houses and stores nearly finished. His people had been in a constant state of alarm on account of the Sioux. This, however, did not worry Henry nearly so much as the appearance of a party of Hudson's Bay men, and another of the rival Canadian (X Y) Company, who both built posts below him on the Red River. "None of them," he says, "dare build above me for fear of the Sioux." The winter passed in keen rivalry among the various traders, broken by a friendly carouse on New Year's night at

Henry's house. "Before sunrise both sexes of all parties were intoxicated and more troublesome than double their number of Saulteurs." "Liquor," comments Henry elsewhere, "is the root of all evil in the North West." Nevertheless, he bowed to what he conceived to be the inevitable, and distributed it freely to his native patrons.

In June, 1803, Henry went down to head-quarters with the brigade, reaching Lake Superior on the 3rd of July. At Rainy River he procured a guide to conduct the canoes by the new route to the mouth of the Kaministikwia, the head-quarters of the Company having been moved since his last visit from Grand Portage to what was soon to be known as Fort William. They left the old Grand Portage route in Lac la Croix, entered Sturgeon River, and after traversing various small waterways crossed Lac des Mille Lacs, from whence they descended the Kaministikwia. "The Kaministiquia route at the beginning of this [nineteenth] century," says Dr. Coues, "corresponds in most of its extent to the present Dawson route as a practicable waterway, with various portages, from Lac la Croix to Thunder Bay of Lake Superior." "Before 1800," he continues, "the route was an 'old' French waterway, which had been abandoned and in a measure lost sight of by the English, who used the Pigeon River route from Grand Portage." This is scarcely accurate, as, so far as our records go, the Kaministikwia route had never been used by the English traders, and was unknown to them, until Roderick McKenzie reopened it in 1797, as described in an earlier chapter.

As to the date of the founding of Fort William, Dr. Coues finds it to vary, with different authorities, from 1801 to 1807, the date usually assigned being 1803. The explanation, however, is simple : " The movement from Grand Portage to Kaministiquia appears to have begun in 1801 ; and building went on in 1802 and 1803, as we see by Henry, but was not expected to be completed till 1804. Moreover, the fort did not receive its present name till 1807, when it was so called in honor of William Macgillivray, then one of the personages of the North West Company."

Henry found great changes when he visited the New Fort in 1803. Fort, store, shop, etc., were all built, and a number of dwelling-houses; building was going on briskly in every corner of the fort ; brick kilns had been erected and were turning out many bricks ; so that everything would be complete and in good order before their arrival the following year.

The 27th of September finds Henry once more at his post on the Pembina, where the fur trade is in full blast. Horses have now become an indispensable part of the fur trader's equipment, somewhat to Henry's disgust, who believes that their introduction has made both his men and the Indians indolent, insolent, and extravagant. To illustrate his argument, he gives an amusing picture of the "bustle and noise which attended the transportation of five pieces of goods" to one of his branch establishments.

" Antoine Payet, guide and second in command, leads
the van, with a cart drawn by two horses and loaded
with his private baggage, cassetetes, bags, kettles, etc.
Madame Payet follows the cart with a child a year old
on her back, very merry. Charles Bottineau, with two
horses and a cart loaded with $1\frac{1}{2}$ packs, his own baggage,
and two young children, with kettles and other trash
hanging on to it. Madame Bottineau with a squalling
infant on her back, scolding and tossing it about.
Joseph Dubord goes on foot, with his long pipe-stem
and calumet in his hand; Madame Dubord follows on
foot, carrying his tobacco pound with a broad bead tail.
Antoine Thellier, with a cart and two horses, loaded
with $1\frac{1}{2}$ packs of goods and Dubois' baggage. Antoine
La Pointe, with another cart and horses, loaded with two
pieces of goods and with baggage belonging to Brisebois, Jasmin, and Pouliot, and a kettle hung on each
side. Auguste Brisebois follows with only his gun on
his shoulder and a fresh-lighted pipe in his mouth.
Michel Jasmin goes next, like Brisebois, with gun and
pipe, puffing out clouds of smoke. Nicolas Pouliot, the
greatest smoker in the North West, has nothing but
pipe and pouch. Those three fellows, having taken
a farewell dram and lighted fresh pipes, go on brisk and
merry, playing numerous pranks. Domin Livernois,
with a young mare, the property of Mr. Langlois, loaded
with weeds for smoking, an old worsted bag (madame's
property), some squashes and potatoes, a small keg of
fresh water, and two young whelps howling. Next goes
Livernois' young horse, drawing a travaille loaded with

reopened it in 179 as desc
chapter.

As to the date of 1e founding
Coues finds it to var, with differ
1801 to 1807, the de usually a
The explanation, hower, is simpl
from Grand Portage o Kaministiq
begun in 1801 ; anc building we.
1803, as we see by Hnry, but was :
completed till 1804. Moreover, the f
its present name ti 1807, when it
honor of William Magillivray, then or
ages of the North Vest Company.

Henry found greachanges wh
Fort in 1803. Fortstore, shop,
a number of dwellig-houses ;
briskly in every corrr of the fort
erected and were irning out r
everything would becomplete an
their arrival the follwing year.

The 27th of Sepember find
his post on the Pebina, wher
blast. Horses havnow beco
of the fur trader'sequipmen
disgust, who believs that th
both his men and he Indi
extravagant. To lustrate
amusing picture of be "bustl
the transportationf five pi
his branch establisnents.

.ion

was
ınd in
ır **the**
ırtage
Souris
ndans,
in an

River
askat-
r four
ugust,
This
e fur
wing

his baggage and a large worsted mashguemcate [what-ever that may be] belonging to Madame Langlois. Next appears Madame Cameron's mare, kicking, rear-ing, and snorting, hauling a travaille loaded with a bag of flour, cabbages, turnips, onions, a small keg of water, and a large kettle of broth. Michel Langlois, who is master of the band, now comes on leading a horse that draws a travaille nicely covered with a new painted tent, under which his daughter and Mrs. Cameron lie at full length, very sick; this covering or canopy has a pretty effect in the caravan, and appears at a great distance in the plains. Madame Langlois brings up the rear of the human beings, following the travaille with a slow step and melancholy air, attending to the wants of her daughter, who, notwithstanding her sickness, can find no other expressions of gratitude to her parents than by calling them dogs, fools, beasts, etc. The rear guard consists of a long train of twenty dogs, some for sleighs, some for game, and others of no use whatever, except to snarl and destroy meat. The total forms a procession nearly a mile long, and appears like a large band of Assiniboines."

A curiously vivid glimpse this into the lighter side of the life of the western fur trader, whose very environ-ment brought him so close to the simplicity and savagery amid which he moved. And the savagery is never far off. Brutality and murder become common-place, and Henry gives little more weight to a shooting affray than he does to the fate of his kitchen garden; rather less, in fact, if only Indians are involved. Note the grim humour of this paragraph, doubly grim because quite unconscious : " Le.Boeuf stabbed his young wife in the arm, Little Shell almost beat his old mother's brains out with a club, and there was terrible fighting among them. I sowed garden seed."

In May, 1804, Henry again started out from Pembina for Lake Superior. June 1st he was on Lake Winnipeg, his own brigade joined by another from the Red River making an imposing array as they swept across the lake eighteen craft abreast, all singing and keeping time with their paddles and oars. He reached Kaministikwia on June 25th, and on September 6th was back once more at his fort on the Pembina. New Year's Day brought the welcome news from Montreal of the union of the North West and X Y companies, which had taken place November 5th, 1804. Another trip was made to Lake Superior in the summer of 1805 ; and in July of the following year Henry left Pembina for the Assiniboine. Two days' journey brought him to Portage la Prairie, and from there he travelled to the Souris River post, on his way to the Missouri and the Mandans, an account of which expedition has been given in an earlier chapter.

May 8th, 1808, Henry finally left the Red River department and turned his face toward the Saskatchewan, where he was to spend the next three or four years. He reached the mouth of Red River in August, and coasted up the west side of Lake Winnipeg. This west side of the lake was but little known to the fur traders, the usual route to the Saskatchewan following the east shore. Henry had never been there before, though some of his men may have been over the ground. In any case they made the journey without mishap. August 18th David Thompson was overtaken, on his way from Fort William to the Columbia, and they reached the mouth of the Saskatchewan together on the 20th. August 24th Henry passed the mouth of Pasquia River, where his uncle had been politely pillaged by Chatique in 1775; and two days later reached the N.W.C. post, Cumberland House. As already mentioned, both the North West Company and the Hudson's Bay Company had forts on Cumberland or Sturgeon Lake, both bearing the same name. They stood about one hundred yards apart, and the North West Company's establishment seems to have antedated its rival by a year or two. Henry says that the former post was kept up less for the purpose of trade than as a depot to supply the northern brigades; that the Hudson's Bay post was the more permanent of the two; and that at this particular point the people from the bay had all the trade in their own hands—"I believe," he adds, "the sole instance of the kind in the North West."

Henry only remained at Cumberland House until sunset, and then hastened on to overtake his brigade. September 2nd he was at the Forks of the Saskatchewan, and turned up the north or main branch, where he found the current stronger than below the Forks, rapids more frequent and some of them dangerous, requiring the utmost exertions of his men at the line and in the canoe

with poles. The stream at this point is contracted between high banks on both sides. The following day he
passed an old establishment known as Fort Providence,
not far from where the town of Prince Albert now
stands. Here he had trouble with a party of half-breeds,
and expresses his conviction, in vigorous terms, that
these people when they live among Indians and
abandon themselves to such a life are the worst of
savages, given to all kinds of roguery and inciting the
natives to every species of mischief.

September 4th Henry passed Hudson House, built
by Turner of the Hudson's Bay Company some years
before. The exact date is uncertain, but David
Thompson mentions the post in 1794. It stood a few
miles below Carlton, where the Hudson's Bay Company
still maintains a post. Pursuing his journey, Henry
camped at the mouth of Battle River, about where the
town of Battleford now stands. Shortly before reaching
the Forks he passed the ruins of Fort Montagne
d'Aigle. Beaver were very numerous on Battle River
in Henry's day, but it was dangerous to ascend the
river on account of the treacherous Slave Indians, who
lived on its upper waters.

Leaving the Battle behind him, Henry continued his
way up the Saskatchewan, following the north bank on
horseback, while his men paddled up in their canoes.
A short distance below present Fort Pitt he forded a
small stream, and the same day reached Fort Vermillion
"in a long flat bottom of meadow, directly opposite
the entrance of Vermillion river." A large party of

Slaves were encamped about the fort, and, despite the unpleasant reputation he had given them, came out whooping and halloing to welcome him as he rode down the hills to the fort. Henry had been there but one day when David Thompson arrived from below, and after a brief rest at the fort continued his way up the river and over the mountains to the Columbia.

Henry wintered at Fort Vermillion, and in the spring of 1809 went down to Fort William. September following he was again in the Saskatchewan country, having spent two months on his upward journey with a brigade of eleven canoes. At Fort Vermillion he found encamped three hundred tents of Blackfeet, most of whom had just returned from an unsuccessful war raid to the Upper Missouri, where they had hoped to find either their Indian enemies or some of the fur traders from the United States, either of whom they considered legitimate prey. They returned in considerable disgust, having been " deprived of their usual spoils in scalps and horses of the former, and missed a supply of beaver and merchandise from the latter, from whom they took considerable booty last year in an expedition of this kind." They had in fact the previous year fallen upon a party of Americans on the Missouri, stripped them of everything, and brought off a quantity of beaver skins, which the Nor' Westers on the Saskatchewan, with the easy ethics of the fur trade, had purchased from them on very reasonable terms.

Henry throws some light upon the capacity of the

various tribes for the deadly fire-water of the white men. The prescription for a nine-gallon keg of " Blackfoot rum" was four or five quarts of high wine and the balance water ; the more sophisticated Crees and Assiniboines must needs have six quarts to the keg; while the hardened Saulteurs were content with nothing weaker than eight or nine quarts.

October 27th Henry set out on horseback for Fort Augustus, passing on his way the ruins of Fort George, built by Angus Shaw of the North West Company in 1792, and abandoned in 1801 ; passing also old Fort Augustus on the north bank of the Saskatchewan. He reached Fort Augustus, where the city of Edmonton now stands, on October 30th, and was back at Vermillion on November 7th.

On the 31st of May both Fort Vermillion and the neighbouring post of the Hudson's Bay Company were abandoned, the rival traders, who here, as in many other parts of the west, seem to have got on tolerably well together, having mutually decided to move up to White Earth River, where a more satisfactory site had been found for their establishments. The scene, as Henry describes it, is full of animation. All day long the exodus continued. Canoes and boats began to leave the old forts at daybreak, loaded with all the paraphernalia of the fur trade ; bags of pemmican, kegs of grease, packs of furs, kegs of liquor, trading goods of all kinds, powder and ball, household furniture and utensils, lay everywhere on the banks of the river ; men and women ran hither and thither, bringing goods and provisions to the water-side, and stowing them on board, with ever a watchful eye on the horses, for fear of thievish Assiniboines. Canoe after canoe left the shore and made upstream, the men breaking into one of the Canadian *chansons* as their paddles dipped into the water; boats and batteaux followed more laboriously, pole and line making slow progress against the swift current of the river. Those who were not on the water made up a cavalcade on land, an imposing array of forty-four horses, some bearing riders, others loaded with packs; here, there, and everywhere were the dogs, sixty of them, getting in everybody's way, and drowning all other noises in their ceaseless clamour. So Fort Vermillion was abandoned by the North West Company, and White Earth House, or White Mud Brook House, reigned in its stead.

A few weeks after Henry had settled down in his new quarters, David Thompson visited him, on his way down to head-quarters from the Columbia by way of Howse Pass. Less welcome visitors were a company of free traders. Henry could stand the opposition of the Hudson's Bay Company, but he had no patience whatever with the unattached traders. His irritation breaks out as he notes their arrival: "Five young vagabonds from Lac la Biche came in to us, on their way, they said, to the Columbia, where they hoped to find beaver as numerous as blades of grass in the plains. . . . I took much trouble in trying to make a division among these freemen, to prevent them from crossing the mountains, where they will be even a greater nuisance to us than they are here." Apparently his efforts were fruitless, for the next day he breaks out even more violently in his journal: "Troubled with those mongrel freemen all day. No dependence is to be placed upon them; they have neither principles, nor honor, nor honesty, nor a wish to do well; their aim is all folly, extravagance and caprice; they make more mischief than the most savage Blackfeet in the plains."

In September Henry started on horseback for Rocky Mountain House, following the north bank of the Saskatchewan, so as to keep at least the width of the river between himself and roving bands of Blackfeet. He took no provisions with him, relying entirely on what he might kill by the way. Moose, buffalo, and antelope were all plentiful. The fresh tracks of a grizzly bear were found—an enormous fellow, judging by the prints of his feet, which Henry found to be fourteen inches long and seven broad. On reaching Rocky Mountain House he was surprised to find it in the possession of the Columbia brigade. The brigade had been stopped and turned back by the Piegans, who "having been severely defeated last summer by the Flat Heads, were determined to cut off the latter's supplies of arms and ammunition, and had kept a strict watch for that purpose." David Thompson was in charge of this brigade, and the obstinacy of the Piegans resulted, as we shall find in the following chapter, in his forcing a way overland from the Saskatchewan to the Athabaska, and exploring a new route to the Columbia through Athabaska Pass.

Henry, not knowing for some time of Thompson's changed plans, resorted to strategy to get the goods and supplies for the Columbia past the Piegans. His difficulties were multiplied by the unexpected arrival at the fort of a number of Hudson's Bay men, from whom it was equally necessary to keep any news of the departure of the Columbia brigade. Fortunately, the Hudson's Bay men arrived thoroughly exhausted by a long day's journey, and slept soundly, while a few glasses of rum all round disposed of the Piegans. The Columbia canoes had already been sent downstream as a blind to rival traders and Indians alike, but their instructions were to return about midnight and pole carefully up the other side of the river. This they succeeded in doing without the Piegans or Hudson's Bay men being any the wiser. But, as the sequel shows, their trouble was all for nothing. Thompson had changed his plans, and the men must return down the river again with the same care as before, it being very important to keep from the Indians any hint of the trick that had been played upon them.

On November 9th Henry rode up the river from Rocky Mountain House to a rising ground on the north side, where Peter Pangman had cut his name on a pine in 1790. This spot was then the utmost extent of discoveries on the Saskatchewan toward the Rocky Mountains. "Of the mountains," says Henry, " we had a tolerable view from this hill. The winding course of the river is seen until it enters the gap of the mountains ; a little east of which appears another gap,

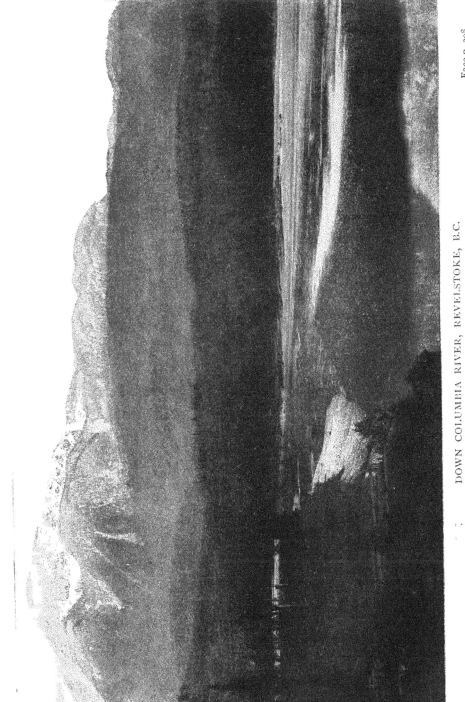

DOWN COLUMBIA RIVER, REVELSTOKE, B.C.

Face p. 308

through which I am told flows a south branch that empties into the Saskatchewan some miles above this place. The mountains appear at no great distance, all covered with snow, while we have none."

Henry describes Rocky Mountain House as standing on a high bank on the north side of the Saskatchewan. The situation, he says, was well adapted to defence, as the blockhouses commanded the fort for some distance. This spot had formerly been covered with aspen and pine, which had been cut down for the use of the place, leaving a large open space, and they now had a grand view of the Rocky Mountains, lying nearly south-west, and apparently running from west-north-west to south-south-east. Up to Rocky Mountain House the course of the river was comparatively clear and unobstructed, but there was a strong rapid almost immediately in front of the fort, and above this navigation even by canoes was slow and tedious by reason of the almost constant succession of rapids. Henry notes the remains of dwellings of the Kootenay Indians, proving that this tribe had formerly lived on the eastern side of the mountains. Thompson had in fact met a party of Kootenays on the eastern side of the mountains in 1800, and induced some of them to return with him to Rocky Mountain House.

In February, 1811, Henry left on a "jaunt in the Rocky mountains." On account of the watchfulness of the Piegans, who were extremely jealous of any movement toward the mountains, being anxious to confine the fur trade as much as possible to their own territory,

Henry had once more to resort to strategy. He gave out that he was going down the river, and started out ostentatiously in that direction for about a mile, then turned off from the road and made a circuit behind the fort, until he had reached the river above, without the Indians having suspected his intention. He had left the fort at 5.30 a.m., and travelled briskly all that day toward the mountains. Two men went with him, and each travelled in a sled drawn by three active dogs. Henry himself was in what he describes as a kind of cariole, made by stretching a wet parchment of moose skins over a wooden frame secured to the sled. Wrapped in buffalo robes, this mode of travelling, except in very severe weather, was far from disagreeable. Dogs have been used for winter travel in the west throughout almost the entire period of the fur trade, and are still the only means of conveyance in winter in the far north. They can travel through a country, and under conditions, that would soon exhaust the endurance of any other animal. The narratives of fur traders and explorers, travellers and sportsmen, early and late, whose business or pleasure has taken them over the limitless plains and through the vast forests of the great north-west, all bear witness to the splendid qualities of the smallest and pluckiest of beasts of burden.

Towards noon the travellers came to a spot where a long reach of the river opening up to the west offered a magnificent view of the mountains, crowned and clothed in glittering snow. In the foreground immense piles of fallen trees lay along the banks of the river, and the yellow and grey banks themselves towered one hundred to two hundred feet above the ice-bound bed of the stream. At 3.30 in the afternoon, after ten hours' steady travelling, Henry and his men camped for the night under a clump of spreading pines.

At 4.30 the next morning they were again on their way. As they travelled up the river the banks rose ever higher above them, presenting faces of perpendicular rock rising sheer from the river on either side. After passing through a gap in an outlying ridge of mountains, the river was found to open out to a width of nearly a mile—it was but sixty yards wide where it broke through the ridge. They were now in full view of the mountains—"the main body of the Rocky mountains ahead of us, upheaved in all shapes and directions." The channels became more numerous and tortuous ; open meadow-lands appeared here and there, and tracks of the buffalo.

The following day Henry overtook a party of hunters whom he had sent ahead, and who had been fortunate enough to kill three mountain sheep and three cow buffaloes. He was glad to rest here for a day, having run on foot the greater part of the way since entering the mountains, there not being sufficient snow on the ground to enable the dogs to draw him in the sled. Buffalo were numerous. They were not the kind found on the prairie, but wood buffalo, "as wild as moose"; they "never resort to the plains, but delight in mountain valleys, where they feed on a short grass which seems to be of an excellent quality."

2 D

Refreshed by his day's rest, Henry set out at daybreak the next morning. The river now became narrow and winding again, the mountains closing in upon its banks. Tracks of mountain sheep could be seen on crags and precipices, where there seemed scarcely sufficient hold for their hoofs. They were sō numerous that the snow on the hills was beaten hard by their frequent passing. A herd of thirty rams was discovered feeding among the rocks, and as the hunters chased them they set off at full speed up the side of the mountain. "At one time," says Henry, "I thought them hemmed in by rocks so steep and smooth that it seemed impossible for any animal to escape being dashed to pieces below, but the whole herd passed this place on a narrow horizontal ledge without a single misstep, and were soon out of sight."

On the fourth day after leaving the fort Henry reached the upper end of the Kootenay plain, a level meadow several miles in length, which attracted the particular attention of explorers and fur traders who went this way through the mountains, by the striking contrast it presented to the wild and rugged mountains that surround it on nearly every side. Henry was now following the same road which Thompson had travelled four years before; he had crossed what are now known as the Palliser and Sawback ranges, and passed Mount Murchison and other notable peaks, and was approaching the eastern end of Howse Pass, between Mount Balfour and Mount Forbes. Shortly before entering the pass Henry abandoned his sled, the

bottom of which was entirely worn out by constant
and rough contact with stones where the snowfall
had been light, and continued his journey on snow-
shoes, to what he presumed to be " the highest source
of the Saskatchewan." About half a mile from the
source of the Saskatchewan, Henry left the river on
his right and entered a thick forest of pines, and after a
walk of two miles came to a small opening " where three
small streams of Columbian waters join. The principal
one comes from the west, and is divided from Saskatchewan waters only by a ridge." From here near the
source of Blaeberry River, where Henry stood, it would
take, he says, three days to walk on snow-shoes to the
banks of the Columbia, but in summer a man might do
it afoot in one. Henry, however, was not at this time
going any farther than the pass, and accordingly turned
his back on the Blaeberry and retraced his steps to the
fort on White Earth River.

Henry had planned a trip south to Bow River on his
return from Howse Pass, to visit the different Piegan
camps, but was warned by friendly Indians not to leave
his fort, as the Fall Indians had formed a plot to murder
him. The Fall Indians had lately been on the warpath
against the Crows, with whom they had fought on the
Yellowstone River. The Crows had cried out derisively
that next summer they would save the Fall Indians the
trouble of coming to war ; they would come themselves
to the Saskatchewan, and would be led by Americans.
The Fall Indians now felt that they were in evil case
indeed. They were already on bad terms with their

eastern neighbours, the Crees and Assiniboines ; if they
went north to the wooded country they would starve ;
starvation faced them also if they crossed the mountains ; in fact retreat was cut off on every side. They
must face the Crows, and face them on unequal terms,
for the Crows were well armed, and had threatened to
bring white men with them, while the Fall Indians had
to fight alone, and, to crown all, the traders had refused
to supply them with guns and ammunition. Guns and
ammunition they must have, and the only way to get
them was to enter the forts under pretence of trade,
take the traders unawares, murder them, and help themselves to what they needed. This they had determined
to do. They had tried to draw the Piegans into the
plot, but the latter told them that it would be madness to
do such a thing ; that they would drive the traders out
of the country; and would then be even more hopelessly
at the mercy of their enemies; finally the Piegans threatened that if the Fall Indians did not abandon their
plot, they would themselves join the traders against
them. This had the desired effect, and the Fall Indians
promised to behave themselves. Henry, however, had
no great faith in their promises, and put his fort into
shape to give them a warm reception if they should
still resort to treachery ; but their valour had evapor-
ated, and the winter passed off quietly.

In May, 1811, Henry left Rocky Mountain House in a
boat with six men, and travelled down the Saskatchewan
to the site of Boggy Hall, where he had expected to
meet a party from the Athabaska. As they did not turn

up, he continued down the river, past Fort Augustus (Edmonton), to Lower White Earth House, where he arrived on May 17th.

Where Henry was, or what he was doing, during the succeeding two years and a half, we can only conjecture, as his journal is missing from May 17th, 1811, to November 15th, 1813, when he arrived at Astoria from Fort William. It is probable that he spent most of this time in the Saskatchewan country, going down to Fort William in the spring of 1813. From Gabriel Franchère it is learned that he left Fort William for Astoria in July of that year. He followed, no doubt, the usual route to the Saskatchewan, and crossed the mountains either by Howse or Athabaska Pass. In the former case he would have reached Astoria by way of the Upper Columbia, the Kootenay, and the Lower Columbia; if he went through Athabaska Pass he must have followed the all-Columbia route from Boat Encampment.

Of the six months spent by Henry at Astoria—the last six months of his life—little need be said here. His time was taken up with the routine of the fur trade. He also found time to visit Clatsop and Chinook villages, and to make short excursions into the surrounding country, which, however, took him no farther afield than the upper waters of the Willamette, and in any event covered no new ground.

H. H. Bancroft, in his *North-West Coast*, says that the Missouri Fur Company sent an expedition to the Upper Missouri and the Yellowstone, in 1808, under Alexander

Henry, who was not only to establish posts on those streams, but was to cross the Rocky Mountains and open traffic with the nations of the western slope. Bancroft goes on to say that Henry erected an establishment at the forks of the Missouri, which he made his head-quarters, but being dislodged by the Blackfeet the following year (1809), passed over the great divide, and built a house on the north or Henry branch of Snake River, one day's journey above its junction with the south or Lewis branch; and that this cabin called Henry Fort, was the first establishment erected in this latitude west of the Rocky Mountains. This startling bit of information, we learn from a foot-note, Bancroft extracted from an address by Thomas Allen at an anniversary celebration, in February, 1847, of the founding of St. Louis, printed in De Bois's *Industrial Resources*, III, 516—rather an indifferent authority for such a circumstantial and positive statement. In the same foot-note Bancroft adds: "The Missouri Fur Company being dissolved in 1812, two years later we find Mr. Henry in charge of a post in the Willamette Valley, engaged in curing venison for the Northwest Company at Fort Astoria, and finally a prominent partner in the Northwest Company. He was drowned in company with Donald McTavish," etc.[1] Elsewhere Bancroft repeats the statement that Alexander Henry was in charge of the N.W.C. post on the Willamette in 1814.[2]

From Alexander Henry's own narrative, it is clear

[1] *North-West Coast*, p. 129.　　[2] *Ibid.*, p. 244.

that he never at any time went farther up the Missouri than the Mandan villages; that he never crossed the mountains by any pass south of Howse; that he was never on the Henry branch (the Clearwater) of Snake River, and probably was never nearer the Snake River itself than its confluence with the Columbia. As we have seen, Henry was on the Saskatchewan in both 1808 and 1809. While he was certainly on the Willamette in 1814, he was never at any time in charge of the Company's post there. It might be added, parenthetically, that in 1814 there was no such place as Fort Astoria, the name having been changed to Fort George when Astoria was turned over to the North West Company in the autumn of 1813.

The fact is that Bancroft hopelessly confused three different traders of the name of Henry. Of the several statements he makes, the only one that actually applies to Alexander Henry is that which refers to his death. Andrew Henry was the man who wintered in 1808–9 at the forks of the Missouri, and built Fort Henry on the Clearwater branch of Snake River; and the trader who was in charge of the Willamette post in 1814 was Alexander's cousin, William Henry, who is frequently mentioned in the former's journals.

On Sunday, May 22nd, 1814, Alexander Henry was drowned, with Donald McTavish of the North West Company and several others, on their way from Fort George to the Company's vessel, the *Isaac Todd*. So abruptly closed the career of one of the ablest officers of the North West Company, after nearly a quarter of a century's service in the west. He was not a great explorer in the sense that Alexander Mackenzie and David Thompson were; he made no such remarkable discoveries as are associated with their names; but he was an untiring traveller, and what is much to the point, he travelled with his eyes wide open, and noted in his voluminous journals everything that aroused his interest. His journals are essential to a full understanding of the course of exploration in North-Western America.

CHAPTER II

ALEXANDER MACKENZIE REACHES THE ARCTIC COAST

ALEXANDER MACKENZIE was born at Stornoway, in the island of Lewis, on the west coast of Scotland, in the year 1763.[1] He came to Canada at the age of sixteen, and immediately determined to enter the fur trade. The fur trade at this time, so far as it was not controlled by the Hudson's Bay Company, was monopolized by several enterprising merchants of Montreal, at the head of whom stood Simon McTavish and Benjamin and Joseph Frobisher. But their supremacy did not remain long unchallenged. Two other Montreal merchants, John Gregory and Alexander Norman McLeod, formed a partnership with two western traders, Peter Pond and Peter Pangman, in opposition to the North West Company, represented by McTavish and the Frobishers. This new organization was afterward known as the X Y Company, and during its brief career kept things very lively in the western fur field. The enterprise and aggressive-

---

[1] It has generally been supposed, on the authority of the *Encyclopædia Britannica* (9th Ed.) and the *Dictionary of National Biography*, that Mackenzie was born at Inverness, in the year 1755. The correct place and date were obtained by Rev. Dr. Bryce from the grandson of the explorer.

ness of the new company attracted to its side the young adventurer from Scotland, and it is not too much to say that a large portion of the success attained by the X Y Company was due to the energy and resourcefulness of Alexander Mackenzie.

After five years' experience in the counting-house at Montreal, and a year at Detroit, where he had an opportunity of familiarizing himself with the practical details of the fur trade, Mackenzie left for the west, reaching Grand Portage in 1785. He was now a *bourgeois*, or partner of the Company, and was given charge of the important Churchill River district. With him in the district was his cousin, Roderick McKenzie, a young man of exceptional abilities. Roderick McKenzie afterward became a partner of the North West Company, and devoted much of his time to the gathering of material for a history of the western fur trade. Unfortunately this history was never published, but the material, in the form of original journals and letters of the traders, from Lake Superior to the Mackenzie River, and McKenzie's own invaluable notes, is still extant, and forms a most important body of data for the future historian. Not the least interesting portion of this material is a series of letters from Alexander Mackenzie to Roderick McKenzie, a number of which have been published in Masson's *Bourgeois de la Compagnie du Nord-Ouest*. Masson also published several of the more important journals and narratives brought together by Roderick McKenzie.

The relations of both Alexander Mackenzie and his

cousin with their rivals of the older Company were on the whole very friendly—in agreeable contrast to some of the other traders, who could not be rivals in trade without becoming bitter personal enemies. Roderick McKenzie had for opponent in 1786-7 William McGillivray, one of the leading members of the North West Company. McKenzie had been directed to establish a post at Lac des Serpents, near and below Ile à la Crosse. McGillivray arrived about the same time. His orders were, he said, to build beside McKenzie; not, in fact, to let him out of his sight. McKenzie had fixed on a place for his fort, on the advice of the Indians, but McGillivray knew of a much better one, and asked McKenzie to visit it with him. They went together, and McKenzie at once recognized that his opponent was right. Here they pitched their tents within gunshot of each other. The next day all hands set to work, and in a short time comfortable lodgings for the winter were completed.

In the spring, after a successful winter's trade, accomplished without serious disagreement, McKenzie and McGillivray agreed to travel in company to their respective head-quarters. They arrived side by side, the crews singing in concert, much to the astonishment of some of the other traders. They both were well received, however. The friendly relations thus established were never broken. McGillivray afterward retired from the fur trade, and in 1814 was appointed a member of the Legislative Council of Canada, in recognition of his services during the war of 1812.

Later he returned to his native Scotland, where he purchased a property, and died there about 1825.

But all the rival traders did not get on so happily together. In the Athabaska department, the North West Company was represented by a Mr. Ross, while the redoubtable Peter Pond looked after the interests of the X Y Company. Pond was an impossible character. He could not keep on good terms even with his friends, while he treated his opponents in the fur trade as personal enemies. He and Ross quarrelled from the very first, and finally, in a scuffle between the two parties, Ross was fatally shot. This serious news being taken down to Grand Portage by Roderick McKenzie, the partners of the two companies grew alarmed, and after discussing the situation together decided to unite their interests. Under the new arrangement Alexander Mackenzie was sent to take charge of the Athabaska district, while Roderick McKenzie went back to the Churchill, now in charge of Patrick Small of the older Company. The two cousins continued their correspondence at intervals. In 1788 Alexander Mackenzie writes his cousin : " I already mentioned to you some of my distant intentions [his projected journey to the Arctic Ocean]. I beg you will not reveal them to any person, as it might be prejudicial to me, though I may never have it in my power to put them in execution." Roderick McKenzie records in his Reminiscences a conversation about this time with Alexander Mackenzie. " He informed me in confidence that he had determined on undertaking a voyage of discovery the ensuing spring [1789] by the water communications reported to lead from Slave Lake to the Northern Ocean, adding that if I could not return and take charge of his department in his absence, he must abandon his intentions." Roderick McKenzie had at that time determined to leave the fur trade. "Considering his regret at my refusal," he continues, "and the importance of the object he had in view, I without hesitation yielded to his wishes, immediately set to work and accompanied him into Athabaska."

Following the usual route by way of Frog and Methye portages, they arrived at what was then known as Mr. Pond's old establishment—the post built by him on the Athabaska River in 1778, about thirty miles above the lake. Here the outfits for the several posts of the Athabaska department were made up and dispatched. Traders had already penetrated to the Lake of the Hills (Athabaska), Great Slave Lake, and the Peace River country, but without making any permanent establishments, and, to judge from one of Alexander Mackenzie's letters, with but indifferent success from a trading standpoint. It was now decided to build a post on Lake Athabaska. Alexander Mackenzie remained at the old establishment for the winter with two or three men, while Roderick with the rest of the party paddled down to the lake to build the new fort.

"On my arrival at our destination," he says, "I looked out for a suitable spot for a new establishment to replace the old one of Mr. Pond. After making every possible enquiry and taking every measure of precaution, I pitched on~a conspicuous projection that advances about a league into the Lake, the base of which appeared in the shape of a person sitting with her arms extended, the palms forming as it were a point. On this point we settled and built a fort which we called Fort Chipewean. It is altogether a beautiful, healthy situation, in the centre of many excellent and never-failing fisheries, provided they are duly attended to at the proper season." The fort was afterward moved to the north side of the lake, and was for many years the most important establishment in the far north-west, being the head-quarters for all the vast territory north to the Arctic and west to the Pacific.

About Christmas, Alexander Mackenzie journeyed down to the lake over the ice, and remained with Roderick at Fort Chipewyan until February, 1789, when he returned to his own post with the winter express, bound for their far-off destination, Grand Portage. By the express he sent a letter down to the partners, announcing the building of the new fort and the opening of an extensive trade with the Chipewyans.

In May, Roderick McKenzie set out in a light canoe for Grand Portage, one of the objects of his journey being to explore a new route from the Churchill to the Saskatchewan, so as to avoid the long and difficult Methye Portage. He followed the Pembina River, a branch of the Clearwater, to the height of land, then crossed over to Swan Lake and the Whitefish River,

FORT CHIPEWYAN, LAKE ATHABASKA

which brought him to La Loche River on the regular route to Ile à la Crosse. This route, however, did not prove satisfactory. On his return journey from Grand Portage, McKenzie tried another route. "I went," he says, "from Isle à la Crosse by Lac Clear to the head of the Athabaska River, which I found to be one continued chain of falls and rapids roaring among rocks and precipices, entirely unfit for the purposes of navigation, so that we had the greatest difficulty with our canoe to find our way through to the landing-place of Portage la Loche." It was clear that Portage la Loche, or Methye Portage, difficult as it was, was the only practicable route from the Clearwater River to Ile à la Crosse Lake.

"When I left Fort Chipewean for Grand Portage," says Roderick McKenzie, "Mr. Mackenzie was preparing for his first voyage of discovery." This was toward the end of May, 1789. In the last letter written by Alexander Mackenzie to the partners before he set forth on his journey, he mentions the arrival at Fort Chipewyan in March of Laurent Leroux "from the other side of Slave Lake, where he had seen a great number of Red Knives and Slave Indians. They traded with him and promised to meet him this summer on the west side of the lake." "I intend," adds Mackenzie, "to pass that way on my voyage for a supply of provisions."

Mackenzie left Fort Chipewyan on June 3rd, at nine in the morning, in a birch-bark canoe manned by four French-Canadian *voyageurs*, two of whom were accompanied by their wives, a young German named

John Steinbruck, and an Indian known as the English Chief, because of the many journeys he had made to the Hudson's Bay Company's fort at Port Churchill. The English Chief travelled with two of his wives in a small canoe, and two other Indians, engaged to act as interpreters and hunters, followed in another. Laurent Leroux also accompanied the party as far as Great Slave Lake, where he expected to meet and trade with the Red Knife Indians. Leroux was himself something of an explorer. In 1786 he and Cuthbert Grant had been sent by Peter Pond from his post on the Athabaska River to build a fort on Great Slave Lake. With the exception of Samuel Hearne's discovery in 1772, this was the first visit of white men to Great Slave Lake. The post was built at the eastern mouth of Slave River. Leroux wintered there in 1786–7 and 1787–8. He also founded, under the orders of Alexander Mackenzie, a post on the north side of the lake, called Fort Providence, about lat. 62° 20′ and long. 114°. Leroux was with David Thompson on the Assiniboine in 1797–8. Some years later he left the fur trade and returned to the province of Quebec, where he died in 1855 at the ripe old age of ninety-seven.

Paddling west along the shore of the lake for twenty-one miles, passing the mouths of the Athabaska, Mackenzie changed his course to north-north-west for nine miles, which brought him to Slave River. He notes the peculiarity of this river, that flows into Lake Athabaska when the water is high on Peace River, and at other times empties the waters of the lake north into Great Slave Lake. The party camped on the banks of the Slave River, and the following morning continued their journey, passing the mouth of the Peace River, described as upwards of a mile broad with a strong current. They landed for the night beside some rapids near the mouth of Dog River, where the Slave River is about two leagues in breadth.

Embarking the following morning at three o'clock, they had to make several portages. Two of these, called the Mountain and the Pelican, entailed hard work. At the latter the whole party was engaged in taking baggage and canoes up the hill. One of the Indian women attempted to run her canoe down the rapids, but lost control, and only managed with great difficulty to leave it in time to save her life, while the canoe with all it contained was dashed to pieces on the rocks. Nine miles farther down another dangerous rapid was passed. Here in 1786 five men who were accompanying Cuthbert Grant to Great Slave Lake were lost in the rapids. The place was known in consequence as the Portage des Noyes. At five in the afternoon camp was made, the men being thoroughly tired. Fortunately the hunters brought in seven geese, a beaver, and four ducks, to comfort the hearts of the weary *voyageurs*.

Notwithstanding this hard day's work, the following morning they were off again at half-past two. Mackenzie knew that the journey before him was a long and difficult one, and if he was to reach the mouth of

2 E

the great river and return during the short season of the far north he must push his men to their utmost strength. And being men of the right sort, almost as interested as himself in the success of the expedition, they needed very little urging.[1] This day, June 6th, they paddled steadily from half-past two in the morning till six in the evening, covering seventy-two miles in spite of a head wind. At six o'clock they landed, unloaded the canoes, and pitched their tents. Nets were set in a small river near by. Half-past three the next morning saw them off once more, on their strenuous race to the Arctic. The weather, although early in June, was so cold that the Indians were obliged to wear mittens. This day they made poor progress, the rain coming down in such torrents that even these determined travellers had to make for shore and get under cover. Geese and ducks still contributed to the evening meal around the camp-fire, but this night fire was an impossibility. The men huddled together under the canvas, smoked their pipes, and rolled over in their blankets for an uncomfortable night's sleep, while the wind howled outside, and the rain drove through the tents. Neither wind nor rain abating, Mackenzie was reluctantly compelled to spend another day in camp.

The morning of the 9th broke foggy but calm. Embarking at half-past two, a few miles brought them to the small branch of the Slave River known as

[1] The officers of the fur-trading companies drove their men at top speed when travelling light. Mackenzie was severe enough, but the lot of the *voyageurs* who manned the canoes of Sir George Simpson was far worse. That autocrat of the wilderness had no mercy at all on his men.

THE MOUNTAIN PORTAGE, SLAVE RIVER

Face p. 418

Embarass River, and after a ten-mile paddle they reached Great Slave Lake, about nine o'clock in the morning. Here they found a great change in the weather. The air was extremely cold. The lake was entirely covered with ice, except close to the shore. The gnats and mosquitoes which had borne them company down the river turned back in disgust, and that was the one redeeming feature in a very uncomfortable situation. The trees on the banks of the river were in full leaf, though the ground was not thawed above fourteen inches in depth. The Indians informed Mackenzie that at a very small distance from either bank of the river there were extensive plains, frequented by large herds of buffaloes ; which confirms Hearne's story, and clearly establishes the fact that the buffalo ranged as far north as Great Slave Lake. Moose and reindeer were reported in the neighbouring woods, and beaver were plentiful around the small lakes and streams. The mud-banks of the Embarass were covered with wild-fowl. Altogether this was a hunter's paradise, and a country to delight the heart of the fur trader.

Coasting eastward between the southern shore of the lake and a long sandbank covered with driftwood and supporting a few straggling willows, Mackenzie reached Leroux's establishment. The canoes were unloaded and tents pitched, as from the appearance of the ice on the lake there was every prospect of their being obliged to remain here for some time. The nets were immediately set, as it was absolutely necessary that the stores pro-

vided for the voyage down the Mackenzie should remain untouched.

For five precious days Mackenzie waited impatiently
for an opportunity to cross the lake. At last a westerly
wind drove the ice apart and opened a passage.
Striking the tents and embarking at sunset, a quick
paddle brought them to a small island eight miles out
in the lake, where they camped for the night. The
next morning a strong wind from the north with vast
quantities of floating ice prevented them from embarking, but about one in the afternoon they succeeded in
getting away, and made about ten miles under difficult
conditions. They camped again on an island; and the
ice closing in, made no progress the following day. The
18th and 19th were equally unfavourable. They were
still ice-bound in the middle of the lake, and to add to
the discomfort of their situation were pestered by
mosquitoes. At last on the 21st a southerly wind drove
the ice to the northward, and at five in the afternoon
they embarked and made fifteen miles through broken
ice, dangerous enough in bark canoes. However, they
got safely to a group of small islands within three miles
of the northern shore of the lake, which was still inaccessible on account of the ice. A number of reindeer that had crossed on the ice to these islands and
been caught there by the thaw furnished the party with
an abundance of fresh meat. Mackenzie sat up all
night observing the setting and rising of the sun, which
he found to be below the horizon four hours and twenty-
two minutes. Even at this time of the year the cold

was so severe that during the sun's disappearance the water was covered with ice an eighth of an inch thick.

The 22nd they coasted to the westward among the islands off the north shore, much impeded by floating ice; and the next day turned north-west up what is now known as the North Arm of Great Slave Lake. This day they traversed a deep bay "which receives a considerable river at the bottom of it"—Yellowknife River —and landing on the mainland in the afternoon, found three lodges of Red Knife Indians. The Indians informed Mackenzie that there were many more lodges of their friends at no great distance, and one set off to fetch them. Leroux purchased of the Red Knives upwards of eight packs of good beaver and marten skins, and the English Chief got from them over a hundred skins on the score of debts due to him, of which he had many outstanding in this country. Forty of the skins he handed over to Leroux to cover his own indebtedness, and exchanged the remainder for "rum and other necessary articles." Mackenzie had several conversations with the Red Knife or Copper Indians, but could get no information from them material to his expedition. They had no knowledge of the great river he sought, beyond the point where it left Great Slave Lake, and as the sequel proved, their knowledge even of that was extremely hazy. In order to save as much time as possible in crossing the bays, Mackenzie engaged one of the Indians to act as guide. This day, the 23rd June, at noon, he took an observation, which gave 62° 24′

north latitude, variation about twenty-six or twenty-seven degrees to the east.

In the afternoon he assembled the Copper Indians, and informed them that he would take his departure the following morning, but that some of his people would remain on the spot until the other Indians who had been sent for should arrive, and that if they brought down a sufficient quantity of skins he would have a fort built here for their convenience. The Copper Indians were delighted; hitherto they had only been able to carry on a trade through the Chipewyans, who gave them little or nothing for the fruits of their hunt.

The morning of the 25th Mackenzie took leave of Leroux, and amid a fusillade of small arms embarked on his journey. Crossing to the western side of the North Arm, he landed on an island, and was much surprised to find that the greater part of the wood with which it was formerly covered had been cut down within ten or fifteen years. On making inquiry of the English Chief he was told that several winters before many of the Slave Indians inhabited the islands in this bay, as there was an abundance of fish throughout the year, but that they had been driven away by the Crees, who continually made war upon them.

From this island their course was south-east from point to point across many small bays on the main shore, in six to ten fathoms of water. Whenever they approached the land they found deserted lodges, marking the ravages of the warlike Crees. On the 26th they continued their course to the south-eastward, and rounding the southern extremity of the North Arm, met a heavy swell from the open lake. ` Here Mackenzie took an observation and found he was in 61° 40′ north latitude. The next three days were spent in sailing with fair winds to the westward along the north shore of the lake, searching everywhere for the outlet of the great river. The Copper Indian who had undertaken to guide them proved to be a broken reed, and at last the English Chief grew so irritated that he threatened to murder him. Finally, however, on the morning of the 29th, they doubled an island—Big Island—and found themselves at the entrance to the river. Passing the point of the long island, their course was southwest by west through a wide channel, so shallow that Mackenzie judged it must be dry when the lake was low. The course of the river now turned to the westward, becoming gradually narrower for twenty-four miles, till it was not more than half a mile wide. The current at the same time increased considerably, and the soundings were three and a half fathoms. The north shore was low, that to the south much higher, and both well wooded. Mackenzie here notes the familiar circumstance that land covered with spruce, pine, and white birch when laid waste by fire subsequently produces nothing but poplar, although that species of tree had never previously been found in the particular locality.

A stiff breeze from the eastward drove them on under sail at a great rate. They held to the north side of the river, where the current was found to be much stronger than on the south side. Horn Mountain was now in sight, which their Copper guide informed them was the home of the Beaver Indians. He added that there were extensive plains on both sides of it which abounded in buffaloes and moose—a statement which, if correct, carries the range of the buffalo still farther to the northward. Great numbers of wild-fowl were found among the islands in the river, and the hunters kept the party well supplied from day to day.

On July 1st the course was westerly, among islands, with a strong current. The river had now narrowed to about half a mile. They passed a stream upon the south-east side—Trout River—and the same day reached the mouth of the River of the Mountain, now the Liard, where Fort Simpson was afterward built. Continuing their course downstream, they concealed two bags of pemmican on an island in the expectation that they would be of service on the return journey, though the Indians assured Mackenzie that it would be quite impossible to return up the river that season. Mackenzie travelled warily, for he had been warned by the Indians of a formidable waterfall about this part of the river.

In fact all the way down the natives—Slave, Dog-rib, and Hare Indians—magnified every rapid into a dangerous cataract, until Mackenzie learned to take their assertions with a big grain of salt. Although they made no hostile demonstrations against the explorer—indeed, generally fled at his approach, and were with difficulty persuaded to come near—they con-

ESKIMO ENCAMPMENT, CHESTERFIELD INLET, HUDSON BAY

FORT SIMPSON, PACIFIC COAST

Face p. 424

jured up all sorts of imaginary horrors and dangers apparently to dissuade him from continuing his voyage. Some of them assured him that old age would come upon him before he could return ; that it would take several winters even to reach the sea ; that he would encounter monsters of horrid shapes and destructive powers; others warned him against a Manitou which swallowed every person that approached it. Unfortunately these stories had a terrifying effect upon the Indians of Mackenzie's party. They were already tired of the voyage in any event. The tireless energy of the explorer was too much for them. Long days of ceaseless toil were more than they had bargained for. They were in terror of meeting the Eskimo. They assured Mackenzie that game would be unobtainable farther down the river, and that they would all assuredly die of starvation. They would willingly have deserted Mackenzie, as their countrymen had deserted Samuel Hearne on his first journey toward the Coppermine, but Alexander Mackenzie was of a more masterful spirit. They soon learned that they must swallow their fears, real or imaginary, and follow the impetuous white man wherever he chose to lead them.

It is interesting to learn from Mackenzie that the Crees had ranged in their war excursions even below the mouth of the Liard. The tribes of the Mackenzie River held them in the same terror as the Sioux inspired in their neighbours of the north-western plains, or the Iroquois among the tribes of the St. Lawrence valley. The primitive state in which Mackenzie found these tribes of the Mackenzie River is illustrated by the fact that they still used stone axes, made of brown or grey stone from six to eight inches long and two inches thick, the inside flat, the outside round and tapering to an edge, and fastened at the middle with green deerskin to a two-foot handle. This axe seems to have been intended more for peaceful than warlike purposes. Their weapons consisted of bows and arrows, spears, daggers, and pogamagans or clubs. The bows were five or six feet long with strings of sinews. The arrows were barbed with bone, horn, flint, iron, or copper, the iron no doubt procured through the more southerly tribes, the copper from the Red Knives. The spear was barbed with bone, and was used for striking reindeer in the water; the daggers were flat and sharp-pointed, made of horn or bone; the pogamagan was made of the horn of the reindeer, the branches being cut off except that which forms the extremity. This weapon they employed both in war and hunting.

On July 2nd Mackenzie came in sight of the Rocky Mountains, at the point where they most nearly approach the river. "We perceived," he says, "a very high mountain ahead, which appeared, on our nearer approach, to be rather a cluster of mountains, stretching as far as our view could reach to the southward, and whose tops were lost in the clouds." A few hours later they were abreast of the mountains, whose summits seemed to be barren and rocky, while their declivities were covered with wood. "They appeared also to be sprinkled with white stones, which glistened in the sun, and were called by the Indians *manetoe aseniah,* or spirit stones." Mackenzie suspected that they were talc, though they possessed more brilliant whiteness, but on his return journey found they were nothing but patches of snow. Sir John Franklin was at this same point on August 6th, 1825. Here the river turns abruptly from a west-by-north course to due north. The mountains cross the river some distance below, and for several hundred miles the river flows between two parallel ranges, the eastern being always in sight. Franklin noticed the same brilliant whiteness in this eastern range. The mountains appeared white as marble in the bright sunshine.

Mackenzie sighted these mountains on July 3rd, and that evening camped at the foot of a high hill which in some parts rose perpendicularly from the river. He immediately ascended it, accompanied by two men and some Indians, and in about an hour and a half with very hard walking gained the summit, which, to his surprise, he found crowned by an encampment. The Indians informed him that it was the custom of the people who had no arms to choose these elevated spots for their camps, as they could render them inaccessible to their enemies, particularly the Knisteneaux or Crees, of whom they were in continual dread. This is the famous "Hill by the River Side" or "Rock by the River Side" so often referred to in the narratives of later explorers, and of which an admirable drawing by Kendall is given in Franklin's Second Expedition.

Since they entered the Mackenzie the weather had been decidedly warm, but it now turned very cold with the suddenness of these northern latitudes. The banks of the river were covered with masses of ice which neither the sun nor the force of the current had been able to remove.[1] On the morning of July 5th they landed on the north bank of the river and surprised a party of natives, who fled to the woods in confusion. After a good deal of parleying, they were persuaded that the white men had no sinister designs, and a present of knives and a few beads and other trinkets completely won their confidence. They proved to be of the Slave and Dog-rib tribes. Mackenzie questioned them closely through his interpreter as to the course and character of the river, but could get nothing intelligible out of them. However, by the gift of a kettle, an axe, a knife, and other small articles, one of them was induced to accompany the party as guide. Re-embarking, they continued their course, and before nightfall passed the mouth of Great Bear River. Mackenzie was struck by the clear greenish hue of its waters, like the waters of the sea. He makes no mention of the remarkable mountain at the entrance to Great Bear River, afterward described by Franklin, whose summit "displays a variety of insulated peaks crowned in the most irregular manner." They camped

[1] The Ramparts, some distance below, " are frequently the scene of great ice jams in the spring, and the dammed-back water is stated to have risen on one occasion over a hundred feet, and on its recession left a boat stranded on the heights above " (R. G. McConnell, Geol. Survey, 1888-9, 106 D).

for the night a few miles below Great Bear River, at the foot of a rocky hill, on the top of which, according to the guide, it blew a storm every day throughout the year.

Mackenzie was still pushing forward with the same extraordinary energy, embarking at four, three, or even two in the morning, and urging his men to their utmost. He was determined at all hazards to complete the great object of his journey, and as the way was long, uncertain, and perhaps hazardous, the season short, and provisions very limited, the utmost expedition was imperative. The Indians grumbled constantly at the killing pace, but, to their honour, the French-Canadian crew stood by him gallantly.

Day after day they paddled down the river, the day lengthening rapidly as they approached the Arctic Circle. Whenever natives were seen on the banks, Mackenzie landed and questioned them as to the course of the river, its distance from the sea, and the character of the surrounding country, but little that was of any practical service could be elicited. Indeed, the Indians were universally shy and suspicious of these white strangers from the south, and always fled at their approach, having to be coaxed back with presents. At one place all fled but one old man, who met them on the beach. He was, he said, too far advanced in years, and too indifferent about the short time he had to remain in the world, to be very anxious about escaping from any danger that threatened him. At the same time he pulled his grey hair from his head by handfuls and offered it to them, imploring their favour for himself and his relations. Mackenzie convinced him that the white men came as friends, not enemies, and he went off to recall the fugitives.

About one hundred and twenty-five miles below Bear River Mackenzie came to what is now known as Sans Sault Rapid. This was the formidable "water-fall" of which he had been warned by the Indians above. As a matter of fact, it is the most serious obstruction to the navigation of the river between Great Slave Lake and the sea, but except at low water presents no serious difficulties even to large craft. At high water the rapid is almost drowned out, and can then be ascended even by the Hudson's Bay Company's steamer. It is not surprising, therefore, that Mackenzie had difficulty in recognizing in this comparatively easy rapid the impassable waterfall of which he had received such highly coloured accounts from the natives.

Another thirty miles or so brought the explorer to one of the most striking points on this remarkable river. Here the banks suddenly contract to about five hundred yards, and for three or four miles the river flows majestically between walls of limestone rising perpendicularly from the water's edge to a height of one hundred and twenty-five feet, increasing at the lower end of the gorge to two hundred and fifty feet. These Ramparts of the Mackenzie, as they were afterwards called by the traders, have been admirably described by later travellers, notably Sir John Franklin,

RAMPARTS OF THE MACKENZIE RIVER

Face p. 430

and Mr. R. G. McConnell, of the Canadian Geological Survey.

One party of Indians met with, of a different tribe from any hitherto encountered, possessed small pieces of iron which they used as knives. These, they said, they obtained from the Eskimo, who no doubt procured them from the Russians on the western coast. They were armed with bows of a peculiar construction, made in two pieces bound with sinews, which were also understood to have been procured from the Eskimo. From these Indians, who seem to have been more cleanly and intelligent than the tribes farther up the river, a guide was procured, who informed Mackenzie that he would sleep ten nights before he reached the sea. He spoke of the upper Indians in terms of great derision, describing them as old women and abominable liars. With the latter part of the description Mackenzie had every reason to agree.

On July 10th he obtained an observation that gave 67° 47′ north latitude, which was farther north than he expected, according to the course he had kept. The difference he attributed to the variation of the compass, which was more easterly than he had imagined. He now for the first time became convinced that the great river emptied into the " Hyperborean Sea," and though it was probable that from lack of provisions he could not now return to Athabaska that season, he nevertheless determined to penetrate to the discharge of the river. The river shortly before had been narrow, flowing rapidly between high banks ; but as they proceeded it widened and ran through various channels formed by islands, some of them little more than banks of mud or sand. Their banks, about six feet above the surface of the water, were faced with solid ice. The channels were so numerous and bewildering that Mackenzie was at a loss which to follow. The guide favoured the easternmost on account of the Eskimo, of whom he was in constant dread, but Mackenzie decided to take the middle channel, as it appeared to be the largest and ran north and south. A snow-crowned range of mountains lay off to the westward, stretching north as far as could be seen. According to Indian report, they were the same as had been seen farther up the river.

The guide now rebelled. He had never been, he said, to the *Benahullo Toe* or White Man's Lake. The Chipewyans too were disheartened and anxious to return. Finally Mackenzie satisfied them by promising that if he did not reach the sea within seven days he would turn back. Indeed, he adds, " the low state of our provisions, without any other consideration, formed a very sufficient security for the maintenance of my engagement." At half-past eight in the evening they landed, and pitched their tents beside a deserted Eskimo camp. Mackenzie sat up all night to observe the sun. At half-past twelve he called up one of his men to view a spectacle which he had never before seen. Surprised to find the sun so high, he thought it the signal to embark, and began to call his companions, who would scarcely believe that the sun had not descended nearer to the horizon, and that it was then but a short time past midnight.

Continuing their course down the middle channel, they landed on the 12th at another deserted Eskimo encampment. The banks of the river were high and covered with short grass and flowers, though the earth was not thawed more than four inches from the surface. The grass and flowers were in striking contrast to the ice and snow that filled all the surrounding valleys. The stream now widened out into what seemed to be a lake, and Mackenzie found his position to be 69° 1' north. Without knowing it, he had already attained the object of his journey, for the body of water before him was the mouth of the middle branch of the Mackenzie.

There was open water to the westward, and the course was steered for a high island about fifteen miles distant, which was reached about five o'clock in the afternoon. No land appeared ahead, and the bay was covered with ice for a couple of leagues. Mackenzie accordingly pitched his tents on the island, ordered nets to be set, and climbed with the English Chief to the highest point of the island. From this elevation he had a wide view in every direction. Solid ice extended from the south-west around to the eastward. As far as the eye could reach to the south-westward he could dimly perceive a chain of mountains, stretching farther to the north than the edge of the ice, at a distance of upward of twenty leagues. To the eastward were many islands. Still Mackenzie did not realize that his

2 F

task was now practically accomplished. He returned to his men, who "could not refrain from expressions of real concern that they were obliged to return without reaching the sea." Indeed, he says, "the hope of attaining this object encouraged them to bear without repining the hardships of our unremitting voyage. For some time past their spirits were animated by the expectation that another day would bring them to the *Mer d'Ouest*, and even in our present situation they declared their readiness to follow me wherever I should be pleased to lead them." The same spirit of discovery, the same fine enthusiasm, which had carried La Vérendrye and his gallant sons through every hardship, inspired these humble French-Canadian *voyageurs*.

But proofs of the fulfilment of his object were now hammering at the doors of Mackenzie's consciousness, though with Scottish stubbornness he refused to listen to them. "We had no sooner retired to rest," he writes in his journal on Monday, July 13th, "than some of the people were obliged to rise and remove the baggage on account of the rising of the water." But he goes off calmly to examine the nets, supposing that this extraordinary phenomenon was nothing but the result of a high wind. In the nets were found a fish about the size of a herring, which none of the party had seen before except the English Chief, who recognized it as being of a kind that abounded in Hudson Bay. About noon Mackenzie took an observation which gave 69° 14' north latitude, and the meridian variation of the compass was 36° east. The longitude he subsequently discovered by the dead reckoning to be 135° west.

The following morning he was awakened by one of his men crying out that he saw a great many strange animals in the water. "I immediately perceived," he says, "that they were whales; and having ordered the canoe to be prepared, we embarked in pursuit of them. It was, indeed, a very wild and unreflecting enterprise, and it was a very fortunate circumstance that we failed in our attempt to overtake them, as a stroke from the tail of one of these enormous fish would have dashed the canoe to pieces." These were the small white whale. "They were frequently seen," says Mackenzie, "as large as our canoe."

About noon an attempt was made to reach the ice, but the wind rising suddenly from the north-east, and the fog closing down with equal suddenness, they were thankful enough to get back to the island in safety. Hoping to find natives, Mackenzie paddled some distance inside the islands, screened from the wind, but without success. Returning, he encamped on the eastern end of the island, which he had named Whale Island, and which still bears the same name on the maps. The island "is about seven leagues in length, east and west by compass, but not more than half a mile in breadth." "This morning," says Mackenzie, "I ordered a post to be erected close to our tents, on which I engraved the latitude of the place, my own name, the number of persons which I had with me, and the time we remained here." From this it would appear that the explorer had at last become convinced that he was really at the mouth of the Mackenzie; though it is not until the next morning that he records in his journal that "being awakened by some casual circumstance at four this morning, I was surprised on perceiving that the water had flowed under our baggage." "As the wind had not changed," he adds significantly, "and did not blow with greater violence than when we went to rest, we were all of opinion that this circumstance proceeded from the tide." An incident that serves, however, to confuse the matter is that a month later, on his way up the river, he upbraided the English Chief for his faithless conduct. "I stated to him," he says, "that I had come a great way, and at a very considerable expense, without having completed the object of my wishes, and that I suspected he had concealed from me a principal part of what the natives had told him respecting the country, lest he should be obliged to follow me." All of which leaves the reader in considerable doubt as to whether or not Mackenzie ever realized the full extent of his discoveries. At any rate, he turned his back on the Arctic without one definite word that would now serve to set the matter at rest.

On the morning of the 16th he sailed once more among the islands, in a final effort to get in touch with the natives—presumably the Eskimo, but without success. The guide imagined that they were gone to their distant haunts, where they were in the habit of fishing for whales and hunting reindeer. His relations, he said, saw them every year, but he did not encourage Mackenzie to expect that he would be likely to find any of them, unless it were at a small river that fell into the Mackenzie from the eastward, at a considerable distance upstream. "We accordingly," says Mackenzie, "made for the river, and stemmed the current." So does he curtly dismiss the primary object of his journey. It has always been inexplicable to those who have studied Mackenzie's expedition to the mouth of the great river that he should, after going into such comparatively minute details of his voyage downstream, say so little, and that so obscurely, as to the conclusion of his journey to the northward. Without a careful reading of his narrative, one might, in fact, readily escape the point where he turns south on his homeward voyage.

On the morning of the 21st they were back at the point where the Mackenzie forks into its several branches before finally emptying the product of its gigantic drainage basin into the Arctic. It had been comparatively easy travelling up to this point, but as soon as they paddled on to the main stream they encountered a current so strong that it became necessary to get out and tow the canoe with a line. The land on both sides was elevated and almost perpendicular, and the narrow strip of shore between the banks and the water's edge was covered with broken stone fallen from the precipice. Altogether it was an uncomfortable path along which to tow even a light canoe. "The men in the canoe relieved two of those on shore every two hours, so that it was very hard and fatiguing duty, but it saved a great deal of that time which was so precious to us." That evening they camped at the same place where they had camped on the 9th, on their way down the river.

The next day Mackenzie had an opportunity of visiting one of the Indian villages, and took advantage of the occasion to closely question the inhabitants, through the medium of the English Chief, concerning the nature of their country. From them he learned that the Eskimo occasionally ascended the Mackenzie River in search of flint stones to point their spears and arrows; that there was a lake at no great distance to the eastward where the Eskimo had their home. The Indians also professed to have heard from the Eskimo of white men to the westward. These white men came in "large canoes," and the Eskimo obtained from them iron in exchange for leather. The "lake" where the Eskimo met these "canoes" was called by them *Belhoullay Toe*, evidently merely a variant in spelling of the name which Mackenzie has already translated as White Man's Lake. From these natives Mackenzie obtained an interesting account of the Eskimo, who were described as wearing their hair short; having two holes perforated, one on each side of the mouth in a line with the under lip, in which they placed long beads that they found in the lake. Their bows were described as somewhat different from those used by the Indians;

ESKIMO IN KAYAKS, MOUTH OF MACKENZIE RIVER

Face p. 438

and the curious statement was made that the Eskimo employed slings from whence they could throw stones with such dexterity that they proved very formidable weapons in the day of battle.

From a Dog-rib Indian, encountered a few days later, Mackenzie obtained further particulars of the White Man's Lake, or *Belhoullay Teo*, as he now spells the name. He had been informed, he said, that there was another river (the Yukon) on the opposite side of the mountains to the south-west, which fell into the *Belhoullay Teo*, in comparison with which the Mackenzie was but a small stream. Emboldened no doubt by the interest which this more or less accurate bit of information excited in Mackenzie, the Dog-rib proceeded to embellish his story with details drawn from his lively Indian imagination. The natives on the banks of this river, he said, were very large, and very wicked; they killed common men with their eyes; and did many other wonderful things. It may be that the "killing with their eyes" was the Indian conception of the white man's strange and deadly weapon; or more probably it was pure fiction.

On the 27th Mackenzie again hears of the White Man's Lake and the river that flowed into it. Meeting another party of Indians, he induced one of them to draw a map of the country to the westward in the sand. "This singular map he immediately undertook to delineate, and accordingly traced out a very long point of land between the rivers, though without paying the least attention to their courses, which he represented as running into the great lake, at the extremity of which, as he had been told by Indians of other nations, there was a *Belhoullay Couin*, or White Man's fort. This I took to be Unalaska fort, and consequently the river to the west to be Cook's River [it was of course the Yukon]; and that the body of water or sea into which this river discharges itself at Whale Island communicates with Norton Sound." Mackenzie tried to induce this Indian to guide him over the mountains to the River of the West, but without success. A further attempt to get light on the river and the tribes who inhabited its borders resulted merely in a fairy tale more preposterous than any that had gone before. The inhabitants of that country were represented as of gigantic stature and adorned with wings; they fed on large birds; and so forth.

On August 2nd Mackenzie was back again at the mouth of Bear River, and a few miles above found the bank of the river to be burning, a circumstance which had escaped his notice on the way down, as he had followed the opposite shore. On closer examination it proved to be a species of coal, to which he conjectured fire had been communicated from an old Indian encampment. Sir John Richardson, however, took a different view — that this lignite, which is excessively combustible, takes fire spontaneously on exposure to moist air. When Franklin passed this way in August, 1825, the banks were burning; they were burning in 1848, when Richardson reached the mouth of Bear River; and they were still burning in 1888, a hundred years after Mackenzie's journey.[1]

Franklin found at the same spot "layers of a kind of unctuous mud, similar, perhaps, to that found on the borders of the Orinoco, which the Indians in this neighbourhood use occasionally as food during seasons of famine, and even at other times chew it as an amusement. It has a milky taste, and the flavour is not disagreeable."

August 14th Mackenzie reached the mouth of the River of the Mountains, which he ascended for about two miles. He describes the stream as very muddy, and forming a cloudy streak along the water of the Mackenzie for some distance downstream, until the contraction of the channel blended the two waters into one. On the 20th an awl and paddle were found on an island in the river, which were recognized as belonging to the Knisteneaux, who were known to have passed this way on a war expedition. Two days later Mackenzie reached the entrance to Great Slave Lake; and at four in the afternoon of the 24th a large canoe was observed ahead with two smaller ones, on overtaking which they were found to contain Leroux and an Indian with his family, returning from a hunting expedition on which they had been out twenty-five

[1] R. G. McConnell's Exploration in Yukon and Mackenzie Basins, Geol. Survey, 1888-9, 98 d. Mr. E. Stewart, Superintendent of Forestry, descended the Mackenzie in 1906, and says in his Report : "Eight miles above Fort Norman (at the mouth of Bear River) for upwards of two miles along the right bank of the river smoke is distinctly observed from fires still burning far down in seams of coal, or rather lignite."

days. On the 30th the entire party reached Leroux's house, where Mackenzie paid off his Chipewyans. Taking leave of Leroux, Mackenzie continued his homeward journey, reaching Fort Chipewyan about three in the afternoon of the 12th of September, after a voyage of one hundred and two days—one of the most remarkable exploits in the history of inland discovery, whether regarded in the light of the results achieved, or of the time taken to cover a journey of nearly three thousand miles.

CHAPTER III

FIRST OVERLAND JOURNEY TO THE PACIFIC

VERY soon after his return to Fort Chipewyan, on September 12th, 1789, Alexander Mackenzie ascended the Athabaska River to the mouth of the Clearwater, where he met Roderick McKenzie on his way back from Grand Portage, and they returned together to Fort Chipewyan, where they spent the winter. In the spring the explorer went down to Grand Portage, where he arrived on July 13th, and writes somewhat dis- *1790* gustedly to his cousin: "My expedition was hardly spoken of, but that is what I expected." He returned to the west, and in March of the following year writes *1791* again to Roderick McKenzie, who was then at the Slave Lake Fort, established by Leroux. He suggests that a party of men be sent down the "River Disappointment" on a trading voyage to the Beaver Indians; and that a post be established at the entrance of Slave River. The name here given to the Mackenzie River is suggestive. Mackenzie still felt that the object of his expedition of 1789 had not been fully accomplished. He asks Roderick to purchase some Indian curiosities for him. He was destitute of such articles, the serious problems of his journey having left no opportunity for such minor considerations; and he adds: "It would be unbecoming a North-Wester to appear below [that is, at Grand Portage or Montreal] so unprovided in that line." One of the things he asks for is the horns of the "small musk buffalo" or musk ox, that singular-looking inhabitant of the barren lands that has excited the interest of so many later travellers.

When Alexander Mackenzie first conceived the idea of his second journey of discovery there is no definite means of knowing. From certain remarks in the journal of his voyage to the Arctic, it would appear that he had even then cherished the idea of an overland expedition to the Pacific, and his subsequent letters to his cousin abound in casual hints pointing to conversations that had taken place on the subject. In August, 1791, he mentions his intention of crossing the ocean, and from other sources it is known that he had about this time determined to spend some months in England perfecting his scientific knowledge. He did not propose to allow any lack of technical equipment to mar the success of this second expedition. Having carried out this design, and returned to Canada with suitable instruments, early in 1792, he hurried on to Fort Chipewyan to make preparations for his great journey. He had determined to ascend the Peace River this season winter there, and as early as possible the following spring make a dash for the Pacific. Two men had already been sent forward to prepare timber for the fort on Peace River.

It having been arranged that Roderick McKenzie

was to remain in charge of Fort Chipewyan and the affairs of the district during his absence, Alexander Mackenzie set forth on October 10th, 1792, for his second and most important tour of discovery. He took with him two canoes laden with necessary supplies, while some of his men followed in several others. Coasting along the southern shore of Lake Athabaska, he entered one of the branches of Peace River known as the Pine River, and reached the main stream on the morning of the 12th. The following day at noon he reached Peace Point, from which, as described in an earlier chapter, the river derives its name. The 17th he reached the fall, where the river is about four hundred yards broad, the fall being about twenty feet high. The next day he passed Loon River, and encamped on Grande Isle. A heavy frost during the night left Mackenzie in some apprehension as to whether he could reach his destination before ice on the river blocked his progress. He therefore determined to push forward with redoubled speed, and embarking at three o'clock on the morning of the 19th, reached the Old Establishment five hours later. This post had been built by a trader named Boyer in 1788, under Mackenzie's instructions. Up to this point the river had already been surveyed by one Vandrieul, on behalf of the North West Company.

Continuing his voyage, Mackenzie overtook a trader named Finlay,[1] who was encamped near the fort of

---

[1] This was John Finlay, who explored the river which bears his name to its source in 1824.

which he was to take charge during the ensuing winter. Here Mackenzie remained for several days, making arrangements for the trade of the post. This was the highest establishment so far made on the Peace River. Taking his departure on the morning of October 23rd, under volleys of musketry, Mackenzie continued his voyage up the river, passing the mouths of several branches, and reaching the mouth of Smoky River on November 1st. Ascending the main stream, a paddle of six miles brought him to the spot where he had determined to make his winter quarters; and he arrived none too soon, for the ice was fast forming on the river, and another day or two's delay would have proved serious. The men who had been sent forward to make preparations for the winter had the timber and palisades ready, and the entire party set to work with a will to build the fort, while the Indians of the neighbourhood were sent to bring in a supply of game. Before Christmas Mackenzie was able to move from his tent into the new building, while the men went on with the erection of a range of five smaller houses for their own occupancy. December 29th they were visited by what is known in the west as a Chinook wind, under the extraordinary influence of which the snow disappeared from the ground as if by magic, and even the ice on the river was covered with water, having the same appearance as when breaking up in the spring. A few hours afterward, the wind changing around to the north-east, they were back once more in the heart of the winter. Similar conditions were experienced early in January.

DOGRIB INDIANS ON GREAT SLAVE LAKE

Face p. 446

About this time Mackenzie was informed by the Indians that they had been hunting at a large lake, called by the Crees the Slave Lake. It was represented as a large body of water lying about one hundred and twenty miles due east of the Fort of the Forks. The Crees on their war excursions from the Saskatchewan to the Peace River country had been accustomed to leave their canoes at this lake, following a beaten track from thence to the Forks. This is the first mention of what is now known as Lesser Slave Lake. A rough cart-road now takes the place of the old war-road of the Crees.

On January 10th, 1793, in a letter to Roderick McKenzie, the explorer says that he has made out the longitude of the fort to be 115° 25' and the latitude 56° 34' 30". In a subsequent letter he corrects both, giving the former as 117° 43'[1] and the latter as 56° 9'. He was not far astray either in latitude or longitude. In 1803 David Thompson fixed the position of this fort as latitude 55° 8' 17" and longitude 117° 13' 14", var. 23½° east. It is probably the same fort, though Thompson says it was five miles above the Forks, while Mackenzie gives it as six.

From the natives Mackenzie learned of a great river on the western side of the mountains, flowing toward the setting sun. As the spring approached he made active preparations for his journey, but experienced a good deal of difficulty in securing Indians to accompany him as guides and hunters. He finally prevailed

[1] 117° 35' 15" in his narrative.

on three to undertake the journey, but one was afterwards induced to desert by another Indian, whose offer
to serve as guide had been rejected. Knowing the
little dependence to be placed on Indian promises,
Mackenzie feared that the others would disappear also,
which would have meant the abandonment of the expedition. It is true these Indians knew no more of the
country to be traversed to the westward than he did
himself; but their instinct for finding their way was as
indispensable as their ability to forage for the party, and
to act as interpreters, in a strange country. It was
therefore with a good deal of relief that he found them
faithful.

May 9th, 1793, having left two men in charge of the
fort until his return, Mackenzie embarked in a twenty-
five-foot canoe which he had built specially strong and
light for the uncertain waterways that lay before him.
With him went Alexander Mackay, one of the most
capable of the Company's men in the Athabaska district, six French-Canadians, two of whom had been
with him on his voyage down the Mackenzie, and the
two Indians. The Indians who were left behind " shed
tears on the reflection of those dangers which we might
encounter in our expedition, while my own people
offered up their prayers that we might return in
safety."

They embarked at seven in the evening, and camped
on an island in the river. At a quarter past three the
following morning they continued their voyage, but at
noon had to land to gum the canoe, which, being heavily

laden, had sprung a leak. In the afternoon the hunters killed an elk and a buffalo, so that they had plenty of fresh meat. Mackenzie was now exploring the upper waters of the Peace River, never before traversed by white men. "The west side of the river," he says, "displayed a succession of the most beautiful scenery I had ever beheld. The ground rises at intervals to a considerable height, and stretching inward to a considerable distance, at every interval or pause in the rise there is a very gently ascending space or lawn, which is alternate with abrupt precipices to the summit of the whole, or at least as far as the eye could distinguish. . . . Groves of poplar in every shape vary the scene, and their intervals are enlivened with vast herds of elks and buffaloes." The current increasing in strength, they had little opportunity to use the paddles and had to resort to poling.

With a strong wind ahead they embarked the next morning at four, leaving all the fresh meat behind, the canoe being already too heavy laden. They were travelling through a country where game was plentiful, and for the present need give no thought to the morrow's meals. This morning they passed the mouth of a small stream flowing in from the east, named by the Indians the *Quiscatina Sepy* or River with the High Banks; and in the afternoon met a party of Beaver Indians on a hunting expedition. It was toward evening, but Mackenzie did not think it wise to land lest the Beavers might induce his Indians to desert the expedition. The Beavers, however, followed along the

2 G

bank, and he had no option but to camp with them. From them he learned that he would reach the foot of the mountains in about ten days.

As they paddled up the river the banks increased in height, until their view of the surrounding country was completely shut off. At the same time the river narrowed from four or five hundred yards to half that width. On the 13th they found tracks of grizzly bears along the shore, but did not see any of the animals, to the relief of the Indians, who held them in great dread. Three days later, however, Mackenzie notes in his journal, "We this day saw two grisly and hideous bears." Buffalo and other large game were still very plentiful, indeed, so much so, that in places the country had the appearance of a barn-yard. At two in the afternoon of May 17th, eight days after their departure from the Forks, they had their first view of the Rocky Mountains, bearing south-west by south, their summits covered with snow. The current was now become very strong, and to lighten the canoe Mackenzie, Mackay, and the two hunters landed and followed up the banks. This day they reached the first serious rapid. In attempting to haul the canoe upstream it was driven violently against a projecting rock and considerably injured. Repairing the breach, they attempted to continue their course, but were finally compelled to return to their starting-point. Traversing the stream to the opposite bank, they found the current equally violent, but as the banks were not so steep they could get foothold, and with a sixty-fathom line managed to pull the canoe up the rapid to the clear water above. Their difficulties were only beginning, however. Climbing a hill, Mackenzie found that, as far as he could see, the river was an almost continuous rapid. There was nothing for it but to go forward. Sometimes hauling the canoe, sometimes carrying it over a rocky point, they made their toilsome and dangerous way upstream, camping at night wherever they could find a little bit of level ground. Sometimes it seemed as if further progress was completely barred, but by heroic efforts they managed to find a way around or over every impediment. At one spot steps had to be cut in the face of the solid rock for a distance of twenty feet. Mackenzie led the way and leaped down to a small rock on the opposite side, receiving those who followed on his shoulders. In this way they worked their way around by slow and painful degrees. At a critical point in one of the rapids a wave struck the bow of the canoe so violently as to break the line. For a moment all seemed lost. Mackenzie looked on with inexpressible dismay, for the loss of the canoe, with all his supplies, meant the abandonment of his enterprise. By a miracle, however, another wave, more propitious than the first, drove her out of the tumbling water, so that the men were enabled to bring her ashore without material injury.

The men were now completely discouraged, and muttered discontentedly that there was nothing for it but to return. As far as eye could see, the river above was one white sheet of foaming water. But Mackenzie

had not come so far to turn back. Paying no attention to the murmurs of his followers, he ordered them
to encamp while he himself set off with one of the
Indians to examine the river above. He followed the
banks as long as daylight lasted, but could see no end
to the rapids and cascades of this Rocky Mountain
cañon, and was finally convinced that it was impracticable to proceed any farther by water. Returning to
camp, he talked the matter over with Mackay, and it
was settled that the latter should the following day
follow the river until he reached navigable water.

At sunset the next day Mackay returned. He had
penetrated thick woods, ascended hills and sunk into
valleys, till he got beyond the rapids, a distance of three
leagues from camp. It was now decided to attempt the
almost superhuman task of carrying the canoe and
baggage overland to the navigable water above. At
break of day on the 22nd the men began to cut a road
up the mountain side. The canoe was then lifted from
the water, and with infinite fatigue, by passing the line
around the stumps of successive trees, they managed to
warp it to the summit of the hill. The same afternoon
the men cut a road through the bush for about a mile,
and they all returned exhausted to camp.

The next day, carrying the canoe and baggage with
them, they made about three miles. The 24th they
continued their painful journey, up and down hill,
cutting away as they went, until finally they reached
the river above the rapids. About two hundred yards
below this point the river rushed with astonishing but

silent velocity between perpendicular banks not more than thirty-five yards apart. Below this again the channel took a zigzag course, the waves dashing with impetuous strength first against one side then against the other, tossed in high, foaming billows as far as could be seen. Mackenzie might well congratulate himself on having surmounted such a gorge.

The 26th they continued their voyage, poling up-stream. The river here widened considerably, being full of small islands. The air was so cold that the men had to wear blanket coats even while they worked at the poles. On the last day of the month they reached the forks of the Peace River. Mackenzie was inclined to follow the Finlay branch, as it appeared to be the most likely to bring him to the point where he hoped to strike the ocean, but an old Indian who had been thus far had warned him on no account to follow this branch, as it was lost in various branches among the mountains and afforded no communication with any considerable stream flowing toward the sea, while the southern branch, according to the Indian, led by a portage to another large river, where the inhabitants built houses and lived upon islands. Mackenzie fortunately decided to follow the advice of the Indian, for, said he, " I did not entertain the least doubt, if I could get into the other river, that I should reach the ocean."

Accordingly he ordered his steersmen to turn up the south branch, to the disgust of his men, who were al-ready more than tired of the ceaseless toil and danger of the enterprise and in no mood to stem the violent current of the Parsnip. "The inexpressible toil these people had endured," says the generous-minded Mackenzie, "as well as the dangers they had encountered, required some degree of consideration." He therefore employed all the resources of his mind to soothe their discontent, making it perfectly plain, however, that he was determined at all hazards to continue his discoveries.

They were only able to make two or three miles up the Parsnip, which was in flood, in an afternoon's hard labour, and were then compelled by sheer exhaustion to land and camp for the night. At sunrise on June 1st Mackenzie had his men embarked, and after some hours' discouraging conflict with the fierce current, found about noon, to his great relief, that it was beginning to slacken. He put to shore to gum the canoe, and while this was being done took an observation which gave 55° 42' 16" N. Continuing the voyage, about evening the current became violent, and Mr. Mackay and the Indians disembarked to lighten the canoe. At sunset they encamped on a point, the first dry land they had found fit for the purpose. During the morning they had passed the mouth of a large river flowing in from the west (the Nation). Mackenzie was struck by the immense number of beavers on this part of the river. In some places they had cut down several acres of large poplars. Their industry knew no bounds. They laboured from the setting to the rising sun.

The second and third of the month Mackenzie worked steadily upstream against a rapid current. He rose with the sun, but had to camp before nightfall, as his men were then completely exhausted by the constant strain at the paddles. At noon on the third he obtained a meridian altitude which gave 55° 22′ 3″, and according to his calculations, he was at this time about twenty-five miles south-east of the forks. The following day the current continued very strong. The river was high and rising rapidly, in many places overflowing its banks. No place fit for a camp could be found until late at night, when they landed on a gravel bank, of which little more appeared above water than the spot they occupied. During the night the water continued to rise, and when Mackenzie awoke in the morning he was just in time to save canoe and baggage from floating downstream, leaving the party stranded helplessly in the midst of the wilderness. Sending the men forward in the canoe, Mackenzie landed with Mackay on the east shore and climbed a neighbouring mountain, hoping to get a view of the surrounding country, but on reaching the summit found himself on an elevated plateau covered with heavy timber. Climbing to the summit of a lofty tree, he saw on the right a ridge of mountains covered with snow, bearing about north-west, and another ridge of high land stretching toward the south, between which and the mountains to the eastward there appeared an opening which was evidently the course of the river. Satisfied with this information, Mackenzie returned to the river-side, but could see no sign of the canoe. The Indian hunters had landed with him, and he now sent Mackay with one of them

downstream, while he proceeded up the banks, in search
of the missing party. As the day wore on without
bringing any response to the signal guns fired at intervals, Mackenzie's anxiety became intense. The Indians
were convinced that the canoe had been upset in the
current, and were already discussing the building of a
raft to return down the river, calculating the number of
days that would be required to reach their homes, when
late in the evening a shot from Mackay conveyed the
welcome news that the canoe had been seen. Though
convinced that the men had taken advantage of his
absence to relax their efforts at the paddles, Mackenzie
was so relieved to find all safe that he accepted their
story of toil and hardship and comforted each with a
consolatory dram.

Without knowing it Mackenzie had passed the mouth
of Pack River, which would have taken him by an easy
route to what was later known as Giscome Portage, and
so to the Fraser. He probably made the same mistake
here that he was to make a fortnight later in passing
the mouth of the Nechaco. Pack River flows into the
Parsnip behind a low, flat island "timbered with spruce
and large cotton-wood," and Mackenzie apparently
paddled up the east side of the Parsnip without seeing
the mouth of this important tributary. Dr. Alfred
Selwyn camped on this island in 1875. "At low water
in the fall," he says, "the northern channel is nearly
dry." It was, perhaps, up this northern channel that
Mackenzie passed at high water in 1793, and thus
missed the junction of Pack or McLeod's Lake River,

ALEXANDER MACKENZIE Esq.

Face p. 456

of which he makes no mention either on his upward journey in June, or on his return journey in August.

For the next four days their course lay up the Parsnip, sometimes paddling, oftener tracking the canoe along the banks of the river, for the water was still rising, and the current so rapid as to make navigation well-nigh impossible. On the 7th Mackenzie found his position to be in lat. 55° 5′ 36″, long. 122° 35′ 50″. He was anxiously looking for the portage which, if the accounts of the old Indian were correct, he should now be approaching. If he could get in touch with the natives some information might, no doubt, be derived from them, but so far he had seen nothing but their deserted camp-fires. On the 9th, however, two Indians appeared on the bank of the river, and after a good deal of parleying with his interpreter, they met Mackenzie on the shore. His account of the meeting with these strange Indians, who were, no doubt, Sikannis, is very interesting. They laid aside their bows and arrows, and when Mackenzie stepped forward and took each of them by the hand, one of them, but with a very tremulous action, drew his knife from his sleeve and presented it to him as a mark of his submission. A flag was shown them as a token of friendship, and they examined it as well as everything about the explorer with minute and suspicious attention. They had heard, indeed, of white men, but this was the first time they had ever met one. Through his interpreter, Mackenzie closely questioned the Sikannis as to the great river he was seeking. They told him that a long portage led to the river, from whence they were just arrived; that they obtained ironwork from another tribe which inhabited the banks of this river and an adjacent lake (the Carriers); that this tribe trafficked with another a moon's journey from their country; that the last tribe (the Coast Indians) lived in houses, and traded at the sea-coast with men like Mackenzie, who came there in vessels as big as islands. One of the Sikannis was induced to guide the party to the great river, but, as it turned out, he knew just about as little of the way as Mackenzie did. June 12th they reached a small lake, the source of the Parsnip. "This," says Mackenzie in his journal, "I consider as the highest and southernmost source of the Unjigah or Peace River, latitude 54° 24′ North, longitude 121° West from Greenwich." If he meant that this was the ultimate source of the Peace he was mistaken—the head-waters of the Finlay being recognized as the source of the Peace River, and of the entire system that eventually finds its way into the Arctic Ocean through the Mackenzie delta. The Finlay is two hundred and fifty miles in length; the Parsnip only one hundred and forty-five. But what of this? How trivial it seems in the light of Mackenzie's wonderful achievement! A little over four years before he had stood at the mouth of the Mackenzie, first of white men to traverse its mighty waters from Great Slave Lake to the sea. To-day he stood at one of its remote sources, two thousand four hundred and twenty miles from its mouth, and again his was the honour of first discovery. Alexander Mackenzie had explored the entire distance from the source of the Parsnip to the Arctic Ocean.

Carrying canoe and baggage over the height of land, a distance of eight hundred and seventeen paces, the party came to another small lake, emptying through a small but tumultuous stream to the southward into the Fraser. These eight hundred and seventeen paces marked the water-parting of two great river systems, one emptying far to the northward into the Arctic, the other into the Pacific. Mackenzie was upon the threshold of another important discovery. He had already achieved the distinction of first crossing the mountains into what was afterward to be known as New Caledonia. He was presently to discover and explore for some distance the third largest river of the Pacific Coast.

The troublesome stream down which he was now about to force a passage was so encumbered by rapids, whirlpools, treacherous rocks, sandbars, and driftwood, that it well earned the name of Bad River which Simon Fraser afterward bestowed upon it. The journey down this river was in fact a chapter of accidents. It began with the shattering of the stern of the canoe on a rock; the steersman losing control, the canoe drove against the bank, and the bow met the same fate as the stern; one of the crew had already been left behind on a sandbar, and as the canoe was driving furiously downstream, the foreman, attempting to arrest her progress by seizing the branch of a tree, was jerked violently overboard and hurled ashore. The canoe rushed on, went over a cascade, and broke several holes in the bottom. Now a complete wreck, it drove on, while Mackenzie and his men hung on to the sides, and with great difficulty brought it into shallow water. While the Indians sat on the bank and wept, Mackenzie stood to his waist in the icy cold water, directing the unloading of the canoe. Finally everything was got ashore with the exception of the balls for their guns, which could not be recovered, having gone to the bottom.

This unfortunate accident brought the discouraged *voyageurs* almost to the point of mutiny. Without a canoe, and no balls for their guns, it seemed to them the height of folly to continue the expedition. Mackenzie waited patiently until a hearty meal and a glass of rum had raised their spirits somewhat, and then put the situation before them with persuasive force. He reminded them that they had engaged for the work with their eyes open; that he had placed before them the difficulties and dangers they would have to face, before they engaged to accompany him. He urged upon them the honour of conquering disasters, and the disgrace that would be theirs if they compelled him to return home without having accomplished the object of the expedition. He appealed to their courage and resolution, the peculiar boast of the Northmen, and told them that he looked to them to uphold the character of their race. He pointed out that the difficulties they had experienced were largely the result of their ignorance of the route; that the navigation was not impracticable in itself; and that the knowledge they had already gained as to the character of the country and its waterways would enable them to pursue the voyage with greater security. Mackenzie's eloquence had the desired effect. He had touched a responsive chord in his shrewd appeal to the racial pride of the French-Canadian *voyageur*. For the present at least, his men would follow wherever Mackenzie chose to lead.

While their enthusiasm was warm he set them to work repairing the canoe, and sent two of the men with an Indian in search of bark. If possible they were also to penetrate to the banks of the great river, and examine the character of the small stream upon whose banks they were encamped, down to its junction with the river. The Indian reached camp late at night with a small roll of bark, and gave a very discouraging account of the character of the Bad River, an account which was confirmed by the two men when they returned the following morning. Nevertheless Mackenzie determined to take the canoe down if there was any way of doing so. Four of the most experienced men were given the task of navigating her, while the rest of the party trudged along the banks with most of the cargo, cutting their way through the bush, wading sometimes knee-high in mud and water, and tormented from daylight to dark by clouds of mosquitoes. Finally at noon on the 17th they found that all further progress was barred by the accumulated driftwood that completely filled the mouth of the stream. Nothing remained but to cut a road across the intervening neck of land which was all that now separated them from the river. The canoe was lifted from the water and carried three-quarters of a mile through a continual swamp, in which they waded up to the middle of their thighs. "At length," says Mackenzie, "after all our toil and anxiety we enjoyed the inexpressible satisfaction of finding ourselves on the banks of a navigable river, on the west side of the first great range of mountains."

In 1806 Simon Fraser, following Mackenzie up the Peace and the Parsnip, reached this same point. He had the same disastrous experience with his canoes on Bad River, their bottoms being smashed almost beyond repair by the time he reached the place where Mackenzie portaged over the neck of land. He was more fortunate, however, in completing his journey to the river. "After the canoes were gummed a little," he says in his manuscript journal, "we continued on, and had better going than we had reason to expect. The river—right branch—is narrow, but plenty of water to bear the canoes, and the current is not strong, which enabled us to continue on with both canoes with their full loads on. At 10 a.m. we arrived at the large river opposite an island, without encountering any other difficulty than cutting several trees that lay across the channel, and we were most happy at having exempted the long and bad carrying place, and seeing ourselves once more on the banks of a fine and navigable river." Here, as well as elsewhere, Fraser indulges in a good deal of rather captious criticism of Mackenzie.

Mackenzie had now completed the first stage of his

journey, and for a time was to enjoy the luxury of a broad, navigable waterway, broken only occasionally by rapids, at least so far as he followed its course. Before eight on the morning of June 18th he embarked with his men, and with the aid of a strong current made good progress, covering about seventy miles before nightfall. He was now on a branch of the Fraser River. Thirty-four miles from his starting-point he reached the great fork of which his guide had informed him, where the Fraser, after flowing north-west for a time, sweeps around in a great semicircle before turning south on its long journey to the sea. The river was here half a mile wide and assumed the form of a lake. Continuing downstream, Mackenzie saw many signs of natives, but for some days could not get in touch with them. On the 19th he reached what was afterward known as Fort George Cañon. The rapids were found to be of considerable extent, and impassable for a light canoe. An Indian portage path led along the left shore, and this was widened to admit the passage of the canoe. The distance was only half a mile, but was over difficult ground, and the canoe had been so often patched that it required almost superhuman efforts to get it across. Four hours were consumed in this laborious undertaking, the fatigue of which, says Mackenzie, " beggars all description." Some miles above he had passed, without noticing it, the mouth of the Nechaco River, afterward explored by Simon Fraser, who rather scornfully notes the omission. It is to be remembered, however, that Mackenzie was paddling along the east bank of the Fraser, and could very easily overlook the Nechaco, which flows in behind a considerable island, on the west side.

The following day Mackenzie landed at a deserted Indian house, of which he gives a minute description. He had seen nothing of the kind west of Michili-makinac, the tribes of the plains contenting themselves with teepees. Mackenzie had never been on the Mis-souri, and was therefore not personally familiar with the houses of the Mandans and their neighbours. This house of the Carrier Indians on the banks of the Fraser, the first of its kind visited by white men, is described as about thirty feet long by twenty wide, with three doors. It appeared to have been built to accom-modate three families. There were three fire-places, with rows of beds on either side, and behind the beds an elevated place for storing dried fish. In the house Mackenzie found a singular-looking machine, cylin-drical in form, fifteen feet long by four and a half feet in diameter, made of long thin strips of wood fastened to six hoops. This he rightly supposed to be a fish-trap ; the familiar salmon-basket of the Carriers, of which an excellent illustration is given in Father Morice's *Northern Interior of British Columbia*. In the course of the day two other houses were observed, built on islands in the river.

On the 21st Mackenzie prudently cached ninety pounds of provisions in a deep hole,[1] to guard against

---

[1] This method of preserving supplies was ingenious. A hole was dug, and the earth and sods carefully deposited on a sheet spread out on the

distress on the return journey. The same day he discovered a party of Indians on the shore, and endeavoured, through his interpreters, to get into communication with them. The Carriers, however, met his friendly advances with a shower of arrows. Mackenzie landed on the opposite bank, determined at all costs to conciliate them. He realized that unless he could convince this first party of his friendly intentions it would be folly to proceed. News of his coming would spread rapidly down the river ; he was already regarded as an enemy, and sooner or later would have to face an attack by overwhelming odds. The Carriers paying no attention to the friendly assurance of his interpreters shouted across the river, Mackenzie conceived the daring project of walking alone up the beach in hopes that the Indians might be induced to come over to him. He, however, took the precaution of sending one of his own Indians through the woods, to keep him in sight, and in case of treachery to fire on the natives. The plan worked admirably. Two of the Carriers came out in a canoe, but stopped when within a hundred yards of the shore. Mackenzie made signs for them to land, holding out looking-glasses, beads, and other alluring trinkets. At length, but with evident apprehension, they approached the shore, stern foremost, but would

ground. Then a tarpaulin was put in the bottom of the hole ; the provisions went in next ; the tarpaulin was gathered up around them, and the hole filled with earth again. Any earth that remained over was thrown into the river. Finally the top of the cache was smoothed over, and a camp-fire made above it, to remove every sign of the excavation. When all this had been accomplished the hidden store was safe from thieves, human or otherwise.

not venture to land. Finally Mackenzie prevailed on them to come ashore. The Carriers examined the explorer, his arms, his clothing, everything that he had about him, with a mixture of admiration and astonishment. They had never seen anything of the kind before. Mackenzie was the first white man who had ever ventured into the Carrier country. The interpreter now cautiously joined the party, and renewed his assurances of friendship. The Indians paddled over to their friends, and after a consultation the white men were invited to come across to the camp. From this party, and from others farther down the river, Mackenzie obtained many particulars as to the character of the country, the course and nature of the river, and the tribes along its banks. The story was discouraging enough. The river was described as emptying into the sea, but far to the southward; its course was broken by many waterfalls and rapids, some of which were impassable; at these dangerous points the river rushed between high, rugged, perpendicular banks, which would not admit of any passage over them; and to add to the depressing picture, the tribes along the river were so malignant that the white travellers could expect no mercy from them. But obstacles of this kind only served to sharpen Mackenzie's determination to win a way to the sea. He induced a couple of the Carriers to accompany him as guides, and the next morning continued his journey. Here and there groups of natives were encountered, but thanks to his guides, although at first their attitude was menacing, they were all eventually brought to a friendly understanding. Many iròn implements, as well as copper and brass ornaments, were seen in the camps, bearing witness to intercourse at first or second hand with white traders on the Pacific coast. One very old man told Mackenzie that as long as he could remember he had heard of white people to the southward; and he had been told, though he did not vouch for the report, that one of them had made an attempt to come up the river and had been destroyed. The Indians described the distance across country to the sea as very short, and Mackenzie himself estimated it as not above five or six degrees. They assured him that the overland journey was not difficult, as they avoided the mountains, keeping along the valleys, many of which were entirely free from wood. The route they were accustomed to follow, when they went to trade with the coast tribes, struck westward from Fraser River, some distance above where Mackenzie now was encamped. The journey occupied no more than six nights, as they counted it. They bartered beaver, bear, lynx, fox, and marten skins for iron, brass, copper, beads, and other articles, which they in turn obtained from white traders on the coast.

Mackenzie was now face to face with an exceedingly difficult problem, and the ultimate success of his enterprise might depend upon how he settled it. Three courses were open to him. He might continue his voyage down the great river, the Columbia as he thought it, the Fraser as it really was; he might return to the West Road River and follow the Indian trail overland to the sea; or he might abandon the whole project and return to the other side of the mountains. The third alternative he dismissed at once. He was not the man to turn back while there remained any conceivable way of attaining his object. ˉ The choice, therefore, remained between the river and a dash overland. The river had the one merit of leading unquestionably to the sea. On the other hand, all that he had heard from the natives strengthened his conviction that its navigation would be attended with almost appalling difficulties, and that it would carry him far to the south of where he had hope to strike the ocean. Not more than thirty days' provisions remained of what he had brought with him, and his ammunition was almost exhausted. The return journey had to be thought of, and that meant the ascent of a tumultuous stream, involving many difficult and dangerous portages, through hostile tribes, who could effectually prevent his obtaining supplies even if they did not destroy the entire party. Altogether the successful termination of his expedition by this route seemed very improbable. Mackenzie decided that his one chance lay overland. If he could find the Indian trail, and push westward at top speed, he might accomplish his object and return before provisions and ammunition were quite exhausted. Having made up his own mind, the next thing was to sound his men. He called them together, and paving the way by a warm commendation of their fortitude, patience, and perseverance, put the case fairly before

them, finally proposing that they should try the overland route to the sea. At the same time, that there
might be no uncertainty as to his unalterable determination to complete his expedition, he told them that
in the event of their failing to secure guides for the
overland journey, he was resolved to return and follow
the river. He was resolved not to abandon the attempt,
even if he had to make it alone. The French-Canadians
responded nobly. They assured him that they would
follow wherever he might lead. A guide having been
procured among the Carriers, arrangements were made
for an immediate departure.

Before leaving Mackay engraved the name of Alexander Mackenzie, with the date, on a tree by the river's
side. This place is notable as the farthest point
reached by Mackenzie down the Fraser. A trading
post was afterward built here by the North West Company, and called Alexandria, in honour of the explorer.
Among the natives in the Carrier village Mackenzie
met a Rocky Mountain Indian and four members of a
tribe from farther down the Fraser—evidently Chil-
cotins or Shuswaps. Having taking leave of his Carrier
hosts, Mackenzie turned the nose of his canoe against
the stream, his objective point being the spot where the
Indian road struck westward toward the Pacific. Much
depended upon his guide, who alone of those in the
party knew where the trail was to be found. It was
therefore with some anxiety that the explorer learned
of the determination of the Indian to push ahead by
land instead of travelling in the canoe. Making the

best of a bad matter, Mackenzie sent Mackay with the two Indian hunters to accompany and keep an eye on him. His anxiety was more than justified when the following morning Mackay and the two Indians were overtaken without the guide. Mackay's story was alarming enough. Soon after they had left the main party, they had met a party of Carriers who appeared to be in a state of extreme rage. The guide asked them some questions, and then set off at such a pace that Mackay had much ado to keep him in sight. When he finally overtook him, the Indian told him that he feared treachery was meditated against the white men. Off they went again at the same breakneck pace, which was kept up until ten o'clock at night, when they all lay down as they were upon the ground, completely exhausted, cold, wet, and hungry. At dawn they continued their journey, and on reaching the lodge of the guide found it deserted. Rushing about for a time like a madman, crying out to his people, the guide set off again in the direction in which he had come, and had not since appeared.

The situation looked serious indeed. It was evident that for some unexplained reason the natives had turned suddenly hostile, and a savage attack might be expected at any moment. The *voyageurs* were seized with a panic, and urged upon Mackenzie the hopelessness of further prosecuting their journey. All they cared for now was to get out of this dangerous country as rapidly as possible. Mackenzie, however, paid no attention to their frightened remonstrances. After an ineffectual effort to get in touch with some of the natives whom he had seen the previous day, he chose a position for his camp which could be readily defended, got the arms in order, filled each man's flask with powder, and distributed a hundred bullets. No attack was made, however, though two or three natives who were observed on the river fled immediately on their approach. Finally, an infirm old blind man was discovered wandering around the camp, from whom an explanation was obtained of the inexplicable behaviour of the natives. It appeared that soon after Mackenzie had left the village below a number of Indians from the north arrived, who denounced the white men as enemies. Their sudden departure up the river seemed to confirm this story, and now the whole Indian population was ready to destroy the treacherous whites. To add to the anxieties of his situation, the guide was nowhere to be found. There seemed to be no object in remaining where they were, and Mackenzie accordingly embarked and continued his course upstream, taking the old man, in lieu of any better guide, with him. A couple of days were lost in building a new canoe, the old one having become quite useless, but on the afternoon of the 29th the missing guide turned up, to Mackenzie's immense relief. He had a plausible explanation of his absence, but nevertheless disappeared again the next morning without leaving any explanation.

The new canoe being completed, it was launched, and Mackenzie continued his search upstream for the mouth of the West Road River, which he understood to be the place where the Indian trail to the coast had its beginning. He reached this river on July 3rd, and now felt more seriously than ever the absence of the fickle guide. He was at a loss what to do. It would be madness to attempt the overland journey without a guide. Yet if he left this spot, which was the rendez-vous, he might miss the natives altogether. Finally it was decided to proceed cautiously upstream, in the hopes of falling in with the missing guide. Fortunately they had not proceeded far before they met him paddling down to meet him, with six of his relatives. These men were prepared to pilot Mackenzie overland, and after caching in two hiding-places a ninety-pound bag of pemmican, two bags of wild rice, two of Indian corn, a keg of gunpowder, and a bale of trading goods, he set out on the last stage of his journey to the sea, on July 4th.

Among the party they carried four and a half bags of pemmican, weighing from eighty-five to ninety pounds each ; a case of instruments ; a parcel of goods for presents weighing ninety pounds ; and one of ammunition of equal weight. Each of the *voyageurs* carried one of these ninety-pound loads beside his gun and some ammunition ; the Indians were only given forty - five - pound bundles, and grumbled at that ; Mackenzie and Mackay carried about seventy pounds each, in addition to their guns. Mackenzie had also the tube of his telescope swung across his shoulders, a troublesome addition to his already heavy load.

So they set forward, over hill and dale, through woods

and swamps, their labours lightened by the conviction that every step brought them nearer their goal. The first night they slept at an Indian village, whither the guide had preceded them. Father Morice has identified this as a village of the Naskhu'tins, which was in Mackenzie's day eleven miles distant from the mouth of the West Road River, or as it is now called, the Blackwater. At sunset an elderly Indian with three companions arrived from the west. He with many of his countrymen had been on a trading expedition to the Coast Indians. According to his report, it did not require more than six days' journey, with light loads, to reach this tribe, and from thence it was not quite two days' march to the sea. To Mackenzie's gratification, he offered to send a couple of young men ahead of the party, to warn the different tribes of their approach, and pave the way to a friendly reception.

At the first Indian camp encountered on the westward journey Mackenzie made the curious discovery of two halfpence hung as ornaments in children's ears. One was an English halfpenny of George III, the other a 1787 coin of the State of Massachusetts Bay. They had evidently reached this out-of-the-way spot from the fur traders on the Pacific coast. From now on evidence multiplied of the traffic with white traders, metal implements and ornaments, pieces of cloth, and many other articles being found in every Indian camp.

The way lay through a comparatively level country, and they were able to make good progress. On the morning of the 6th they fell in with the great road to the sea, which here followed the north bank of the Blackwater, and the same day came up with a party of Indians, who informed Mackenzie that he was approaching a river, of inconsiderable size, which emptied into an arm of the sea, and that in this bay a great wooden canoe with white people arrived about the time when the leaves begin to grow, or the early part of May. This was good news indeed, though as a matter of fact many a long mile had yet to be travelled before the explorer would have sight of the salt water.

At 2 p.m. on July 9th they reached what Mackenzie supposed to be a new river, but which was in reality still the Blackwater. He left the main stream at what is known as the Upper Cañon, where the Blackwater takes a great bend to the south, and following a small branch, had again reached the river about long. 124°, about the entrance to Kluscoil Lake. Here Mackenzie prudently cached half a bag of pemmican for use on the return journey.

Continuing his journey, on the morning of the 10th he crossed the river and followed a small branch that leads to the Cluscus Lakes, where a post of the Hudson's Bay Company was afterward built. Beyond lay a range of beautiful hills covered with verdure. At noon Mackenzie obtained an altitude, which gave 53° 4' 32" north latitude. He found a small fishing village, the inhabitants of which called themselves Sloua-cuss-Dinais, or Red-fish Men, and from them he learned that he was still several days' journey distant from the sea. The stock of provisions was now running low, and it became necessary to reduce the daily allowance by one-third, a measure very unwelcome to the men. On the 12th they again reached the Blackwater, which, according to the natives, was navigable for canoes from the Fraser up to and beyond this point with the exception of two rapids. The rapid pace, the inclemency of the weather, which had been rainy almost continuously since they left the Fraser, and apprehensions of attack from the Indians, were beginning to tell upon the spirits of the *voyageurs*. Mackenzie was himself worried over his diminishing supplies and the uncertainty of his guides, but had to stifle his own uneasiness in order to encourage his men. They had been in worse situations before, he told them, and had always managed to pull through in safety ; they could not now be far from the sea, and must soon be among the Coast Indians, who, being accustomed to trade with white men at the coast, would be disposed to treat them with kindness. The *voyageurs* plucked courage from the optimism of their leader, and pushed forward with renewed energy.

Mackenzie's course was now from Eliguck Lake, near the head-waters of the Blackwater, across a considerable hill to a group of small lakes, beyond which he forded Dean River. From here, under the guidance of some friendly Indians, he crossed the Tsi-tsutl Mountains, and late at night on the 17th reached the banks of the Bella Coola after an extremely exhausting march. He slept that night at a village of the Coast Indians, where he and his men were hospitably entertained. After feasting sumptuously on salmon and other delicacies, Mackenzie and his party laid themselves down to rest with no other canopy than the sky. " I never," says Mackenzie, " enjoyed a more sound and refreshing rest, though I had a board for my bed, and a billet for my pillow."

Eloquent testimony is borne by the explorer to the intelligence and kindliness of the people of this village. No sooner had he awakened in the morning than roast salmon and delicious berries were brought to him Mackenzie examined their houses and the ingenious weirs which they had constructed across the river to catch the salmon. Connected with their salmon fisheries were many curious superstitions. Fish was their only animal food. One of their dogs having picked and swallowed the bone of a deer from Mackenzie's campfire, he was beaten by his master until he disgorged it. One of the *voyageurs* also having thrown a deer bone into the river, a native immediately dived and brought it up, and, having burnt it in the fire, instantly proceeded to wash his polluted hands. Their prejudice against venison was so strong that they objected to Mackenzie taking it in a canoe, lest the salmon might smell it and abandon the neighbourhood, leaving them to starve. They, however, willingly furnished him with a couple of canoes and a supply of roast salmon, with which to continue his journey.

Taking leave of these friendly Indians, Mackenzie continued his journey down the Bella Coola, aecompanied by seven of the natives, who were marvellous canoemen. " I had imagined," says Mackenzie, "that the Canadians who accompanied me were the most expert canoemen in the world, but they are very inferior to these people, as they themselves acknowledged." One of their exploits was to shoot the canoe over a fish weir without taking a drop of water. A run of two hours and a half down the rapid current brought the party to the great village of the Coast Indians. They landed a little above the village and walked through the woods. As they came within sight of the village the guides signed to Mackenzie to take the lead. The natives could be seen running from house to house in a state of wild excitement, some armed with bows and arrows, others with spears. Did this mean a hostile reception? At any rate, there was nothing now but to go forward. Without a sign of fear, Mackenzie and his men marched into the village, and as they approached, the villagers threw down their weapons and crowded around the white strangers. Suddenly an elderly chieftain broke through the press and embraced the explorer, to his surprise. Another, following closely upon his heels, unceremoniously brushed the old chieftain aside and paid Mackenzie the same compliment. He again was followed by a younger Indian. Meanwhile the curious crowd were pressing so closely on every side that it was impossible to move. Now, however, they swung back to admit a young chieftain, who, advancing with dignity to the explorer, broke the fastenings of the splendid robe of sea-otter skins that he wore and threw it around Mackenzie. There could be no doubt now that he had won their hearts. They had invested him with one of the most precious of their possessions.

The old chieftain now led the way to his own house, where mats were spread for the white men. The chief and his counsellors seated themselves opposite. Native dishes were ceremoniously placed before them—roasted salmon, cakes made from the inner bark of the hemlock sprinkled with sweet salmon oil, which were found very palatable. The feast lasted for three hours, the curious tribesmen meanwhile standing around in a circle. Mackenzie, not to be outdone in courtesy, presented the chief with a pair of scissors to trim his beard, a blanket to the young man who had given him the sea-otter robe, and other articles to the minor chiefs

There could be no doubt that the explorer was regarded as a great medicine man. Tales of his marvellous possessions had preceded him to the village, and the natives stood around in open-mouthed astonishment as he explained the object and properties of his astronomical instruments. The following morning the old chief came to Mackenzie's lodge complaining of a pain in his breast. Mackenzie, who had found it wise on many previous occasions to humour the credulous belief of the Indians in his powers as a healer of all physical ills, now gave the sick man a few drops of Turlington's Balsam on a lump of sugar, which he swallowed without hesitation. Having tested the white man's powers on himself, the old chief carried him off to another part of the village, where his son lay suffering from a violent ulcer. To his consternation, Mackenzie was requested to touch the sick man and make him whole. Knowing that it at least could do him no harm, he again had recourse to the precious balsam. The effects not being immediately apparent, which perhaps was not surprising under the circumstances, Mackenzie found on returning to the sick man later in the day that the native doctors had again taken him in charge, and were vehemently practising their skill and art on the unhappy patient. They blew on him, and then whistled ; they rubbed him violently on the stomach ; they thrust their forefingers into his mouth, and spouted water into his face. He was next carried on a plank into the woods, where a fire was kindled, and the native physicians resorted to the heroic, and possibly effective, treatment of scarifying the ulcer with red-hot instruments. The patient bore the cruel pain like a stoic, but the scene was too much for Mackenzie, who hastily withdrew.

The explorer was now anxious to hasten his departure. He had not yet completed the object of his journey, and had little time to waste if he was to return to the east before winter. But the chief and his followers seemed loth to let him go. To his request for canoes and guides to conduct him down to the sea they turned a deaf ear. Finally he stumbled upon an effective argument. Their superstitious fears had invested the astronomical instruments with magical powers, and these fears naturally turned toward the most vital factor in their lives—the salmon. They were apprehensive that the salmon might be frightened from that part of the river. Therefore when Mackenzie got out his instruments to take an altitude, they were as anxious as they had formerly been reluctant to hasten his departure. A canoe was instantly provided, and four of the villagers were assigned the duty of guiding the party down to the coast. Before he-left, however, Mackenzie had an opportunity of examining the chief's own canoe, a somewhat remarkable vessel, built of cedar, forty-five feet long, four feet wide, and three feet and a half in depth. . It was painted black and decorated with white figures of fish of several species. The gunwale, fore and aft, was inlaid with the teeth of the sea-otter. In this canoe, said the chief, he had travelled ten winters before a considerable distance toward the midday sun, that is toward the south, with forty of his people, when he saw two large vessels full of white men, by whom he had been kindly received. They were, he said, the first white people he had ever seen. Mackenzie conjectured that they were the ships commanded by Captain Cook.

Leaving the village where he had been so hospitably entertained, the explorer continued his voyage down the Bella Coola. Making brief visits to other villages on the way, he rapidly descended the current, and about half-past six in the evening came within sight of the mouth of the river where it discharges into North Bentinck Arm. He estimated the distance from the great village upwards of thirty-six miles, which made pretty rapid travelling. At a village a short distance above the mouth of the Bella Coola he spent the night.

BELLA COOLA BAY, PACIFIC COAST

Face p. 480

At eight o'clock the following morning, July 20th, Mackenzie reached the mouth of the river and found himself at last on salt water. The tide was out and had left a large space covered with seaweed. The surrounding hills were involved in fog. The bay appeared to be from one to three miles in breadth. As he paddled along the shore he saw a great number of sea-otters, or what he supposed to be sea-otters; he afterward concluded that most of them were seal. Porpoises disported themselves in the water, while white-headed eagles soared aloft. At two in the afternoon the swell was so high and the wind so boisterous that he could not proceed with his now leaky vessel. He therefore landed in a small cove on the north side of the arm. Mackenzie was now exceedingly anxious to secure an observation, but continuous cloudy weather prevented him. Provisions were getting perilously low, and he was by no means sure that he could count on the natives to assist him. Twenty pounds of pemmican, fifteen of rice, and **six** of flour, among ten half-starved men, in a leaky vessel and on a barbarous coast, made the situation critical. Yet he would not return without getting an observation.

At six on the morning of the 21st Mackenzie left the small bay which he had named Porcupine Cove and continued his way down the North Arm, crossing the entrance to South Bentinck Arm and landing at the cape which Vancouver had visited some time before and named Point Menzies. Here he had an altitude, and here also **he** for the first time met with any hostility on

2 I

the part of the Coast Indians. Three canoes arrived with fifteen men in each, who entered into conversation with the guide. They examined the white men and their belongings with an air of indifference and disdain, and one in particular treated Mackenzie with studied insolence. The secret of his hostility came out when he told Mackenzie that a large canoe had lately come into this bay, manned by white men, one of whom, whose name he pronounced *Macubah*,[1] had fired on him and his friends, and another named *Bensins* had struck him with the flat of his sword. From his insolent behaviour Mackenzie did not doubt that he had deserved the punishment. However, he was to give the explorer more than a little trouble before he was rid of him.

Leaving Point Menzies, Mackenzie followed the main channel to the westward, landing at the ruins of an Indian village. He had been followed by ten canoes of savages, whose attitude was so hostile that Mackenzie prepared to defend himself from an attack. About sunset, however, they departed, taking with them several small articles which they had managed to pilfer while ashore. By an observation he found the longitude of the place to be 128° 02′. The guide now urged Mackenzie to depart, as the natives, he said, were as numerous as mosquitoes and as malignant. The alarmed *voyageurs* joined their remonstrances to his, but Mackenzie was determined not to leave the place until he

[1] This evidently referred to Lieut. Johnstone, an officer of Vancouver's expedition, who made an examination of this part of the coast in boats, in 1793, and was at Point Menzies the last of May of that year.

had determined its position. Finally he succeeded in getting an observation, which gave 52° 21′ 33″ by an artificial horizon, and by the natural horizon 52° 20′ 48″ north latitude. By these he knew that he was at the entrance to Vancouver's Cascade Canal. His object now being accomplished, he prepared to return; but before entering the canoe he mixed some vermilion in melted grease and painted in large characters on the south-east face of the rock on which he had slept the previous night this brief memorial: " Alexander Mackenzie, from Canada, by land, the twenty-second of July, one thousand seven hundred and ninety-three."

Of the return journey little need be said. Early on the morning of the 23rd he reached Porcupine Cove. As he drew near the village at the mouth of the Bella Coola he was met by a number of Indians with daggers in their arms and fury in their faces. Among them he recognized the same troublesome individual who had already done so much to thwart him, and who now took the occasion to repeat his former grievance against Macuba and Benzins. Nothing but Mackenzie's resolute attitude, and the familiarity of the natives with the deadly power of fire-arms, now saved the party from annihilation. Upon Mackenzie presenting his gun the Indians fled into the wood. He was determined, however, to teach them a lesson, and drawing his men up in front of the village, which he appropriately named Rascal's Village, he insisted on the restoration of everything that had been pilfered, and demanded as well a supply of fish, as the conditions of his departure. The

Indians, who were by this time thoroughly cowed, complied with all his demands. Mackenzie paid for the fish and continued his voyage up the river. On the 25th he reached the great village and got a cold reception from the old chief, but a few presents had the effect of restoring the white men to favour. Procuring here a supply of fish, he continued his way up the river, travelling by land, and about eight the following morning reached the upper village, where he was cordially received by the chief, Soocomlick.

Resting at the Friendly Village for a few hours, Mackenzie crossed the mountains, and following the same route which he had traversed on his way down, regained the Fraser on August 4th, about a month after his departure. Ascending the river and passing the forks, he encamped on August 15th by the side of Bad River. Two days later he had the satisfaction of embarking on the waters of the Parsnip, and on the 19th reached the main stream. Five days later, at four in the afternoon, he landed at his fort on the Peace River. "Here," concludes Mackenzie, "my voyages of discovery terminate. Their toils and their dangers, their solicitudes and sufferings, have not been exaggerated in my description. On the contrary, in many instances, language has failed me in the attempt to describe them. I received, however, the reward of my labours, for they were crowned with success."

CHAPTER IV

NINETEEN YEARS IN THE WEST

IN his preface the editor of Daniel Williams Harmon's *Voyages and Travels in the Interior of North America* compares Harmon's achievement with that of Alexander Mackenzie, rather to the advantage of the former. While admitting that Harmon's narrative is unequal to Mackenzie's in minuteness of geographical detail, he claims that, putting aside the voyage to the North Sea, Harmon's explorations were more extensive than those of Mackenzie. He means, of course, that within the limits covered by both Harmon surveyed a larger area than Mackenzie.

This is probably true, for during the nineteen years that Harmon spent in the west, during which period he never came east of Fort William, he was almost constantly on the move, and his journeys covered nearly every section of what is now Western Canada, from Lake Superior to Northern British Columbia, and from the International Boundary north to Great Slave Lake. At the same time, there can be no comparison between the two men so far as actual discovery is concerned. Harmon undoubtedly added something to what was known of the geography of the west, and he added a good deal more to what was known of the languages, character and customs of the north-western tribes and those of the Pacific coast, fifteen of which he says he had visited and become familiar with ; but for the most part his travels took him over fairly well-known ground, and none of his journeys approached in importance, even remotely, the two famous expeditions of Sir Alexander Mackenzie.

It remains true, however, that Harmon fills a place, and not an inconsiderable place, in the story of Western American exploration. This much would be clear even if nothing remained of Harmon's but his map, for that map, based, as the editor says, on that of Sir Alexander Mackenzie, shows many important additions and corrections, and was probably at the time it was published the most complete and accurate map of the northern half of the continent. At the same time, while Harmon corrected some of the errors of his predecessors in exploration and map-making, he himself managed to slip up occasionally, and in one case at least was completely led astray by Indian report. His map shows in Northern British Columbia or New Caledonia an immense lake extending in a north-easterly direction from about 54° 40′ N., 125° 30′ W., to 56° N., 124° 30′ W. This lake, which the natives called Musk-quâ Sâ-ky-e-gun or Bear's Lake (Great Bear Lake on his map), Harmon describes as the source of Finlay's or the North Branch of Peace River. The real source of the Finlay River is a small body of water, Thutage Lake, near the height of land, 57° N., 127° W. Harmon's

Great Bear Lake was "so large that the Indians never attempt to cross it in their canoes," and was situated nearly due west from the junction of the Finlay and Parsnip rivers, at a distance of about one hundred and fifty miles.   Those who resided at the east end affirmed that it extended to the Western Ocean, but on his map Harmon places the western end well inland, four or five degrees, in fact, east of the head of Observatory Inlet.   Elsewhere he describes a large river of New Caledonia which enters the Pacific several hundred miles north of the mouth of the Fraser, and "arises near Great Bear's Lake."   This could only have been the Skeena, one branch of which rises in Babine Lake, the largest body of water in Northern British Columbia, and another near a very small lake called Bear Lake, a little north of 56°, and east of 127°.   This little lake with the significant name will be referred to again.

In Simon Fraser's manuscript journal of 1806, in the Bancroft Collection, a similar account is given of this singular lake.   Possibly Harmon may have got the story from Fraser, or they may both have been deceived by, or misinterpreted, Indian reports.   In Fraser's journal, as quoted by H. H. Bancroft, under date of the 23rd of April, 1806, the arrival of a party of Indians from Finlay River is recorded, who report that that stream does not begin its course in a series of rapids, as had been supposed, but near a large lake called Bear Lake, "where the salmon come up, and from there is a river that falls into another much larger, according to their report, than even the Peace River, that glides in a north-west direction." "We cannot," concludes Fraser, "imagine what river this is; by their description and the course it runs it cannot be the Columbia, and I know of no other excepting Cook's." Fraser had not yet explored the great river that bears his name, and which at this time was supposed to be part of the Columbia. In a foot-note Bancroft disposes of the problem of Bear Lake off-hand. "It is Babine Lake here referred to."[1] But a later investigator takes quite another view. The Reverend A. G. Morice, who is thoroughly familiar with the geography and history of Northern British Columbia, flatly contradicts Bancroft, though it must be confessed that the criticism he brings against Bancroft of so peremptorily solving the question might with almost equal justice be applied to himself. "The lake above mentioned," he says, "is simply Bear Lake, sometimes called Connolly by a few strangers, and the river that exercises the mind of Fraser is the Skeena."[2] Father Morice has personally ascertained that this small Bear Lake is one hundred and eighty miles from the head-waters of the Finlay. In the light of all the evidence it does not appear that he has finally disposed of the question. It may be that this insignificant lake and the great body of water spoken of by Fraser and Harmon are identical, but in that event there must have been more than the usual exaggeration in the accounts of the Indians. From some points of view

[1] *History of the North-West Coast,* II, 96.
[2] *History of the Northern Interior of British Columbia,* 56–7.

Babine Lake meets the situation much more closely, and it is by no means certain that Bancroft's conjecture was wrong. On the other hand, the theory might even be advanced that Harmon and Fraser were deceived by some confused stories of one of the great inlets or channels along the coast. All that is certain is that nothing very closely resembling the immense lake they describe has any existence in Northern British Columbia.

Harmon, a New Englander by birth, entered the service of the North West Company in 1800, and the same year left Montreal for the west with one of the canoe brigades. He reached Grand Portage on June 13th. Three years before Harmon's visit the group of Montreal merchants known as the X Y Company, who had entered into a vigorous opposition to the North West Company, had built a fort at Grand Portage, about two hundred rods from the establishment of the North West Company. Harmon's description of the latter is practically the same as the one quoted in an earlier chapter, from an anonymous writer who was at Grand Portage in 1793. "Every summer," says Harmon, "the greater part of the Proprietors and Clerks, who have spent the winter in the Interiour come here with the furs which they have been able to collect during the preceding season. . . . The people who come from Montreal with the goods go no farther than this, excepting a few who take those articles to the Rainy Lake which are intended for Athabaska, as that place lies at too great a distance from this to permit people who

reside there to come to this place and return, before the
winter commences. Those who bring the goods from
Montreal, on their return take down the furs, etc., from
the north." Harmon, brought up in the pious atmosphere of a New England home, was shocked to find
the traders treating the Sabbath with no more consideration than any other day of the week. "People
who have been long in this savage country have no
scruples of conscience on this subject." The men were
engaged in making and pressing packs of fur to be sent
down to Montreal. But all was not work at Grand
Portage. One evening "the gentlemen of the place
dressed and we had a famous ball, in the dining room.
For musick we had the bagpipe, the violin and the
flute, which added much to the interest of the occasion.
At the ball there was a number of the ladies of this
country; and I was surprised to find that they could
conduct themselves with so much propriety, and dance
so well."

Harmon remained a month at Grand Portage and
then left for the interior. He was kept busy for a day
or two at Fort Charlotte, at the western end of the
portage, sending off canoes laden with supplies for Fort
des Prairies. He left Fort Charlotte on July 15th
in two canoes manned by six *voyageurs*, and threading
the intricate series of small rivers, lakes, and ponds that
then formed the route to Rainy Lake, reached Rainy
Lake Fort on the 24th. Here were encamped many
Chippeways, who maintained themselves on the excellent sturgeon and white fish caught in the lake, which

they supplemented with wild rice. "This," says Harmon, "is thought to be nearly as nourishing as the real rice, and almost as palatable. The kernel of the former is rather longer than that of the latter, and is of a brownish colour." On the 29th he crossed Lake of the Woods, or Woody Lake as he calls it, and entered the Winnipeg River, noting as he descended the "majestick and frightful waterfalls" that break its course. On the last day of the month he reached the North West Company's post at the mouth of the river, and notes the presence of an establishment of the Hudson's Bay Company at the same place.

Harmon's destination had been the Saskatchewan, but it was now decided that he should take charge of a new fort in the Swan River country. He therefore waited at the mouth of Winnipeg River for the Swan River brigade, and spent the interval very agreeably in pigeon-shooting. He was now for the first time introduced to that most important food pemmican, the bread of the western wilderness. Pemmican "consists of lean meat dried and pounded fine and then mixed with melted fat. This compound is put into bags made of the skins of the buffalo, etc., and when cold it becomes a solid body. If kept in a dry place it will continue good for years." Harmon describes it as very palatable and nourishing. Sometimes sugar or dried berries were added to improve the flavour of the pemmican.

On August 10th the long-expected brigade arrived from Grand Portage, and Harmon embarked for his Swan River post. Skirting the shores of Lake Winnipeg the brigade reached what is known as Sturgeon Bay, on the western coast, on the 17th, and immediately ascended Dauphin River to Lake Manitoba, from whence they portaged over into Lake Winnipegosis. At the entrance of another little river called the Dauphin, connecting with Dauphin Lake, they stopped to make up an assortment of goods for the Dauphin River post.[1] Harmon mentions that a French missionary was stationed at this place before the British occupation. "I am told," he says, "that there are some Indians still living who recollect prayers which were taught them by the missionary." This was probably one of the Jesuit fathers who went west with La Vérendrye, or possibly with Saint-Pierre.

On October 9th Harmon entered Swan River, which he found very shallow and encumbered with rapids, and reached Swan River Fort the following day. Travelling had been very unpleasant up the river. For about four miles of the way the men had to get out of the canoes and drag them up the shallows, while Harmon trudged along the bank in an uncomfortable mixture of snow, mud, and water. The Hudson's Bay Company had had an establishment here a few years before, but had abandoned it, and now the North West Company had a monopoly of the fur trade in the Swan River district. Sending several men to build a fort about fifty miles up the river, Harmon remained at the Swan River Fort for a few days, waiting for a guide to conduct him to Fort Alexandria. On the 18th two men arrived from

[1] Somerset House on his map.

Alexandria, and Harmon left with them for that place. The route lay across an open country broken occasionally by clumps of small timber. On the 22nd they crossed Swan River on a raft and got into a somewhat more hilly country, almost destitute of timber. The following afternoon they reached Fort Alexandria, "built on a small rise of ground on the bank of the Assiniboine, or Upper Red River, that separates it from a beautiful prairie about ten miles long and from one to four broad, which is as level as the floor of a house." On the whole the fort was delightfully situated, and as game was plentiful Harmon was content enough to spend the winter there. It is worth noting that although horses had only been acquired by the Assiniboines and Crees within a comparatively short period,[1] they were so numerous in 1800 that well-built, strong, and tolerably fleet animals could be bought for a mere trifle.

At Fort Alexandria Harmon had his first experience of the life of the western fur trader, and the picture he draws is not altogether an inviting one. The Indians who visited the fort were Crees and Assiniboines. Men, women, and children drank all they could get. "At some times ten or twelve of both sexes may be seen fighting each other promiscuously, until at last they all fall on the floor, one upon another. To add to the uproar a number of children, some on their mothers'

[1] Edward Umfreville, writing in 1789, says "they were originally imported by the Spanish on the western side of the Continent, and it is but lately that they have become common among the Nehethawa [Cree] Indians."

shoulders, and others running about and taking hold of their clothes, are constantly bawling."

Against this unpleasant picture of the Indian in civilized society may be placed another of a vastly different kind. During the winter Harmon had set out for a camp of the Assiniboines on a trading expedition. When they approached within about a mile of the camp, ten or twelve of the chiefs met them on horseback and conducted them to the village, where they were received with every demonstration of joy. The principal chief sent his son to invite them to his tent. "As soon as we had entered it and were seated, the respectable old chief caused meat and berries and the best of everything which he had, to be set before us. Before we had eaten much, we were sent for to another tent, where we received a similar treatment; and from this we were invited to another; and so on, till we had been to more than half a dozen. At all these we ate a little, and smoked our pipes." "Hospitality to strangers," concludes Harmon, "is among the Indian virtues. During several days that we remained with these people, we were treated with more real politeness than is commonly shown to strangers in the civilized part of the world." The Indian brand of hospitality was in rather marked contrast to that which the civilized white men offered in their forts.

The next three years Harmon spent in the Upper Assiniboine and Swan River country, moving about from fort to fort, trading with the Indians, hunting buffalo, and adding to his knowledge of the country. In March, 1804, he started out on a trading expedition over the western plains. He travelled for ten or twelve days, camping with wandering bands of Assiniboines, until he reached the country of the Rapid Indians (Atsinas), apparently somewhere about the South Saskatchewan. "A white man," he says, "was never before known to penetrate so far." No doubt Harmon thought so, but there is evidence to the contrary. It has already been seen that Anthony Hendry traversed this very region fifty years before.

In the autumn Harmon left Fort Alexandria for Montagne à la Basse,[1] some distance down the Assiniboine, to obtain a supply of goods for the winter trade. He made the return journey in twenty-one days. Montagne à la Basse was fifty miles above McDonnell's House at the mouth of the Souris, and stood on a high bank commanding an extensive prospect. On November 24th Harmon received a letter from Chaboillez, at Montagne à la Basse, informing him that Lewis and Clark had reached the Mandan villages, and that as soon as navigation opened they designed to continue their journey to the Rocky Mountains, and thence descend to the Pacific Ocean.

Harmon was back again at Montagne à la Basse in April, 1805, and while there Chaboillez induced him to undertake a tour of discovery. He was to leave that

---

[1] Should be Bosse, according to Dr. Coues, from the French word meaning hump, knob, etc., applied in this case to the hill or bank on which the fort stood.

place about the beginning of June, accompanied by six or seven Canadians and two or three Indians, and proceed by way of the Mandan villages and the Missouri to the Rocky Mountains. It was expected that they would return from their excursion the following November. Harmon, however, fell ill about the time he had planned to start for the Rocky Mountains, and the journey was abandoned. Dr. Coues, in referring to this project, in a foot-note to his Henry and Thompson, says that Harmon had " made up his mind to go to the Pacific via the Missouri River at the Mandans," and that "had he done so, he might have given Lewis and Clark a close race for their laurels." There is nothing in Harmon's own statement, or elsewhere so far as can be seen, to justify such a conclusion. The time allowed for the expedition—six months at the outside—would have been barely sufficient for a journey to the Rocky Mountains and back; and certainly would not have sufficed for an expedition to the Pacific and back even under the most favourable conditions. Moreover, it is stated in Harmon's Journal that Larocque attempted to make this same journey, and as already seen, Larocque's expedition was to the Rockies, not to the Pacific. Only one party attempted to reach the Pacific by way of the Missouri, previous to the successful Lewis and Clark expedition, and that attempt was made long before Harmon's day, by the sons of La Vérendrye.

Toward the end of June, 1805, Harmon left the Assiniboine country, and returned by way of Red

River to Lake Winnipeg, and on the 16th of July arrived at the mouth of the Kaministikwia, where he remained for a few days at the New Fort as it was then called, afterward known as Fort William.

On the 22nd he again left for the interior, his destination now being the Saskatchewan. On September the 5th he reached Cumberland House, not the establishment of that name built by Samuel Hearne for the Hudson's Bay Company, but the neighbouring fort of the North West Company, built, Harmon tells us, thirty years before by Joseph Frobisher. Leaving Cumberland House, he continued up the Saskatchewan, and turning up the south branch, arrived on September 21st at South Branch Fort, about one hundred and twenty miles above the Forks. This fort had been built the previous summer.

In coming up the river Harmon had seen the remains of a number of trading establishments, some abandoned as long as thirty years before. One, a few miles below the South Branch Fort, had been abandoned fifteen years since, on account of an attack by the Rapid Indians. A near-by fort of the Hudson's Bay Company suffered at the same time. The Indians, to the number of one hundred and fifty horsemen, first attacked the Hudson's Bay fort, killing the few people who were there, with the exception of one man who managed to hide. After plundering the fort and setting fire to it, they turned their attention to the North West Company's establishment, two hundred rods distant. Here, however, they met with a different reception. The

2 K

North West men had been warned in time, and had shut the gates of the fort. The garrison consisted of three men, with several women and children. The three men pluckily defended the fort from the block-houses and bastions until nightfall, when the Indians withdrew, carrying with them a number of dead and wounded, while the little garrison sustained not a scratch. In the morning the fort was abandoned, the traders embarking their women and children and all their property in several canoes, and paddling two hundred miles down the river to a point below the Forks, where they built another fort.

In September Harmon returned to Cumberland House, where he passed the following winter. He mentions that the Hudson's Bay house was within a hundred yards of the North West fort, and was in charge of Peter Fidler, of whom we have already heard. The traders on the Lower Saskatchewan lived mainly on fish, of which they obtained an abundant supply by means of spread nets. Sturgeon were caught in these nets anywhere from ten to one hundred pounds in weight. Trout, catfish, and pike lent a slight variety to the universal fish diet.

July, 1807, saw Harmon again at the New Fort. The seven years for which he was under engagement to the North West Company had expired, but the free life of the fur trader, with its strange admixture of hardship and adventure, danger and pleasure, had taken too deep a hold on him, and he decided to turn his face once more toward the western wilderness, that wonderful land of stupendous distances, of great lakes and rivers, limitless plains, and gigantic mountains. His decision is, however, made the occasion of one of those fits of moralizing which one finds scattered so thickly throughout his narrative, and which always appear so incongruous in their relation to the text that one is convinced they must have been introduced by the reverend and well-meaning editor, who seems to have been singularly lacking in the saving sense of humour.

Harmon wintered at Lake Nipigon, where he was again subjected to a monotonous diet of fish. In the spring he returned to Fort William, and left the same day for the Athabaska district, in company with J. G. McTavish. In descending the Winnipeg River they met David Thompson, on his way back from the Columbia River. On the 12th of August they reached Cumberland House, and turned north to the Churchill by way of Portage de Traite or Frog Portage. Paddling up the Churchill—English River as the Canadian traders called it—they reached Ile à la Crosse Fort on the 25th. Harmon describes it as a well-built fort standing on the north side of the lake, with an excellent kitchen garden attached. Leaving the fort, five days later they crossed Methye Portage, and dropped their canoes into the waters that ultimately empty into the Arctic. Harmon, like every other traveller who has passed this way, is enraptured with the wonderful view from the summit of the portage down the valley of the Clearwater.

On the 6th of September they paddled out of the Clearwater River on to the broad waters of the Athabaska ; and the following day reached Fort Chipewyan. This fort, afterward removed to the northern side of Atha- baska Lake, was at this time situated on a rocky point, at the south-western end of the lake. It was the general rendezvous for all the traders in the Athabaska district and beyond. On the 21st Harmon notes that ever since his arrival men from almost every corner of the district had been flocking in, some coming from more than a thousand miles down the Mackenzie River, others from Great Slave Lake and Peace River. The same day, Simon Fraser arrived from his adventurous voyage down the Fraser River to the sea.

On the 22nd of September, Harmon left Fort Chipe- wyan, and entering Peace River, paddled up to Fort Vermillion, passing on the way, about sixty miles below the fort, a waterfall about twenty feet in height. This modest little cataract is apparently the one described by the irrepressible Peter Pond to Isaac Ogden, of Quebec, as " the largest falls in the world." The river at this point, said Pond, is at least two miles wide. Harmon says thirty rods. Quite a discrepancy.

Continuing up the river, Harmon reached Dunvegan[1] on the 10th October, and wintered there. He was never more comfortably situated. Buffalo, moose, deer, and bear furnished the larder, as well as the produce of a tolerably good kitchen garden. The fort was

---

[1] Dunvegan was, and in fact still is, situated on the left bank of the Peace River, about lat. 56°, long. 118° 40'. The fort was named after the " cold, bleak, rock-built castle of the McLeods of Skye."

equipped with a fair collection of books ; and, to crown all, Hermon had as companions for the winter several traders whom he describes as "enlightened, sociable, and pleasant." What could man want more? What mattered it that on December 20th the thermometer registered forty degrees below zero, so long as a good fire blazed on the hearth? Others, however, were not so fortunately situated, for on the 20th March Harmon gets word of the death of several Canadians in the vicinity of Great Slave Lake, from starvation, those who survived having lived for several days on the flesh of their dead companions. Commenting on this, Harmon mentions the case of an Indian woman who was reported to have eaten no less than fourteen of her friends and relations during one winter.

Harmon remained at Dunvegan until October, 1810, when he was requested by the Company to cross the mountains and take charge of the New Caledonia department.

John Stuart, who was at that time in charge of the New Caledonia department, had asked to be relieved, but Harmon persuaded him to remain, he himself becoming second in command. Accompanied by Stuart, and a number of men, in four canoes, he ascended the river, reaching St. John's Fort on the evening of the third day, and Rocky Mountain Portage Fort five days later. Some of the Sicannies, a mountain tribe, helped them over the portage. These Indians, whom Harmon describes as quiet, inoffensive people, seem to have been unfortunately situated. To live, they had to get down to the habitable country on one side of the mountains or the other. They spent, or attempted to spend, the summer months on the Pacific side of the mountains, and the winter on the eastern side. On the western side they were attacked by the Tâcullies[1] and Atenâs ; when they returned to the eastern slope the Crees and Beaver Indians gave them an equally hot reception. Being driven from the salmon streams on one side, and the game country on the other, they frequently had to live for weeks at a time on roots picked up in the mountains. Between the devil and the deep sea, the wretched Sicannies fell upon many evil days, and not infrequently ended in starvation.

Harmon left the western end of the Rocky Mountain Portage on the 17th, and the following week was spent in the heart of the mountains, following the river through the pass now known as Peace River Pass. Just as they got clear of the mountains they passed the mouth of Finlay's Branch, and continued up the South Branch—now the Parsnip River—through a thickly timbered country, to McLeod's Lake Fort. Here they left the canoes, and travelled overland to Stuart's Lake, a distance of one hundred miles to the westward. The fort at Stuart's Lake was pleasantly situated on rising ground, at the east end of the lake. Fifty miles due west lies Fraser's Lake, where a small fort had been built in 1806. Harmon came here and remained until the spring of 1811, when he returned to Stuart's Lake. Stuart's Lake Fort he made his head-quarters, and here he

[1] Carrier tribe.

remained for the next six years, building up a profitable trade for the Company, studying the character and customs of the Tâcullies and other tribes of the vicinity, and making occasional excursions, of no very great length, into the unexplored country to the west and south.

The Tâcullies, or rather these particular members of the tribe, were new to the white man and his ways, and Harmon tells that when they first witnessed a New Year's celebration they " hid themselves under beds, and elsewhere, saying that they thought the white people had run mad, for they appeared not to know what they were about.   It was the first time that they had ever seen a person intoxicated."

In December, 1812, Harmon left Stuart's Lake on an expedition to the country of the Nâte-ote-tains,[1] a tribe that had up to this time had no intercourse whatever with white men.   Seven days' hard travel brought him to their first village, the inhabitants of which " were not a little surprised and alarmed to see people come among them whose complexion was so different from their own."   Men, women, and children came out to meet Harmon, all armed, some with bows and arrows, others with axes and clubs.   They made no hostile demonstration, however, and as soon as they understood the object of the visit, Harmon and his men were treated with the utmost respect and hospitality.

Continuing his journey, Harmon passed through four other villages of the Nâte-ote-tains, from whom he learned that a large river flowed through their country

[1] Babine Indians.

and emptied into the Pacific (probably the Skeena), and that white traders ascended this river for some distance in barges, to trade with another tribe who lived along its banks. These white men Harmon conjectured to be Americans, who had come around Cape Horn to the North Pacific Coast, where they were carrying on a coasting trade with the Indians.[1]

In November, 1812, Harmon notes the arrival of John Stuart and J. G. McTavish from Fort Chipewyan. The latter with his men purposed wintering near the source of the Columbia, and descending it in the spring to its mouth, where they were to meet Donald McTavish, who had sailed from England for the mouth of the Columbia in October. On the 1st of May John Stuart left Stuart's Lake, with six Canadians and two Indians, with the intention of joining J. G. McTavish on the Columbia, and if possible discovering a water route from Stuart's Lake to the Columbia. On the 25th of September Harmon received a letter from Stuart describing his journey to the Columbia, which had been successfully accomplished. He had descended the Columbia for eight days, when the canoes had to be abandoned and a land journey of more than one hundred and fifty miles undertaken to a lake called O-ke-nâ-gun, the modern Okanagan, south of the Fraser River, and about 50° N. and 119° W. From Okanagan Stuart wrote that he could go all the way by water to the ocean by making a few portages, and he

[1] According to Father Morice, these were simply Indians from the coast, not white men.

hoped to reach the Pacific in twelve or fifteen days at farthest.

On the 7th of November Joseph Larocque, who had accompanied McTavish and his party on the voyage down the Columbia, arrived at Stuart's Lake Fort. They had met Stuart and his company on their return, and Larocque, with two of Stuart's men, had come to Stuart's Lake by the very roundabout route of Red Deer River, Lesser Slave Lake, and Dunvegan—a route which entailed two crossings of the mountains, eastward through the Yellowhead Pass, and back by the Peace River Pass.

In May, 1819, Harmon finally left New Caledonia, and following the same route by which he had come in, at last reached head-quarters at Fort William on August 18th, and returned from thence to the east, after an absence of nineteen years in the wilderness.

CHAPTER V

EXPLORING THE CAÑON OF THE FRASER

IN the story of Western American exploration no incident is marked by more indomitable pluck than the descent of the fearful cañon of the Fraser by Simon Fraser and John Stuart. Viewing the tumultuous waters to-day from the safe vantage-point of a car window, one gets a faint idea of the appalling difficulties surmounted by these Scottish-Canadian discoverers. The steadfast courage, endurance, and resourcefulness needed to carry them through this notable exploit were extraordinary even in an age and among a race marked by these characteristics.

Simon Fraser was born at Bennington, Vermont, about the year 1776. His father, a Scotchman by birth, and a captain in Burgoyne's army, was captured with that ill-fated general and imprisoned at Albany. After his death the widow with her young son crossed the boundary and settled at Three Rivers, in what is now the province of Quebec, afterward removing to St. Andrews, Cornwall. Simon entered the service of the North West Company at the age of sixteen, and about ten years after became a *bourgeois* or partner of the Company. At different times he was stationed in nearly every section of the western fur country, from Grand Portage to New Caledonia. His restless temperament, even more than the exigencies of his occupation, kept him constantly on the move. If he kept any journals of his first fourteen years of service in the North West Company, they are no longer extant. Up to the year 1806 his life can only be traced indistinctly by means of occasional references in the journals of David Thompson and other contemporaries. He wintered 1795–6 at Lac la Ronge; was agent for the Company at Grand Portage in 1797; and at Fort Liard, Athabaska, in 1804. He signed the Montreal agreement that same year. In June, 1805, he passed Cumberland House on his way west to the Rocky Mountains. Crossing the mountains by the Peace River Pass, he ascended the Parsnip to a lake which he named after Archibald Norman McLeod. Here he established a small outpost. In the spring of 1806, accompanied by John Stuart, he crossed over from the head-waters of the Parsnip to the Fraser River, which he descended to the Nechaco. Here they left the main stream and turned up the Nechaco to the mouth of a tributary now known as Stuart River. Fraser seems to have given the name to the entire stream. Paddling up Stuart River, they came to a considerable lake, which was named, like the river, after John Stuart. Near the outlet of the lake a post was established, afterward known as Fort St. James. Of Fraser's encounter with the Carriers on the shores of the lake, and of their first introduction to the properties of tobacco and soap, an interesting and amusing account is given by Father Morice.[1] In August Stuart with two men was sent overland to another lake about forty miles to the south. After exploring the lake he was to descend to the confluence of the Nechaco and Stuart rivers, where Fraser would meet him. This was done, and Stuart's report being favourable as to the prospects of a trading establishment on the new lake—which he had named after his chief—they both turned up the Nechaco, and built Fort Fraser near the outlet of Fraser Lake. Leaving two or three men here, Fraser and Stuart returned to Lake Stuart, where they wintered.

In the spring of 1807 Jules Maurice Quesnel and Hugh Faries arrived from the east with instructions to Fraser to explore the great river, the Tacouche Tesse, then still supposed to be the Columbia. Fraser and Stuart descended to the forks, or the confluence of the Nechaco and Fraser, where they built a post and named it Fort George in honour of the King. It became the starting-point for their great expedition down the river to the sea. All preparations having been made, they left Fort George on May 28th. With Fraser went Stuart and Quesnel and nineteen *voyageurs*, as well as two Indian guides, in four canoes.

Their troubles began almost immediately. Fifteen miles from Fort George they came to what was afterward known as Fort George Cañon. Attempting to run the rapids, one of the canoes was nearly wrecked against the rocky bank of the river. In the afternoon they had

---

[1] *Northern Interior of British Columbia.*

fine going with a smooth current, and passed the mouth of a river on the right which they named Bourbonneur.

Sunday, the 29th, they embarked at four in the morning; cached a bale of dried salmon on an island against their return, and three additional bales a few miles farther down; ran through the Cottonwood River Cañon without misadventure; and camped for the night at the mouth of a river, which on the return journey was named Quesnel after one of the party. The village of Quesnel now stands about the spot where Fraser encamped.

Embarking again at the first touch of dawn, they ran down with a strong current. The view on either side was altogether charming. The plains rose gradually from the banks of the river until in the distance bounded by hills thickly clothed with evergreens. Behind these rose other hills, and then again others, giving the scene the appearance of an immense amphitheatre. This day they passed the site of the future Alexandria— Mackenzie's farthest point to the southward. Beyond this all was new, unexplored, undiscovered. Native houses appeared here and there on the banks; then a group of Indians, who watched the approach of the white men with evident alarm. As they drew near the shore they could see couriers posting off on horseback with the news to the Indians below. Fraser thought it wise to remain here until a number of the natives should collect, to whom he could explain his intentions. These were of the Atnah tribe, and among them was a boy who understood a little of the Carrier language and could therefore act as interpreter. His mother was of the Tahowtin nation, which Masson incorrectly identified with Harmon's Nate-ote-tain. Father Morice explains that the Nate-ote-tain or Nato-o'tin are the Babines, while Fraser's Tahowtin were a sub-tribe of the Carriers known as the Lhtha-o'ten.

In the afternoon some of the Atnahs and Tahowtins arrived on horseback. They were friendly, but gave a very discouraging account of the river below, which they described as a succession of falls and cascades enclosed by impassable cliffs. They advised Fraser to abandon the attempt. No, said he, he was determined to force a passage down the river, and was yet to be convinced that it was not possible. Then, said they, if he would go, the Great Chief of the Atnahs lived at the next village, and had there a slave who had been to the sea and might be procured as a guide. The Atnahs and Tahowtins had heard of fire-arms, but had never yet seen any. They asked Fraser to show his and explain its use. Fraser produced the gun, and to give them an illustration of its effectiveness told his men to fire at the trees. Terrified at the report, they fell on their faces, and when they had sufficiently recovered their wits to examine the marks of the bullets in the trees, their uneasiness was increased. They naively assured Fraser that the Indians in that country were good and peaceable, and would never make use of their arms to annoy white people.

The Great Chief of the Atnahs did even better than had been promised for him. Not content with sending his slave, he volunteered himself to accompany the explorers. He was well known to the tribes below, he said, and his presence would ensure their security. Fraser gladly accepted the offer. Embarking, they ran down some minor rapids, and late in the afternoon came to one much more formidable than any yet encountered. It was about two miles in length. On either side the cliffs rose sheer from the water's edge. The channel was contracted to forty or fifty yards, and through this narrow gorge the immense body of water rushed turbulently, its foam-crowned waves dashing hither and thither against the rocky walls. Yet, as it was next to impossible to carry the canoes over the precipitous banks, it was decided to attempt to run the rapid. Fraser ordered five picked men from the crews to man a light canoe, and, not without serious misgivings, watched them push out into the stream.

Only for a moment could they control her. Over the first cascade she rode in safety. Then the men lost all power. Drawn into an eddy, she was whirled about like a reed, while her crew could do nothing more than keep her afloat. Swinging around for a time, she flew out into the current, over the breakers, now escaping a jutting rock by a hair's-breadth, again in imminent danger of crashing into the bank. Finally she was forced against a low, projecting rock. The men sprang out and managed to hold the canoe, while Fraser came to their assistance.

How to reach them, though, was the problem. The situation was perilous for all. The bank was extremely high and steep, and the rescuing party had to drive their daggers into the face of the cliff to check their speed. Unless they were to abandon the canoe and baggage, there was nothing for it but to drag everything up the face of this perpendicular bank. Steps were cut in the wall with the daggers; a line was fastened to the front of the canoe; some of the men scrambled to the summit with the line, while the rest supported it upon their shoulders. As they drew and pushed it up their lives hung upon a thread. One false step, or the breaking of the line, would hurl the whole party into the furious waters beneath. With infinite labour, however, and the utmost care, they managed before dark to get the canoe to the top of the cliff. There was nothing for it now but to carry everything overland. It was a superhuman task—climbing the steep face of a mountain with eighty or ninety pound packs; but these wiry *voyageurs*, inured to every hardship, accomplished what would have been impossible to ordinary travellers.

The natives watched the proceedings with interest and curiosity, no doubt wondering what particularly mad freak brought the white men to such an outrageous exploit. They assured Fraser that the navigation of the river for some distance below was impracticable, and advised him to leave his canoes in their charge and proceed overland to the banks of a great river that lay off to the south-east (the Thompson), which would bring him to the lower waters of the Fraser, and from thence he would have smooth going to the sea. The plan looked inviting, but Fraser would have none of it.

SIMON FRASER, ESQ.

Face p. 512

His instructions were to trace the Fraser to the sea, and that he was determined to do at all cost. The crew stood by him to a man.

Here the explorer encountered for the first time a tribe which he calls Chilk-odins, who inhabited the banks of a large river flowing in from the west (the Chilcotin River). The river had risen eight feet within twenty-four hours—nothing unusual with that torrent-like stream, says Father Morice. With the aid of the Indians, two of the canoes were hauled laboriously over the ridge. Fraser had intended to leave the other canoes and part of the provisions behind, the Indians having promised him horses ; but with native perversity they broke their engagements, and there was nothing for it but to haul another canoe over, so that all the party might proceed by water. With difficulty he managed to secure four horses, which were of some service in the heavy work of portaging, though one of them went over the cliff into the river with Stuart's desk and the medicine chest and was lost. The natives, while not over-generous in other respects, were prodigal of advice, but Fraser preferred to follow the dictates of his own judgment. One interesting bit of information they supplied, however. White people, they said, had lately passed down the first large river to the left. "These," comments Fraser, "were supposed to be some of our friends from the department of Fort des Prairies." It was of course David Thompson's party, and the river was the Columbia. Fraser must have wondered what this great river could be, for it must be remem-

2 L

bered that he still laboured under the misapprehension that the river he was himself descending was the Columbia. It was not, in fact, until he reached the mouth of the river, and found that it debouched far to the northward of where the Columbia was known to empty, that he realized his mistake.

Sunday, June 4th, Fraser continued his journey down the river, which turned out to be quite as dangerous as the Indians had painted it. He notes a precipice of immense height which seemed to bar the river ahead— now known as Bar Rock. Running several minor rapids, he came to one which indeed looked impassable. Examining it by land, it was found to be a succession of immense whirlpools; but again the choice was between running the rapid or abandoning the canoes. The latter were therefore unloaded, and the canoes went down light. Between the whirlpools and the rocks the course was hazardous in the extreme. "It was," says Fraser, "a desperate undertaking," but fortunately they got through without either breaking or sinking the canoes.

This was only half the task. The packs still remained to be brought down by land. The only passage lay along the face of a huge precipice, on loose stones and gravel which constantly gave way under their feet. One of the men, losing the path, got into an intricate and perilous situation. With a large pack on his back he got so engaged among the rocks that he could move neither backward or forward, nor yet unload himself without imminent danger. Seeing his predicament,

Fraser crawled on hands and knees to the spot and managed to cut the thongs that held the pack, dropping it over the precipice into the river. For two miles their way lay along this perilous pathway, and before they reached the lower end the shoes were worn from their feet, and they arrived bruised, bleeding, and utterly exhausted.

Day after day the same story is told. The river was one long series of dangerous rapids, down which they ran with their lives in their hands. The dangers of the river were matched by those of the land. When the portages were not treacherous, they were at least long and exhausting. The men were harassed by fatigue. From daylight to dark, when not on the river, they were toiling with heavy packs up steep hills, down into deep ravines, around steep precipices; a pair of moccasins did not last a day; when the moccasins went they had to stumble along over sharp rocks and thorns without any protection.

On the 6th they came to a waterfall which seemed to afford no passage. Cascades and whirlpools hemmed in by huge rocks offered a dreary prospect. Quesnel and six men were sent to examine both sides of the river for a carrying place. After an absence of three hours they returned and reported that there was a beaten path on the opposite side, but it was four miles long and through a very rough country. They crossed over, and after consultation decided to try the river. The canoes were put in the water and tracked down to the fall. Portaging over a point, they ran several small rapids and encamped for the night.

The morning of the 9th they reached a rapid that threw all that they had hitherto encountered into the shade.

" Here the channel contracts to about forty yards, and is enclosed by two precipices of immense height which, bending towards each other, make it narrower above than below. The water which rolls down this extraordinary passage in tumultuous waves and with great velocity had a frightful appearance. However, it being absolutely impossible to carry the canoes by land, all hands without hesitation embarked as it were *à corps perdu* upon the mercy of this awful tide. Once engaged, the die was cast. Our great difficulty consisted in keeping the canoes within the medium or *fil d'eau*, that is, clear of the precipice on one side and from the gulfs formed by the waves on the other. Thus skimming along as fast as lightning, the crews, cool and determined, followed each other in awful silence, and when we arrived at the end, we stood gazing at each other in silent congratulation at our narrow escape from total destruction."

Reaching comparatively quiet water, they paddled on to an Indian encampment. Here the natives drew a chart of the river below, which they represented as a chain of insurmountable difficulties. They asked Fraser why he had not taken the advice of the old chief and gone overland. The river below, they said, would be found impracticable both by land and water. He would have in many cases to climb up and down dangerous precipices by means of rope ladders. These had been

VALE, B.C., FRASER RIVER

placed there by the Indians, and there was no other way. But Fraser, though weary and discouraged, was not yet beaten by any means. Having got so far, he would find some means of completing his journey. He prevailed upon one of the local Indians to go with him as guide, and continued his course until late in the evening. One rapid succeeded another in rapid succession. Inaccessible cliffs rose to the sky on either side. "I scarcely ever saw anything so dreary and dangerous in any country," exclaims Fraser. "At present, while writing this, whatever way I turn my eyes, mountains upon mountains whose summits are covered with eternal snow close the gloomy scene."

The morning of the 10th Fraser sent two men ahead to examine the river, and their report confirming what the natives had said as to its impracticability, he decided at length to abandon the canoes. Erecting a scaffold for the canoes, he covered them with branches to shield the gum from the sun, and cached such articles as could not be made up into convenient packs. By five o'clock on the 11th all was ready. Each man shouldering an eighty-pound pack, they set forward on foot toward the sea. A hard day's travel brought them to the banks of a small stream, where they encamped. The next day, continuing their route, they were suddenly confronted by a party of Askettihs (probably the Lillooet Indians), who, mistaking them for enemies, presented their bows and arrows in readiness for an attack. Discovering their mistake, however, they shook hands and accompanied the explorers to their evening

518 THE SEARCH FOR THE WESTERN SEA

camp, where they brought gifts of dried salmon, berries, and edible roots. These Indians said that the sea was about ten nights' journey from their village. One of the old men, a very talkative fellow, and reputed to be a great warrior, had been to the sea and seen "great canoes" manned by white men. He observed that the chiefs of the white men were well dressed and very proud, for, continued he, getting up and clapping his two hands upon his hips, then striding about the place with an air of importance, "this is the way they go."

June 14th Fraser reached the forks, or the point where the Thompson joins the Fraser. Here the chief men of the Askettih village came out to meet him, "dressed in coats of mail." The old chief harangued them in his own language; they answered in theirs; and it needed the services of three interpreters to settle the affair. When the conference was over the ambassadors returned to their camp. Fraser and his party followed and encamped on the right bank of the Thompson,[1] directly opposite the Indian village. The tents had no sooner been pitched than the Indians came over in canoes. "I had to shake hands with over one hundred of them," says Fraser ruefully, "while the old chief was haranguing them about our good qualities." Fraser had the inexpressible satisfaction of learning that from this point the river was navigable to the sea; a statement which his subsequent experience scarcely

---

[1] So named by Fraser in honour of his fellow-explorer of the North West Company, who at this very time was tracing the course of the mighty Columbia.

justified. During the night the old chief with his countryman the pilot and the Tahowtin interpreter deserted and returned to their own country, leaving the explorer in a rather awkward situation. However, the natives seemed friendly, and after some negotiation were prevailed upon to furnish a canoe. At the Askettih or Lillooet village Fraser again heard of the Columbia—"at some distance to the east there is another large river which runs parallel with this to the sea." The village was rudely fortified, one hundred feet in length by twenty-four, surrounded by palisades eighteen feet high, slanting inwards, and lined with a shorter row supporting a bark roof.

The day following his arrival at the forks he set forward on the final stage of his journey. The heaviest packages were loaded in the canoe, and in it embarked Stuart with two of the natives who had agreed to act as guides. The rest of the party went on foot, each man bearing a heavy pack on his back. Among the first Indians met with Fraser found a new copper kettle and a gun of large size, both he thought probably of Russian manufacture. The following morning he fell in with another band of Indians, among whom were two of a tribe called Suihonie. They were exceedingly well dressed in leather, and on horseback. Fraser noticed that one of them wore a silver brooch "such as the Salteux wear." Stuart meanwhile was finding the river by no means easy going. The current was exceedingly swift, and constantly broken by dangerous rapids. From the mouth of the Thompson the explorers were travelling over a portion of the river that is familiar to every traveller who crosses this part of the continent. The Canadian Pacific Railway, which follows the Thompson to its junction with the Fraser, crosses the latter stream a few miles below the forks, and from thence down to Westminster Junction the traveller is never for any length of time out of sight of the river.

On the 19th Fraser was conducted by the Great Chief of the Hacamaugh, a tribe whose country lay between the Columbia and the Fraser, to an encampment of the tribe. The scene was singular enough, as Fraser describes it. " He took me by the arm and conducted me in a moment up to the hill to the camp. Here his people were sitting in rows to the number of twelve hundred, and I had to shake hands with the whole! Then the Great Chief made a long harangue, in the course of which he pointed to the Sun, to the four quarters of the world, and then to us; he afterwards introduced his father, who was old and blind, and carried by another man, who also made a harangue of some length. The old blind man was placed near us, and he often stretched out both his hands, through curiosity, in order to feel ours."

On the 21st one of the men had an extraordinary escape from drowning. Having with several of his companions in three canoes attempted to run an exceptionally dangerous part of the river, one of the canoes filled and upset in the first rapid; the foreman and steersman managed to get clear of the wreck and swam ashore, but this man was unlucky enough to go under with the canoe. Unable to get clear of the thwarts, he remained in this critical situation until the canoe drifted into smooth water and righted sufficiently to enable him to crawl out. Although he had swallowed a quantity of water, he managed to crawl to the upper side of the vessel, which had again drifted out into the current. "Here," he says, "I continued astride the canoe, humouring the tide as well as I could with my body to preserve my balance, and, although I scarcely had time to look about me, I had the satisfaction to observe the two other canoes ashore near an eddy, and their crews safe among the rocks. In the second or third cascade (I do not recollect which) the canoe plunged from a great height into an eddy below, and striking with great violence against the bottom, split in two. Here I lost my recollection, which, however, I soon recovered, and was surprised to find myself on a smooth, easy current, with only one half of the canoe in my arms." So he floated down through rough water until the current carried him into an eddy at the foot of a steep precipice. Utterly exhausted, he lost his hold, a large wave washed him among the rocks, and another hoisted him clear on shore. When he recovered consciousness, he managed somehow to climb up the almost perpendicular face of the cliff and regained his companions. He had drifted, in an upturned canoe, for three miles through a succession of rapids, cascades, and whirlpools, and by extraordinary good fortune lived to tell the tale.

On the 26th they came to a portion of the river beyond which navigation seemed impracticable. They had already had to do a good deal of portaging; the men were weary and dispirited; and provisions were perilously low. All hands had to proceed by land, over an exceedingly rugged and difficult country. " I have been for a long period among the Rocky Mountains," says Fraser, "but have never seen anything like this country. It is so wild that I cannot find words to describe our situation at times. We had to pass where no human being should venture; yet in those places there is a regular footpath impressed, or rather indented upon the very rocks by frequent travelling. Besides this, steps which are formed like a ladder or the shrouds of a ship, by poles hanging to one another and crossed at certain distances with twigs, the whole suspended from the top to the foot of immense precipices and fastened at both extremities to stones and trees, furnish a safe and convenient passage to the natives; but we, who had not had the advantage of their education and experience, were often in imminent danger when obliged to follow their example." To climb, with a ninety-pound pack on one's back, up or down these dizzy ladders, must indeed have been a trying experience. As it was impossible to portage the canoes over such country, Fraser resorted to the desperate expedient of setting them adrift. They were recovered some distance down the river, more or less damaged, but not beyond patching.

On the 28th they came to a village of the Achinrow tribe, where they were received with much kindness.

Neat mats were spread for their reception, and plenty of salmon, in wooden dishes, were placed before them. The houses of these Indians were remarkably well constructed. They were made of planks three or four inches thick, each plank overlapping the adjoining one a couple of inches. The posts, which were very strong and rudely carved, received the cross beams. The walls were eleven feet high, covered with a slanting roof. The Achinrows told Fraser that from their village the river was navigable to the sea, and this time the statement proved to be well founded.

The old canoes having been abandoned some little time before, Fraser now procured new ones, and continued his journey. Before he left he learned from the natives that white men had come from below to the foot of the rapids some time before. They showed him marks indented in the rocks which they said the white men had made, but which Fraser thought were nothing but natural marks.

Embarking on the morning of June 30th, the party made their way downstream under comparatively easy conditions. The same day they reached the mouth of the Coquihalla, where the town of Hope now stands, and saw in the distance a mountain which the natives called Stremotch—Mount Baker. They encamped at sunset on the banks of the river, in the midst of a grove of gigantic cedars, some of which were five fathoms in circumference. Mosquitoes surrounded them in clouds, and they had to go supperless to bed—a dreary prospect. At the mouth of the Coquihalla they had seen seals, and a native who had come up from the coast assured them that they might reach it the following day.

Setting forward again at four o'clock the next morning, they landed at a village where the natives regaled them with fish and berries, as well as dried oysters. The Indians who had conducted them this far now went off with their canoes, and Fraser had difficulty in securing others. Finally the chief of the village consented to lend his large canoe and to accompany the party himself. The tide was now observed to rise two and a half feet. The explorer was nearing the end of his journey. But he was not yet at an end of his difficulties. The river Indians had been at war with those of the coast, and told Fraser that if he went down to the sea the coast Indians would certainly destroy him. They indeed painted their enemies in such lurid colours that the *voyageurs* grew alarmed and declined to go any farther. Fraser, however, like Mackenzie, was not a man to be so easily turned from his purpose. Peremptorily ordering his men to embark, he pushed off, without the Indian guides, and continued his journey.

Two miles below the village they came to a point where the river divides into several channels. Looking back, Fraser found that a number of the Indians were pursuing him in their canoes, armed with bows and arrows, spears and clubs, singing their war songs, beating time with their paddles upon the sides of their canoes, and evidently bent upon mischief. Fraser, however, continued his way with apparent unconcern, and the natives thought better of their meditated attack. Proceeding on his way down one of the channels, he at last came in sight of a gulf or bay of the sea, which the Indians called Pas-hil-roe. It is described as running in a south-west and north-east direction, and containing several high and rocky islands whose summits were covered with snow.

Directing his course toward the right shore, he ascended a small winding river to a little lake, by the side of which stood an Indian village called by the natives Misquiame. Landing, he found only a few old men and women, the others having fled into the woods at the approach of the white men. After an hour spent in examining the village, consisting of a number of houses under a common roof, fifteen hundred feet in length by ninety in breadth, Fraser and his men prepared to embark, but found that in the meantime the tide had ebbed and left the canoe high and dry. While they were dragging it down to the water the Indians plucked up courage and appeared at the edge of the wood howling like wolves and brandishing their war clubs. Finally Fraser got away, and continued his course to a second village, but did not think it prudent to disembark. His provisions being completely exhausted, he determined to return up the river to the friendly Indians, intending if supplies could be obtained to return and explore the mouth of the river and the adjacent coast. It was now evening, and the tide being in his favour he ran rapidly upstream until eleven, when he encamped within six miles of the friendly village. The men, being extremely tired, lay down to sleep on the shore where they landed, but were roused before long by the tide washing around the camp. Early the next morning they embarked and reached the chief's village at five.

An Indian named Little Fellow, who had accompanied them as guide and who had remained behind at one of the lower villages, returned during the morning with discouraging tales of the natives below, who he said were determined to destroy the entire party if they returned down the river. Fraser was so anxious to get at least within sight of the sea that this alone would not have deterred him, but unfortunately the villagers would not let him have a morsel of provisions, and the owner of the canoe insisted that his canoe should be immediately restored. While he was in the village one of the men came running to inform him that the natives were pillaging the canoe. Alarmed at this report, he hastened to the shore, and found the Indians, among whom were several from the lower villages, in an ugly humour. Fraser, knowing the character of the men he had to deal with, pretended to fly into a violent passion, thrust them violently aside, and abused them roundly, exactly, as he says, in their own fashion. Peace and tranquillity were instantly restored, but it was evident that it would not be safe to remain here any longer, and it would be madness to go down to the sea with no prospect of provisions. Very reluctantly, therefore, Fraser turned his face homeward. "I must acknowledge," he says, "my great disappointment in not seeing the main ocean, having gone so near it as to be almost within view." He had hoped to have settled his position by an observation for the longitude. However, he found that his latitude was nearly 49° (as a matter of fact he was some minutes north of 49°), and as the mouth of the Columbia was known to be in 46° 20', or thereabouts, it was evident that this great river was not the Columbia. "If I had been convinced of this," remarks Fraser, somewhat disgustedly, "when I left my canoes, I would certainly have returned." There of course spoke the fur trader. He had been sent to explore what was believed to be the Columbia, as an important route from the interior to the sea-coast, or vice versa. He had discovered an impracticable waterway. Yet geographically Simon Fraser had accomplished a notable task, under exceedingly difficult and trying circumstances. Twenty years afterward George Simpson descended the Fraser from Stuart Lake to the sea, and with somewhat characteristic assurance claimed the honour of first discovery, or rather of having first explored the river from Stuart Lake to the sea. He must surely have been aware of Fraser's achievement. The fact that Fraser did not actually come within sight of the sea—his farthest point was probably somewhere about where the city of New Westminster now stands —cannot detract from his just title to be recognized as the discoverer of the river that has ever since borne his name.

In connection with the misconception of Fraser, and also of Alexander Mackenzie, as to the true character of this river, it is somewhat curious that at the very time Fraser was struggling down what he thought was the Columbia, David Thompson was paddling up the true Columbia, without knowing it. The error was natural enough in both cases. Looking at the completed map of the Pacific coast as we have it to-day, we may wonder at first how they could have been led into such a mistake. But it must be remembered that in the days of Fraser and Thompson all that had actually been discovered was the upper waters of this unknown river and the mouth of the Columbia. What more natural than to suppose that this mighty river, pointing down so significantly to where the mouth of the Columbia was known to be, was itself the Columbia? And on the other hand, how could David Thompson have imagined, until he had traced its entire course, that the river which he reached by way of Howse Pass, and which flowed not south, but north, was in reality the Columbia?

CHAPTER VI

DAVID THOMPSON, ASTRONOMER, GEOGRAPHER, AND EXPLORER

THREE names must ever stand first in the annals of exploration in Western Canada: La Vérendrye, Mackenzie, Thompson. Of these three only one, Alexander Mackenzie, has received the meed that was his due. Parkman, it is true, did something toward awakening public interest in the splendid achievements of La Vérendrye and his sons; and Dr. Elliott Cones made an equally praiseworthy effort to secure recognition for David Thompson; but the fact remains that both La Vérendrye and Thompson are to-day, as in the past, little more than names to the great majority of readers. This, no doubt, is due to a large extent to the fact that the original journals of both have never yet appeared in print, except in very fragmentary form; while Mackenzie's narrative was published during his lifetime and gained immediate recognition. The journals of the La Vérendryes may be published before long; but it is to be feared that, unless the Canadian Government can be induced to shoulder the responsibility, there is small chance of Thompson's journals seeing the light, their very voluminousness making the project too expensive for any private publisher. In their original form they fill forty volumes of manuscripts, and cover the amazing period of sixty-six years, from 1784 to 1850. Yet it reflects slight credit on Canada and Canadians that the names of these men, representing all that is best in the two races, should have been allowed to sink into oblivion, while men of infinitely less worth have been honoured both during their lifetime and afterward. The people of the United States show a finer appreciation of the value of original discoveries. They delight in honouring the memory of the heroic pathfinders of their country; and it is sufficiently humiliating that such slight recognition as Canadian explorers have had in their own country is largely due to the interest and enthusiasm of American historians.

A brief account has been given in an earlier chapter of Thompson's journeys and explorations during the eight years that he passed in the service of the Hudson's Bay Company. It now remains to follow him through the much longer and more important period of his service with the North West Company. He was left, in the previous chapter, on his way down to Grand Portage to offer his services to the partners of the North West Company. He arrived there July 22nd, 1797, and lost no time in putting himself in communication with the Canadian traders. He had met three of the partners of the North West Company on his way down and had talked the matter over with them. The partners were glad to have the services of a man like Thompson. More far-sighted than their rivals, they realized the value and importance of exploration, even from a purely commercial point of view; and as a matter of fact Thompson seems to have appeared on the scene just when his services were most needed. "The Company desired," says Mr. Charles Lindsey, who made a special study of the subject in connection with his Investigation of the Unsettled Boundaries of Ontario, "to learn the position of their trading houses with respect to one another, and also to the 49° of North latitude, become, since the treaty of 1792, the boundary line between Canada and the United States, from the north-west corner of the Lake of the Woods to the Rocky Mountain, in lieu of the line from the former point of the head of the Mississippi, as designated by the treaty of 1783. The source of the Mississippi was then known only to the Indians and a few fur traders, and was supposed to be further north than the Lake of the Woods. Mr. Thompson was instructed to survey the 49th parallel of latitude, to go as far as the Missouri River, visit the ancient villages of the agricultural natives who dwelt there, to inquire for the fossils of large animals, and to search for any monuments that might throw light on the ancient state of the countries to be travelled over and examined. He received orders on all the agents and trading posts of the Company for men and whatever else he might require."

Setting out from Lake Superior with four canoes on August 9th, 1796, equipped with a sextant of ten inches radius, with quicksilver and parallel glasses, an excellent achromatic telescope, one of a smaller kind, with drawing instruments and thermometers, all by Dollond, Thompson crossed the Grand Portage, taking five days to carry canoes and supplies over the eight miles of very difficult road to Pigeon River. He followed the usual route through Rainy Lake and Lake of the Woods, and reached Lake Winnipeg on September 1st. Coasting around the southern and south-western shores of the lake, which are here mostly low ground rising occasionally in limestone cliffs fifty feet high, he reached Pigeon Bay and ascended Dauphin River, a small stream about thirty yards wide and three feet deep. Both the soil and timber improved in quality as he proceeded, but deer and beaver were scarce. From Dauphin River he paddled through St. Martin's Lake to Lake Manitoba and by way of Meadow Portage to Lake Winnipegosis, where he camped near the mouth of Little Dauphin River. Coasting up the west side of the lake, he ascended Swan River to Swan River House, an establishment of the North West Company. The two following months Thompson spent in travelling on horseback about the Assiniboine country, during which time he surveyed the upper waters of the Assiniboine to its source, and also Red Deer River. On November 28th he set out on his Mandan tour, already described in another chapter.

On the 25th of February, 1798, Thompson started on foot, with a dog-team to carry his supplies, on a long and arduous journey to the head-waters of the Mississippi, and thence to Lake Superior. This expedition lies outside the present narrative, but it is worth mentioning that by it Thompson made the first scientific examination of the upper waters of the Mississippi. He reached Lake Superior in May, surveyed a portion of the south shore of the lake, reached the Falls of Ste. Marie on the 28th, and leaving there in a light canoe, reached Grand Portage on June 7th.

On the 14th of the following month he once more started for the interior, returning to his former field north of the Saskatchewan. On the 18th of August he was at Cumberland House, where he met Peter Fidler of the Hudson's Bay Company, almost as indefatigable an explorer as himself, and a man of character and resourcefulness, of whom we get tantalizingly brief glimpses in the journals of the fur traders. Why was there not a Boswell at Cumberland House to record the meeting between these two remarkable men—both the product of exceptional conditions and an exceptional environment?

From Cumberland House Thompson set out again on a long canoe journey to Lac La Biche, a small body of water emptying through a river of the same name into the Athabaska. His course was by way of the Sturgeon-Weir River and Frog Portage to the Churchill, which he ascended to Lac La Ronge, where it will be remembered Peter Pond had wintered in 1782, and where, Thompson tells us, Simon Fraser wintered in 1795–6. Again ascending the Churchill, he reached Ile à la Crosse Lake on September 6th, and turned up the Beaver River, which he followed to the mouth of a small tributary, Green River. The North West Company already had a post on Green Lake, at the head of this stream. From this post, Thompson took horses and travelled overland to Fort George on the Saskatchewan, and turning north again, reached Beaver River, which he ascended to Little Beaver River, and following this branch to its source in Beaver Lake, crossed the portage and found himself at Lac La Biche on October 4th. Three days later he commenced to build a fort on a small bay on the west side of the lake, the position of which he afterwards ascertained to be lat. 54° 46′ 23″ N. and long. 111° 47′ W.[1] This proved a favourable position for a trading post, lying as it did on Athabaskan waters, and separated only by a short portage from a tributary of the Churchill. Here Thompson spent the winter. Toward the end of March, 1799, he travelled to Fort Augustus on the North Saskatchewan, a mile and a half above the mouth of Sturgeon River, where he remained until the 10th of April.

On the date last mentioned Thompson left Fort Augustus with a party of three men and five horses, and journeyed north-westward until he reached the Pembina River. Sending the horses back to the fort, he proceeded to explore the Pembina in a canoe. On the 25th April he reached the junction of the Pembina with the Athabaska, and continuing down this river to the mouth of Lesser Slave Lake River, paddled up the latter to Lesser Slave Lake, making a survey of the river as he went. Returning to the Athabaska, he travelled downstream to the mouth of the Clearwater. On the 10th of May he turned up the Clearwater,

[1] According to Dr. Coues, Tyrrell says, 54° 56′ 30″ and 112° 12′.

crossed Methye Portage, and reached Ile à la Crosse Fort on May 20th. Here he was married, on June 10th, to a girl of fourteen, Charlotte Small. This important event did not prevent him from, according to his usual custom, fixing the position of the fort, which he found to be in 55° 26′ 15″ N., 107° 46′ 40″ W. During the summer he went down to Grand Portage, whether on his honeymoon or for some more prosaic purpose Thompson does not say. At any rate he was back at Fort George on the Saskatchewan in September, and remained there until March, 1800, when he travelled overland to Fort Augustus, and on the last day of the same month started for Rocky Mountain House, which he reached seven days later. This establishment, built by John McDonald of Garth in 1802, and one of five bearing the same name, was situated on the north bank of the Saskatchewan, something over a mile above the mouth of the Clearwater River. This was, as Dr. Coues points out, the "uppermost permanent post the North West Company ever had on the Saskatchewan, and thus always the main point of departure for the crossing of the mountains by any of the passes about the sources of this great river." Its position, by Thompson's observations, was in lat. 52° 22′ 15″ N., long. 115° 07′ W. Thompson had planned to cross over by land to the upper waters of the Red Deer River, an important tributary of the South Saskatchewan, but was prevented by an accident. He, however, sent four of his men on the same journey. A boat had been built for them, and in this they apparently descended the Red Deer to its

junction with the South Saskatchewan, where Chesterfield House was afterward built by the Hudson's Bay
Company, and followed the South Saskatchewan down
to the forks, being the first white men to traverse a
large part of this route. Thompson himself spent the
summer on the North Saskatchewan, and on the
5th October left Rocky Mountain House for what he
calls his "Journey to the Kootenaes Rocky Mt., 1800."
He took with him five French-Canadians and a couple
of Indian guides, all on horseback. The route lay in
a south-easterly direction, across the Clearwater, and
several tributaries of the Red Deer, until they struck
the Red Deer itself, which they ascended to the mouth
of Williams Creek, in lat. 51° 41' 41", long. 114° 56' 40".
Here Thompson encamped, and the following day rode
west, about twenty-two miles to the foot of the mountains, where he met a chief of the Kootenays with
a number of his followers. He accompanied the Indians
to their camp, and prevailed on some of them to come
back with him to Rocky Mountain House.

On November 17th of the same year Thompson
again left Rocky Mountain House, with Duncan
McGillivray of the North West Company and four
men, on a journey to the upper waters of the Bow
River. As far as the Red Deer his route was the same
as on the previous trip, but in the present case he
crossed the Red Deer and continued on a little east of
south until he struck Bow River, about where the town
of Calgary now stands. Turning down the Bow, he
crossed it and struck what is now known as Highwood

RUINS OF ROCKY MOUNTAIN HOUSE, SASKATCHEWAN RIVER

FORT ST. JAMES, 1875

Face p. 536

River, on November 22nd. Crossing this stream, he arrived at a camp of the Pikenow or Peikans, and after spending a day with them ascended the river to another camp of the same tribe, who told him that it was only ten days' journey overland to the Missouri. He started on his return journey on the 26th, and two days later reached the Bow River, which he ascended to the mountains, reaching the Gap in lat. 51° 03′ 04″, long. 115° 21′, where he could look to the eastward over limitless plains stretching out to a remote horizon, and to the westward over a sea of mountains and snow-capped peaks. Returning, he reached Rocky Mountain House on December 3rd.

It appears from Thompson's journal that some time during this year (1800) Duncan McGillivray made a journey to the westward from Rocky Mountain House, in the course of which he reached the source of the North Saskatchewan, near the summit of the Rocky Mountains in Howse Pass, and crossing the summit, came to a stream flowing toward the south-west. From here he returned to Rocky Mountain House. This journey, to which Mr. Tyrrell draws attention, is important as establishing the first discovery of Howse Pass by Duncan McGillivray. The credit for this achievement has sometimes been given to David Thompson.[1]

Thompson spent the winter of 1800–1 at Rocky Mountain House, and in June of the latter year made

[1] Howse Pass was examined by Dr. Hector in 1859. See his report in Palliser's Journals. London, 1863.

another journey into the mountains, to a point in lat. 51° 57' 24", long. 116° 27' 54", from whence he returned to the fort.

From the autumn of 1801 to the autumn of 1802 his journals are missing, but in November, 1802, he was at Lesser Slave Lake, where he fixed the position of the North West Company's fort at the west end of the lake in lat. 55° 32' 36". Early in 1803 he arrived at Fort of the Forks on Peace River, five miles above the mouth of Smoky River, where he remained, making short explorations into the surrounding country, until the 15th of March, 1804, when he descended the Peace River on the ice to Horse Shoe House (lat. 57° 8', long. 117° 39' 49"), and as soon as the ice broke up, continued down the river by canoe to Lake Athabaska, where he rested for a few days at Athabaska House (lat. 58° 42' 50", long. 111° 8' 30"). Ascending the Athabaska River, on his way to Ile à la Crosse, he passed Peter Pond's old fort on May 17th, 1804. He surveyed the river to the mouth of the Clearwater, which he reached on May 19th. Paddling up the Clearwater and crossing Methye Portage, he was once again at Ile à la Crosse Fort; and from there descended by the usual route to Lake Superior, and took up his quarters at the New Fort at the mouth of the Kaministikwia — afterwards Fort William — to which place the head-quarters of the Company had been removed since Thompson last visited Lake Superior.

Never content to remain idle for any length of time, we find Thompson again on the move before the end of

July. Leaving Kaministikwia, he followed the new route through Lac Mille Lacs and Lac la Croix, to Rainy Lake, Lake of the Woods, and Lake Winnipeg. On the 1st of September he was at the mouth of the Saskatchewan, and eight days later at Cumberland House. From this time until June, 1806, Thompson was busily engaged in travelling about the country between the Saskatchewan and the Churchill, to the eastward of Cumberland House and Frog Portage, mapping out new routes, establishing new posts, carrying on his meteorological journals, and fulfilling his commercial duties as a fur trader. On the 14th June, 1806, he set out from Cumberland House for the Kaministikwia. On the 11th of September we know that he was again at Cumberland House, for Harmon mentions meeting him there. One month later he arrived at Rocky Mountain House, then in charge of Jules Quesnel, who two years later accompanied Simon Fraser on his perilous journey down the Fraser. Thompson spent the winter trading with the Indians and making preparations for a long-planned journey through the mountains, a journey which was to bring him to the most important period of his life as an explorer. For the next five years we shall find him almost continuously on the western side of the Rocky Mountains, threading his way through the tangled wilderness of the Pacific slope. He is much more difficult to follow on this side of the Rocky Mountains than on the eastern side. It is true we still have the benefit of his careful surveys and astronomical observa tions, but he is now traversing entirely new ground, and unravelling the most intricate river system on the continent. The student is further puzzled by the fact that while many of the geographical names found in Thompson's journals and on his map are also found on modern maps, they are applied to entirely different streams and lakes, while other of his names are entirely obsolete. For this reason the list of Thompson's place-names with their present equivalents, in the Introductory Chapter, will be found helpful in following Thompson through this most important field of his explorations.

On the 10th of May, 1807, Thompson left Rocky Mountain House on horseback, following the north bank of the Saskatchewan, while his assistant, Mr. Finan McDonald, brought the provisions up the river in a canoe. On June 3rd they reached Kootenay Plain, " a wide, open flat on the north side of the river within the mountains," which Thompson placed in lat. 52° 02′ 06″. On June 6th they reached the forks, and turned up the south branch, which they ascended for three miles. Navigation then became impossible for the canoe. Thompson remained here until the 22nd, making preparations for his journey across the mountains. Provisions and equipment were packed on the horses, and the party set out for the summit, which they reached at one o'clock on the same day. Thompson found the point at which he reached the height of land to be in lat. 51° 48′ 27″. One gets an idea of the magnitude of the rivers that drain this great western country when it is remembered that to within a few miles of the point where Thompson now stood in the heart of the Rocky Mountains, he had followed one and the same river, the Saskatchewan, for a distance of 1100 miles. The country he is now entering is radically different from the one he leaves behind, and the rivers of course correspond. The quiet, easy-going, navigable rivers of the plains gave place to the turbulent and treacherous streams of the Pacific slope. Explorer or trader who navigates these wild rivers must have his wits about him if he would come safely through.

A few miles south of the summit Thompson reached the upper waters of a small tributary of the Columbia, now known as Blaeberry River, "whose current," he notes in his journal, "descends to the Pacific Ocean"; and he piously exclaims, "May God in His mercy give me to see where its waters flow into the ocean, and return in safety." He camped near the summit on the 23rd, waiting for Finan McDonald and the rest of his party, who arrived the following day. He then descended Blaeberry River to the main stream, this portion of which he named the Kootanie. Duncan McGillivray had, as we have already seen, reached the Blaeberry River in 1800, but had gone no farther. Thompson was the first white man to stand upon the banks of the Upper Columbia. He reached the river on June 30th, and fixed his position in lat. 51° 25′ 14″, long. 116° 52′ 45″. He camped here for twelve days, building canoes. On the 12th July he packed everything into these and paddled upstream to a lake which he called Kootanae, now Windermere Lake. Here, or rather about a mile below the northern end of the lake, he unloaded his canoes and built a fort—Fort Kootanae, or, to adopt the modern spelling, Kootenay—on the west side of the Columbia, in lat. 50° 32′ 15″, long. 115° 51′ 40″, var. 24½° E. Mr. Tyrrell states that there is now a village of Shuswap Indians about opposite where the old fort stood. At this fort Thompson spent the winter, trading with the Indians, and taking meteorological and astronomical observations.

In April, 1808, he continued his exploration toward the south, and finally reached the source of the Columbia in Upper Columbia Lake. This notable achievement was but an incident to Thompson. From the head of the lake he could see the waters of another great river flowing turbulently to the south, and made up his mind to follow it. The canoes were carried over the intervening flat terrace to the banks of McGillivray's River (Kootenay). This portage, which Thompson also named after his friend McGillivray, is marked on his maps as two miles; Dr. G. M. Dawson says about a mile and a half. A canal now connects the two great rivers at this point. Thompson descended the Kootenay, passing the mouth of St. Mary's River a little below the present Fort Steele on the 24th April, and the mouth of the Tobacco River three days later. Continuing downstream, he followed the river around the great bend, portaging past Kootenay Falls on May 6th, and on the 8th reached a camp of Flatheads and Kootenays, where he remained a few days. Setting out again on the 13th, he passed the mouth of a river which he named after

Finan McDonald, now Moyie River, and the next day entered Kootenay Lake. Returning up the river to the Indian camp, he ascended the bank of Moyie River on horseback, following approximately the present railway line from Yahk to Cranbrook, and rejoining the Kootenay about the mouth of St. Mary's River on May 18th. He crossed the Kootenay and ascended its right bank to the portage, from whence he reached the fort on the 5th of June. Packing the winter's crop of furs, he descended the Columbia to Blaeberry River and crossed the mountains, reaching Rocky Mountain House on the 24th of June. He descended the Saskatchewan to Cumberland House, where he arrived on July 9th, and reached Rainy Lake House on the 2nd August.

On the 27th of October we find him again crossing the mountains by the same pass. He killed two buffalo at the height of land, and saw a herd of cows some distance down the western slope—one of the very rare recorded instances of buffalo being found on the Pacific side of the mountains. He reached the Columbia on the last day of the month. As on his previous journey, he crossed the mountains with horses. These he now sent through the woods, while he ascended the Columbia in a boat to a point near the mouth of the Spilimichene River. From here he sent Mr. Finan McDonald on to establish a post at Kootenay Falls, while he went on horseback to Kootenay Fort, where he wintered.

In April, 1809, he once more crossed the mountains,

with forty packs of furs. At the Kootenay Plain he built a canoe and paddled down the Saskatchewan to Fort Augustus, where he was on June 24th. Sending the furs down the river, he himself returned to the mountains, meeting Mr. Howse of the North West Company west of Kootenay Plain. Mr. Howse, after whom he had named Saskatchewan Pass, was on his way back to Fort Augustus from an exploring trip to the mountains. Thompson reached the Columbia on August 13th, and ascending it to McGillivray's portage, entered the Kootenay on the 20th, and nine days later was at the place where he met the Flatheads in 1808. Here he remained until September 6th, when he set out on horseback to the southward, crossing the Cabinet Range, by the Indian road, to Kullyspell Lake (Pend d'Oreille), on a peninsula on the east side of which he built a fort, Kullyspell House, in lat. 48° 12′ 14″. On the 27th September he left the new fort on an exploring trip around the southern side of the lake, to where the Saleesh River, or Pend d'Oreille, leaves the lake. This river has its source about lat. 49° 25′ N., long. 114° 50′ W., and flows thence to the Flathead through the very heart of the Rocky Mountains across the international boundary to Flathead Lake, thence south and west to its junction with the Missoula 47° 18′ and long. 114° 45′. Thence at Clarkes Fork it flows north-west to Lake Pend d'Oreille and from Lake Pend d'Oreille west, north, and west to its junction with the Columbia in 49° N., 117° 35′ W. Exploring this for some distance, in fact well into what is now the State of

Washington, he returned to the fort on October 6th. Clarkes Fork falls into the Columbia at 49° N.—i.e. on the international boundary. Five days later he set out on horseback in the opposite direction, following the Pend d'Oreille from where it enters the lake in a south-easterly direction ; then, leaving the river, rode north-east and north-west, until on the 21st he reached the Kootenay above the falls, or about the site of the present town of Jennings. Here obtaining canoes, he descended the river past Kootenay Falls to the Great Road of the Flatheads, where he left the river and journeyed overland to Kullyspell House, which he reached on October 29th.

Early in November he again ascended the Pend d'Oreille, and built Saleesh House in lat. 47° 34′ 35″, long. 115° 22′ 51″, near the mouth of present Ashley Creek, in Montana. He wintered here, or rather made it his head-quarters, from which he explored the sur-rounding country, on one of his trips ascending Clarkes Fork to the junction of Flathead River with the Missoula, returning in April, 1810, to Kullyspell House. Once more he started north by the Kootenay and Columbia, and made Howse Pass on June 18th. He descended the Saskatchewan, passing the ruins of Fort Augustus, which had been destroyed by the Blackfeet since he had last seen it, and met Alexander Henry at White Mud Brook House, on White Earth River. He reached Cumberland House on July 4th, and on the 22nd was at Rainy Lake.

Returning to the far west, Thompson reached Alex-

2 N

ander Henry's new establishment on White Earth River on September 6th; on the 15th he was at Old White Earth House, and from there went down the Saskatchewan to Boggy Hall, between Brazeau River and Wolf Creek, or rather the site of Boggy Hall, for the post had been abandoned in the fall of 1808. Near here Henry found him on October 15th, encamped on the top of a hill three hundred feet above the river, in a grove of pines so thickly set together that he could not see the tent until within ten yards of it. Some of Thompson's canoes had been stopped and turned back by the Piegans, who were self-constituted guardians of Howse Pass, and as a result Thompson had decided to find a new way through the mountains farther north, by way of the Athabaska River. A party of "freemen" (that is, traders working on their own account) and Nipissing Indians had penetrated the Rocky Mountains by way of the Athabaska Pass a few years before, but for all scientific as well as practical purposes, the expedition upon which Thompson was just setting out was the real discovery of Athabaska Pass.

Thompson sent some of his men up the Saskatchewan for horses, and on October 29th left Boggy Hall for the north. This journey was to test his courage, endurance, and leadership to the utmost. From start to finish it was a desperate fight against almost overwhelming odds. Starvation dogged his footsteps continually; more than once the party were in danger of being frozen to death; formidable obstacles presented themselves at every turn; and nothing but the masterful spirit of their leader kept the men from mutiny. The first week in November brought him to Pembina River. On the 7th two of his men arrived at Henry's Fort for provisions. They reported that Thompson was cutting his way doggedly through a wretched, thick woody country, over mountains and gloomy muskegs, and that the party were at the point of starvation, animals being very scarce in that quarter. On the 1st of December, however, Thompson reached the Athabaska, and ascended it to a point in lat. 53° 23′ 37″, mean long. 117° 44′ 15″, where he built a hut for his goods, and a meat shed. Unfortunately, however, there was nothing to put into the shed. His provisions were about exhausted, and until others could be obtained he dared not attempt the pass. Some of his men were sent hunting; others in search of birch to make sledges and snowshoes for the journey; while still another party went overland to Rocky Mountain House on the Saskatchewan, for provisions, dogs, and horses, of all of which they were entirely destitute. "It is seventeen days," says Henry, "since they left Mr. Thompson on Athabaska River at the foot of the mountains. On their way here they ate an old horse and five dogs, but had been some time without food, and were worn out with fatigue and hunger." Henry gave them what provisions he could spare, but he himself was in sore enough straits, having no more meat in store than would answer for eight days' rations, and of other provisions not a mouthful. "Our hunters are lazy," he says, "and when we shall see an Indian to bring a supply, God knows."

Meanwhile Thompson was having a desperate time on the Athabaska. Provisions were scarce; the thermometer ranged from 30° to 36° below zero; the men were ready to desert at any moment.[1] Notwithstanding, on the 29th of December he started out from his camp, determined to force his way through the mountains to the Columbia, at any cost. Provisions and supplies were loaded on sleds, drawn some by one, some by two dogs, according to the load; beside these, 208 lb. of pemmican and other provisions were loaded on four horses. So the party set out, making its way slowly up the frozen bed of the Athabaska toward the pass. On the first of the New Year, 1811, the thermometer registered 24° below zero, and the travelling was so bad that the dogs could not move the sleds. Some of the provisions were accordingly cached, and the loads reduced by one-third, and on they went, spurred to their utmost by the untiring Thompson, to whom difficulties and dangers were but incentives to greater effort. On the 4th they came to a bold defile, through which issued the branch of the Athabaska now known as Whirlpool River. This was "the canoe road to pass to the west side of the mountains." On the 8th

---

[1] In a letter to Alexander Fraser, dated Athabaska River, Foot of the Mountains, 21 December, 1810, Thompson says: "I am now preparing in this hard season to cross the mountains and gain my first post near the head of the Mississourie, a march of about 34 days, and a part of it over a dangerous country for war. . . . If all goes well and it pleases good Providence to take care of me, I hope to see you and a civilized world in the autumn of 1812. I am getting tired of such constant hard journeys; for the last 20 months I have spent only bare two months under the shelter of a hut, all the rest has been in my tent, and there is little likelihood the next 12 months will be much otherwise."

they were at the head-waters of Whirlpool River, between mountains two to three thousand feet high.
Two days later they crossed the height of land, in lat.
52° 08′ 38″ W. On the 11th they began to descend the
western slope, along the course of a small stream.
Thompson, having no paper, sent a report of his progress to the partners of the Company on boards, to be
copied at the nearest post and forwarded. The snow
getting deeper and softer as they descended the pass,
the dogs could no longer haul the loads, and Thompson
abandoned everything except what was absolutely essential. He had much difficulty in keeping up the spirits
of his men, but at last, on the 18th of January, they
were within sight of the Columbia. Thompson, the indefatigable, would have pushed on at once to Kootenay
House, but his men were by this time thoroughly
dispirited. He turned back, therefore, to the junction
of Canoe River with the Columbia, where he spent the
remainder of the winter.

In the spring of 1811 he explored the Columbia to
the mouth of Blaeberry River, and continued over the
old ground to the source of the Columbia. Crossing
McGillivray's Portage to the Kootenay, he was once
more at the Great Kootenay Road on May 19th. This
road, according to Mr. Tyrrell, strikes up a stream from
the south-east bend of the Kootenay River; apparently
it is the one called "Kootanae Road" on Thompson's
map. It ran from about the position of Jennings, south
to the Pend d'Oreille. Another Indian road, also indicated on Thompson's map, as the Lake Indian Road,

ran from somewhere in the neighbourhood of Bonner's Ferry, south of Pend d'Oreille Lake. Following one of these roads—it is not clear which—Thompson reached the Pend d'Oreille west of the lake, travelled over another Indian road, the Sheetshoo, to the Spokane River, and on June 15th reached Spokañe House, in lat. 47° 47′ 4″, about where the city of Spokane now stands. This post had apparently been built by Thompson or one of his assistants some time before. From here he descended the Spokane River to the Columbia, and ascended the latter river to Ilthkoyape or Kettle Falls, visited many years afterward by Paul Kane, who describes them as the highest on the Columbia, about one thousand yards across and eighteen feet high, the immense body of water tumbling amongst the broken rocks rendering them exceedingly picturesque and grand. He explains the origin of its name (note similar condition at Chaudiere, Ottawa). Resting here for a few days, Thompson started down the Columbia, and reached the mouth of Snake River on July 9th, 1811. Down to this point he was travelling over entirely new ground. From Snake River to the mouth of the Columbia, Lewis and Clark had preceded him in 1805. At Snake River Thompson took formal possession of the country. The entry in his original manuscript journals, as noted by Dr. Coues in his Henry-Thompson Journals, is as follows: "$\frac{1}{2}$ a mile to the Junction of the Shawpatin (Snake) River with this the Columbia, here I erected a small Pole, with a half sheet of Paper well tied about it, with these words on it—Know hereby that this country is claimed by Great Britain as part of its Territories, and that the N.W. Company of Merchants from Canada, finding the Factory for this People inconvenient for them, do hereby intend to erect a Factory in this Place for the commerce of the Country around.—D. Thompson." Alexander Ross, in his *Adventures of the First Settlers on the Oregan or Columbia River*, says that he was at this place on the 14th of August, 1811, when "early in the morning, what did we see waving triumphantly in the air at the confluence of the two great branches, but a British flag, hoisted in the middle of the Indian camp, planted there by Mr. Thompson as he passed, with a written paper, laying claim to the country north of the forks, as British territory."

Thompson reached the mouth of the Columbia on July 15th or 16th. Alexander Ross and Gabriel Franchere both state that it was on the 15th, but Mr. Tyrrell points out that Thompson's record of his observations seems rather to point to the 16th as the date of his arrival. The famous Astoria had been founded at the mouth of the Columbia a few months before. The following year, when it was handed over by the Pacific Fur Company to the North West Company, the name was changed to Fort George.

Thompson remained at Astoria for a few days and then started up the river, reaching the mouth of the Willamette, near the present town of Portland, on July 24th. From here he ascended to the mouth of the

Snake River, and turned up that river as far as lat. 46° 36′ 13″, long. 118° 50′, where he arrived on August 8th. From this point he left the river and travelled overland to Spokane House, where he was on the 12th of the same month. He then descended the Spokane to its mouth, and followed the Columbia north to Kettle Falls, the farthest point he had previously reached in this direction. From here he wrote a letter to Harmon, dated August 28th, informing him of his voyage down the Columbia to the sea. This letter only reached Harmon on the 6th of the following April, at his post on Stuart's Lake in what is now Northern British Columbia. It had come by the Indian post. Paul Kane in his *Wanderings of an Artist* describes this rather primitive mail delivery. "The gentlemen in charge of the various posts have frequently occasion to send letters, sometimes for a considerable distance when it is either inconvenient or impossible for them to fit out a canoe with their own men to carry it. In such cases a letter is given to an Indian, who carries it as far as suits his convenience and safety. He then sells the letter to another, who carries it until he finds an opportunity of selling it to advantage; it is thus passed on and sold until it arrives at its destination, gradually increasing in value according to the distance, and the last possessor receiving the reward for its safe delivery. In this manner letters are frequently sent with perfect security, and with much greater rapidity than could be done otherwise." One wonders what the less rapid method could have been like. Thompson's letter took

exactly seven months and eight days in getting from
Kettle Falls to Stuart's Lake.

From Kettle Falls Thompson continued up the
Columbia, through the Lower and Upper Arrow lakes
to Boat Encampment, at the mouth of Canoe River,
which he reached about the beginning of October, 1811.
He had now completed his greatest achievement as an
explorer. During the four and a quarter years that had
elapsed since he first stood on the banks of the Columbia,
at the mouth of the Blaeberry, he had surveyed every
inch of the great river from source to mouth, eleven
hundred and fifty miles ; and as far down as the mouth
of Snake River was the first white man to explore its
waters. In 1807 he had ascended the river from Blaeberry to Kootenay House ; in 1808 he had explored
from there to the source, and followed the Kootenay to
Kootenay Lake ; in 1810 he had reached the most
northerly point of the Columbia, by way of Athabaska
Pass, and ascended the river to Blaeberry ; in 1811 he
had descended the Columbia to its mouth ; and the
same year reascended it to the mouth of Canoe River,
thus completing his survey.

From Boat Encampment Thompson went over the
Athabaska Pass to the head waters of the Athabaska.
In April, 1812, he is back again at Kettle Falls on the
Columbia, and on May 6th once more at Boat Encamp-
ment. On that day he set out on foot over the pass,
reaching the house of Mr. William Henry on the
Athabaska (lat. 52° 55′ 16″) on the 11th. Two days
later he descended the Athabaska to the mouth of

Lesser Slave River, went up that to the lake; returning, he continued down the Athabaska to the Red Deer, turned up the Red Deer to the lake of the same name, crossed the portage to Beaver River, and descended the Beaver to lat. 54° 22′ 14″, long. 110° 17′, where the survey is abruptly broken off. It is probable that he followed the usual route from there to Cumberland House, and so on to Lake Superior. At any rate, we find him at Fort William in August of the same year, when he finally took leave of the great west. He returned to Montreal and settled at Terrebonne, where for two years he was engaged in preparing for the North West Company his great map of Western Canada. This very remarkable map, now in the possession of the Crown Lands Department at Toronto, and portions of which were copied from Dr. Cones' Henry-Thompson Journals, is on a scale of about fifteen miles to an inch. It was compiled mainly from Thompson's own observations and surveys covering a period of twenty years, but embodies also Turner's surveys of Athabaska Lake and Slave River, Alexander Mackenzie's track through the mountains and down the Fraser as far as Alexandria, and John Stuart's survey of the Fraser down to the sea.

"David Thompson," says H. H. Bancroft, "was an entirely different order of man from the orthodox fur trader. Tall and fine-looking, of sandy complexion, with large features, deep-set studious eyes, high forehead, and broad shoulders, the intellectual was well set upon the physical. His deeds have never been trumpeted as those of some of the others, but in the westward explorations of the North West Company no man performed more valuable service or estimated his achievements more modestly. Unhappily his last days were not as pleasant as fell to the lot of some of the worn-out members of the Company. He retired almost blind to Lachine House, once the head-quarters of the Company, where Mr. Anderson [whose inedited *North-West Coast* is one of Bancroft's main sources] encountered him in 1831 in a very decrepid condition."

Anderson must, however, have misjudged the physical condition of the veteran explorer, for it is known that in 1831 Thompson was still actively engaged in his profession. He surveyed Lake St. Francis on the St. Lawrence River in 1834; three years later he made a survey of the famous canoe route from Lake Huron to the Ottawa, which had been traversed by explorers and fur traders from the early days of the French regime, and was still in active use; and later still he surveyed Lake St. Peter on the St. Lawrence. We learn from Mr. Tyrrell that his last years were spent either in Glengarry County, Ontario, or in Longueuil, opposite Montreal, where he died on the 16th of February, 1857, at the age of nearly eighty-seven years. It is a remarkable fact that, in spite of the constant hardships they had to endure, many of these western fur traders and pathfinders lived well into the seventies, some into the eighties, and a few even into the nineties. Thompson's wife survived him by only about three months, dying on the 7th May, 1857. They were both buried in Mount Royal Cemetery at Montreal.

Although Bancroft had formed such a favourable opinion of David Thompson's work as an explorer, it is clear that he had only a very vague knowledge of the extent of his explorations. In his *History of British Columbia* (p. 134) Bancroft says: "Old Fort Kamloop was first called Fort Thompson, having been begun by David Thompson, astronomer of the North West Company, on his overland journey from Montreal to Astoria, by way of Yellowhead Pass, in 1810"; and in his *History of the North-West Coast* (II, 122) he gives a detailed account of this purely imaginary part of Thompson's explorations. "Thompson," he says, "crossed the mountains at some point south of Peace River—probably he came through Yellowhead Pass to Mount Thompson—and after a preliminary survey of his surroundings he regarded the north branch of Thompson River as more likely to prove an important tributary of the true Tacoutche Tesse of Mackenzie than the stream to which he afterwards gave the name of Canoe River. The more he examined this stream the more he became satisfied, from the description given by Stuart and Fraser, that this was not the river descended by them. Nor was it until he had reached Kamloops Lake, and had there seen all the tributaries of this river taking their decided westward course in one large body toward the defile where he knew the Fraser to be, that he became convinced that he had not been navigating the Columbia." Thompson thereupon,

according to Bancroft, retraced his steps to the head-
waters of Thompson River, crossed over to Canoe
River, and descended that stream to a point some distance above its junction with the Columbia. Here he
wintered, and in the spring of 1811 paddled downstream to the Columbia, and from there descended the
Columbia to its mouth, which he reached on July 15th,
1811. With the single exception of the date of
Thompson's arrival at the mouth of the Columbia,
which is about correct, Bancroft is hopelessly at sea.
As we have already seen, Thompson crossed the moun-
tains in 1810–11 by the Athabaska Pass, not the
Yellowhead. According to Bancroft, he crossed the
Yellowhead Pass to the head-waters of the North
Thompson River, descended that river to Kamloops
Lake, a distance of one hundred and eighty-five miles,
returned to the head-waters of the river, crossed to
Canoe River, and descended that river some distance to
his winter quarters, and all this before winter had set in
On the other hand, Thompson's own narrative proves
conclusively that up to the 10th January, 1811, he was
still on the eastern side of the mountains, and it was
not until the middle of January that he reached the
mouth of Canoe River, by the Athabaska Pass. In the
spring of 1811 he did not, as Bancroft states, descend
the Columbia to its mouth from Boat Encampment, but
ascended it to its source—quite a different matter. He
did of course descend to the mouth of the Columbia,
but it was by way of the Kootenay, not by way of the
Arrow Lakes. As we have seen, the portion of the

Columbia between Kettle Falls and Boat Encampment was explored for the first time on Thompson's upward journey from Astoria, in August and September, 1811.

It is evident that Bancroft had not seen Thompson's own journals at Toronto when he wrote his Histories of British Columbia and the North West Coast. He probably placed together what scraps of information he could gather from the journals of Thompson's contemporaries in the fur trade, and the result furnishes a warning as to the pitfalls that beset this method of writing history. Most historians are forced at times to resort to circumstantial evidence, because they cannot obtain direct evidence, but nine times out of ten they guess wrong, as Bancroft did here.

The explanation of Bancroft's mistake is simple enough. It is all in the Thompson journals. David Stuart, under instructions from Thompson, left Astoria in July, 1811, with a party of nine or ten men, to explore the Okanagan, or Ookenaw Kane as it appears on Thompson's map. He reached the mouth of the Okanagan on August 31st, where he established Fort Okanagan. Leaving several of his men to winter here, he with three others pushed up the Okanagan, which he ascended to its source, some two hundred and fifty miles. He crossed over to the river afterward known as Thompson, but which is named Sheewap on Thompson's map, and descended it to the mouth of the north branch, where he established a post among the Shuswaps, and returned February 26th, 1812. He reached Astoria on May 11th, and left again about the end of June, with a large party, for Fort Okanagan. Ascending the Okanagan, he spent the winter of 1812–13 at Fort Thompson. The position of this fort is clearly indicated on Thompson's map, on the north side of the river, between the forks. Probably during the winter of 1812–13 Stuart descended the Thompson to its junction with the Fraser, as its course is clearly laid down on Thompson's map. It is a rather amusing commentary on Bancroft's story that while the main Thompson River is carefully mapped by Thompson, from source to mouth, on Stuart's surveys the North Thompson is represented only for a very short distance from its mouth. Clearly neither Stuart nor Thompson had explored it at any time.

One cannot close this sketch of David Thompson better than by quoting Dr. Coues' fine tribute: "The world can never be allowed to forget the discoverer of the sources of the Columbia, the first white man who ever voyaged on the upper reaches and main upper tributaries of that mighty river, the pathfinder of more than one way across the Continental Divide from Saskatchewan and Athabaskan to Columbian waters, the greatest geographer of his day in British America, and the maker of what was then by far its greatest map."

CHAPTER VII

THE AFTERMATH

THE long story of the exploration of North-Western America has now been told, from Hudson and La Vérendrye to Mackenzie, Fraser, and Thompson. There remains but to trace briefly the history of subsequent explorations. In its broader aspects the story closed with that brief but pregnant inscription painted by Alexander Mackenzie on a rock washed by the waters of the Pacific Ocean. All that followed was in a sense but the filling in of the details. Yet this must not be understood as minimizing the importance and value of subsequent explorations. The search for the Western Sea had been crowned with success ; but there remained immense areas of what is now the Dominion of Canada to add to the sum of geographical knowledge. For a hundred years to come this important field was to be traversed in every direction by fur traders and explorers, from the Missouri to the Arctic, and from Hudson Bay to the Pacific. A comparison of Arrowsmith's earlier maps with the last Canadian Government maps reveals the immense amount of geographical work accomplished in this field during the nineteenth century. Its main features are to-day fairly well known ; many of its

vast areas have been traversed by well-equipped recon-
naissance surveys. Nevertheless it would be quite
inaccurate to assume that there remain no large unexplored areas in Canada. Seventeen years ago the
late Dr. George M. Dawson surprised the unscientific
world by the statement that between one-third and one-
fourth of the entire area of the Dominion still remained
unexplored, and even this computation was based upon
a very liberal interpretation of work actually done. He
assumed that along each reasonably accurate line of
exploration a belt of country about fifty miles in width
was removed from the unexplored category. No explorer, however competent, could know much about the
country twenty-five miles away from his route on either
side; still he would have obtained a general idea of the
character of the land. Drawing broad belts of this
kind across the map, and ignoring all districts under
7500 square miles, there still remained sixteen large
unexplored areas, of which the aggregate was computed to be about 954,000 square miles. This was in
1890. Seven years later Dr. Dawson again referred to
the subject, and was able to announce that the aggregate blank spaces on the map of Canada had been very
materially reduced in the meantime; largely, it may be
said, owing to the splendid work accomplished by the
Geological Survey, of which he was then the very
capable head. Another decade has gone by since then,
with a further shrinkage of the unexplored areas. Yet
there remains an enormous amount of exploration still
to be accomplished before the map of Canada, and

2 O

especially of North-Western Canada, can be said to be even approximately accurate.

In the preceding chapters the history of exploration has been brought down to the beginning of the nineteenth century, or say to the close of the first decade of that century. It remains to survey very briefly the achievements of the succeeding ninety years.

Broadly speaking, these later explorations are confined to the northern half of the immense field with which this story has to deal. Lat. 60° may be taken as its southern boundary, with an extension to 55° in the extreme west to include what is now Northern British Columbia.

Fifty years after Hearne's journey to the Coppermine, and thirty-one years after Mackenzie had reached the mouth of the great river that bears his name, Captain (afterward Sir) John Franklin reached Fort Providence, on the north side of Great Slave Lake, on his way to the Arctic coast of America. The expedition which he commanded had been sent out by His Majesty's Government to explore the coast to the eastward of the mouth of the Coppermine; to correct as far as possible the very defective geography of the northern interior of the continent; to take astronomical and meteorological observations; observe the dip and variation of the needle; and study the curious phenomena of the aurora borealis.

Franklin, accompanied by Dr. John Richardson, George Back, and Robert Hood, all of whom distinguished themselves on this expedition, and two of whom led subsequent expeditions to the same Arctic coast, sailed from Gravesend in May, 1819, on board the ship *Prince of Wales*, and reached York Factory by the end of August.

Following the Hayes route to the interior, they arrived at Norway House on October 6th, and Cumberland House sixteen days later. Here they remained until the middle of January, when they left for the north with dog-sleds and snow-shoes. The long journey to Fort Chipewyan, at the western end of Lake Athabaska, was made in two months and eight days. Here they remained until July 18th, when they took their departure for Old Fort Providence.

Up to this point Franklin had travelled over familiar ground, following in the footsteps of Pond, Mackenzie, and other early explorers. Mackenzie had preceded him to the Arctic, but Franklin was to blaze a new trail from Great Slave Lake to the sea, by way of Yellowknife River and the Coppermine. With the exception of the vague mapping of Hearne's journey and the fragmentary reports of fur traders and Indians, nothing was known of the immense country that lay between Great Slave Lake and the mouth of the Coppermine. Ascending Yellowknife River with his somewhat unruly party of French-Canadian *voyageurs* and Indians, he reached his winter quarters, near Winter Lake, and built there a small wooden building, which was dignified with the name of Fort Enterprise.

In June of the following year, 1821, he crossed the height of land and descended the Coppermine to the sea. Not far from Bloody Fall, the scene of the horrible massacre so vividly described by Hearne, he encountered a band of Eskimo, but found great difficulty in getting in touch with them. The Eskimo had perhaps reason enough to doubt the good intentions of Franklin's Indians, and knew little or nothing of the white men.

From the mouth of the Coppermine Franklin and his party turned to the eastward along the bleak Arctic coast of the continent. A month later he had completed the exploration of Coronation Gulf, Bathurst Inlet, and Melville Sound, from the mouth of the Coppermine around to a point on the north-west coast of Kent Peninsula, which he named Turnagain. At the foot of Arctic Sound, west of Bathurst Inlet, he had discovered the mouth of a river which he named after Robert Hood, and as the season was now too far advanced to explore the coast farther to the eastward, he returned to the mouth of Hood River and ascended it to Wilberforce Falls. The shallowness of the stream made further progress impossible. The large canoes were therefore abandoned, and the party set out overland for Fort Enterprise, practically without supplies and with very little prospect of securing game by the way. It was now the end of August, winter was rapidly approaching, and travelling was exceedingly slow and difficult. Before they reached the banks of the Coppermine, instruments, books, and specimens had been left behind to lighten the loads, and they were thankful to eat what even the wolves had left behind. Several days were lost in getting across the Coppermine.

Back with three men pushed on ahead, reached Fort Enterprise, and continued on to the south in search of Indians and supplies. A few days later Franklin with another small detachment reached the fort. The fort gave shelter, but nothing more. Food there was none, but he was too exhausted to move. Meanwhile Richardson, Hood, and a Scotch sailor named Hepburn had fallen behind. They were presently joined by a *voyageur*, Michel. Day after day they struggled forward, with nothing to eat but lichen scraped from the rocks. Michel, crazed with hunger, shot poor Hood, and threatened the others. In self-defence Richardson shot the murderer. Some days afterward the two survivors crawled into the fort in the last stages of exhaustion. Back had not yet returned. He was trying desperately to reach Fort Providence. On November 3rd he fortunately met some Indians, and the following morning an ample supply of provisions was hurried back to Fort Enterprise. On December 11th the survivors reached Fort Providence. The following July Franklin was back again at York Factory, having travelled by land and water, as he says, five thousand five hundred and fifty miles, some of the distance at least under conditions of the most extreme hardship.

Three years after his return Franklin was placed in command of a second expedition, the object now being to explore the Arctic coast west of the Coppermine. With Franklin went Richardson and Back, as well as a young naval officer named Kendall. They wintered, 1825–6, on Great Bear Lake, where they built Fort Franklin, and in June descended the Mackenzie to the head of the delta. Here the party separated, Franklin and Back taking the western arm of the river, Richardson and Kendall the eastern. His experience on the former expedition having convinced Franklin that canoes were not adapted to the navigation of the Arctic coast, he had provided himself with two stout boats which he named the *Lion* and the *Reliance*. Richardson was similarly equipped with the *Dolphin* and the *Union*.

From the mouth of the Mackenzie, Franklin explored the coast west to Gwydyr Bay, near Point Beechey, a distance of three hundred and seventy-four miles. Meanwhile Richardson had turned east and surveyed the coast to the mouth of the Coppermine, a distance of nearly a thousand miles, naming the great strait separating the mainland from Wollaston Land after his two stout little boats. Early in August he ascended the Coppermine to Bloody Fall, and, abandoning the boats and superfluous stores, continued up the river for some distance, and then struck overland to Great Bear Lake. Here he fell in with a party of Indians who guided him around the lake to Fort Franklin, which he reached on the 1st of September, and before the end of the month the entire party were together once more, having accomplished very much more in the way of exploration than on the first expedition without a tithe of the hardships.

In 1833 Captain Back returned once more to the sub-arctic region of America, to search for traces of the expedition that had sailed in 1829 under Captain Ross.

In August, 1833, Back reached Great Slave Lake, and having been instructed to descend the Thlew-ee-cho-dezeth or Great Fish River (now Backs River), which had never yet been explored, made his way to the eastern end of the lake, found the entrance to Hoar Frost River, ascended it to Cook Lake, thence to Walmsley Lake and Artillery Lake. Lockhart River brought him to Clinton-Colden Lake and Aylmer Lake. Following the north shore of Aylmer Lake, he portaged over the height of land and discovered a small lake, which he called Sussex, and which proved to be the source of the river he was seeking.

It was impracticable to complete his exploration that year, and having descended the river as far as Musk-Ox Lake, he turned back to the east end of Great Slave Lake, where he built Fort Reliance and settled down for the long winter.

June of the following year found him prepared to resume his journey to the northern coast. Word had been received of the safety of Ross and his party, and Back's energies could now be devoted solely to the interests of geographical discovery. By the end of the month he reached Musk-Ox Lake and continued his way down the great river, henceforth to bear his own name. It was hard going, for the river was not only broken by many turbulent rapids, but the lakes into which it expanded every little while were still more or less covered with ice. July 13th he reached Lake Beechey, and was disappointed to find the course of the stream turn abruptly to the south-east. Indian reports had led him to expect that this river emptied into Bathurst Inlet, but it now looked as if it must flow into Hudson Bay. However, he must trace it to its mouth, wherever that might be. Indications of Eskimo multiplied as he advanced, but the natives themselves were not met with until near the end of the journey, when the expedition was approaching the sea-coast. A few days before Back's anxiety as to the probable outlet of the river had been relieved by a decided trend to the north, and July 29th he reached the mouth of the river, which, "after a violent and tortuous course of five hundred and thirty geographical miles, running through an iron-ribbed country without a single tree on the whole line of its banks, expanding into fine large lakes with clear horizons, most embarrassing to the navigator, and broken into falls, cascades, and rapids, to the number of no less than eighty-three in the whole, pours its waters into the Polar Sea in latitude 67° 11′00″ N., and longitude 94° 30′ 0″ W."

Before returning to Fort Reliance, Back explored the coast as far as Point Ogle, the extreme north-eastern point of Adelaide Peninsula, and gave names to a number of capes and islands between Point Ogle and the mouth of the river. The return journey up the river occupied a little more than a month. He reached Fort Reliance on September 27th, 1834.

An officer of the Hudson's Bay Company, Thomas Simpson, took up the thread of exploration in the far north four years after Back had completed his journey. In actual achievement Simpson is fairly entitled to rank first in this particular field. His total explorations covered an immense stretch of the Arctic coast. He not only connected Franklin's farthest west with Point Barrow, the most easterly point reached by Elson in 1826, but also succeeded in filling in the important gap between Turnagain and Ogle.

Starting from Fort Confidence, at the eastern end of Dease Bay, Great Bear Lake, on June 15th, 1839, Simpson, with his companion Warren Dease, descended to the mouth of the Coppermine and coasted around to Point Turnagain. Continuing his way to the eastward, he completed the exploration of Kent Peninsula, sailed inside Melbourne Island and through the maze of islands in Labyrinth Bay. He rounded Adelaide Peninsula, landed on Ogle Point, and on Montreal Island found a cache left there by Back five years before. He then explored the coast to the north-eastward as far as the mouth of Castor and Pollux River, which he reached on August 20th. Returning from thence, he reached the mouth of the Coppermine on the 16th of the following month, and Fort Confidence eight days later.

Simpson also explored a portion of the southern coasts of Victoria Land and King William Land, as Richardson had already done with Wollaston Land. One of the most important results of Simpson's work was the final settlement of the question as to the existence of a water-channel separating these great Arctic islands from the mainland. His discoveries therefore had an important bearing upon the search for a North-West Passage—but that matter lies outside our field.

Anxiety as to the fate of Sir John Franklin led to several overland expeditions to the Arctic coast which indirectly resulted in important geographical discoveries. In 1846–7 Dr. John Rae crossed the isthmus from Repulse Bay to Committee Bay and explored the coast of the Gulf of Boothia from a point a little south of Cape Inglefield around to Ross Peninsula. In 1854 he connected the discoveries of Simpson from Castor and Pollux River to Cape Porter.

Richardson's expedition of 1848, while important in other respects, did not add very materially to what was already known of the Arctic coast of the continent. Mention, however, must be made of Anderson's expedition in 1855 to the mouth of Backs River, from Great Slave Lake. The later journeys of Warburton Pike, J. B. and J. W. Tyrrell, and David T. Hanbury through the barren grounds have already been sufficiently alluded to so far as this narrative is concerned.

To summarize the results of these several expeditions, it will be seen that between 1821 and 1854 the northern coast of the continent was explored from Point Barrow in the west to Melville Peninsula in the east. In the interior, Great Bear Lake was discovered and partially explored, as well as Backs River, the major portion of the Coppermine, and a number of less important lakes and rivers. Mackenzie's slight and Hearne's serious errors in fixing the position of the mouths of the two great rivers they respectively discovered were corrected; and the Arctic coast of North America at last assumed a definite character. Incidentally a great deal was learned of the geological features of this region of the far north, as well as of its flora and fauna, the character of the tribes that inhabited it, its physical features and climate. Valuable data were also acquired as the result of astronomic and magnetic observations.

Turning to the far west—to that vast territory lying north of the Peace River and the Skeena, and west of the Mackenzie, which now constitutes Northern British Columbia and the Yukon Territory—the last hundred years have seen a succession of important explorations, conducted by men of untiring pluck and energy under exceptionally difficult circumstances. If the history of exploration in the far west is divided into three periods, the first may be said to belong to the North West Company, the second to the Hudson's Bay Company, and the third to the Geological Survey of Canada. The first has already been dealt with in earlier chapters. It remains to tell briefly the story of far-western exploration by officers of the Hudson's Bay Company; and afterward by officers of the Geological Survey.

The Stikine River was first discovered at its mouth, by Captain Cleveland, of the sloop *Dragon*, in April, 1799, but this was nothing more than a visit to the delta of the river, and it was not until 1834 that any portion of its upper waters was explored. In that year J. McLeod, a chief trader in the service of the Hudson's Bay Company, ascended the Liard to Simpson Lake, in what is now Yukon Territory. Returning to the forks of the Liard and Dease rivers, he ascended the latter to Dease Lake (the lake and river were so

named by McLeod in honour of Warren Dease), crossed
the height of land to the head-waters of the Stikine,
which he called the Pelly River, and followed it westward as far as the famous Indian bridge at the foot of
Thomas Fall. This frail construction, afterward appropriately named Terror Bridge by Robert Campbell,
was too much even for the steady nerves of McLeod
and his men, and they decided to return to the Liard.
As mentioned by Dr. George M. Dawson, in his
elaborate Report on an Exploration of the Yukon
District, the geographical information obtained by
McLeod was incorporated in Arrowsmith's 1850 map,
on which, however, the upper part of the Stikine is
named Frances River, is placed much too far north, and
is not connected with the Stikine. The name Frances
appeared again on the 1854 map, as an alternative to
Stikeen, but subsequently fell into disuse. "McLeod's
route," says Dawson, "from the head of Dease Lake,
crossed the Tanzilla within a few miles of the lake and
followed its left bank, recrossing before the main Stikine
enters the valley, probably by an Indian suspension
bridge, which is reported still to exist (1887), within a
mile or two of this point. On careful consideration of
the facts, there can scarcely be any doubt that the Tooya
River was McLeod's furthest point, and the Indian
bridge probably crossed it near the position of the
present bridge, though it may have been at some
point further up the stream which has not yet been
mapped."

An effort was made two years later to continue

McLeod's exploration down the Stikine, but nothing was accomplished owing to the hostility of the Indians. In 1838 Robert Campbell, another officer of the Hudson's Bay Company, accompanied only by a half-breed and two Indian boys, succeeded in establishing a trading post at Dease Lake, where he spent a wretched winter. "We passed," he says, "a winter of constant danger from the savage Russian [coast] Indians, and of much suffering from starvation. We were dependent for subsistence on what animals we could catch, and failing that, on *tripe de roche*. We were at one time reduced to such dire straits that we were obliged to eat our parchment windows, and our last meal before abandoning Dease Lake, on 8th May, 1839, consisted of the lacing of our snow-shoes."

In 1824, ten years before McLeod discovered the upper waters of the Stikine, another officer of the Hudson's Bay Company, John Finlay, explored the river that bears his name from the place where it becomes known as the Peace River to its source in Thutage Lake.

Two years later Fort Connolly was built by Douglas on Bear Lake, at the head of the Skeena River ; and an overland route was subsequently established from Fort Connolly to the Liard and to Fort Simpson on the Mackenzie.

Returning to the north again, we find that Robert Campbell was commissioned by Sir George Simpson in 1840 to explore the north branch of the Liard to its source and endeavour to reach the head-waters of the

Colville. Pursuant to these instructions he left Fort Halkett on the Lower Liard in May, 1840, with a canoe and seven men. Ascending the river far into the heart of the mountains, Campbell entered a beautiful lake which he named Frances Lake, after Lady Simpson. Leaving his canoe there, he shouldered blankets and gun and ascended the valley of a stream to its source in a lake ten miles long, both of which he named Finlayson. From here he struck across to a river which he called the Pelly, in honour of Sir H. Pelly, a Governor of the Hudson's Bay Company. Constructing a raft, he drifted downstream for a few miles, and then returned to Frances Lake, where some of his men had in the meantime constructed a house afterward known as Fort Frances.

In June, 1843, Campbell, having provided himself with a birch-bark canoe, descended the Pelly to the mouth of a large tributary which he named the Lewes, where he met a party of Wood Indians. From them he got such a discouraging account of the natives lower down the main stream that he decided to turn back. In 1848 Campbell built Fort Selkirk at the confluence of the Lewes and the Pelly; and two years later descended the Yukon to the mouth of the Porcupine, which he ascended, crossed over to the Mackenzie, and so reached Fort Simpson. Dr. Dawson points out that one result of this journey was to show that the route from Fort Selkirk by way of the Porcupine River to the Mackenzie was preferable to that originally discovered. The Porcupine had itself been discovered in 1842 by J. Bell, of the Hudson's Bay Company. In 1846 Bell descended it to its confluence with the Yukon.

In concluding this brief sketch of the explorations of the fur traders in the extreme west and north-west, one cannot do better than quote Dr. George M. Dawson's eloquent tribute. " The utmost credit," he says, " must be accorded to the pioneers of the Hudson Bay Company for the enterprise displayed by them in carrying their trade into the Yukon basin in the face of difficulties so great and at such an immense distance from their base of supplies. To explorations of this kind, performed in the service of commerce, unostentatiously and as matters of simple duty, by such men as Mackenzie, Fraser, Thompson, and Campbell, we owe the discovery of our great north-west country. Their journeys were not marked by incidents of conflict or bloodshed, but were accomplished, on the contrary, with the friendly assistance and co-operation of the natives. Less resolute men would scarcely have entertained the idea of utilizing, as an avenue of trade, a river so perilous of navigation as the Liard had proved to be when explored. So long, however, as this appeared to be the most practicable route to the country beyond the mountains, its abandonment was not even contemplated. Neither distance nor danger appears to have been taken into account, and in spite of every obstacle a way was opened and a series of posts established extending from Fort Simpson on the Mackenzie to Fort Yukon."

Some idea of the extreme remoteness of these fur posts west of the Mackenzie River may be gained from a statement of the time required to convey goods to them from London, and carry furs back to the same market. The goods were sent from London to York Factory one season; carried inland to Norway House the next; reached Peel River the third, and were hauled over the mountains to La Pierre's House ; arrived at Fort Yukon the fourth. The fifth season, the returns in the shape of peltries were carried to Peel River ; the sixth, they reached Fort Simpson on the Mackenzie ; and the seventh, they arrived at their destination. Seven years from the time the trading goods left London to the time the furs bartered in exchange reached the same place.

Important as are the explorations of the Canadian Geological Survey, they can only be briefly alluded to here. The late Dr. George M. Dawson spent many years in the exploration of the far west. From 1876 to 1879 he was engaged on surveys both in Northern and Southern British Columbia, as well as on the Queen Charlotte Islands, the report of the latter embodying a mass of exceedingly valuable data in ethnology and archæology. In 1887 Dr. Dawson carefully explored the Yukon district, and the results obtained form the basis of our present knowledge of much of that great region.

Mention has already been made, in earlier chapters, of the explorations of Dr. Robert Bell and Mr. A. P. Low, the present director of the Survey, around Hudson and James bays, and between these bays and Lake Winnipeg ; as well as of the work of the Tyrrells in the

FORT EDMONTON

FORT ELLICE, 1879

Face p. 576

far north. Various officers of the Survey have also from time to time added materially to our knowledge of the geographical and other features of the Lake of the Woods district, the Winnipeg country, the great plains lying between the Saskatchewan and the Missouri, the wooded country north of the Saskatchewan, the valley of the Peace River, the region about Great Slave Lake and Lake Athabaska, and the Rocky Mountains. The results of these explorations and surveys are to be found in that invaluable series of reports published annually by the Geological Survey of Canada. No one who has not had occasion to examine these reports carefully can have any conception of the enormous amount of information they contain as to the character of this broad country, its physical features, resources, history its fauna and flora, its native inhabitants and their manners and customs. From the particular point of view of this book, they contain the records of numerous large and small surveys performed by the devoted and efficient officers of the Geological Survey. Thanks to their enthusiasm and careful work, accurate information is now available as to the character of many large districts that were a few years ago practically unknown. The time is coming, though it must still be a good many years ahead, when the unexplored areas will diminish to the vanishing point, and the long story of the exploration of North-Western America will come to a final close.

2 P

APPENDIX

MEMORANDUM BY ALEXANDER HENRY
ON AN OVERLAND ROUTE TO THE PACIFIC [1]

SIR,

I have sent for your Perusal and Amusement a Rout from Quebec or Montreal across the Contenent to the Westernmost Extremity of America, I have also Annexed an Estimate of the expence which I think Sufficient.

if his Majesty Should think Proper to Incourage the Undertaking, and think me a Proper Person to Command, this Hazardous Interprize, knowing the possibility and from the Great desire of Continuing, that Discovery which I have already began, I would except of it—having from Experience by Residing and Traveling amoungst the Natives Acquired the different Languages of the Nations, or Tribes, Inhabiting those Interior Parts, and often from Nessecity been Obliged to Learn the different Methods Practis'd for Procuring Subsistance by fishing and Hunting and having already pass'd the greatest part of the Rout as farr as the Rivers which Descends to the Sea, as farr North as Sixty degrees—but if his Majesty Should not think proper to Incourage the Discovery at present, this Rout may be Usefull some other day, which if so my expectation will be fulfilled, always being happy in Communicating any thing to you that may be of Use to the . . . public—

Mr. James Phyn, Merch't
Old Broad Street is my Correspondant, who can give you any Information concerning me you Require.

I am Sir your
Most Humb'e Serv't.
ALEX'R HENRY.

Montreal, 18 Oct'.
(1781).
To Joseph Banks Esq'r.

[1] The original is in the library of M. Phiteas Gagnon, of Quebec.

A Proper Rout, by Land, to Cross the Great Contenant of America from Quebec to the Westenmost extremity by Alex'r Henry founded on his Observations and Experience, during the Space of sixteen Years, Traveling with the Natives, in least known, and before Unknown parts of that Extensive Country.

Everything Neccessary be prepared to Sett from Quebec or Montreal the beginning of May if possible and Proceed to Michilimakinac where the Provisions are laid in for the Voyage and Canoes purchased from the Savages proper for Transporting over Carrying places and Navigating in Small Rivers, and Lakes, and Proceed frome thence to St. Marys the Entrance of Lake Superior, and Coasts, along the North Side, of said Lake untill you arrive at the Great Carrying place 150 leagues from Makinac, Near the Westermost Extremity of said Lake, where the Carrying place is Twelve Miles over and no other Method of Transporting Canoes and Goods, but by Canadians, who are very Expert in that bussiness, This may be done, by the Twentieth of July, and Ready to depart, from whence you ascend Grozell River for Ten leagues, passing severall Carrying places, From an Acre, to a League long, here you come to the Lands height, where the Watters seem to be at a Stand, and a Number of Small Lakes, from half a League to Five leagues long, This being the Extremity of the River St. Lawrence,—likewise those which, Discharges themselves at York Fort in Hudson's Bay —you continue Carrying from one Lake, to another, for about 20 Leagues, when you Perceive the Watters running to the Westward in Small Streams not Sufficient to Carry Canoes drawing only Six Inches of water, The Farther you Proceed down these small Rivilets the more they Encrease in Size, untill you come to Saganagaw, where they become Navigable, which, is about Sixty leagues from the Great Carrying place and Thirty Carrying places, This being, the most difficult Part of the Voyage, on Acco't of the Fatiguing the men, and Shallowness of the Rivers, and Breacking the Canoes, which are only made of Bark, not much thicker, than a Crown Piece. This Lake is about Fifeteen Leagues long. From here you must Proceed to Lake Lapluye or Rain Lake, distant from Saganagaw Sixty Leagues, between which are Fourteen Carrying places, from fifty yards, to a mile, the face of the Country is very poor and Rocky. This Lake is about Twenty Leagues long, and Ten wide. The Borders of this Lake is Inhabited by the Chipeways, being the most Westermost part of there Territories, at the Extremity of this Lake, is a Carrying place called the Chaudier, from hence you Continue down a fine River without a Carrying place for Forty Leagues about Two hundred yards wide, fine Rich lands each Side being the first from the Carrying place fit for Cultivating, where Provisions might be Raised at a Moderate Expence to Supply the trade in the Interior parts. This River Empties itself into Wood Lake, which is Reckoned thirty Leagues long—full of Islands, and many deep bays, the Borders of this Lake appears, Mountaineous and Barren, here the Natives begins. to speak the Kristinoes Language, this part of the Country abound in wild oats, or wild Rice, the most valuable of all Spontaneous Productions growing in water and Marchy places not fit to Produce any other Vegetable Substances, without which the Inhabitants could not Subsist, nor Travelors, Proceed far in the Country for want of Provisions, its Utility and Culture, is Worthy, the attention of the Curious, a Stock of this, must be laid in here To Conduct you, to your wintering ground, which is purchas'd from the Natives for European Manufactors from the westermost discharge of this Lake Commences the River Winipigon, a Very large River from one mile to Three miles wide,—a Rocky Mountaneous Country. The Navigation is Dangerous on Account of the falls, and Rapids, Twenty Carrying places, most of them, Great Falls, from Twenty to Fifty foot Perpendicular, This River is Reconned, Eighty leagues Long, Great Quantity's of Sturgeon in the Lower parts of this River, Very Good food, This River falls in a Lake, from whence it takes its Name, Lake Winipigon one hundred and Twenty leagues long, but not Equal, In Width, to Lake Superior or Huron by the time the Canoes gets to this Place, The Stormy Season, will set in, which generally begins the first of September,

(I was Twenty Eight days Crossing this Lake). From the Entrance of which must Coast along the North Shore for near Forty Leagues, where the Lake forms partly a Strait, and then must Cross to the South side and many Deep bays, which are very Dangerous at this Season, Untill you arrive at the Entrance of the River Bourbon, which falls in Lake Winipigon. This Lake discharges itself into Hudsons bay, at York Fort, (Contrary to the Travelers here to fore, who make the Great Discharge from Lake Bourbon). at the Entrance of this River is a Rapid, where the Canoes, and everything must be Carryed over by the men. two miles long, and assend this River to Lake Bourbon, about Twenty Leagues, from the Grand Rapid, a very strong Current, all the way, and four Carrying places. This Lake is Eighteen leagues long. The Lands, appears poor, the Soil bad, it is Remarkable. There is no Cedre found to the Northward of this Lake, from thence, you enter the River Pasquyaw, a fine Large River, the Current Strong, but no falls or Carrying Places, to Impede the Navigation for Canoes for Three hundred Leagues, each side, of this River for Fifety Leagues are Generally covered with Watter, occasioned by the Melting of the Snow in the Spring, but these parts abound with wild fowls, Duck, Geese, Swans, in Such abundance that the Savages brings Canoe Loads, which is a Great Relief, as Provisions—about this Time, begine to be Scarce—and Proceed up this River untill you arrive at a Small Discharge, which falls into the River Pasquyaw from the North, Called the English River, from a Fort being built near it, by hudsons bay Company Called Cumberland Fort, from the Entrance of pasquyaw River to the Village is Fifty leagues, and from the Village to Cumberland fort, Sixty leagues, the banks of the River, from Pasquyaw Village appears higher and of a Clay Soil, only covered with Small brush in different places—The Great Plains, not being farther distant than ten or fifeteen Leagues, which abounds with buffeloes, and Supplys the Numerous Inhabitants, with every thing necessary for food and Cloathing, the Source of this River is unknown, but the inhabitants about Eighty leagues above this, Report the

Course Incline more from the Southerd, Coming through the Great plains, from the Stony Mountains, from whence the Rivers take there Rise, which falls into the South sea, the Course from Lake Superior, to this place near Northwest, the English River, only Two leagues long, when you enter Sturgeon Lake, Eighteen Leagues long—when you enter bad River called so on Account of its Rapids, fifteen leagues long untill you arrive at Beaver Lake, which is Ten leagues, here the People must winter, being the only Place where provisions can be had abounding with Fish of every kind, that every man can Supply himself with food—for the winter which is very Severe, the Ice, five foot thick, in the Lake, through which holes are made with Chisles proper for that purpose, and nets, sett under, by which means the fish are taken, the Winter here very long, the latter end of October, the Lakes frizes. & Snow fall and Continues so untill the Latter End of May, before the Rivers becomes Navigable but the Lake generally, not before the middle of June. Proceed from Beaver Lake up Kenoche, or Pike River, to a Lake of that Name, here, the Men must Supply themselves with fish, the River being so plenty, they can take any Number of them they chuse Lake Kenoche; five Leagues long, & from thence from Lake to Lake, & Sometimes, a small Rapid River and Carrying places, untill you arrive at the Great River Missinebe Eighty Leagues North from Beaver Lake. Two hundred Leagues West from Churchill, or Prince of Wales's fort—the Northermost of Hudson's bay's factory's, from Beaver Lake, to this River, is seven Carrying places, from Two hundred yards, to half a Mile Long the Lands Level, but the Soil, not Rich, at this Place the Missinebe's River is two miles broad, a Gentle Current from hence, Guides must be procured, as the Natives Inhabiting these parts, Seems, Sepparated, and unconnected with the Southern Indians, theire Language, differing but little from the kristinay the passages very difficult, to find in the River on Acco't of its great breadth, and Number of Islands—and great Lakes, here the Canoes must be Refitted, and when Ready, proceed up this River, In the Streights of which, are great Rappids, and Dangerous places from the great body of Watters, Coming, down from the Melting of the Snow, in this Season, & proceed to Orrabuscaw Carrying place, Two hundred and fifty Leagues, from where you fall on the Great River, Course, near West, Supposed to be in Sixty Degrees Lattitude, Day nineteen hours long, the Twenty second of June, the North side of this River, appears a Barren, Mountaneous Country mostly bare Rocks, great quantity of fish in this River, the Natives appear, as you Proceed to the Westward, to Increase in Number, at this Carrying place, Provisions must be procured from the Natives Dry'd mouse and Rein Deer, to Subsist the people while Carrying over this Carrying place which is Twelve Miles long, & as far as Orabuscaw Lake, it will take six days to Carry over, at the other End of which, you fall on the River Kiutchinini which runs to the Westward, takes it Rise to the Northward of this Place, Current, Gentle, the Land Low and Marshy—Great plenty of Wild fowl in the fall—The Season by this time will be advanced, it will be Necessary to prepare for Winter, Build Houses &c, the frost very Severe, Imploy the Natives to hunt, for the Subsistance of the men—which is mostly Flesh, Dry'd Buffloes meat, & mouse Deer, It is not only, the Provisions for the winter Season, but, for the Course of next Summer, must be provided which is Dry'd Meat, Pounded to a Powder & mixed up with Buffeloes Greese, which preserves it in the warm Seasons here, every Information must be procured from the Savages, Relating to the Course of this River, the Inhabitants of the Lower parts the Orabuscaws, makes war on the Kitchininie therefore, it Will be Necessary to Procure a Peace between the two Nations which would be no difficult matter for the Natives, from all Parts, hearing of Europeans being here, will come in the winter Season to bring Provisions on Acco't of European Trinkets, by which means, Intelligence may be Procured, and Conveyed to any Distant parts, it is Common for these wandering Tribes to Remove two hundred Leagues in the winter Season. and Carry their Tents, Family's and everything belong to them, when every thing is Ready, and Provisions Procured for the Summer, as no Dependance can be put, on what you are to receive in an unknown part. Every precaution should be taken, but very often, must expect to be dessappointed.

A New sett of Interpretors & Guides must be Procured, which can always be had, from the Difft Nations and Proceed down this Great River, Untill, you come to the Sea—which cant be any very Great Distance. Suppose it Should be Thirty, or Forty Degrees of Longitude Unless, some Accidents should Entervene, it can be done in Thirty days, which will be in July, here an Establishment may be made in Some Convenient Bay, or harbour, where Shipping, may come to. In the mean Time a Small Vessell may be Built, for Coasting, and Exploaring the Coast, which can be no Great Distance from the Streight, which Seperates the two Contenants, the Greatest difficulty is procuring provissions for another winter on the Sea Cost, I always found, where the Savages found Subsistance for themselves, there was a Possibility, of procuring from them, or, by the Industry of the Canadians, who are very Expert in fishing, and hunting Risques, there are always expected in Enterprizes of this kind, the Farther North, and West, The Furrs are Finer, & in Greater Abundance, and doubt not but, a Convenient port, may be found, for Establishing a Profitable Trade with the Natives in these parts,— which if once fix't Discoverys may be carried on with more ease, and less Risque, when it is thought Necessary to Return it must be done in the same manner, only they will return in two years to England, by the way of Hudsons bay being much the Shortest way back. There are many National advantages which may Result from Discovering and Surveying these Remote, unknown Parts of America, and having a Communication, from other Rich Country's in the East and easily, Conveyed across to Hudsons bay, where British Manufactorers, might be sent, To Thousands on the Continent, & fetch large Profits & a Valuable New Commerce be opened and Secured to his Majesty's subjects—as there is at Present no appearance of a North west passage, for Ships— An Estimate of the Expences, Attending the Voyage I here annex—

(Turn over)

Ten Canoes Navigated by Forty men will be
  sufficient which can be Engaged at £6 p.
  month Two years advance which is for four
  years £5760
10 Canoes at £20 each   200
Provissions for 40 men for 12 months at 2/ a
  pr. Diem   1460
Equipments for the Mens outfit at £10 each .   400
Transporting from Montreal to Makinac .   .   500
Merchandize, for Purchasing Provisions & presents to the Natives for 4 years, amunition etc   4800
Guides and Interpretors for 2 years .   .   .   200

                  Sterling   £13,320
                                  is sufficient

The above Expence, without some Extraordinary, should
Entervene, The Two Years Wages advance must be paid the
Men as an Encouragement, for them, & to Enable them to
purchase their Necessaries, for so long a Voyage. The Remainder at their Return, being the only Expence Remaining,
as Cash is of no Use to them, after, they pass the Great
Carrying place from Lake Superior. The only Persons
Necessary to attend such a Journey, Should be an Experienced Man to Conduct the Expedition, who must be
properly Authorized as Commander in Chief, & and have the
whole Regulating in all Matters, whatsoever Ingaging, Discharging, Paying, Purchasing Provisions, Marching, Incamping
& ordering in every way whatsoever, after him there should be
another Employed who understands Mathematics & if possible
Botany and Drawing in the Same Person, as any unnecessary
becomes a Great charge, Especially one who is unaccustomed to
live in the manner of the Inhabitants of the Country—Through
which they must pass, if not used already to Fatigues they
should be young & of a good Constitution as they must
Expect many severe Trials. Two Clerks or Overseers Who
are to act as Commissary's, People of this Country, who must
be acquainted with Voyaging and Conducting men chosen by
the Commander of the Expedition. Orders to be given to

the Commander in Chieff, & to the Lieu't Governors of the Upper Posts to aid and ajust all in their Power in Purchasing provisions, & Engaging Men, & any other Matter Necessary for the Voyage, Likewise to the Officers of the Hudsons bay Company, as that would be much the nearer way to Return to England. Likewise I annex the Distances, as near as can be ascertained without Mathematical Observations.

From Montreal to Michillimakinac . .	250 leagues
From Makinac to the falls of St. Mary, Entrance of Lake Superior . . .	30 ,,
From St. Mary's to the Great Carrying Place West end of Lake Superior . .	120 ,,
From the G. Carrying place to Saganagas .	60 ,,
From Saganaga to Rain Lake . . .	60 ,,
Rain Lake	20 ,,
From Rain Lake to Wood Lake . .	40 ,,
Wood Lake	30 ,,
	610 leagues
From Wood Lake to the Entrance of Lake Winipigon	80 ,,
From the East End of Lake Winipigon to the W. End	120 ,,
From thence to the Entrance of Lake Bourbon	20 ,,
Lake Bourbon	18 ,,
From the Entrance of the River Pasquyaw to the Village	50 ,,
From the Village to Cumberland Fort .	60 ,,
From thence to Beaver Lake . . .	33 ,,
The Lake	10 ,,
From the N. End of Beaver Lake to where you come to the Missinebe . . .	70 ,,
From there to the Great Carrying place at the head of the River Missinebe . .	250 ,,
Carrying place	3 ,,
From thence to Orobusca Lake . .	40 ,,
	1364 leagues

The Carrying Place at the head of the Missinebe River according to the best of my Calculation Lays in 60 Degrees North Latitude & 140 West Longitude from London.

Montreal 18 October, 1781.
To Joseph Banks, Esq'r. G.R.S.

ALEX'R HENRY.

MEMORANDUM BY ALEXANDER DALRYMPLE ON THE ROUTE FOR DISCOVERIES[1]

2nd Feby. 1790.

The season being so far advanced renders a voyage round Cape Horn *inexpedient*, I do not say *impracticable*, for admitting a Vessel to sail the beginning of March, we cannot fairly suppose less than three months to double Cape Horn, which brings it to June, the beginning of winter in South Latitude. Allow three months more to the N. W. Coast of America. This brings it to September, which is the beginning of winter there. But altho' it is therefore an inexpedient season to proceed round Cape Horn on discovery of that Coast It admits a question whether It would not be better under the disadvantage to make the voyage *immediately* than to *procrastinate:* for altho' their arrival on the Coast of America would not be at the most proper season for Discovery, there would be some advantage in the passage round Cape Horn, for the Lion's Voyage P. 4, says it is commonly found that the winds in the winter months are favourable to go round Cape Horn from Europe and unfavourable to come out of the South Seas, and by the Journal of Winds at the Falkland Islands this opinion seems to be confirmed as the Easterly winds seem, at least, as frequent as *Westerley* in *June more frequent* in *July*.

Admitting therefore that the Vessel came upon the Coast of America so late even as October we know by experience of the Prince of Wales and Princess Royal who remained on the Coast till after the middle of Novr., that it is practicable to remain on that Coast so late, but these Vessels were at

---

[1] Canadian Archives, series Q, vol. 49, p. 368.

Calamity Harbour in Lat. 54° 12′ North and the present object of Discovery is *De Fouca's Strait* in 48½ N. Lat., and if they can find a convenient harbour on that Coast to winter in, much progress may be made by land during the winter towards effecting a communication; and if they choose they can proceed to the Sandwich Islands & return at the early part of Spring.

But however much I may be an enemy to *Procrastination*, on any *account*, my opinion is that the present operation ought to be by *Hudson's Bay* in preference to Cape Horn.

The antient idea of a N. W. Passage was by the Hyperborean Sea on the N. of America, altho' I am very far from meaning any imputation on Capt. Cook's memory or abilities, I cannot admit of a *Pope* in Geography or Navigation.

It is alledged that the Esquimaux's extend to the most remote parts of the North Coasts of America. This the Language given in Cook's voyage proves incontrovertibly in western parts; and it is beyond dispute that the Esquimaux's are confined to the Sea Coasts & its vicinity; that they are not to be found where there is not a communication with the sea, is self evident from the nature of their Boats &c., & therefore the argument is almost demonstrative that there is a *Sea Communication*, *navigable* for their Boats, from *Labrador* & *Greenland* to the utmost extremity of *America* & the Islands.

Whether the Sea Communication is navigable for *more* than *Boats*, is a matter well worth examining.

Every modern discovery tends to corroborate the old reports, and in the earliest maps, long before Hudson's voyage, the *Bay* or *Sea* which bears *his name* is Distinctly marked, tho' represented of much less dimension than it is.

In these maps a channel is represented as communicating the N. W. part of that Sea which corresponds to *Repulse Bay*, with the *Hyperborean Ocean;* and this sea communication is conformable to all the Indian Maps, which continue the Sea coast from *Churchill* in *Hudson's Bay* to the *Copper River*.

Captain Meares, who was frozen up in Prince-William-Sound, remarks, that there are no *High Islands* of *Ice*, such as are

found in *Cross-Sound* in a much lower Latitude. His inference is a natural one, that *Cross-Sound* is a Sea communication
to a higher Latitude where these *High Islands* of *Ice* are
found.

Capt. Portlock learnt from the Indians at his *Harbour*, to
the *South-ward* of *Cross-Sound*, that there was a *Sea* beyond
the mountains, which environ that Harbour, to the Eastward
and the concurrent opinion, of all those who have visited the
Coast for many degrees to the Southward, is that the whole is
only a Range of Islands.

The opinion therefore of a N. W. Passage is strongly con-
firmed by the concurrence of the antient Reports, the Indian
Maps, and the opinion of those who have recently visited the
N. W. Coast. The only allegations to the contrary that Capt.
Middleton represents *Repulse Bay* to be shut up, and that
Capt. Cook & Capt. Clerk could not find a Passage by the
Strait of *Anian* now called *Behring's Strait*.

Whoever looks into Capt. Middleton's Journal will, I am
confident prefer the *positive testimony* of the Indian Maps, to
his *conjecture*, and without controverting the Inference drawn
from Capt. Cook's voyage. This can by no manner of argument prove the *Sea*, from Repulse Bay round to the Westward
is *unnavigable*.

The many great Rivers of Asia disemboguing into that Sea
which lyes on the North of It, bring down multitudes of Drifts,
which will tend to congregate Ice. That Ice may be so
accumulated between Asia and the opposite Coast (the extent
Northward of both which is unknown) as to prevent a passage
that way. But we have no Reports to indicate any considerable Rivers falling into the *Hyperborean Sea* from *Repulse Bay*
to the meridian of Cross-Sound & both Mr. Hearne and the
Canadian Traders represent the northern part of America as
destitute of Timber.

The allegation concerning the *Bar* of *fixed Ice*, admitting
this as a *Fact*, instead of an *Hypothesis*, as it is by some
alledged to be, make nothing in favour of what it is brought
to prove, for we know the sea is navigable at *Spitzbergen* to
80° N. Lat. and we have no reason to believe the Coast of the

Hyperborean Sea, from Repulse Bay westward extends to 70° N. Lat. The Canadian Traders represent it to lye in 68½ N. & Mr. Hearne only alledges it to be in 72° N. Lat. The Danes have a settlement in Davis's Strait in 73° 15′ N. Lat., and there is no one circumstance, either in Mr. Hearne's Journal or in the Canadian Reports, to countenance an opinion that the Country on the west of the Northern part of the Hudson's Bay is uninhabited in winter; on the contrary Mr. Hearne set out in December from Churchill, where the climate seems to be more temperate than at Albany, altho' the latter be much further to the South, and this is a strong presumption of a Sea to the Northward.

But even supposing for a moment, what is not supported by any probable inference, that the navigation westward by the North of Hudson's Bay is impracticable, then we are to consider the matter as confined to an Examination by Land.

The Canadian Traders represent the distance from Quebec to the extremity of Lake Superior to be 750 Leagues or 2250 Geographical miles, & from thence to the Great Slave Lake 1000 leagues, or 3000 more, in the whole 1,750 Leagues or 5250 Geographical miles. Altho' this distance be admitted to be greatly exaggerated, still the estimation operates equally in favour of Hudson's Bay when compared with the distance from thence.

I will suppose the distance in a direct Line may be admitted in miles instead of Leagues, because I would give the fairest computation, this gives 1750 miles thro' a country full of falls & rapids to impede the navigation.

We shall take it however only to the Island in the Arathapescow Lake at 1350 Geographic miles.

This distance from Hudson's Bay is only 600 miles, of which above 200 is the *Chesterfield Inlet known* to be navigable. The Canadian Trader represents the *Arathapescow* Lake to extend 100′ to the Eastward of the Island, Mr. Hearne 90′; and a very considerable portion of the remaining 300 miles is occupied by the *Dobaunt* and other Lakes.

By Hudson's Bay the Discoverers would profit by the information of Mr. Turnor whom the Hudson's Bay Company have sent into those parts and from whose Astronomical abilities we may reasonably expect competent Information, whereas Peter Pond's allegation (as reported by Mr. Holland) "that the *Observations* of the Latitude in his *last Journey* agreed to a *second* with the positions in his *former* map" laid down by Estimation, betrays his *ignorance* or impudence and invalidates any Reports coming from him.

Supposing some person of knowledge and veracity to be sent with him it is probable Pond would *hide* that Person as is at present alledged of a person whose merits raised his Jealousy.

It is also to be considered that Pond is a native of the United States, and cannot therefore be deemed to be attached to this Country. He also pretends to the Sovereignty of the Lands adjacent to the Arathapeskow Lake, so that by encouraging him we may be fostering a Viper in our bosom.

Should the Vessel by going to Hudson's Bay find no Sea communication practicable, she would return back to England by the beginning of October in time to proceed by Cape Horn, in prosecution of the Voyage on the west side, with the advantage of all that Local knowledge which their Observations and enquiries in Hudson's Bay had obtained.

I am given to understand that the Wages and Provisions for a Vessel of 120 tons & 30 men would not exceed £100 p. month, so that the expence of this attempt would be small.

The most eligible mode of promoting the enterprise would be by sending one vesssel round Cape Horn without delay & another to Hudson's Bay; and the Hudson's Bay Company have expressed their readiness to co-operate with Government as the Esquimauxs on the West side of the Bay, are on Friendly Footing with the Hudson's Bay Company's Agents, some of them might probably be induced to accompany the Adventurers in their Canoes. Mr. Hearne mentions that the Esquimauxs winter at a *very great Lake*, called *Yathked*, situated to the S. W. of the *Chesterfield Inlet*, & it is not improbable they may be induced under the English Influence to accompany some of our People across those Lakes & by those Rivers which the Indian Maps represent as connecting Hudson's Bay & the Arathapescow Lake, which would obviate the objection made to the navigation from the Northern Parts of Hudson's Bay, as being a country destitute of Birch-wood for making *Bark Canoes*.

I cannot omit mentioning the propriety of having *Dogs* as a *watch;* for the Indians coming upon their enemies like a Tiger by stealth, The Alarm would be given and their Brutal Ferocity prevented.

CAPTAIN HOLLAND'S PLAN TO EXPLORE FROM QUEBEC[1]

The following Plan strikes Mr. Holland as most Eligible for carrying into Effect the proposed Expedition for Discovering, and Exploring the Interior parts of the Northern and Western Quarter of America: Lying between Lake Aurabusquie, or Arathepeskow and the Line of Coast discovered by Capt. Cook:

First. That the Party to be employed should consist of not less than sixteen Persons, including a Surveyor and Assistant: Four Men having some knowledge of Boat Building; Eight Canadians, and Two Indians, for navigating Two, or sometimes Three Canoes, in order at Times, or as occasion may require to be enabled to Detach one, on any separate work which may present itself, such as exploring Rivers, sketching in the side of a Lake opposite to that taken by the Main Party and Chief Surveyor with whom Two Canoes must constantly be stationed for fear of accidents to either; and by keeping the Duplicates, Plans, observations, Journals &c. separated less injury would be sustained by the loss.

One of the great Obstacles to impede such an Expedition, would be the want of Provisions. It will therefore be necessary that a sufficient Quantity (for at least Three years consumption) should be deposited at Aurabusquie, to be conveyed thither from the King's Stores at Fort Michilimacinac, and as our Canoes, from the smallness of their size would not be able to contain the Quantity requisite, a Party, and Canoes,

---

[1] Canadian Archives, series Q, vol. 49, p. 381.

might be spared from the Fort, to aid in the transporting of it to Aurabusquie; from whence our chief operations ought to commence.

The Track from Lake Superior thither being known (and an accurate survey not the object in view) all that appears necessary between those Places is the ascertaining the Latitude and Longitude of some Principal Posts in our Route; and making such Sketches as may be useful to Persons who may follow. This I presume will be all that can be done in the course of the Ensuing Summer, supposing the Party to depart from Quebec about the end of May; at which Place, and at Montreal; a Month at least will be consumed in making the necessary Preparations Prior to our Departure. Little further during the winter season can be done at Aura-busquie, than exploring the Surrounding Country; making Observations; gaining Intelligence; and preparing for pursuing our Route in Spring; which I think should be by mounting the Slave River; thence North West Coasting the Slave Lake (which by Information gained at Quebec from Persons who have been in that Country) is not less than ten Degrees of Longitude; That it Discharges itself into a River which takes its course N. West, and that its Distance from thence, to Prince Williams Sound or Cook's River, does not exceed Fifteen Degrees of Longitude.

After reaching the mouth of Cook's River, or whatever other River, we may fall in with on the outset, It will be advisable to stretch along the Coast, to the South East, to observe the course of all such rivers as may appear of import-ance; untill we shall be joined by the Party, intended to depart from Hudson's House, who I apprehend will follow the Coast to the North West, and explore the rivers in like manner untill our Junction.

----

2 Q

ESTIMATE OF EXPENSE NECESSARY TO EQUIP
A PARTY ON AN EXPEDITION TO THE NORTH
WEST PARTS OF AMERICA TO BE EMPLOYED
IN EXPLORATION AND DISCOVERY

£

A Surveyor at   Pr Diem   .   .   .

One Assistant at 10s. P r Diem makes Pr
Annum 182 10

Four men to understand Boat Building 3s. pr.
Diem 219

Eight Canadians for navigating & Transporting
Canoes, Provisions &c 365

Two Indians at 2s. Pr Diem 73

Sixteen Rations of Provisions for the above
Party. The Ration consisting of: 16 ounces
of Bread, 1 lb. of meat, 1 Pint of Rum .

Necessary Disbursements not included in the
above . . . .

Astronomical and other Instruments . . 150

Indian Trinkets 150

Canoes, Oil Cloths, Tackling &c . . . 40

Arms, Ammunition, Hatchets, Nap Sacks, &c.

LIST OF INSTRUMENTS, &c.

List of Instruments necessary for making Astronomical and
other Observations by the party intended to cross from
Canada to the Pacific Ocean. Prepared by Mr. Holland,
February, 1790.

A Transit Instrument.

A Time Piece.

Telescopes {A Refractor} of sufficient power to observe the
{A Reflector} Eclipses of Jupiter Sattelites.

A Thermometer graduated considerably below the Freezing
Point.

A Barometer constructed for measuring Heights.

A Theodolite, Azimuth and Hadley.

CAPTAIN HOLLAND TO EVAN NEPEAN

LONDON, *July 25th*, 1790.

SIR,—Presuming from the advanced state of the season, that little more can be done this year towards prosecuting the intended exploration of the Interior parts of the North West of America; than in making such arrangements at Quebec during the winter as will enable us to leave that place the Instant the Ice breaks up in Spring; to effect which I conceive it of material consequence to have the necessary Instruments and other articles to be procured in this Country shipped this season for Canada, for the following reasons, That after Sunday next the 1st of August the direct communication by shipping to Quebec closes till next Spring; when from numberless impediments their arrival is frequently retarded till near the commencement of June at which time we should be near Michilimacinak. Submitting the above with all deference to your superior judgement.

I have the honour to be, Sir,

Your most devoted, most obedient

and most humble servant,

JN. F. DE B. HOLLAND.

A BIBLIOGRAPHY

OF THE

EXPLORATION OF NORTH-WESTERN AMERICA

THE following bibliography does not pretend to be even approximately exhaustive. It is designed merely to suggest the extent of the material available for a study of the field. So far as it goes, however, it is not confined to the period of time covered in the Search for the Western Sea, but embodies also later explorations.

GENERAL WORKS

Dawson, S. E. *Canada and Newfoundland.* London. 1897.

Greswell, W. P. *Geography of Canada and Newfoundland.* London. 1891.

Selwyn and Dawson. *Descriptive sketch of the physical geography and geology of Canada.* Montreal. 1884.

Lucas, C. P. *Historical geography of the British Colonies.* Vol. V. Canada. Oxford. 1901.

Winsor, Justin. *Narrative and critical history of America.* Boston. 1886–9. 8 vols.

Thwaites, R. G. *Jesuit relations and allied documents.* Cleveland. 1896–1901. 73 vols.

Larned, J. N. *Literature of American history.* Boston. 1902.

Charlevoix, P. F. X. de. *Histoire et description générale de la Nouvelle France.* Paris. 1744. 3 vols. Trans. with notes by J. G. Shea. New York. 1886. 6 vols.

Garneau, F. X. *Histoire du Canada.* Quebec. 1845–52. 4 vols. Trans. by Andrew Bell. Montreal. 1860.

Sulte, Benjamin. *Histoire des Canadiens-Français.* Montreal. 1882–4. 8 vols.

Kingsford, William. *History of Canada.* Toronto. 1887–98. 10 vols.

596

Parkman, Francis. *France and England in North America.* ⁊
     Boston. 1898. 11 vols.

Fiske, John. *The discovery of America.* Boston. 1892.
     2 vols.

Bancroft, H. H. *History of the Pacific States of North
     America.* San Francisco. 1882-90. 21 vols.

Wrong, G. M. *Review of historical publications relating to* ⁊
     Canada. Toronto. 1896.

Canadian Archives reports. By Douglas Brymner and Arthur ⁊
     G. Doughty. Ottawa. 1873.

Royal Society of Canada, transactions. Montreal and Ottawa.
     1883.

Geological Survey of Canada, reports. Ottawa. 1842.

*Memoir upon the voyages, discoveries, explorations, and surveys
     to and at the west coast of North America and interior of
     the United States west of the Mississippi River, between
     1500 and 1880, etc.* Washington. 1889.

Documents relating to the boundaries of Ontario. Toronto.   ⁊
     1878.

Mills, David. *Report on the boundaries of Ontario.* Toronto.   7
     1873.

Lindsey, Charles. *Investigation of the unsettled boundaries of*   ⁊
     Ontario. Toronto. 1873.

Manitoba Historical and Scientific Society, transactions.   ⁊
     Winnipeg. 1879.

Petitot, E. "Géographie de l'Athabaskaw-Mackenzie et des   ⁊
     grands lacs du bassin Arctique." In *Bulletin de la
     Société de Géographie.* (Paris.) Tome X. 1875.

Dawson, G. M. "The larger unexplored regions of Canada."   ⁊
     In *Ottawa Naturalist.* 1890.

White, James. *Altitudes of the Dominion of Canada.*
     Ottawa. 1901.
     Dictionary of altitudes in the Dominion of Canada. Ottawa.   ⁊
     1903.

Geographic Board of Canada. Sixth report. Ottawa. 1906.

Harrisse, Henry. *Discovery of North America*, etc. London. 1892.

Harrisse, Henry. *Notes pour servir à l'histoire, à la bibliographie et à la cartographie de la Nouvelle France et des pays adjacents, 1545–1700.* Paris. 1872.

CARTOGRAPHY

Phillips, P. Lee. *List of maps of America in the Library of Congress.* Washington. 1901.

Winsor, Justin. *The Kohl collection of maps relating to America.* Washington. 1904.

Maps accompanying the annual reports of the Geological Survey of Canada.

Bellin, J. N. *Remarques sur la carte de l'Amérique septentrionale, comprise entre le 28ᵉ et le 72ᵉ degré de latitude.* Paris. 1755.

Dalrymple, A. Charts of the north-west coast of North America. London. 1789–91.

Marcel, Gabriel. *Cartographie de la Nouvelle France.* Paris. 1885.

Scadding, Henry. "On the early gazetteer and map literature of Western Canada." In *Canadian Journal of Science*, etc. Toronto. 1878.

Marcel, Gabriel. *Reproductions de cartes et de globes relatifs à la découverte de l'Amérique du XVI au XVIII siècle.* Paris. 1894.

"Notes on maps examined with a view to illustrate the boundaries of Canada," etc. In *Documents respecting boundaries of Ontario*, p. 135.

Dawson, S. J. "Memorandum on early maps." In *Documents respecting boundaries of Ontario*, p. 273.

Bartholomew, J. G. "Maps of North America." In *Scottish Geog. Mag.*, 1891, p. 586.

White, James. Map illustrating explorations in Northern Canada. Ottawa. 1904.

White, James. Map of Canada showing routes of explorers. Ottawa. 1907.

Arrowsmith, A. Map exhibiting all the new discoveries in the interior parts of North America, etc. Jan. 1, 1795, with additions to 1811. (This is one of several maps by Arrowsmith, of North America, or North-Western America.)

Devine, Thomas. Map of the Hudson's Bay Territory. Toronto. 1857.

Christy, Miller. Map showing the tracks of explorations into and about Hudson Bay. In his ed. of Foxe and James. Reproductions of Foxe's and James's charts are also included in this edition.

Maps showing the explorations of Hudson, Hearne, Carver, Mackenzie, and Harmon are published with their respective narratives.

La Vérendrye, P. G. de. Two maps by La Vérendrye, or prepared from his notes, dated respectively 1737 and about 1740, are in the Library of Parliament MSS., Ottawa. A third, of which a facsimile will be found in Lindsey's *Boundaries of Ontario*, is in the French Archives at Paris.

Pond, Peter. In the Library of Congress there is a copy of a map by Peter Pond, dated about 1785; and another map by Pond, dated about 1789, is reproduced in the 1890 Report on Canadian Archives.

Fidler, Peter. A map laid down from the sketches and observations of Mr. Peter Fidler for J. G. McTavish, Esquire, by G. Taylor, Junior. (This MS. map is now in the office of the Geographer of the Interior Department, Ottawa.)

Turner, Philip. Chart of lakes and rivers in North America. 1790. (Copy in the Kohl Collection, Library of Congress.)

Thompson, David. Map of the North-West Territory of the Province of Canada, etc. Made for the North West Company in 1813–14. (The original is in the Crown Lands Department, Toronto. Portions of it have been reproduced in Coues' Henry-Thompson Journals.)

HUDSON BAY

Hakluyt, Richard. *Principal navigations, voyages, traffiques, and discoveries.* Ed. by Edmund Goldsmid. Edinburgh. 1884–90. 16 vols.

Purchas, Samuel. *Hakluytus posthumus or Purchas His Pilgrimes.* Glasgow. 1905–6. 20 vols.

Rundall, Thomas. *Narrative of voyages towards the North-West in search of a passage to Cathay, 1496 to 1631.* London. 1849.

Gilbert, Sir Humphrey. *A discourse of a discoverie for a new passage to Cataja.* London. 1576.

Frobisher, Sir Martin. *A true discourse of the late voyages of discoverie for the finding of a passage to Cathaya, etc.* London. 1578.

The three voyages of Martin Frobisher in search of a passage to Cathaia and India by the North-West, 1576–8. London. 1867.

Davis, John. *Voyages and works of John Davis the navigator.* A. H. Markham. London. 1880.

Hudson, Henry. *Detectio Freti of Hessel Gerritz.* Amsterdam. 1612.

Asher, George M. *Henry Hudson the navigator.* London. 1860.

Markham, C. R. *Voyages of William Baffin, 1612–22.* London. 1881.

Gosch, C. C. A. *Expedition of Jens Munk to Hudson's Bay.* London. 1897.

ɔ Christy, Miller. *The Voyages of Luke Foxe and Thomas James, 1631–2.* London. 1894. 2 vols.

ɔ Radisson, Pierre Esprit. *Relation du voiage du sieur Pierre Esprit Radisson au nord de Lamerique es annees 1682 et 1683* (with trans.). Canadian Archives Report. 1895. Note A.

ɔ Hudson's Bay Company. Committee appointed to inquire into . . . the countries adjoining Hudson's Bay. . . . Papers presented to the Committee. London. 1754. Report from Committee, with Appendix. 1749. 2 vols.

Report from the Select Committee on the Hudson's Bay
    Company. . . . London. 1857.

ɔ Oldmixon, John. *British Empire in America*, etc. London.
    1708. 2 vols.

ɔ Jérémie. "Relation du detroit et de la baye d'Hudson." In
    Bernard's *Recueil de Voiages au Nord*. Amsterdam.
    1724.

ɔ Coats, W. *Geography of Hudson's Bay, 1727-51*. Ed. by ɔ
    John Barrow. London. 1852.

Robson, Joseph. *Account of six years' residence in Hudson's*
    Bay, 1733-6 and 1744-7. London. 1752.

Ellis, Henry. *Voyage for the discovery of a north-west passage,*
    etc., 1746-7. London. 1748. 2 vols.

Voyage for the discovery of a North-West passage by Hudson
    Streights, etc., 1746-7, in the ship "California," Captain
    Smith. London. 1748.   J. S. ? ⟨ ⟩

Middleton, Christopher. "Voyage for the discovery of the y
    North-West Passage." In Coat's *Hudson's Bay*.

Dobbs, Arthur. *An account of the countries adjoining*
    Hudson's Bay. . . . London. 1744. See also Middleton's
    Defence ; Dobbs's *Remarks upon Middleton's Defence;*
    Middleton's *Answer ;* and Dobbs's *Reply*.

Chappell, Edward. *Narrative of a voyage to Hudson's Bay in*
    1814. London. 1817.

Lyon, G. F. *A brief narrative of an unsuccessful attempt to*
    reach Repulse Bay . . . in the year 1824. London.
    1825.

Belcourt, G. A. *Department of Hudson's Bay*. In Minnesota
    Hist. Soc. Coll., I., 207.

Bryce, George. *Remarkable history of the Hudson's Bay* ɔ
    Company. London. 1900.

Willson, Beckles. *The Great Company*. London. Toronto.
    1899.

M'Lean, John. *Notes of a twenty-five years' service in the* y
    Hudson's Bay territory. London. 1849. 2 vols.

Ballantyne, R. M. *Hudson's Bay.* London. Edinburgh. 1848.

Bell, Robert. "Report on Hudson's Bay," in *Geol. Survey Report*, 1879; "Exploration on northern side of Hudson Strait," *Geol. Survey*, 1898.

Markham, A. H. "Hudson's Bay and Strait." In Royal Geog. Soc. Supp. Papers, Vol. II, pt. 4. 1889.

Low, A. P. "Exploration of part of the south shore of Hudson Strait and Ungava Bay," in *Geol. Survey*, 1898; "The east coast of Hudson Bay," *Geol. Survey*, 1900; "Explorations in James Bay," *Geol. Survey*, 1887.

Gordon, A. R. *Report on the Hudson Bay expedition.* Ottawa. 1885.

Wakeham, Wm. *Report on the second Hudson Bay expedition.* Ottawa. 1898.

Low, A. P. *Report on expedition to Hudson Bay and the Arctic Islands.* Ottawa. 1906.

Kellsey, Henry. See *Hudson's Bay Report*, 1749; Robson's *Hudson's Bay.*

Hendry, Anthony. MS. journal in Archives at Hudson's Bay House, London; copy in Canadian Archives, Ottawa.

Hearne, Samuel. *Journey from Prince of Wales Fort in Hudson's Bay to the Northern Ocean, etc., 1769-72.* 1795. London.

Bell, Robert. "Explorations of the Churchill and Nelson rivers," in *Geol. Survey*, 1878; "Boat route from Norway House to York Factory," *Geol. Survey*, 1877; "Explorations to south of Hudson's Bay," *Geog. Journal*, London, 1897.

Low, A. P. "Exploration of country between Lake Winnipeg and Hudson Bay." In *Geol. Survey*. 1886.

Klotz, Otto. *Exploratory survey to Hudson's Bay.* Ottawa. 1884.

Tyrrell, J. B. *Report on the Doobaunt, Kazan, and Ferguson rivers and the north-west coast of Hudson Bay.* Ottawa. 1897.

NORTHERN CANADA

Mackenzie, Sir Alexander. *Voyages from Montreal through the continent of North America, 1789 and 1793.* London. 1795. 1801.

See also Masson's *Bourgeois de la Compagnie du Nord-Ouest.*

Franklin, Sir John. *Narrative of a journey to the shores of the Polar Sea in 1819–22.* London. 1823.

Franklin, Sir John. *Narrative of a second expedition to the shores of the Polar Seas, 1825–7.* London. 1828.

Murray, A. *Historical account of discoveries and travels in North America,* etc. London. 1829.

Tyler, P. F. *Historical view of the progress of discovery of the more northern coasts of America.* Edinburgh. 1833.

Account of the several land expeditions to determine the geography of the north-west part of the American coast. 1831.

Back, Sir George. *Journal of the Arctic land expedition to the mouth of the Great Fish River and along the shores of the Arctic Ocean, in the years 1833, 1834, and 1835.* London. 1836.

King, Richard. *Narrative of a journey to the shores of the Arctic Ocean in 1833, '34, and '35, under the command of Captain Back, R.N.* London. 1836.

Simpson, Thomas. *Narrative of the discoveries on the north coast of America . . . 1836–9.* London. 1843.

Simpson, Alexander. *Life and travels of Thomas Simpson.* London. 1845.

Rae, John. *Narrative of an expedition to the shores of the Arctic Sea, 1846 and 1847.* London. 1850.

Richardson, Sir John. *Arctic searching expedition . . . 1848.* London. 1851. 2 vols.

Anderson, James. "Descent of Back's Great Fish River, 1855." In *Royal Geog. Soc. Jour.*, Vol. XXVI. 1856.

Anderson, James. "Extracts from Chief-Factor James Anderson's Arctic Journal. Communicated by Sir John Richardson." In *Royal Geog. Soc. Jour.*, Vol. XXVII. 1857.

See the list of works on Arctic subjects, in John Brown's *North-West Passage*, etc., London, 1860, p. 448, for further references on the various land expeditions to the Arctic coast of America.

Pike, Warburton. *Barren Ground of Northern Canada.* London. 1892.

Tyrrell, J. B. "The Barren Lands of Canada." In *Ottawa Naturalist.* 1897.

Tyrrell, J. W. *Across the Sub-Arctics of Canada.* London. n.d.

Whitney, Caspar. *On Snow-shoes to the Barren Grounds.* New York.

Hanbury, David T. *Sport and travel in the Northland of Canada.* London. 1904.

Gilder, W. H. *Schwatka's search, 1879–80.* New York. 1881.

Campbell, R. *Twenty years in isolation in the Sub-Arctic territory of the Hudson's Bay Company.* London. 1901.

Bell, J. M. "Great Bear Lake and Great Slave Lake regions." In *Geol. Survey Rep.* 1899. C.

McConnell, R. G. "Exploration in the Yukon and Mackenzie basins." In *Geol. Survey.* 1888–9. D.

FRENCH EXPLORERS IN THE WEST

Charlevoix, P. F. X. de. *Histoire et description générale de la Nouvelle France.* Paris. 1744. 3 vols.

Trans. with notes by John Gilmary Shea. New York. 1866–72. 6 vols.

Bougainville's "Memoir on the French Posts." 1757. In Margry's *Découvertes*, etc. Trans. extracts in *Documents relating to Boundaries of Ontario*, p. 80.

De La Potherie. *Histoire de l'Amérique Septentrionale.* Paris. 1722. 4 vols.

Jeffreys, Thomas. *History of the French dominions in North and South America.* London. 1761.

Cauchon, Joseph. "Remarks on the North-West Territories of Canada," etc. In *Journals of Leg. Ass. of Canada.* 1857.

Hodgins, J. G. "Discoveries and trade of the rival French and English colonists in the Hudson Bay Territories." In *British American Mag.* 1864.

Tassé, Joseph. *Les Canadiens de l'Ouest.* Montreal. 1878. 2 vols.

Taché, Mgr. A. *Esquisse sur le Nord-Ouest de l'Amérique.* Montreal. 1869.

Trans. by D. R. Cameron. Montreal. 1870.

J Margry, Pierre. *Découvertes et établissements des Français dans l'ouest, etc., 1614-98.* Paris. 1879-88. 6 vols.

Dugas, G. *L'Ouest Canadien . . . jusqu'à l'année 1822.* Montreal. 1896.

Dugas, G. *Histoire de l'Ouest Canadien de 1822 à 1869.* Montreal. 1906.

Winsor, Justin. *Cartier to Frontenac. Geographical discovery in the interior of North America . . . 1534-1700.* Boston. 1900.

Laut, Agnes C. *Pathfinders of the West.* New York. 1904.

Petitot, E. *Traditions Indiennes du Canada Nord-Ouest.* Alençon. 1887.

Butterfield, C. W. *History of the discovery of the North-West by John Nicolet in 1634.* Cincinnati. 1881.

Jouan, Henri. *Jean Nicolet, 1618-42.* Trans. by Grace Clark. In Coll. Wisconsin Hist. Soc., Vol. XI.

See also accounts of Nicolet, by Garneau, and Ferland, in Vol. X; and in Vol. I of Minnesota Hist. Soc. Coll.

Dulhut, Daniel Greysolon. Journals and letters, in Canadian Archives.

See also article on Dulhut in Minnesota Hist. Soc. Coll., Vol. I; and in *Harper's Magazine*, Sept., 1893.

Radisson. *Voyages of Peter Esprit Radisson; being an account of his travels and experiences among the North American Indians from 1652 to 1684,* etc. Ed. by G. D. Scull. Boston. 1885.

See also Sulte, Bryce, Prud'homme, and Dionne, in *Trans. Royal Soc. Canada;* J. V. Brower's *Minnesota: Discovery of its area, 1540–1665;* H. C. Campbell, in *American Hist. Review,* 1896, and *Proc. of Wisconsin Hist. Soc.,* 1895; Coll. Wisconsin Hist. Soc., Vol. XI; Oldmixon's *British Empire in America,* I, 385; Jérémie's *Relation;* De La Potherie's *Histoire de l'Amérique Septentrionale;* Agnes Laut's *Pathfinders of the West.*

Bobé's *Memoir on the Western Sea.* Canadian Archives MSS. Ottawa.

De Noyon, and De La Noüe. Canadian Archives MSS. Ottawa.

La Vérendrye, P. G. de. Journals and letters. Canadian Archives MSS.

See also Pierre Margry's articles in the *Moniteur,* Paris, 1852, trans. in *Documents relating to Boundaries of Ontario,* p. 68; *Revue Canadienne,* May, 1872; Sulte, in *Revue Canadienne,* 1873; Prud'homme, and Burpee, in *Trans. Royal Soc. Canada;* F. de Kastner's *Les La Vérendrye père et fils,* Quebec, 1904; E. D. Neill, in *Contr. to Hist. Soc. Montana,* Vol. I, p. 266. La Vérendrye's Journal, 1738–9, will be found, with a trans., in *Report on Canadian Archives,* 1889.

Saint-Pierre, J. R. L. de. "Journal, 1750–2." *Report on Canadian Archives,* 1886.

La France, Joseph. In Dobbs's *Hudson's Bay;* and *Hudson's Bay Report,* 1749.

BRITISH WESTERN EXPLORATIONS

North West Company. The origin and progress of the North West Company of Canada, etc. London. 1811.

Narrative of occurrences in the Indian countries of North America. London. 1817.

Masson, L. R. *Les Bourgeois de la Compagnie du Nord-Ouest*, .J
etc. Quebec. 1889-90. 2 vols.

Stations of the Hudson's Bay Company and the North West
Company respectively, at the period of their coalition,
1820-1. In *Documents relating to Boundaries of Ontario*,
p. 401.

See also Masson manuscripts (North West Company) in
McGill Library, Montreal; and Canadian Archives,
Ottawa; "Memorials on North-Western exploration,"
Archives Report, 1890, p. 48; Mackenzie's General history
of the Fur Trade, in his *Voyages;* Bancroft's *North-West
Coast;* and Bryce's *Hudson's Bay Company*.

Begg, Alexander. *History of the North-West*. Toronto. .J
1894-5. 3 vols.

Hind, H. Y. *The North-West Territory*. Toronto. 1859. .J

Dalrymple, Alexander; and Henry, Alexander. Memoirs on
the routes for western discoveries. See Appendix.

Hind, H. Y. *Sketch of the overland route to British Columbia*.
Toronto. 1862.

Fleming, Sir Sandford. "Expeditions by land to the Pacific." .J
In *Trans. Royal Soc. Can.* 1889.

Bell, C. N. "Some historic names and places of the North-
West." In *Trans. Manitoba Hist. and Sc. Soc.* 1885.

Bryce, George. "Five forts of Winnipeg," in *Trans. R.S.C.*,
1885; "The Assiniboine and its forts," in *Trans. R.S.C.*,
1892; "The Winnipeg country," in *Trans. Man. H. and
S. Soc.;* "The Souris country," in *Trans. Man. H. and
S. Soc.*

Catlin, George. *Manners, customs, and conditions of the North
American Indians*. New York. 1841. 2 vols.

Dugas, G. *Un voyageur des pays d'en haut*. Montreal.
1890.

Beers, W. G. "The 'Voyageurs' of Canada." In *British
American Mag.* 1863.

Prud'homme, L. A. "Le Bison." In *Revue Canadienne.* Oct., 1906.

Upham, Warren. "The Glacial Lake Agassiz of Manitoba." In *Geol. Survey Report.* 1888-9. E.

Carver, Jonathan. *Travels through the interior parts of North America, in the years 1766, 1767, and 1768.* London. 1778.

Fifteen subsequent editions, in English, French, German, and Dutch, are described in Pilling's *Bibliography of the Algonquian Languages,* and seven others mentioned, making twenty-three in all.

See also articles by J. G. Gregory in Parkman Club Publications, No. 5, 1896; D. S. Durrie, in Wisconsin Hist. Soc. Coll., VI, 268; Minn. Hist. Coll., I; E. G. Bourne, in *American Hist. Review,* Jan., 1906.

Henry, Alexander. *Travels and adventures in Canada and the Indian Territories between the years 1760 and 1776.* New York. 1809.

New ed., ed. by James Bain. Toronto. 1901.

Pond, Peter. Memorial in *Archives Report,* 1890.

See also Masson's *Bourgeois de la Compagnie du Nord-Ouest;* and Mackenzie's *General history of the Fur Trade;* also *Archives Report,* 1889, p. 29.

Umfreville, Edward. *Present state of Hudson's Bay,* etc. London. 1790. Also his MS. journal in the Masson MSS., McGill Library.

Fidler, Peter. His MS. Journals, covering twenty-five or thirty years, also four or five vellum-bound books, being a fair copy of the narrative of his journeys, Fidler bequeathed in his will to the Hudson's Bay Company. No trace of them can now be found. See Bryce's *Hudson's Bay Company,* p. 282; and *Geol. Survey,* 1886, 8 E.

Turner, Philip. His journal of explorations, 1790-2, is said to be in the Hudson's Bay Archives. See Winsor's *Kohl Collection of Maps,* p. 74.

Thompson, David. MS. Journals in Crown Lands Department, Toronto. See Dr. Coues' *New light on the history of the greater North-West;* J. B. Tyrrell's *Brief narrative of the journeys of David Thompson,* Toronto, 1888; " Extracts from journal of David Thompson," by J. F. Whitson, in *Proc. of Assoc. of Ontario Land Surveyors,* Toronto, 1904; Lindsey's *Boundaries of Ontario,* p. 225.

Henry, Alexander. *New light on the history of the greater North-West. The manuscript journals of Alexander Henry . . . and of David Thompson . . . 1799–1814.* Ed. by Elliott Coues. New York. 1897. 3 vols.

Missouri Journals. In Masson's *Bourgeois de la Compagnie du Nord-Ouest.*

See also Catlin's *North American Indians;* Maximilien's *Travels;* Lewis and Clark Journals.

Pike, Z. M. *Exploratory travels through the western territories of North America.* London. 1811.

Keating, W. H. *Expedition to St. Peter's River, Lake Winnepeek, Lake of the Woods, etc., in 1823.* London. 1825.

Beltrami, G. J. C. *Pilgrimage of discovery to sources of the Mississippi.* London. 1828.

Franchere, Gabriel. *Narrative of a voyage to the north-west coast of America,* etc. Trans. and ed. by J. V. Huntington. Redfield. 1854.

Kane, Paul. *Wanderings of an artist among the Indians of North America.* London. 1859.

Palliser, John. Journals, detailed reports, etc. London. 1863.

Hind, H. Y. *Narrative of the Canadian Red River exploring expedition of 1857.* London. 1860. 2 vols.

Dawson, S. J. *Report on the line of route between Lake Superior and the Red River Settlement.* Ottawa. 1868.

Hind, H. Y. *Report of the Assiniboine and Saskatchewan exploring expedition.* Toronto. 1859.

Dawson, S. J. *Report on the exploration of the country between Lake Superior and the Red River Settlements,* etc. Toronto. 1859.

2 R

Butler, Sir W. F. *The Great Lone Land.* London. 1872.

Butler, Sir W. F. *The Wild Northland.* London. 1873.

    See the following reports of explorations by officers of the Canadian Geological Survey, in the Annual Reports of the Survey : A. R. C. Selwyn, Observations in the North-West Territory from Fort Garry to Rocky Mountain House, 1873 ; Robert Bell, Report on the country between Red River and the South Saskatchewan, 1873 ; G. M. Dawson, Report on the Bow and Belly rivers, 1883 ; A. C. Lawson, Report on the Lake of the Woods region, 1885, and on the Rainy Lake region, 1887 ; J. B. Tyrrell, Report on North-Western Manitoba, 1890, on Lake Winnipeg, 1898, on the country between Athabaska Lake and Churchill River, 1895 ; D. B. Dowling, On the west shore of Lake Winnipeg, 1898.

OVERLAND TO THE PACIFIC

Mackenzie, Alexander. See his *Voyages.*

Fraser, Simon. Journal, in Masson's *Bourgeois de la Compagnie du Nord-Ouest.*

    See also Bancroft's *North-West Coast,* Vol. II, chaps. iv and v.

Stuart, John. Journal. See Bancroft's *North-West Coast,* Vol. II.

Thompson, David. MS. Journals. Coues, Tyrrell, etc.

Harmon, D. W. *A journal of voyages and travels in the interior of North America,* etc. Burlington. 1820.

    See also Bryce's "Notes and comments on Harmon's Journal," in *Trans. Hist. and Sc. Soc. Manitoba,* 1883.

Cox, Ross. *Adventures on the Columbia River,* etc. London. 1831.

Ross, Alexander. *Fur traders of the far west.* London. 1855. 2 vols.

McLeod, Malcolm. *Peace River,* etc. (Archibald McDonald's Journal.) Ottawa. 1872.

⌐ Simpson, Sir George. *Narrative of a journey round the world,* ⌐
    in 1841–2. London. 1847.

Milton and Cheadle. *North-West Passage by land.* London. ⌐
    1865.

Begg, Alexander. *History of British Columbia.* Toronto· ⌐
    1894.

Papers relating to the affairs of British Columbia. 1859–62.

Begbie, Judge. *A journey into British Columbia.* 1859.

Morice, A. G. *History of the northern interior of British* ⌐
    Columbia, 1660–1880. Toronto. 1904.

Waddington, A. "Geography and mountain passes of British
    Columbia." *Jour. Royal Geog. Soc.* 1868.

Coleman, A. P. "Mount Brown and the sources of the
    Athabaska." *Jour. Royal Geog. Soc.* 1895.

    See the following in the Reports of the Geological Survey :
    James Richardson, Explorations in British Columbia,
    1873–4; A. R. C. Selwyn, Explorations in Northern
    British Columbia, 1875–6; John Macoun, The Lower
    Peace and Athabaska rivers, 1875–6 ; G. M. Dawson,
    Explorations in British Columbia, 1875–6, 1876–7,
    1877–8; Fort Simpson to Edmonton, 1879–80 ; Robert
    Bell, The Athabaska River, 1882–3 ; R. G. McConnell,
    Peace River to Athabaska River, 1890–1 ; G. M. Dawson,
    West Kootanie district, 1888–9.

Wheeler, A. O. *The Selkirk Range.* Ottawa. 1905. 2 vols. ⌐
    See also the voyages of Cook, Vancouver, etc., to the North-
    West Coast.

INDEX

2 T

WILLIAM BRENDON AND SON, LTD.
PRINTERS, PLYMOUTH